YOU GOT NOTHING COMING

JIMMY LERNER

YOU GOT

notes from a

NOTHING

prison fish

COMING

broadway books
new york

BROADWAY

Broadway Books titles may be purchased for business or
promotional use or for special sales. For information, please write to:
Special Markets Department, Random House, Inc.,
1540 Broadway, New York, NY 10036.

BROADWAY BOOKS and its logo, a letter B bisected on the diagonal,
are trademarks of Broadway Books, a division of
Random House, Inc.

Visit our website at www.broadwaybooks.com

PRINTED IN THE UNITED STATES OF AMERICA

Book design by Jennifer Ann Daddio
Photo courtesy of Photodisc

Library of Congress Cataloging-in-Publication Data
Lerner, Jimmy, 1951–
You got nothing coming: notes from a prison fish / by
Jimmy Lerner.—1st ed.
p. cm.
1. Lerner, Jimmy, 1951– 2. Prisoners—Nevada—Biography.
3. Prisoners—Biography. 4. Prisons—Nevada. 5. Prisons. I. Title.
HV9468 .L47 2002
365'.45'092—dc21
[B]   2001037396

First edition published 2002

ISBN 0-7679-0918-6

1   3   5   7   9   10   8   6   4   2

CONTENTS

FOR THE LERNERS:

My mother, Elaine,

brother Michael,

sister Lisa,

my daughters, Alana and Rachel,

my former wife and now dear friend,

Lydia Dotres Lerner,

and in memory of my father,

Dr. Larry Lerner,

whose unconquerable spirit

sustains me still.

ACKNOWLEDGMENTS

Sunday, August 26, 2001

As I peer through the bars of my cell window, looking up past the razor-wire fences and concrete guntowers, my spirit soars, lofted by the love and support of all the people who helped make this book possible.

First, I would like to thank my good (and great) friend Barry Demant, who not only suggested this book but kindly encouraged me during its awkward construction, one four-page letter to him at a time.

My gratitude goes out to literary agents Brian DeFiore and Mark Roy for having the courage (and conviction) to make this adventure possible.

You Got Nothing Coming owes whatever integrity it may possess to Gerry Howard at Broadway Books, who refused to accept anything less than my best and most emotionally truthful efforts. (And who also kicked much of my "sideways stuff" to the curb.)

▸ To a teacher who comes into the prison every day and leaves it a slightly more humane place for his having been here: Vito Perrone. May you forever cast your hopeful pearls before swine, believing in the power of Shakespeare and Bilbo's ring.

My heartfelt thanks to a Virginia City man whose life seems to be a sustained act of generosity: Shaun Griffin, poet, editor, artist, and patron saint of prisoners everywhere. Thank you for more than a decade of your Wednesday "Razor Wire" workshops—for proffering the gift of poetry and intuitively understanding that to redeem just one life is to redeem a universe.

Thank you to my good friend Larry Anderson, who was down for me when I was down. Your visits always leave me feeling a little lighter, a little braver.

To Dr. William "Cousin Billy" Hunter: your letters and love help to keep me (more or less) sane.

To Mildred ("Aunt Noogie") Hunter: for reaching out to me across the decades with your love and support.

To Scott Freeman, Nevada's best and brightest criminal defense attorney: for your faith, for your friendship.

And last, but certainly not least, to my new and very special friends in Nevada: Ray Horner, whose friendship and visits I cherish beyond words; Cathy Spinetta, whose letters and laughter are an ongoing gift.

I wish you all joy.

AUTHOR'S NOTE

What follows is a true story. Except for the members of my own family and my friends Barry Demant and Mr. Brown, the names and other identifying details for all of the characters, whether inmates or not, have been changed. I have occasionally created a composite scene based on actual events I participated in or observed. Because I am still a (reluctant) guest of the Nevada Department of Prisons, I have disguised the location of my crime and the county jail as well as the location and description of this prison. In addition to protecting both the guilty and the innocent, I have done this mostly to protect myself. I hope it works.

YOU GOT NOTHING COMING

PROLOGUE

The prison shrink thinks I should talk about why I killed the Monster. Then maybe the nightmares will go away.

And maybe I will stop screaming in my sleep.

"It's all in my diary," I tell him. "The guards took it during the last shakedown."

"May I read it?"

"Do I have a choice?"

"I'm afraid not."

"Then be my guest. May I go back to my cell now? I think my fifty-minute hour expired a long time ago."

I never talk about the Monster.

Or Suicide Watch Cell No. 3.

Where I woke up long ago . . .

PART ONE

THE ABYSS

This way to join the lost people . . .
abandon all hope, you who enter!
—DANTE, *LA DIVINA COMMEDIA, INFERNO*

Naked.

I am naked in Suicide Watch Cell No. 3.

The white paper coverall lies on the concrete floor, ripped in so many places I must have shed it like a snakeskin while I slept.

I hope they do not blame me.

There are no windows in my cell, and of course they took my watch, but I can estimate the time by the food trays. Three times a day an unseen hand shoves a plastic tray through a slot in the bottom of the solid steel door.

If it's a handful of Rice Krispies and a dented orange (invariably encrusted with a thick white mold), then it must be breakfast time. Yesterday they gave me a few Cocoa Puffs instead of the Krispies. The chocolate puffs were all embedded in the white mold like sprinkles on a vanilla ice cream cone.

Not yummy, but I love chocolate.

Peanut butter and jelly means it's about noon, and macaroni and cheese must signify Happy Hour here on the nut wing of the Las Vegas county jail. I no longer pound on the cell door whenever I hear footsteps outside.

I think it makes them mad.

At night I can hear screams and wild sobbing from the other cells. Keys jangle whenever the cop approaches my cell door, but he rarely responds to the questions I try to shout out through the door. Like, "What time is it?"

Maybe the cop, wise to the workings of the devious criminal mind, regards this as a trick question.

Go figure.

My paper suit may have been less than fashionable, but it was certainly functional, and, most important, it was *mine*. When all you have in this world is a half roll of toilet paper and a little piece of gray soap the size of a Chiclet, any property loss is an occasion for mourning.

When the food slot opens for breakfast, I seize the opportunity to announce my nakedness to my unseen captors.

"Guard! Guard!" My mouth is practically pressed against the cold steel door.

"What the *fuck* do you want? There's no *guards* here, asshole! I'm a *deputy* sheriff." The voice behind the door has a weary, practiced contempt to it.

"Sorry, Sheriff, it's just that my paper suit has fallen apart and I would appreciate it if I could possibly get another one." I feel like Oliver Twist pleading for some more soup.

"That's *Deputy*, asshole. Now step back from the fucking door before I chain your ass to the toilet!"

In a cell measuring eight by six feet, stepping back from the door involves taking one baby step back before banging into the stainless-steel toilet and sink unit. I'm not permitted any books or newspapers, and up until about an hour ago my requests for paper and a pen have been laughed at. This absence of frivolous distractions has afforded me countless opportunities to study the graffiti in the cell with a single-minded focus.

FUCK THE POLEASE is scrawled in red (blood?) on the wall above the sink. The cinder block next to my steel cot is a mural of misery and enigmatic engravings: LORD PLEASE LET ME GO TO THE LIGHT is somehow carved into the gray wall. Directly above it is a somewhat less spiritual sentiment: EAT A HOLE YOU'LL SUCK A POLE!

I'm still trying to figure that one out.

There are dozens of crudely drawn swastikas and what I presume to be gang names: TREY STREET DEUCES and BAD BLOODS and the puzzling NAZI LOW RIDERS. Scratched into the metal cell door above the food slot is SMOKE A ROCK YOU'LL SUCK A COCK. I feel fairly confident in concluding the latter admonition is by the same author who was inspired to write about pole-sucking.

The only institutional inscription is stenciled in huge black letters at the top of the sliding steel door: SW3. When I was first taken here shortly after my arrest, shuffling pathetically in my ankle shackles and handcuffs secured to a belly chain, I asked the cop what it meant.

The cop—excuse me, the *deputy* sheriff—a bored and beefy young man, had apparently been asked this before. He answered by shoving me into the cell before saying, "Suicide Watch 3, asshole, and don't even *think* of offing yourself during my shift."

Offing myself? That sounded not only preposterous but so, well, late sixtyish. Nevertheless, I was scared shitless.

"There must be some mistake. I'm not suicidal." I suspect the cop had also heard this before.

"Oh, that's right, *excuse us*—you're fucking *homicidal*! There's no *mistake,* dickwad. You were arrested on a Murder One *with* a deadly weapon. That's a *capital* crime in this state, so you get to stay in suicide watch with the other killers and J-Cats until you're transferred to the joint. *Then* you can fucking kill yourself."

"J-Cats?" Curiouser and curiouser—I felt like Alice fallen into the rabbit hole.

"Category J—the fucking crazies. I just love chatting with you, *convict,* but now get on your fucking knees and face the wall. When I uncuff your left wrist, *immediately* place your hand on top of your head . . . good . . . now your right hand on top of your head, eyes front and don't get up, don't *move* until you hear the cell door slam behind you. You think you can remember all that, *college* boy?"

At the age of forty-seven, with distinguished (or so I imagine) gray streaks on my temples, I am hardly a boy, but I decided this was not the time to object.

"Yes, Officer, but the murder charges were dropped to manslaughter, so why am I still in—"

"Don't *Officer* me dickbrain, I'm a *deputy* sheriff, and if you have any more stupid fucking questions, why don't you ask your little nutsack New York lawyer?"

Behind me the steel door hissed and rolled shut—*thwunk*—a tomb being sealed. I climbed up on the steel bed, which was bolted to the concrete cell wall. Grateful to be unshackled for the first time since my arrest, I stretched out on the steel slab, waiting, wondering if the cop would come back with some kind of mattress or sheets or even a blanket.

Closed my eyes.

And wept like a lost child.

Freddy Shapiro was my lawyer. We had been friends as far back as P.S. 92 in Brooklyn and also shared an apartment in New York when we were both going through our hippie cabdriver phase in the early seventies. Freddy, a small man with a startling facial resemblance to Woody Allen, still clung stubbornly to the Radical Lawyer Look with long gray hair falling in a circle from his mostly bald head.

Three days ago Freddy had sat across a table from me in the jail's tiny conference room reserved for inmates and lawyers. Two cops stood guard outside the door, observing through the glass walls.

Freddy placed a thick legal document on the desk.

"Jimmy, this is the formal plea bargain agreement. Just like we talked about. The D.A. drops the Murder One and you get one to six years for voluntary manslaughter and a consecutive one-to-six sentence for the use of a deadly weapon. Jimmy, you have no criminal jacket, no arrest record. This is a two-to-twelve sentence, and with good behavior, you'll be out in two."

I tried to imagine what two *years* in prison would be like. Couldn't.

"Freddy, I know we went over this, but with all the evidence you say is in my favor, you still don't think we should go to trial?"

In answer, Shapiro reached into a thick folder and put a dozen large color photographs on the table. Facedown.

"Jimmy, we can still go to trial and you probably have a *ninety* percent chance of an acquittal. But that's still a *ten* percent chance of a guilty, which is a death sentence. A lethal injection."

"Freddy, you know how much I hate needles."

"That's pretty funny. But save the gallows humor for a state where they hang you. Listen, my friend, a jury is unpredictable—they can do *anything*. Do you really want to roll the dice for your life when you have this definite deal in front of you? Two years for sure versus maybe a chance of taking the needle?"

"But the self-defense we talked about, the—"

Freddy flipped over the color photographs.

I had to avert my eyes.

"We go to trial and the district attorney will bring out *at least* two witnesses who will say you threatened to kill this guy just *hours* before he died. The D.A. will also show the jury these pictures. Crime scene photos. Of your victim. He will wave them in their faces and under their noses and shout that the evidence, the pictures, don't support an argument of self-defense. Take a close look, Jimmy, just the way the jury will. Take a look at all the blood and look *especially* at the way the—"

I looked down at the pictures, at all the blood and the rest of it, and felt a fist plunge like a hot knife into my stomach—a sickening stab of fear and disgust.

I had to look away. This was pure horror.

My voice finally emerged in a strangled exhalation of breath.

"All right, Freddy . . . where do I sign?"

The food tray slot snaps open sharply and a clean white paper jumpsuit is shoved through, followed by the usual plastic airline tray containing a peanut butter and jelly sandwich and half an apple, the flesh the color of mud. On the other side of the cell door the deputy's voice, dim and muffled, says, "Lerner! Get your convict ass dressed. First thing tomorrow you're rolling it up—you're catching the train."

After Suicide Watch Cell No. 3, this is great news, maybe the best news I have received since my accountant explained I could carry over a capital loss on my taxes for *three* years. "Catching the train" is the expression here for being transported to prison. Fine with me. Anything has to be better than slowly growing suicidal in a county jail suicide watch cell with no windows and no one even watching.

"Thanks for the suit, Deputy. You think I could get a piece of paper and a pen? I'd like to write my daughters and let them know."

A long pause outside the cell door, then the familiar jangling of the keys. A minute later the slot is opened and four sheets of lined paper and a pencil slide across the concrete floor.

"If you decide to stab yourself to death with the fucking pencil, do me a favor and wait until my shift is over in ten minutes."

I push the food tray toward the toilet and snatch up the precious writing materials. The pencil turns out to be a stub without an eraser, like the ones you get at the golf course.

"Thanks, Deputy. Don't worry, I'm really not suicidal." The food flap shuts tight.

I write the girls a brief note, figuring I can get an envelope and a stamp at the state prison. I have no idea when I'll be able to use a phone again.

The three remaining sheets of paper I start filling up with these words. I have decided that if I am to keep my sanity in the days and perhaps years to come, I will need a personal therapist, even if it's only in the form of this . . . what? Diary? Journal? Maybe it's going to be a really long letter to my kids, to read when they are older, or just some notes to the outside world.

As my teenage girls would say—*whatever.*

For now I decide to just start addressing these letters to my best friend, Barry Demant, who both suffered and laughed with me during my eighteen years at the phone company. Years where I happily crouched in a cubicle, crunching numbers and coaxing a series of computers into spewing out hopeful marketing and product proposals.

With lots of incomprehensible charts and graphs with arrowed vectors and critical milestones overlapped by three-dimensional bubbles representing microsegmented target markets.

I miss my job, Barry.

I miss my little girls.

A violent pounding on the cell door. The nerve-jangling steel snap of the food slot, and another plastic airline tray hurtles across the concrete, collides with the far wall, releasing a spray of Rice Krispies. The fuzzy white orange rolls like a tennis ball under the toilet.

"Ten minutes for chow, convict, then roll it the fuck up! Train's coming for all you fish!" The deputy's voice recedes down the corridor, then repeats the instructions to another reluctant guest in another cell. I'm so hungry I collect every errant bit of cereal from the floor and wolf it down with the help of a handful of suspiciously cloudy cold water from the rusted sink. I manage to wipe most of the white sludge from the orange onto my paper pants leg before peeling it. Devour the distinctly unjuicy fruit, seeds and all, in three bites.

Not yummy.

The cell door slides open and the same beefy young deputy flings a bright orange coverall against my chest.

"Lerner! Get the fuck out of your J-Cat costume! A new fish like you is gonna get eaten in the joint anyway—no need to advertise you been locked down with the nutcases." At that moment I had no idea what a huge favor the cop was doing for me. A fish with a "J-Cat jacket" in the joint does not inspire much respect on the yard.

I'm out of the paper J-Cat suit and into the orange jumpsuit in seconds. PROPERTY OF THE LAS VEGAS COUNTY JAIL is inscribed in black letters on the back. Like somebody would actually want to steal one of these things?

The deputy stands at the cell door, smoking an unfiltered cigarette, watching me dress. I haven't had a cigarette since being taken into custody, and I suddenly want one more than anything, except maybe some bacon and eggs and an English muffin dripping warm with butter. I have always suspected that high cholesterol is one of those made-up medical scares designed to keep us from life's small pleasures.

"Deputy, can I have a cigarette?" With the enhanced status conferred by the cloth jumpsuit, I can feel the old confidence surging through me. The deputy, who looks like he started shaving this morning, removes a Camel from the pack, hands it to me.

"Sure, why not? By tonight in the joint, you'll probably be *married* to the convict with the most cigarettes."

"Thanks, Deputy, but I hope to remain celibate in prison." This witticism provokes a puzzled scowl from the cop as he nevertheless lights my cigarette.

"*Celibate?* Ha! A skinny fish like you, never been down, never even been arrested before, *fuck!*—the cons in the joint will be *celebrating* around your asshole. Now roll it up!"

"Roll it up," I have come to learn, means the same thing to all convicts in all jails and prisons: *you are moving!* Gather up your state issue—sheets, towel, blanket, mattress—and personal belongings, if any, and go somewhere and wait. And wait.

Since I was not burdened with any of these state amenities (unless my toilet paper roll could be considered a towel), I proceeded directly to the cuff-and-chain exercise. Hands on head, facing the wall, while the deputy trussed me up like a Christmas turkey.

The cop a few feet behind me, I marched down a long corridor past other cells, then finally into an open rotunda area where a long steel bench was bolted to a wall beside a door marked PROPERTY. A red line painted on the floor separated the bench from an administrative area bustling with cops and clerks at desks. Behind the clerical area a short hallway led to the world of light and freedom—the parking lot.

Seven other inmates, six in orange jumpsuits, belly chains linked to ankle shackles and cuffed hands, are chattering away on the bench, clearly excited to be getting on the prison "train." Six young white guys, one skinny black teenager in a yellow jumpsuit. With the exception of the black kid, who leans back against the wall, languid and aloof as a cool breeze, they all seem desperately anxious to catch up on old times. Like they're at some high school reunion from hell or Old Home Week at Convict U., these white boys are all shouting at once.

"What's *up*, dawg? Whatchu down for this time?"

"Caught a new case outta Reno, dawg, looking at a fucking *nickel*. Pure bullshit—know what I'm sayin'?"

"Yeah, dawg, caught a P.V. myself."

"Parole in Nevada is a trick bag, bro! They violating motherfuckers from the jump, all bogus shit, dawg, y'unnerstan' what I'm sayin'?"

"It's *scandalous,* dawg!"

"It's *outta line!*"

"*Way* outta line!"

"That's what I'm talking about, y'unnerstan' what I'm sayin'?"

"This bitch back in Kansas musta dropped a fucking *dime* on my convict ass—y'unnerstan' what I'm sayin'?" This reference to the apparent treachery of a woman triggers a fresh outcry from the convict choir on the Group W bench.

"That's outta line, dawg, falling behind some bitch *snitch*!"

"That ain't *right*, Kansas, know what I'm sayin'?"

I'm starting to figure out that all this "know what I'm sayin'" stuff is not really a question, or even a rhetorical device—it's just white noise designed to fill in conversational gaps.

The chorus of convict righteous indignation swells and washes over me as I lean back against the wall, crushed between the black teen and the huge white boy they call Kansas. I'm definitely a stranger in a strange land and they all know it, studiously ignoring me while secretly sizing me up.

With the exception of Kansas, all the white boys look like they emerged from the same sad inbred trailer park community where breakfast is an intravenous injection of methamphetamine followed by a Hostess Twinkie. Five speed-thin, heavily tattooed young guys with a total of maybe twenty-five teeth among them. Greasy, matted shoulder-length hair (secured by filthy rubber bands) and five identical goatees scraggily aspiring to a bad-ass look. The goatees, in addition to lending a certain satanic aura, serve the aesthetic purpose of concealing the almost total absence of chins.

Kansas is decidedly different. A skinheaded giant with a three-inch blue swastika tattooed on his neck, his massive head and shoulders dwarf everyone else on the bench. His dark brown goatee is razor-trimmed, and there appears to be an actual jawline with teeth and a chin beneath it. Handsome in a bald Arnold Schwarzenegger kind of way.

And undisputedly the leader.

"Dawgs, we got *nothin'* comin' now." Kansas sums up the collective woe with this observation, which rouses the heretofore stuporous black kid to speech.

"Y'all be *tripping,* muthafuckin' white boys acting like dey going to a punk-ass *par-tay*! Only party y'all fittin' to be at, be the *par-tay* up yo white asses, and *all* yo friends be *comin',* know what I'm sayin'? That's right, *all* yo frens is comin'!"

And all the white boys lean forward on the bench, chains rattling in outraged solidarity. They shoot Murder One stares at the solitary black face, while glancing at Kansas as if for guidance. *Kansas, hey, dawg— you gonna let this punk-ass nigger dis us, bro?*

Kansas unleashes a roar of laughter that's so violent the swastika on his neck starts to vibrate.

"Fucking *T-Bone*! *Whassup,* Bone? I heard they caught your black ass in some crack house. Whatchu down for, Bone?" For the first time I notice that T-Bone's yellow jumpsuit is stenciled, front and back, with large black letters: CAPTURED ESCAPEE. This designation, along with the yellow color, is the jailhouse equivalent of a designer label, demanding special status for the wearer.

"*Aiiight* now, Kansas! What up! I hear you talking shit 'bout *catching* a pee-vee! Like a pa-*role* violation be some kind of muthafuckin' *cold*! You white boys be something *else*! When Mighty Whitey falls, it's always behind some bogus bullshit, know what I'm sayin'? Yo, Kansas, this time they're fittin' to strain me up and put me in a muthafuckin' *cross* behind an ax-*cape* charge! Shee-*it*! Cain't a muthafucka *walk* up out of a fire conservation camp to get hisself some *pussy*? There's no muthafuckin' *fences,* no *walls* at a fire camp! How the fuck they tryin' to call that an ax-*cape*? I call it a muthafuckin' *conspiracy* against the black man!"

Kansas just takes in this little speech, leaning forward, looking directly at T-Bone as if he empathizes with every word. I recognized this active listening technique from a corporate seminar last year titled

"Enhancing Interpersonal Communication Skill Sets." They also lectured about how important it is to be able to "pick up minimal environmental cues." I don't remember any giant Nazi skinheads in the audience, but I may have been hung over that day.

"That's right, Bone, a *straight-up* conspiracy! That's fucking *scandalous,* bro!" Kansas's validation of the Bone's pain is apparently a signal to the other white boys to start their echoing routine.

". . . straight-up conspiracy, dawg, that's outta *line!*"

"*Way* the fuck outta line!"

"That ain't right, dawg. The Bone didn't even climb no fences, no fucking walls—just *walked* outta the camp. That ain't no *escape!*"

"It ain't right—Bone got *nothin'* comin' now, dawgs."

"The motherfucker just went out to get some pussy and now he's all strained up!"

The Bone, delighted by this unexpected flood of sympathy, shakes his bushy head mournfully.

"Well, it ain't nothin' nice, know what I'm sayin'?"

All these dawgs seem to know what the Bone is saying, so he now gives a dismissive wave of his hand. "Hey, but it's all *good*—it's all good in the hood, *wood!*"

At the mention of "wood," the white boys tense up, swiveling their badass goatees in the direction of Kansas again. Will this wood (short for "peckerwood"?) insult go unpunished?

Kansas, Chairman of the Convict Board, just laughs again.

And all the white boys laugh with him.

The cops were in a big hurry to get everybody rolled up. Now that they have collected the precious blankets and sheets and towels (from those deemed nonsuicidal enough to have them), they seem content to busy themselves at their desks with paperwork while we wait in cuffs and leg shackles on the bench for a couple of hours. *Hurry up and wait* seems to be the standard operating jailhouse philosophy. We're ostensibly waiting for the property sergeant to collect our jumpsuits and give us back the clothing we were wearing when arrested or sentenced.

I recall the same philosophy from my army days, a lifetime ago, except we had spiffier uniforms and really cool boots.

And guns.

Speaking of boots, or shoes, I seem to be the only one on the Group W bench without any. All of my new colleagues are wearing blue canvas slip-ons. Of course, the dawgs eventually focus on my bare feet—once they finish analyzing a recent *Jerry Springer Show* and then debate the realism of WWF violence and finally swap heated opinions about the future of NASCAR (bright).

Kansas leans his monstrous bulk forward on the bench, his left shoulder crushing my ear in the process. I manage to push my glasses back on before they slip off.

"Hey, dawg, didn't they give you no fucking shoes?" And everyone on the bench leans forward, chains clattering, to study my feet, as if for some precious clues. *Here it comes,* I thought. The deputy remembered the paper SW suit but forgot about giving me shoes.

"No," I answer. Keep my answer short. *Never complain, never explain,* another mantra I picked up somewhere in the army, or maybe at the phone company. Or wherever it was I received training in cover-ups.

"Whatchu mean *'no,'* dawg?" The giant leans back against the wall so that his big blue swastika is now level with the top of my head. My initial (and possibly suicidal) impulse is to provide the same response I used to delight in giving my little girls when they questioned a parental "no": *What don't you understand, the "n" or the "o"?*

I wisely decide to stifle this impulse.

"They said I had to wait to get them from the property sergeant."

This was technically true, but the Kansas Nazi isn't buying it. He stares down at my feet with the intensity of a cat contemplating a baby bird that has just fallen out of its nest. "The jail gotta give ya *shoes,* dawg! It's like a fucking rule or something. Except for the J-Cats. J-Cats got nothin' coming. You a fucking J-Cat? What cell they been keeping you in? We ain't seen you out for chow or nothing."

My wife, before she elected to become my former wife, once observed that relationships that begin with a lie tend to not flourish. So I opt for an honest answer.

"SW3." And all the dawgs on the Group W bench (I just can't seem to shake *Alice's Restaurant*) fall silent, again awaiting the reaction of the Kansas Nazi.

It is T-Bone, the *Captured Escapee,* who mercifully breaks the ominous silence.

"They ain't just putting J-Cats up in there. Suicide Watch also be for muthafuckas with *capital* crimes and shit, like cold-ass killers. I ain't trying to put nobody on front street, but my homeboy, C-Note, was locked up in there. The state ain't fittin' to be cheated out of *killing* a muthafucka, know what I'm saying? C-Note said they had his ass strained up *tight* in that SW muthafucka. Cain't even come out the cell to eat. Ain't *nothin'* nice about it."

Kansas and the choir dawgs greet this outburst from the Bone with wide-eyed wonder. The Bone apparently knows something about jail that even Kansas doesn't. Kansas studies me with a new respect.

"That's *scandalous,* dawg! Fuck, they still gotta give you shoes, though. Just because a man fucking wastes someone don't mean his feet don't get cold. That ain't *right!*" The tension broken, all the dawgs erupt in outrage.

"That's fucking outta line, bro. They got to give you shoes. You oughta file a fucking grievance or something!"

"*Sue* their state asses!"

"*Way* the fuck outta line!"

"Man's a *righteous* con!"

"Fo *sho*!" adds the Bone, proud to have instigated this rich level of sharing.

The chorus probably would have regaled me for an hour had the Camel-smoking deputy not interrupted.

"LISTEN UP, DICKWADS!" Clipboard in hand, the cop surveys the bench like a drill sergeant disgustedly appraising a busload of new recruits. Satisfied the dawgs have ceased their howling, the cop starts issuing orders:

"I want all you cum-sucking maggot convicts down on your fucking knees, *right now*!" Chains rock and roll as we drop.

"FACE THE FUCKING WALL—HANDS ON YOUR HEADS!" We somehow manage this without smashing into each other.

"All right, jerkoffs! After I uncuff you, you still don't move, you keep your hands on top of your heads *until* your name is called—then you proceed to the property counter, pick up your civvies, and change in the holding cell to your left. There will be a cavity check in the holding cell for the benefit of any ignorant motherfucker that thinks he can ass-keister a hypo or crack pipe or even a naked photo of his sister Kate doing the shimmy."

This last advisory completely lost the dawgs. "Po-lease best not be disrespectin' *my* sister," the Bone mutters.

"Shut the fuck up! Any of you retards even *think* of bolting, or even moving too fast, well, we got something for your convict ass."

Behind the cop there is the sickening sharp crack of a shotgun snapping into a killing position. The muzzle pokes down at us from a Plexiglas enclosure built into the opposite wall about fifteen feet above the floor. We all peek. From my position by the bench it seems the barrel is trained directly on my head. All the muscles in my stomach and parts south cramp as the copper taste of fear rises to my mouth.

Satisfied with the efficacy of the sound effects, Deputy Camel con-

tinues. "Any motherfucker tries to slow-play me or the property sergeant, I'll lock your ass down all day and fuck your train! *Face the fucking wall, I said!*"

Behind me I hear the familiar jangling of keys as the deputy moves
down the kneeling row to uncuff and unchain us, one by one. My
hands on top of my head, knees on the hard concrete floor, I stare at
the wall, careful not to move. I'm the first one called.

"*LERNER* . . . JIMMY! Pick up your shit and get in the holding
cell." I stand slowly and take four steps to the Property Office counter.
The property sergeant, a pudgy little cop in military-style khakis, hands
me a clear plastic bag containing the suit, shirt, tie, underwear, socks,
and shoes I wore to court for my sentencing.

The cop slides a clipboard across the counter. "Sign here for your
shit." I am trying to read the paper detailing my pathetically meager
worldly treasures when the property cop slams his pudgy little hand
down on the clipboard.

"This ain't the fucking library! Just sign for your shit and get in the
fucking holding cell. Bring back the jumpsuit, and if it's fucked-up,
torn, stained, or anything, your inmate account will be charged."

"My *inmate account*?" I am genuinely baffled. And must look it because the property cop now suspects he is being "slow-played," which I
gather is a bad thing. He starts screaming, veins popping out of his
neck.

"YOUR FUCKING BOOKS! WHAT ARE YOU—A GOD-
DAMN FISH? NOW SIGN FOR YOUR SHIT AND GET THE
FUCK OUTTA MY FACE!"

I am not completely inexperienced at being bullied by low-level bu-
reaucrats, and there's no way I am signing this paper without first making sure that the three hundred in cash that was in my wallet when I
was booked is listed. I am not opposed in principle to the occasional
contribution to the Police Benevolent Association, but I prefer to be a
willing participant in such transactions.

Behind me, the unmistakable raspy sound of a shotgun shell being ratcheted into a chamber. And a new voice.

"Is there a problem here, Sergeant?" A tall cop, apparently a lieutenant, if the gold bars on his collar mean anything here, joins me at the property counter.

"Sir!" The little property sergeant leaps to his feet—the overall effect on his stature is negligible. "This convict is *slow-playing* me, won't sign for his property."

This deus ex machina manifestation of a higher authority strikes me as an opportunity to escalate the issue. Years of corporate training in detecting windows of opportunity (and ignoring them) are now paying off.

I keep my tone calm, professional. "Sir, I am just trying to verify that the property form reflects both the property *and* the money that was turned in." I imagine the lieutenant perceives me as a veritable model of reasonableness in contrast to the rabid property cop.

"You shut the fuck up!" the lieutenant shouts at me before turning his attention to the miniature cop. "Give me the clipboard." He glances at the property form and takes a minute to go through the contents of the plastic bag.

"Looks like all your property is present and accounted for, Mr. Lerner. Your wallet, belt, tie, pen, and watch will be sent with you on the train. The prison won't let you keep the pen—it's metal—but they might let you have the belt and the watch. The tie and the wallet you can probably kiss good-bye, but they will let you know your disposal options when you get to the Fish Tank."

I've already figured out from listening to the dawgs on the bench that the Fish Tank is the convict name for the intake processing unit at the prison. Like a boot camp barracks before being sent overseas or to a permanent station.

"I appreciate your checking this, sir, but what about the money that was in my wallet?"

The lieutenant lets out a world-weary sigh that suggests he has been here before. Done this.

"Sergeant, where is Mr. Lerner's cash receipt record?"

The sergeant immediately bobs down beneath the counter—no slow-playing the boss—and emerges with a pink form and a stammer.

"Su-sir, I was ju-just getting it when the con started sweating me, giving me shit, slow-playing."

The lieutenant ignores him, hands me the pink cash receipt record after taking a quick look at it. "Is three hundred dollars the correct amount?"

"Yes, sir, thanks for your help."

"Then everything is in order. The funds will be transferred to your state prison books. Now please sign the form and proceed to the holding cell for a strip search." The lieutenant pivots on his spit-shined boots like he's on some imaginary parade grounds and marches smartly (if a bit stiffly) back to the booking area, where an endless stream of new guests arrive with handcuffs and bad attitudes.

The holding cell is nothing more than a large windowless metal box where up to twelve inmates can sit in airless comfort on one of the three steel benches bolted to the cinder block walls. The fourth wall is distinguished by an ancient toilet and sink. They are so thoroughly rusted and discolored that at first I have no idea what I am looking at. The smell rising from the toilet provides me with the missing clue.

"All right! Strip, then hand me the jumpsuit." Young Deputy Camel motions me to a bench while he stands guard at the open cell door. He is wearing a pair of those thin plastic disposable gloves that I associate with a prostate check. I suddenly find myself feeling insanely nostalgic for my regular internist's familiar friendly finger up my butt.

Naked, I reluctantly hand over my orange coverall to the cop—it took me so long to graduate from paper to cloth that I now find myself *coveting* the orange suit. The deputy's gloved hands squeeze, shake, and caress every square inch of the fabric (searching for *what?*—a smuggled

Cocoa Puff?) before tossing it into a barrel outside the holding cell. I gather the property sergeant won't get to deduct any dry-cleaning bills from my books.

"All right, now stand up and push your ears forward—leave your glasses on—back and forth." I do my best Dumbo imitation, and when no guns or ninja swords drop from behind my ears, the deputy goes through the rest of the strip search checklist.

"Lift up your equipment . . . good . . . turn around, bend over, and spread your cheeks . . . now cough . . ." I wait in paralyzed horror for the prostate probe that never comes. The cop just says, "Good. Now stand up, turn around, and open your mouth."

This doesn't sound good, either, but I suppose it's better than, say, "*Kneel* and open your mouth," which is what I imagine to be the prison version of "Welcome to your cell." I have watched too many prison movies, because the cop just says, "Take your fingers and rub them across your gums . . . good . . . now run your fingers through your hair . . . shake your head. Now get into your civvies and take a seat on the bench outside."

A New York minute later I'm back on the bench in my generic blue Men's Wearhouse suit, which no one would mistake for an Armani, even with the label inside. Freddy Shapiro advised me to dress "professionally but not stylishly" at my sentencing appearance before the judge. "You never want to dress better than the judge," counseled Freddy. "Sometimes it pisses them off and they're *already* pissed off." So Freddy wrote down my size and went shopping for me, billing me only two hundred and fifty dollars for the hour of his time. Which means I really got to wear a five-hundred-dollar suit. But hey, what are old friends for?

The bench dawgs, of course, go nuts at the sight of a suit—not to mention my corporate-issue black wing tips. Kansas lets out a bizarre yelp of pain.

"*Owwww!* Check this dawg *out!* Hey, bro, you a lawyer or something?"

"Or something," I answer, which provokes the peanut gallery into action.

"Muthafucka be *stylin'*!" exclaims the Bone, who is now inexplicably sporting a clear plastic shower cap over the top of his big Afro hairdo. Then all the tattooed, goateed, chinless, toothless white boys get into the act. They are all in blue jeans and T-shirts. Some of them must have been barefoot when arrested because plenty of jailhouse blue canvas slip-ons are still in evidence.

"Check out the *shoes*! Them leather, dawg?"

"The dude's gotta be a lawyer, know what I'm saying?"

"Probably had a real lawyer, not like your punk-ass public pretender."

"Fuck you, bro, I coulda had a fucking real lawyer, didn't wanna waste the money, y'unnerstan' what I'm saying?"

"You mean you couldn't find no real lawyer who would take an ounce of crank and some food stamps!"

"Keep talking outta the side of your neck, dawg, and I'll stamp your fucking face into dog food, and that ain't no bullshit."

"Come on wid it, dawg—I'm sitting here, bring it on down, motherfucker."

The Bone shakes his shower-capped head sadly. "White boys be *trippin'*. Selling wolf tickets they can't cash. This old dude here in the suit might be *O.G.*—know what I'm sayin'? *Original* Gangsta! *Old* school! That's what I'm talkin' 'bout, the motherfuckin' *O Gee*!"

Following another fifteen-minute flurry of wolf tickets—which I take to mean threats, probably of an idle nature—young Deputy Camel does the chain, handcuff, and ankle shackle routine again. Shouts up to the shotgun cop.

"ACCESS—EIGHT CONVICTS OUT!"

Two sets of sliding steel doors separate, and then we are in the parking lot, blinking like deranged owls in the blazing June sun.

Our "train" awaits. Actually it's an eight-passenger van with NEVADA DEPARTMENT OF PRISONS prominently lettered in black on both sides of it. Another cop with a shotgun watches from an outside catwalk as we shuffle like old men in a dry season toward the train.

The deputy guides me into the van, placing his still plastic-gloved hand on my head so I don't bang it as I bend to squeeze into the front row. Once again, I am sandwiched between the big blue swastika and the Bone's plastic shower cap. A Plexiglas partition with heavy-gauge metal mesh separates the prison guard driver and his escort from the guests.

The Bone immediately starts whining.

"Cain't a muthafucka get some A-condition'? It be hot as a crack ho's mouth up in here!" Both cops and all the dawgs laugh, then we are rolling, chains rattling, cuffs biting into flesh, leaving Las Vegas.

The dawgs are all barking at once, selling wolf tickets to each other, everyone excited to just be *outside,* on the move, even if it's only the short drive to the state prison. Whenever the Bone's shower cap isn't obstructing my view, I gaze out the tinted sealed window on my left.

The neon and concrete of the casinos soon fade to a vast empty sky and endless miles of desert. Feels like watching one's life trickle out like sand from an hourglass. Thinking my life is really over now, that things can't possibly get any worse than this.

Then things got worse.

I wake up in the stifling-hot van to the curses and groans of the Dawg Chorus. Like a nightmarish desert mirage, the state prison compound looms ahead. Barbed wire, guntowers, more barbed wire, and concentric circles of fences, all topped with swirls of razor wire.

There is nothing alive. Nothing green, nothing growing, not even cactus. Just the fading desert sun beating down on what appears to be a medieval fortress of blackened stone structures.

Six 100-foot-high concrete guntowers surround the outermost fence perimeter. The towers are strategically placed to allow rifle and shotgun coverage of the inner prison yard as well as the surrounding miles of desolation beyond the barbed-wire fences.

The van comes to a stop at a checkpoint just in front of a main gate formidable enough to have kept the barbarians out of Rome for another thousand years.

Over the top of the Bone's plastic shower cap I watch as a guntower guard steps out onto a small railed terrace and points a rifle down at the van. Once again my stomach is seized with a sickening iron grip. Or perhaps it is my soul, assuming I still have one.

Our driver shouts out his window to the checkpoint guard: *"Incoming! Eight fish, Clark County!"* A moment later the massive gate swings open and we are cruising through the main yard. The van neither slows nor stops for a cluster of inmates who seem to be taking a leisurely stroll along the cement walkway. The convicts simply leap to either side, most of them landing on their feet in the sand and dirt. All of them screaming at the van.

"Motherfucking fish train!"

"Hey, C.O., we're *walkin'* here—that shit's outta line!"

"That's some fucked-up shit! Damn near busted my fucking grill!"

"It weren't nothin' nice."

The atmosphere in the van sinks into a grim silence as we approach a two-story concrete building charred with decades of grime. The building is segregated from the main yard by both distance and its own razor-wire fence enclosure and gate.

The sign on the gate says, UNIT 7A—INTAKE. I remember reading about the Jews who disembarked from the cattle car train in front of the main gate of Auschwitz. They were greeted by a sign in German that roughly translated as "Work Will Make You Free." Trying to think positive, I reassure myself that no matter how bad conditions are in this prison, it's certainly *not* an extermination camp. My mind gropes for a positive affirmation, settles for *I can survive this—I will survive this!* This determined sentiment seems more appropriate to my current situation than one of the affirmations I picked up at a seminar once: "I am a beautiful, intelligent, loving person whom people cannot help but love!" Try reciting that fifty times a day to the mirror in your bedroom.

Then try believing it.

The van proceeds through the gate and a small dirt yard containing a dilapidated concrete basketball court, both metal hoop rims twisted into pretzel shapes. We stop in front of the two-story cellblock, the Fish Tank.

Like all the buildings in the main yard that we just passed, the Fish Tank appears to have been built with limited federal funds—sometime shortly after the Civil War. Blighted, crumbling, the gray walls discolored by broad swaths of brown and black streaks, the Fish Tank resembles a putrefying brick of Swiss cheese, complete with jagged holes in the concrete. Suppurating fissures in the snail-gray walls spew out the unlovely aroma of fresh sewage, suggesting a certain institutional indifference to the benefits of modern plumbing.

Kansas leans forward to massage the swollen flesh on his ankles where the leg shackles have chafed for hours in the heat. Sweat spills in rivulets from his shaved head down over his neck swastika and onto my right shoulder.

"Fuck me," he moans. "Fuck me *again!*" His county jailhouse enthusiasm for the train ride is all but gone. "We're in the jackpot now, dawgs—thirty fucking days of this Fish Tank trick bag."

In the two back rows of the van the dawgs commence whimpering.

"Cain't get no store, no yard, no nothin' in the fucking Tank."

"It's like a supermax lockdown. Worse—don't even get no yard time, no weight pile, no nothin'."

"We got nothin' comin' now."

"It ain't nothin' nice," adds the Bone, punctuating the collective discontent nicely.

Then the van is suddenly surrounded by a half dozen shouting guards in khaki uniforms. The doors are opened and we are yanked out by belly chains and shirtfronts with a disturbing lack of gentleness.

"UP AGAINST THE FUCKING VAN! HANDS ON YOUR HEADS!"

I am slammed so hard against the van that the only reason my teeth don't rattle is that my glasses have slid down into my mouth. I clench the frame to keep them from dropping to the ground. I make the mistake of using my right hand to shove the glasses back in place.

"I SAID HANDS ON YOUR HEAD! ARE YOU FUCKING DEAF OR STUPID?" I get both cuffed hands on my head but not before receiving another unpleasant directive from high above me. There is a cop with a shotgun ensconced in another one of those Plexiglas bubbles embedded in the concrete wall about twenty-five feet over our heads.

"MOVE AGAIN AND I'LL BLOW YOUR FUCKING HEAD OFF! DON'T LOOK AT ME—EYES FRONT!" I decide to study the dirt streaks on the roof of the van.

After a couple of trembling minutes the guards unchain and uncuff us. Another county jail van rolls up, this one marked WASHOE COUNTY JAIL, and eight or nine more startled fish are roughly hauled out and subjected to a similar welcome.

All this micromanagement is taking a severe toll on my already challenged nervous system. And my system is not accustomed to dealing with anxiety without my prescription for Xanax or Valium—or at least a self-prescribed shot of Jack Daniel's chased down with a Heineken. Not to even mention my wake-up dosage of Prozac and then for beddy-bye, a near coma-inducing combination of Ativan and trazodone.

No, my fear now is unadulterated. And I seem to have inexplicably lost all desire to medicate myself. Lost it around the same time I killed the Monster.

I'm idly wondering if this is what my friends at Alcoholics Anonymous refer to as a "bottom" when I'm shoved from behind and we are herded in front of the steel doors.

"Lower access!" shouts one of the guards. Two sets of sliding steel doors open sequentially, and sixteen new fish are marched inside the Fish Tank.

For a moment I'm blinded by the swift transition from the sunlight to the cavernous gloom of the Fish Tank. Like stepping from the light of a dazzling day into the darkness of a movie theater. Except this theater is broiling hot and filled with the stench of sweat, urine, and something worse—the thick oppressive odor of fear and despair.

Forty cells on each floor, or "tier," are arrayed in a compressed horseshoe pattern around a lower-tier staff office and the upper-tier Plexiglas-enclosed gun bubble. A steel handrail runs around the upper-tier catwalk, probably as a reminder to convicts that there is an unpleasant thirty-foot drop to the concrete floor below. If the fall doesn't kill you, I suspect the fetid puddles of water on the floor might.

Once my eyes adjust, I spot one of the reasons for the stygian ambience. Most of the fluorescent bulbs in the ceiling are burned out. All of the steel cell doors are marked in foot-high black numbers, cells 1 to 40 on the lower tier and 41 to 80 above. A large communal shower stall takes up a portion of the central lower tier, directly opposite the lower guard station and Bubblecop's pod directly over it.

"Get behind the red line!" Bubblecop screams down at us, angling the barrel of the shotgun down for emphasis. We all step back from the open door of the staff office where a thick red line is painted on the floor a few feet in front of the door. Like mindless moths to a lightbulb, we'd all been drawn to the cool flood of air-conditioning washing out from the door.

A middle-aged cop with a crew cut, a clipboard, and the approximate dimensions of a fire hydrant emerges from his cool sanctuary.

"Listen up! Most of you ain't real fish—you been down before—so you know the drill." Here the cop pauses to make eye contact with several of the dawgs from the Group W bench. "Welcome back, dickheads," he says sweetly, flashing a grotesque parody of a smile.

"Before I give you losers your cell assignments, you're all going to shower—*with* disinfectant—then pick up your state issue and proceed next door for intake processing. You slow-play me and I will personally fuck you. You horseplay in the shower and you will be shot. Now . . . MOVE!" We all shuffle toward the showers as if still encumbered by the cuffs and chains, everyone conscious of the Bubblecop with the shotgun.

"Stop right there . . . now strip! Leave your mangy-ass clothes on the floor—you'll get them back later." The group striptease is accomplished with much cursing, groaning, and the selling of wolf tickets.

Then the screaming begins.

All around us and above us, convicts are standing and shouting from behind their cell doors, faces pressed up against the square glass windows. The spectacle of sixteen naked, sweating bodies has apparently inflamed the current guests, inspiring them to scream out their respective welcomes.

"Yo, fish! *Love* your shoes." *Please don't let him be referring to my wing tips.*

"Hey, bitch, come on up to my crib when you done—I got something for you."

"Don't drop the soap, dawg!"

"Hey, hey, *flaco*! You a pitcher or a catcher, homes?"

"Yo, fish—yeah, *you*, skinny-ass with the glasses! Y'ever been hit in the shitter?"

I would like to presume they are all just glad to see us.

The squat crew-cut cop—STRUNK, according to his little plastic nameplate—positions himself and his clipboard between the shower stall and the queue of naked fish. We're all trying, without much success, to avoid stepping into the puddles of brown water that are fed from the overflowing toilets behind the cell doors. From every third or fourth lower-tier cell, like little toilet tributaries, the sludge streams out from under the doors.

"Control!" Strunk yells up to Bubblecop, who peers down through a narrow horizontal opening in the glass.

"What's up?" Bubblecop asks, kneeling down with his shotgun in an effort to hear Strunk above the bedlam of convict shouts coming from the locked cells.

"Porters!" shouts Strunk, and Bubblecop rises, takes a couple of steps back to a huge desk console, and pushes some buttons. Cell doors 1 through 5 are electronically cracked open. Ten "porters"—convicts clad in blue jeans, blue work shirts, and white tennis sneakers—spill out from the cells and assemble in front of a long steel table set up against the wall adjacent to the showers.

"Sixteen fish setups," orders Strunk. From cardboard boxes beneath the table the porters start pulling out Day-Glo-orange coveralls (no white paper suits, thank God), gray blankets, towels, sheets, soap bars, and small plastic bottles of "disinfectant" shampoo. To each separate pile a plastic coffee mug is added. A small plastic comb, a tube of toothpaste, and a toothbrush are dropped into the mugs.

Incredibly the plastic cups are designer mugs with vertical gold jailhouse bars against a deep blue background. HARD TIME is printed over the bars and below that, in smaller print, BETWEEN A ROCK AND A HARD PLACE. I love it. It's the first sign of prison humor.

"Sporks," says Strunk, using the same tone a surgeon might employ when demanding a scalpel. The porters start dropping plastic orange spoons with forklike prongs into the cups. *Sporks?* A combination spoon and fork?

Go figure.

"Skell! Lay it down for these fish." An emaciated porter with a shaved head and a gray stubble of stunted beard shambles to the head of the table. His age is what a medical coroner might describe as "indeterminate," after issuing a death certificate to a corpse that has washed up under a bridge. Strunk hands Skell the clipboard, then disappears into the air-conditioned staff office.

Skell surveys the new fish with the practiced eye of an old street hustler before favoring us with a ghastly, toothless grin.

"All right now," announces Skell, obviously pleased to be in charge of something. "You fish are gonna step up to the table, put your clothes in the plastic bags—make sure you write your name on the bag with the marker. I ain't lookin' to get crossed out by the Man behind some fish be saying he got ripped off by the porters—y'unnerstan' what I'm telling you?"

Kansas, who has apparently heard enough, steps over the red line. If not for the tattoo mural on his back and chest (a bare-chested woman astride a motorcycle covers his back), he would look like a Greek statue (on steroids) come to life. The neck swastika further detracts from this classical image.

"Fuck you, Skell! We *unnerstan'* that you ain't nothing but a punk-ass porter, skid-row motherfucker, so quit trying to act like you're *about* something."

"GET THE FUCK BACK BEHIND THE RED LINE!" Bubble-cop is on his feet, the shotgun muzzle protruding through the opening. Kansas leisurely gets back in line, slow-playing Bubblecop.

A clearly chastened Skell pretends to study the clipboard before resuming his little orientation speech. His closely shaven skull is studded with large scabs and bright red patches.

"Hey, Kansas! We missed you, dawg! What's up?" Skell flashes some gums at the giant and then starts picking at one of his skull scabs with a broken black fingernail. His efforts are quickly rewarded by a generous flow of blood and pus which trickles down his forehead, slowing briefly at the barrier of eyebrows before resuming its disgusting downward journey into the hepatic-yellow eyes.

Skell mops up this mess with a swipe of his blue shirtsleeve, just as casual as a jogger wiping sweat from his brow. The dawgs from the Group W bench and the newcomers from the Washoe County van all go crazy.

"That's *sick*, dawg! Damn—you ain't touching my shit."

"Fuck, dawg! You are one *foul* motherfucker!"

"That's outta line, dawg!"

"*Way* outta line!"

The Bone, who has been busily renewing his old gang ties with the Washoe convicts, all of whom are black, shakes his shower cap in dismay.

"That's one *nasty-ass* white boy!"

This remark ignites a corresponding black chorus from the back of the shower line.

"Muthafuckin' Skell ain't *sheeit*! I be knowing his pale ass from county—got the muthafuckin' *AIDS* or somethin'."

"Whatever Mighty Whitey got, it ain't nothin' nice."

"That's what I'm talkin' about—punk touch my shit and I gonna bust a fuckin' grape."

"Nigger, *puh-leese*!! You couldn't bust a grape in Napa wid jo cleats on!"

All the dawgs, black and white, with the exception of your clueless narrator (*bust a grape?*), explode in laughter, prompting Bubblecop to scream "SHUT THE FUCK UP!"

An unperturbed Skell resumes his speech, the fingers of his left hand absentmindedly continuing to explore the scabrous topography of his skull.

"All right now, everybody gonna pick up one towel, a bar of soap, and a bottle of this lice-killer shampoo. You got to rub this shampoo shit all over your dome and your skin—unnerstan' what I'm sayin'? If you don't use the whole bottle, the cops will make you do it again." Skell glances up at Bubblecop as if to confirm this threat.

Bubblecop starts shouting orders.

"Pick up your shit! Four at a time—MOVE!"

We surge forward, trampling the red stripe on the concrete floor. Skell and the other porters take up positions behind the table, Skell bargaining with each convict before handing over the towels.

"Whatchu need for the Wranglers, dawg?"

"Kick me down a can of Bugler tobacco, dawg."

"No Bugler this week, bro. How 'bout half a bag of 4 Aces?"

"Fuck that half-bag bullshit—I look like some fuckin' fish to you? How 'bout *two* bags of 4 Aces and a jar of Folgers for the Wranglers *and* my wedding ring?"

"Lemme see the ring, dawg."

"Hey, bro, that's eighteen-karat gold—straight up!"

"*Aiight,* dawg, gimme the ring."

I reach the table and start stuffing the suit into the bag when Skell hisses at me, holding the towel just out of my reach.

"Whatchu need for them shoes, dawg?"

"Nothing today, thank you, I'm fine."

"*Fine?*" Skell looks like I just slapped him in the face. "You talkin' outta the side of your neck, dawg?"

"Excuse me?" What is this repugnant creature talking about? My hand involuntarily goes to my neck, though.

"*Fine?*" Skell now tries to look amused, his yellow eyes flickering over his fellow scavengers, enlisting them in his little game. "How you gonna be *fine,* dawg? 'Less you talkin' some sideways shit. *Fine?* Hello! You're in fucking prison, dawg!" This cracks up the porters as well as some of the fish. Skell tries again.

"How 'bout a full bag of 4 Aces, dawg, or maybe you don't smoke?

Tell you what—I'll give you twenty stamps for the shoes." I shake my head, considering, as the naked dawgs behind me start muttering impatiently.

A frustrated Skell hisses once more. "Whatchu *want,* dawg?"

What do I want? I want to not be standing naked in a puddle of convict piss, waiting to take a group shower with a bunch of criminals. I want a time machine, travel back a year, before all this madness began. I want a trip to Disneyland, a bowl of ice cream. I want to wake up in my own bed back in Danville, California, and laugh about this obvious nightmare.

I want to hold, to hug, my little girls.

"Can you get me some paper and a pen?" I ask.

Skell is momentarily astonished but quickly recovers. "Pens are contraband in the Fish Tank, dawg. How 'bout I hook you up with a pencil and, say, half a pad of writing paper?"

"Deal," I say, snatching the towel, soap, and shampoo.

The shower produces only cold water (why am I not surprised?), but given the suffocating heat in the Fish Tank, I am grateful for it. Three of the Group W dawgs who preceded me into the shower are shrieking in pain as the disinfectant burns eyes and skin.

The convict catcalls rain down on us from upper-tier cells.

"That white fish got *ass!*"

"Dat's what I'm talkin' about—par-*tay* tonight!"

"Yo, fish! *Fish!* Dey fittin' to be a party tonight!"

"A muthafuckin' par-tay in yo butt!"

"In yo mouth!"

"And *all* yo friends is *coming!*"

Whatchu need, dawg? I look up through the veil of ice water, check on Bubblecop's position—he's back to studying the desk console—then pour the disinfectant down the drain. Body lice will probably be the least of my problems.

Whatchu want, dawg?

Right now, I just want to die.

Freshly showered, deloused, and resplendent in our or-ange jumpsuits, we are marched by Strunk through another set of slid-ing steel doors and into the fish processing area. It's similar to the bullpen in the county jail—a couple of benches for the fish, five World War I–vintage desks manned by convict clerks in blue, a separate area for photo ID and fingerprinting. The clerks are all pecking away at an-cient Royal typewriters. The upper tier is apparently reserved for middle management, with two small glassed-in offices (presumably air-conditioned) for the intake sergeant and unit caseworker.

The ubiquitous Bubblecop, having shifted from a view of the shower to a new perch overlooking the benches, has upgraded his weaponry. Possibly bored by the limited mayhem potential of the shot-gun, he has switched to an M-16 rifle.

The moment we entered the bullpen all the black convicts took seats on one bench and Kansas and his all-white choir claimed the other bench at the bottom of the steel staircase. Once again I was squashed between Kansas and one of the cookie-cutter no-chin cons.

After a few minutes the intake sergeant emerged from his upper-tier office and stood at the railing, gazing down at us like the pope survey-ing the throngs of faithful in St. Peter's Square. Except the sergeant's eyes do not radiate Christian love and forgiveness. Something more akin to loathing.

The intake sergeant is an unimpressive figure with an amazingly un-kempt bush of a black beard and a crumpled khaki uniform bearing ev-idence of a moist and hasty lunch. If not for some teeth, the sergeant would have fit in very nicely on our bench.

With an impatient, very unpapal wave of his hand, the sergeant signaled for silence from the benches.

"Listen up, fuck sticks! This is the *only* advice you are going to get in the joint."

"Fuck sticks?" Kansas was indignant. "That's outta line, dawgs. That's straight-up *disrespectful!*"

"Po-lease be *trippin',"* whispered the Bone.

The sergeant glared down at the benches till the dawgs hushed. "Rule number one," he continued, "y'all got *nothin'* coming! Rules number two to two thousand—see rule number one." The sergeant paused to let us bask in this bit of penological cleverness.

"My name is Sergeant Grafter. I am a *correctional officer*—not a fucking prison guard and not a cop. You will address me as 'C.O.' or 'Sergeant.' Your other hosts, including C.O. Strunk here, you will address as 'C.O.' . . ."

C.O. Strunk, who may have only heard this speech two thousand times before, stifled a yawn and sat down behind one of the war surplus desks.

". . . 'cause you are *convicts*! Your job here is to lie, cheat, steal, extort, get tattoos, take drugs, sell drugs, shank, sock, fuck, and suck each other. Just don't let us catch you—that's *our* job." Grafter then consulted his clipboard with obvious distaste, while I reflected on my presumed job with fresh clarity.

"The warden and prison medical director have asked me to pass along a . . . health advisory. This prison has a combined HIV and hepatitis C infection rate of 60 percent. If you choose to just say yes, and use drugs, and you will—that's your job—then snort them, smoke them, or swallow them, but don't shoot them." Grafter irritably perused the rest of the memo before crushing it into a ball and tossing it over the rail.

"So if you must get some cock action, let the con sitting next to you suck *your* dick. Also, there are plenty of homosexual prostitutes on the yard, some of 'em with better tits than your old ladies." This got a big laugh from both benches, which only encouraged Grafter.

"You stick your dick into one of these HIV homos and get the AIDS—and you will—you got nothin' comin' from the state. The prison infirmary is full of dying faggots and cocksuckers. Some of you geniuses might think getting a tattoo is okay if you supply the artist with a fresh needle. Wrong! Every day we confiscate two or three tat guns off the yard—from deep inside someone's keister." Some nervous titters from the bench as a few of the white dawgs unsubtly readjust their butt cheeks on the steel bench.

"Finally, don't cross the red lines unless you like getting shot. Above all, *don't get caught!* We catch you, you got nothin' comin'."

The uplifting welcome speech over, Grafter and Strunk ran us through the intake maze: Fingerprints (two sets, one for the state and one for the FBI), even though we all were just printed in the county jails. We were given our prison number, called back numbers, and photographed holding the cardboard number signs beneath our chins. All of this was accompanied by helpful comments from Grafter.

"Carry your photo ID cards with you at all times. Failure to produce your ID card when ordered to do so by a correctional officer will result in disciplinary action, which could include solitary confinement in the Hole."

Having just seen the cesspool they call the Fish Tank, I couldn't imagine how the Hole could be worse. But then again, what do I know? I'm just a fish.

The convict clerks called us to the desks, four at a time, under the supervision of Strunk and Grafter.

"Occupation?" asked a toothless (don't they give these guys dentures?), goateed clerk of one of the toothless, goateed white dawgs.

"I'm a cook," said the fish, not without some pride. The clerk just smirked.

"Dawg, the only thing you ever cooked was your morning wake-up shot."

The fish protested. "Nah, dawg, straight-up business, on my skin, bro! I was a short-order cook."

"Where at, dawg? Last place of employment?"

"Uh . . . it's been a while, dawg. I been down all year in county, know what I'm sayin'?"

"Aiight, dawg. 'Unemployed' is what I'm puttin' down."

"That's cool, dawg. I'm down with that."

The next four fish also belonged to that vast fraternity of unemployed short-order cooks. Then Sergeant Grafter shouted out the next fish on his list.

"Lerner! Jimmy! Six-one-six-three-four!" I took the just-vacated chair by the clerk's desk, clutching the plastic bag that still contained my suit, shirt, underwear, and socks. The shoes, of course, were gone long before I stepped out of the shower. The sergeant gave me the option of "donating" the suit to a local charity or having it shipped home at my expense. "Of course, if you have it shipped home, we put a freeze on your spending account till we deduct the shipping and handling fees."

"How long would the freeze last?" I asked.

"Oh, usually about four months. That's four months you'll go without being able to buy anything from the canteen."

"I'd like to donate it."

"A wise decision."

The clerk inserted a personnel card into the typewriter.

"Race? Forget it, dawg. Caucasian." A painfully slow pecking ensued.

"Age?"

"Forty-seven." The clerk, twenty-something going on eighty, looked up from his labors.

"Kinda old to be up in the mix, dawg, know what I'm sayin'?"

"I unnerstan' what you're sayin', dawg." Damn! I was picking up on the convict jargon, know what I'm sayin'?

"Height?"

"Six feet."

"Weight?"

"One sixty-five."

"Scandalous, dawg. When you hit the yard, better check out the weight pile, bulk up a bit, know what I'm sayin'?"

"Thanks, that's one of my top priorities."

The clerk gave me a puzzled glance. "You talkin' sideways, dawg, 'cause I don't need no fuckin' fish leaking outta the side of their neck on my shit."

"Nah, dawg. Straight-up business." The clerk, temporarily placated, went back to studying the card.

"Aiight then. Got any tattoos? No sense lyin' 'bout it—the police gonna check you anyway."

"No tattoos."

"Occupation?"

"Office worker," I answered, knowing better than to give the job title that's been on my business card since the last corporate restructure: Strategic Planning Manager. One of the hidden benefits of constant downsizing, right-sizing, reengineering, restructuring, and market repositioning was that I received new business cards after every corporate bloodbath.

"Ya mean like a clerk in an office, dawg?" The convict clerk's speculation was actually much closer to the truth than my job title. Among my male peers in the company, we routinely referred to each other as "glorified clerks," except when we got really honest and called each other "gofers," "ass-kissers," "butt-wipes," and "dick-lickers."

"Yeah, dawg, just type in 'clerk.' "

"Aiight, Pops. Watch your back in the Fish Tank now. Got some psycho J-Cats comin' in for processing from Lake's Crossing to-morrow."

"Lake's Crossing?"

"Guess you ain't from around here. Lake's Crossing would be the Nevada Prison for the Criminally Insane. They get overcrowded they pack the J-Cats in with the rest of the fish."

"Aiight, dawg, thanks." I was particularly pleased with my enunci-ation of "aiight," remembering that a contracted "all right" should rhyme with "tight."

I was just starting to feel like I was making progress in building rap-port with these dawgs when Grafter read out the cell assignments. Following some unwritten rule, he scrupulously placed the blacks with the blacks, the white dawgs with the white dawgs. He didn't ask for any preferences, such as nonsmoking cell or a vegetarian cellmate.

I was assigned to cell 47, upper tier, lower bunk. I had no problem with either the lower bunk or the upper tier. My problem was the dawg he assigned to cell 47, upper bunk: Neck Swastika Boy and Goliath of the Trailer-Trash Tribe—Kansas.

Mr. Lapidis, a former boss (and self-appointed "mentor") back at the phone company, once shared his management philosophy with me: "There are no such things as problems; problems are merely opportu-nities in disguise."

My new, unchosen lifestyle was about to be blessed with an abun-dance of opportunities.

I just prayed that they didn't include any "par-tays."

With or without all my friends coming.

Following in the wake of the new fish, Kansas and I trudged up the steel staircase to the upper tier of the Fish Tank. We had

been given yellow plastic footlockers, called tubs, to store our "state issue." On top of the tubs we placed our blankets, sheets, towels, and
three-inch-thick vinyl pallets that the prison generously referred to as
mattresses.

Kansas was also carrying a small cardboard box containing whatever
county jail treasures Grafter had decided he could keep. As I had expected, Grafter kept my wallet and my belt but gave me back my wrist-
watch, which now read 10:30 P.M. I was also given a large brown envelope
(after Grafter removed the metal clasp) containing my legal paperwork—
plea bargain agreement, Notice of Judgment, and my Presentence
Investigation Report, which the cops and cons refer to as a PSI.

Bubblecop waited till all the new inmates stood silently in front of
their respective cell doors before pushing a button on his desk console.
Crack! The cell doors all popped out an inch from the walls, sliding
open on the tracks on the concrete floor.

Clearly an old hand at this ritual, Kansas grabbed the handle of cell
47 and yanked till it slid open a few feet.

"Fuck, dawg! This is *outta line!*" Kansas said, tossing his burdens on
top of the lower—*my*—bunk and sitting down. "Last time I was down,
these was one-man cells—*fuck!*"

Strunk was screaming from the lower tier.

"LOCK IT DOWN! LOCK IT THE FUCK DOWN!"

Like a well-conditioned Pavlovian dog, Kansas extended one tree-
limb-size arm (requiring me to move against the wall) and yanked the
door across its tracks.

Thwunk! The door locked tight, sealing me in with this skinhead
giant who had just usurped my bunk. The cell was identical in dimensions to my old SW3 studio apartment, except for the additional rec-
tangular metal slab bolted to the cinder block wall about five feet above
the floor.

Eight by six feet with a twelve-foot-high ceiling containing a fluorescent bulb protected by a wire-mesh screen. An integrated stainless-

steel toilet (no seat cover) and sink unit. Cinder block walls yellow-brown from decades of cigarette smoke. Lots of moronic graffiti.

The one improvement over my county jail cell was the small square window cut into the concrete above the upper bunk. Heavy-gauge metal wire was woven into the glass.

It was the window that decided me not to contest the lower-bunk issue with Kansas. That, plus personal health concerns.

Sitting on the steel tray of the upper bunk, I could look up at the immense desert night, glittering with stars. If I could remember not to lower my gaze, perhaps I would forget the guntowers and razor-wire-topped fences below.

I've always had a mild case of claustrophobia, but until cell 47 in the Fish Tank it had never been more than a minor inconvenience. With the beds jutting out three feet from the wall, only one man at a time could comfortably stand up.

With the exception of one occasion when I had to have an MRI, I simply avoided enclosed and cramped places. I did not view forsaking such hobbies as spelunking and deep-sea diving for treasure *inside* sunken Spanish galleons as a lifestyle sacrifice. Even during my MRI when they slid me into the cylinder, I managed to be calm. I think I would have behaved very bravely even without the shot of Valium the doctor insisted on administering, claiming my shaking and sobbing would interfere with obtaining a clear image. Radiologists are not known for their people skills.

Of course, I had heard of the chronic problem of prison over-crowding. I had even voted for a bond issue once to finance new prison construction. The issue had seemed academic, vague, as far removed from my life as the latest atrocities being reported in the Balkans. The issue had a bit more immediacy now, or, as my old boss, Lapidis, would have said, "granularity."

With my phone company–financed M.B.A. mind I considered the problem from a monopolist's perspective, while trying to make up the "bed" as best I could. As guest demand exceeded capacity, the prison, unconstrained by market forces such as competition and customer price sensitivity, simply bolted a second slab of steel a few feet above the original one and called it a bed.

Problem solved.

"LIGHTS OUT!" screamed Strunk, and Kansas flicked off the switch. Moonlight bathed the upper bunk, and soon Kansas was emitting the peaceful snores of a man who had just arrived home to the comfort of his own bed after a long and tumultuous journey out in the world.

For thirty days in the Fish Tank, Kansas never shut up. The unifying theme of almost all of Kansas's remarks was a simple one: Nevada prisons are crawling with punks, J-Cats, snitches, and child molesters (called Chomos). The Kansas pen where he served five years ("Did a nickel there, dawg") was home only to "righteous, stand-up cons." Whenever Kansas sensed that I wasn't giving my undivided attention to his Kansas penitentiary anecdotes, he would reach up and pound the bottom of my steel tray.

"Yo, O.G.!" *Yogee!* "You awake, dawg?"

"I am now." I didn't bother to move. It was too hot and Kansas never required eye contact to register his latest observations on the "punk-ass" nature of Nevada penology. Besides, I had been studying the patterns of mold and wall sweat on the ceiling.

Our conversations had a surreal, incorporeal quality.

Kansas in his new state-issue boxer shorts, on his back on the lower tray, addressing the underside of my steel tray where he judged my head to be.

"You ain't no *Chomo,* are you, dawg?"

"Excuse me?" I had been gazing out the sealed window to the small Fish Tank yard. A summer sandstorm was raging across the basketball court and weight pile. Beyond the Fish Tank fenced-in yard, general population inmates huddled against the concrete walls of the nearest buildings, trying to shield their faces with blue shirts they had fashioned into Lone Ranger masks.

"Y'unnerstan' what I'm sayin' to you, O.G.?" Kansas rapped his knuckles (also tattooed) against my tray for emphasis. "You some kind of fucking Chomo? 'Cause I don't put up with no child molesters in my house, know what I'm sayin'? Back in the pen in Kansas we threw the fucking Chomos off the top tier, y'unnerstan'?"

This time I did roll away from the window. Poked my head over the edge of the tray.

"No, Kansas, I'm not a child molester—you know what I'm here for." Kansas glared up at me with his patented cold convict stare. His Murder One look. Of course, I didn't flinch—that would be considered "punk-ass bitch" behavior. Very un-Kansas.

"I know what I *heard,* dawg. Lemme see your paperwork, your Notice of Judgment and shit."

I tossed the envelope down to him. Waited for Kansas to pass judgment.

A few minutes later, "Shit, O.G.! You must of had a real lawyer . . . pled a Murder *One* down to a voluntary *manslaughter* . . . plus they hit you with a deadly weapon enhancement." I rolled back against the sweating wall to check the progress of the sandstorm. The entire prison was enveloped in a brown whirlwind.

". . . and they got your shit running wild, O.G. That's outta line."
"Running wild?"
"Yeah, dawg—bowlegged sentences, y'unnerstan' what I'm sayin'?"
"No."

Kansas idly stroked some sweat into his neck swastika and perused my criminal history until he was satisfied that I hadn't raped any babies.

"Running wild—*bowlegged*—that's *consecutive* sentences, O.G. You got one to six for the manslaughter *and* another one to six for the deadly weapon. Whatchu do, dawg? *Cap* the motherfucker? What was the weapon, your punk-ass *attaché* case—ha!"

Before I could answer, Strunk was screaming outside the cell door. "*COUNT!* STAND THE FUCK UP FOR COUNT!"

Every day throughout the prison at 6 P.M. there is a "standing count," officially called an Inmate Health and Welfare Inspection. I climbed down carefully and stood a few inches behind the tattoo mural that was Kansas's back. We both faced the cell door till Strunk peered through the window before moving on to the next cell.

Kansas, of course, was dissatisfied with the process.

"They can't count for shit here, O.G. In Kansas they line ya up *outside* the cell door, stand the cons up on their front porches, outside the house, three, four, *five* fucking times a day. Y'unnerstan' what I'm sayin' to you, O.G.?"

"I understand. Listen, Kansas—"

"And I'm talking about a hardcase fucking joint! None of this pussy barbed-wire *fences* neither, dawg, got fucking *walls* five hundred foot high, *scandalous,* dawg, on my skin, bro, that shit is just outta line. Y'unnerstan' what I'm sayin', O.G.? This ain't shit—"

"Kansas!" I couldn't take it anymore. "Listen, I understand. How can I put this? It's not really necessary for you to ask me if I understand what you're saying *every* time you say something."

"Whatchu sayin', dawg?"

"I'm saying all this 'y'unnerstan' what I'm sayin' ' stuff is driving me crazy—you can just *assume* that I understand what you're saying. Tell you what—if I don't understand what you're saying, I'll ask for a clarification, how's that?"

Suddenly, Kansas's blue eyes were a blaze of cold fire. He took one half-step toward me, and my back was instantly pressed against the cell wall. Looming over me was a rock, the neck swastika pulsing violently with an angry vein.

"How 'bout I *clarify* your sideways-talking mouth into chopped meat, you *fish* motherfucker! Nobody comes outta the side of their neck at me! Specially not no fuckin' fish! I been *down,* behind the walls all my life, dawg—did *hard* time all over this country. I ain't no fish, I ain't no chump, and I sure as fuck ain't no *punk*! You unnerstan' what I'm sayin'?"

When I was first promoted into management at the phone company, I, along with a group of Future Leaders, was required to attend a four-hour "seminar" titled "Managing the Difficult Employee." Years later, having earned the reputation of Difficult Employee myself, I was sent off (under threat of a "diminished career path") to a three-day "retreat" near Big Sur, California. The theme was "Building Rapport with Key Stakeholders." One of the techniques they shared with us was Mirroring and Echoing. The idea was that by parroting the body language and speech patterns of a habitually hostile "stakeholder," one could instantly achieve rapport.

Looking up at Kansas, a very hostile stakeholder, I opted for the Echoing technique.

"Aiight, dawg, listen . . . I'm not looking to disrespect you, I know you been *down,* dawg. I'm not talkin' outta the side of my neck, neither. All I'm sayin' here, bro, is that we need to maybe work on our communication. Know what I'm sayin'?"

Miraculously the vein beneath the swastika stopped throbbing. The psychotic blaze of his eyes subsided to a small campfire. He backed off a full step and I was able to peel myself off the cell wall.

"Aiight, O.G. I know what you're sayin'." Kansas ducked under the edge of my top tray and inserted his mass of tattooed muscle on his bunk. "All *I'm* sayin' is that you are a fuckin' fish—I'm tryin' to teach you something so you don't get killed in here, y'unnerstan'? You ain't never been down, never done no time. You got no sleeves, no stand-ups, and no cold jacket—y'unnerstan' what I'm sayin'?"

"Uh, not completely—what's this business of 'sleeves'? Not to mention the other things you're talking about." Kansas loved nothing better than to be cast in a mentor mode when it came to the art of doing time.

"Sleeves, dawg? *Tats!* That's what I'm talkin' about. Any of these woods out there takes one look at your bare, skinny-ass arms, he fuckin' *knows* from jump street that you're a fish, a fuckin' *mark,* dawg—y'unnerstan'? Any righteous white boy that's been down more than a few days got full sleeves, tattoos from the neck down to the wrist, know what I'm sayin'?"

To illustrate his point, Kansas extended his elaborately webbed arms. Straight out of Bradbury's *Illustrated Man.* Not a square centimeter of virgin skin. Snakes, skulls, and more swastikas in all shapes and sizes. His colossal chest boasted a single massive canvas: the Grim Reaper slashing down with his scythe at a naked prostrate woman. The woman, with long dark hair and breasts the size of mutant cantaloupes, bore a strong resemblance to the bare-breasted motorcycle girl on Kansas's back.

I wondered, not for the first time, if Kansas had some relationship issues. Decided our rapport had not yet reached a deep enough level for me to pursue my thought.

"What's the initials on your shoulder stand for?" I asked.

"You really are a fish! That's SWP—Supreme White Power." Kansas stroked his shoulder with obvious pride. Sensing I was on safe conversational ground, I then asked about the knuckle tattoos—NLR.

"That's my motorcycle gang, O.G.—Nazi Low Riders." Kansas studied the back of his right hand as if to confirm his statement.

"Motorcycle? I thought low-rider was a kind of car."

Kansas lay back on the steel tray, closed his eyes, sighed. "Yeah, well, O.G. I was drunk when I got that tattoo, y'unnerstan' what I'm sayin'?"

"I think I do, dawg."

"Aiight, O.G. I'm gonna bust some z's, y'unnerstan'?"

"You're going to take a nap?"

"Right on, dawg. Tell you what—when we get up outta this fucking Fish Tank, I'll get a tat gun and hook you up with some righteous artwork on your scrawny-ass chest. You might be doin' some serious time, O.G. Don't wanna look like a fish."

I considered explaining to Kansas that most Jews of my generation were allergic to tattoos. And Nazis. Again decided the rapport levels were not yet rich enough.

"Thanks, Kansas, but I'll pass. My mother would kill me if I got a tattoo, and she's in her seventies."

Kansas opened his eyes as I climbed up on my tray.

"I know what you're sayin', O.G. I just wish my mom had killed me when I was born."

A moment later Kansas was snoring, oblivious to the unending din outside the cell: shouts, screams, laughter, even the occasional muffled sob from behind some cell door.

Of this strange beginning, my friendship with Kansas was born.

I am happy to report that (so far—knock on wood) I am surviving the Fish Tank with my rectal chastity intact. The promised "par-tay in the butt" (with everybody coming) hasn't materialized.

My cellmate, Kansas ("cellie," he explained, is the proper prison term for a roommate), says I'm too mature to be a prime target for unsolicited affections. Actually, what Kansas said was, "O.G., ain't nobody looking to fuck an old fart like you, especially when we got lots of tight-ass young fish in here—y'unnerstan' what I'm sayin' to you?"

It also appears that I am stuck with the nickname O.G.—"original gangsta"—that the Bone semifacetiously awarded me back in county jail. Kansas and his trailer-trash dawgs have adopted it, so I guess I better get *down* with it.

Besides, it beats being called "bitch."

Y'unnerstan' what I'm sayin'?

During the thirty-day intake processing phase, new fish are locked down twenty-four hours a day, seven days a week. I had always had the idea (based on books and movies) that prisoners were legally entitled to a limited amount of fresh air and exercise. Nevada prisons neatly circumvent any such requirement by a "classification system."

Once an inmate is assigned to general population and given a job (usually in the kitchen or laundry), he gains some freedom of movement throughout the yard. He is "classified."

Fish are unclassified. Nonpersons.

Kansas explained it this way. "We got nothin' comin'. Punk-ass cops think they're running a fucking supermax lockdown in the Fish Tank. It's outta line. No books, no canteen, no weight pile, no yard time, gotta eat in your fucking cell—it's *scandalous*! They try to pull this lockdown shit in Kansas and the shit would've jumped off big-time, unnerstan' what I'm sayin'? This fucking bullshit is outta line! In Kansas we'd of jacked up a few cops. We . . ."

And on and on. Know what I'm sayin'?

We are let out of our cells for ten minutes every *other* evening after chow. During this so-called "tier time," we can take a shower or line up to use one of the three phones on the lower tier.

Bubblecop pushes some buttons every ten minutes to crack open only three cell doors at a time. In case a fight breaks out or the Shit Jumps Off (a riot), Bubblecop will only have to shoot six fish.

The ten-minute limit imposed a tough choice. With Fish Tank temperatures rarely dropping below 100 degrees, we all wanted to take a cool shower. Of course, every fish also desperately longed to use the phone. No way to do both in ten minutes. Eight minutes actually— subtract two minutes for travel time to and from the showers and phones.

Even though I was a graduate of the phone company's Time Management, Prioritization, and Multitasking training (with a framed certificate on my cubicle partition wall), it was Kansas who solved the equation. Kansas, who has managed more prison *years* than I have managed multitasking minutes.

"Here's whatchu do, O.G. Same as me. You shower using the sink. Use the state soap and towel, dab a little with the toilet paper, and you are good to go. The *second* that punk-ass Bubblecop cracks open the crib, you fucking *fly* down the stairs and grab the phone. If some con tries to chump you off, pressures you, sweats you, you fuckin' *stick* 'im! Stick 'im right through the fucking throat!"

I peered down from my tray to see Kansas busily sharpening the handle of his state toothbrush by scraping it back and forth across the rough surface of the concrete floor. A plastic prison shank was under construction.

Don't leave your cell without one.

Kansas glanced up at me and grinned. "A Bic pen works better, but until Skell brings me one I gotta work with the materials at hand, know what I'm sayin'?"

"Kansas, that seems a little extreme, don't you think? *Stabbing* a guy over a phone call?"

Kansas paused in his labors to admire the now lethally pointed end of the toothbrush. "It ain't about the phone call, O.G. It's about

Respect." "Respect" is one of Kansas's favorite words and he always pronounces it as if it were capitalized—like "God."

"Well, I think I'll try it without the toothbrush," I said.

"Aiight, O.G. Do whatchu gotta do, dawg—do it your fucking fish
way. Maybe you'll get to talk to your kids or your mom in about ten
years."

The instant the cell door popped open, I was moving like a cat
(think of speed, not the grace) down the upper-tier catwalk, the steel
guardrail on my left. Behind me I could hear the rapid footsteps of
other fish on the same mission.

"NO RUNNING!" Bubblecop screamed, pointing the muzzle of a
rifle through the opening in the glass. I slowed down, took the stairs
two at a time, and had my hand on the phone receiver when behind me
another hand reached out and closed like a steel band on my neck.

The hand was huge, black, and squeezing hard.

I turned to confront the stuff of every white boy's prison nightmare:
Big Black Bubba, except this monster looked more like Jabba the Hut
from one of the *Star Wars* movies.

"The phone be *mines!*" Jabba said, increasing the pressure on my
neck. A sharpened toothbrush would have availed me doodley-squat
against this black giant. I would have needed a small hydrogen bomb.
Maybe two.

Even taller than Kansas but fat. Fat beyond all reason. Fat beyond
belief.

Seven feet tall, at least a quarter ton of flab and bad attitude wearing filthy gray boxer shorts the size of a circus tent. An incongruously
tiny cornrow head formed the apex of this mammoth.

It was as if God, in a playful mood, had taken a giant spatula and
slapped the behemoth's body together, piling one layer of jiggling lard
on top of another. For six days. On the seventh He either rested or just
ran out of enough clay to shape a full-size head.

The grip on my neck didn't relax until I released the phone. The lips on the tiny head moved.

"I's just fittin' to call my bitch—why don't you just get on line there behind the Bone. Wait yo turn befo' I bust yo dome."

T-Bone, wearing nothing but boxers and his shower cap, glanced up at Bubblecop, who was conveniently on the phone, the rifle resting across his lap. The Bone voiced his disapproval at the state of prison phone etiquette.

"Yo, Big Hungry—*Hunger!* That ain't right. Cain't a muthafucka make hisself a phone call without y'all acting up and shit? Mighty Whitey look down here, he fittin' to trip and shoot all our asses."

The abomination known as Big Hungry ignored the Bone, started punching in the numbers for the collect call to his bitch. T-Bone tried to console me. "Go haid, O.G. Yo be befo' me. Cain't no muthafucka reason with the Hunger when he fittin' to talk to his bitch."

The Hunger never did connect with his bitch that night. A mighty white hand reached out and pressed down on the switch hook. Tattooed in blue on the backs of the three fingers were the initials "N," "L," and "R."

"Yo, Big Hungry—what's up? There a problem here?" Kansas was as casual and friendly as a life insurance salesman at a high school reunion.

Big Hungry's mouth dropped open, dazzling us with two gold front teeth. A moment later the phone dropped from his bear claw and dangled on its steel cable.

"*Whassup,* Kansas!" cried the Hunger, suddenly the soul of congeniality. "I thought you was out on pa-*role!*"

"Was out seven months, Hunger—caught a fucking P.V. You ain't sweating my dawg, are you?"

Hunger tilted his tiny head back and laughed so hard his cornrows vibrated along with the rest of his gelatinous bulk. "*She-it,* Kansas! Pa-*role* violation—that's some fucked-up shit! Nah, ain't nobody sweatin' your boy. I was just fittin' to take a shower." The Hunger lumbered off like a tame black bear. Kansas slid the toothbrush shank back under the elastic band of his underwear and climbed up the stairs to our cell.

With three minutes remaining before lockdown, I was able to reach my mother in Florida, who promised to call my girls and give them my address so they could write.

In answer to a mother's worried questions, I quickly assured her that my health was fine and I had plenty to eat. Right before Bubblecop screamed "Lock it down," my mother promised to send me a subscription to the Sunday *New York Times* so I could stay more or less current with the outside world.

"Thanks, Mom. I love you."

"I love you, Jimmy. Please take care of yourself in there."

Click.

My mother had a lifelong affection for the *New York Times.* As her life grew longer, she became more and more interested in the obituary section. She would drink her coffee at the kitchen table, reading the entries with intense fascination, then glance up to share the news with me.

"Jimmy, remember Hymie Goldblatt—had that little appetizer store on Flatbush Avenue?"

I was happy to play straight man for my mom. "Yeah, Mom, what about him?"

"Dead! *Massive* heart attack."

"Sorry to hear that—he always gave me fresh chopped liver."

A few minutes later, "Jimmy—remember Lenny Lipschitz?"

"I think so. Didn't he teach that SAT preparation course?"

"That's the one."

"What about him?"

"Dead! Massive *stroke.*"

And Mom would peek slyly up at me from the paper, both of us smiling at our shared morbid sense of humor.

Bubblecop was still screaming "Lock it the fuck down" when I pulled the cell door shut behind me and climbed up on my cookie tray.

Kansas was raving and ranting from the bottom bunk.

"Ya see, O.G., even when we was trying to show the niggers some respect, started calling them 'toads' instead of 'niggers,' they still act like fuckin' animals. Fuck, dawg! In the Kansas pen a big fat black motherfucker like the Hunger would have been shanked from the jump, y'un-nerstan' what I'm sayin'? No stand-up con going to put up with his shit. Next time, dawg, you gotta stand up for yourself, you gotta . . ."

I lay back and closed my eyes, trying to tune Kansas out. Through the cinder block wall I could hear someone in the cell next door pounding something hard against the wall. Then some muted sobs.

I missed my mommy.

Among the highlights of the Fish Tank calendar were the three meals a day. We would be let out of our cells to descend the stairs to the lower tier and pick up the trays that were wheeled in on steel carts by Skell and the porters.

Strunk used a small hand counter to ensure that the number of trays handed out matched the latest fish head count. From high above, Bubblecop discouraged anyone from cutting ahead in line by occasional screams and brandishing a mini-14 through the horizontal slots in the glass bubble. Bubblecop preferred the mini-14 for mealtimes, since the magazine could hold forty rounds, any one of which would destroy a man's appetite. Permanently.

We filled our Hard Time cups with milk for breakfast (coffee is a "privilege" reserved for general population inmates, who eat in the main chow hall), purple Kool-Aid for lunch, and orange Kool-Aid at dinner.

After the culinary delights of the Las Vegas county jail served SW3
style, the breakfasts seemed wonderful to me: biscuits and gravy, hot oatmeal (served cold), sometimes a hard-boiled or scrambled egg, and always a piece of fruit, usually an apple or an orange (and no white mold).

About a dozen five-sided steel tables were bolted to the floor of the
lower tier, each small side extruding its own metal stool. These tables
were reserved for the porters and other nonfish inmates who were temporarily housed in the Tank.

New fish eat in their cells. We were given ten minutes.

Using our sporks and our bunks as dining room tables, Kansas and
I devoured every morsel on our trays that wasn't made of Styrofoam. I
sat cross-legged on the upper tray listening to Kansas bitch from the
bottom bunk.

"This shit is outta line, O.G. In Kansas we got fucking *sausage*! We
got *bacon*. Y'unnerstan' what I'm sayin' to you?"

I was absurdly pleased by the utility of the spork, having just
spooned in a mouthful of oatmeal and a chunk of egg at the same time.
Talk about multitasking.

"I understand, Kansas. Back in Kansas you were served steak and
eggs every morning followed by lime sherbet to clear your palate before
the lobster bisque—"

"Keep up with that sideways shit, O.G., and I'll just reach up and
snatch your old ass down here and peel your fucking onion."

"My *onion*? Would that be Kansas-speak for my head?"

"You pick shit up fast, O.G. All I'm sayin', dawg, is that you can't
get no fucking *pork* in this punk-ass prison. The fucking Muslims,
motherfucking sand niggers, raised so much shit about it being against
their so-called *religion* that *nobody* can get ham. No bacon, no
sausage—nobody got *nothin'* comin' because of these freaks." Kansas
was working himself up into one of his psychotic rages. I automatically
went into my Mirroring and Echoing mode.

"That's outta line, Kansas."

"O.G. This shit is so outta line it's *off the hook*, know what I'm sayin'?"

"It's fuckin' *scandalous*, dawg!"

"That's what I'm talking about, O.G."

"I'm down wid that, bro."

"O.G.?"

"What's up, dawg?"

"If you don't stop trying to talk like me, I will kill you, unnerstan' what I'm sayin'?"

I had clearly reached the limitations of Mirroring and Echoing.

"All right, Kansas. Sorry—I get carried away sometimes."

"That's cool, dawg, I ain't sweatin' you."

"Aiight then."

Our ten minutes of quality time over, the cell door cracked open and we put the empty trays outside it (on the "front porch") for the porters to pick up.

Kansas timed this routine perfectly, not closing the door until Skell had dumped our trays into a plastic garbage bag and handed Kansas another tray. Skell expertly positioned his cadaverous body to block Bubblecop's view. A fresh trickle of blood leaked from a scab on Skell's shaved head.

Kansas put the tray—heaped generously with biscuits and eggs (no sausage, though)—under his bunk, then slow-played sliding the door shut.

"Good looking out, Skell. Make sure you don't get crossed out behind this."

"Ain't no thing, Kansas—got the fucking tray count *wired*, dawg, y'unnerstan' what I'm sayin'? The kitchen dawgs *owe* me. Fuck, I could getchu some—"

"CELL 47! LOCK IT THE FUCK DOWN NOW!" Skell took a quick peek behind him at Bubblecop's mini-14 before slithering off to the next cell. Kansas locked us down.

"Yogee, want some eggs? Biscuits?"

"Thanks, Kansas, but I'm full."

"Full? Straight-up business, dawg? 'Cause I take care of my cellies, know what I'm sayin'? It ain't no big thing, ain't even a chicken wing."

"Okay, I'll take a chicken wing."

"There you go again, leaking outta the side of your neck." Then Kansas was sporking away with a savage concentration.

"Aiight, O.G. I'm hungry as a hostage."

Kansas *had* to have at least two trays per meal and he got them. By the 6 P.M. head count he would have pumped out eight hundred sit-ups and five hundred push-ups. Between exercise sets he would fart out the aroma of rotten eggs.

Leaving me to watch the sandstorms out the window and try to remember who said "hell is other people."

When Kansas wasn't bragging about being the "Shot-caller" back in the Kansas pen, he was yelling out the door to his wood dawgs in the other cells. When he just wanted to chat with our neighbor in cell 46, a sunken-cheeked crankhead called Big Bear, he'd scream through the air vent in the cell wall.

"Yo, Bear, *Big* Bear! What's up, dawg?" Since the air ventilation system hadn't been burdened with any actual air in decades, Big Bear's response came through the metal grille clearer than an advertised Sprint call.

"Yo, Kansas! Just kickin' it. What's up, dawg?"

"Same old same old." Which Kansas rendered as *sameol' same-o.*

"Aiight then, Kansas."

"Aiight, Bear." End of conversation.

Big Bear looked more like a longhaired tattooed squirrel than a bear, but prison nicknames are funny that way. These vent exchanges with Big Bear were usually initiated by Kansas, who would first pound his fist against the common wall to get Bear's attention. The pounded-wall response signaled that the jailhouse dial tone was activated.

It took Kansas and Big Bear mere seconds to unearth such news-worthy nuggets as both dawgs were kicking it, or things were sameol' same-o. Both of them would return compulsively to this exhausted ver-bal terrain dozens of times a day.

Kansas had two techniques for yelling through the door. If he didn't want the cops to spot his face at the wire-reinforced cell window, he would drop to the floor and shout under the door. There was about an inch of space between the concrete floor and the bottom of the steel slider. When especially bored, Kansas enjoyed lying on his stomach and making animal noises through the opening. He did a great dog imita-tion, a passable cow, and a lousy cat.

Usually, not caring who saw him (the "no yelling out the door" rule was rarely enforced), Kansas would just stand in front of the door and scream. Sometimes all day long.

About that time I became an expert in constructing earplugs from wet toilet paper. I could still detect some zoo noises, but the plugs muf-fled the shrillest of the screams.

I was starting to believe that this was just part of the punishment.

Every day at 9 A.M. the nonfish residents of the Fish Tank were let out of their cells for one hour. As soon as Bubblecop could crack open the cells, convicts would race out to grab the phones or a seat at one of the tables. Cards, checkers, chess sets, domino games, and paperback novels would miraculously materialize.

Other inmates rushed through the now-opened double sliders to play basketball or handball or lift weights in the tiny fenced-in Fish Yard. When Kansas wasn't monopolizing the cell door, I watched all these privileged activities with a painful envy.

More than anything, I wanted to get my hands on a book—*any* book. An abandoned storeroom on the lower tier had been converted to a library of sorts—four shelves of torn-up paperbacks, ancient *National Geographic* magazines.

The nonfish loved the old *National Geographic*s, flipping furiously through the photos in search of bare-breasted native women. Pages of particular cultural interest were ripped out and shoved down underwear. Once safely back in their cells, the convicts would no doubt peruse the swollen breasts to the accompaniment of hand organ music.

The prison used the lower tier of the Fish Tank to temporarily house convicts that were being "reclassified," or simply because of overcrowding in other cellblocks or institutions. The nonfish residents included inmates awaiting formal disciplinary hearings for lapses in judgment ranging from theft and extortion to rape and mayhem. If convicted on the charges, they would be transferred to the "Shoe," a mangled but user-friendly acronym for the Security Housing Unit, or SHU. Most cops and convicts just called it the Hole.

The J-Cats, the criminally insane transfers from the nuthouse prison, were being warehoused while the state legislature debated funding construction of additional facilities. Even the J-Cats got their one hour out.

"*Yogee!* Check out the baby-fucker!" Kansas slid onto his tray to permit me a peek out the window.

"What baby-fucker?" All I saw was a group of nonfish in blue state shirts playing cards or reading at the tables.

"The fucking *Chomo* in the *wheelchair,* dawg. The *librarian.*"

Wheeling his way out of the book storeroom was a frail elderly con whom I had heard Bubblecop call Lester. Of course the inmates called him Lester the Molester.

Kansas, my self-appointed Guide to Hell and historian of sordid prison trivia, was only too happy to enlighten me.

Lester Rheems arrived here about twenty-five years ago with a child molester "jacket" (reputation). He had been tried and convicted of raping his son starting when the child was three years old and continuing until the boy was fourteen.

Lester was immediately inducted into the Peckerwood Test Pilot Program. He was tossed off the upper tier of the Fish Tank without benefit of wings, and his spinal cord was shattered on the concrete below. Lester has been the Tank librarian ever since, supervising his collection of paperbacks from a wheelchair. Lester, like many Chomos in this prison, has a "private" cell—in his case, a handicapped-accessible eight-by-six "house." (Convicts call their little cages here houses. For many of them, especially the lifers, it is home.)

As soon as a Chomo checks into the Fish Tank, every convict knows about it. The paperwork of Chomos hits the yard before they do, leaked by either the guards or the convict clerks in intake processing.

Sometimes the prison will place the Chomos in protective custody, a segregated maximum security cellblock which also houses snitches, J-Cats who won't take their medications, some HIV-positive homosexual prostitutes, and, incredibly, the *victims* of rape and violence in prison. The P.C. unit is home to the fastest-growing segment of the inmate market—teenagers terrified of general population.

Every few days the county jail vans pulled up to discharge a fresh load of fish. Kansas enjoyed watching the shower-and-disinfectant ritual through the window. He would also mentally catalog the clothes and sneakers that Skell either stole or bartered for.

"Check it out, O.G. Here come some more youngsters. P.C. meat—*scandalous!*" Kansas sat down on the toilet to make room for me at the cell door window.

It was a scene I had lived through just two weeks before: naked fish lined up for their showers, trying to step around the cesspools that bubbled out beneath the lower-tier cell doors. Among the latest batch were the protective custody candidates: children, some barely in their teens, trying to act nonchalant beneath the avalanche of shouts, hoots, and whistles cascading down on them from every cell.

Kansas, who loved nothing more than screaming out the cell door, was uncharacteristically silent, assessing the baby fish with the hard eyes of a born extortionist.

"Looks like I'll be selling a lot of life insurance in here, O.G." Kansas smacked his lips and favored me with a wolf's grin.

"Term or whole, Kansas?"

"Better shut your sideways hole, O.G. If these youngsters don't P.C. up like punk-ass bitches, they can pay, say, a carton of tailor-mades a month. That is, if they want somebody to keep the Chomos and J-Cats off 'em—y'unnerstan' what I'm sayin', O.G.? Fuck, dawg, you *know* they got mommies and daddies that will be sending money every week."

"I thought a lot of these kids were here for *killing* Mom and Dad." Every now and then I enjoyed raining on Kansas's parade.

Kansas adjusted his giant haunches on the steel toilet. A sad expression flickered across his face, and I didn't attribute it to any sudden sympathy for orphans.

"O.G., I'm a righteous convict, y'unnerstan'? If the youngsters got no cash, then they can play lookout or even become soldiers for me. They P.C. up, they got *nothin'* comin'. P.C. in this joint is as bad as the Fish Tank or the fucking Hole—those dawgs sit in their fucking houses twenty-four-seven. Fuckers never see the light of day. Nevada Fucking Prisneyland, O.G.! Homos, snitches, Chomos, straight-up J-Cats, and children all P.C.'d up together, scandalous shit, dawg! Back in Kansas no stand-up con, no *righteous* dawg—not even the fucking snitches— would ever P.C. up, would never . . ."

And on and on.

In the Fish Tank the days curl like dying leaves.

Big Hungry was behind me as I carried my breakfast tray up the stairs. Kansas was already back in the house.

"The banana be *mines!*" The Hunger simply reached up and snatched the banana off my tray.

"KEEP MOVING! LOCK IT DOWN!" Bubblecop pointed the assault rifle right at me in case I was crazy enough to make an issue out of the stolen banana. The philosophy of most of the prison guards is that inmates should work out their internal disputes among themselves, but *not* in front of the cops.

I turned away from the Hunger, continuing up the stairs to the catwalk. My tray felt like it weighed a hundred pounds, even without the banana. Big Hungry was dogging my steps like a hungry black bear.

"Where yo *daddy* be now, O.G. punk-muthafucka? Ain't no *Kansas* to take yo back now—whatchu fittin' to do, O.G.? Goan busta grape?"

"LOCK IT THE FUCK DOWN NOW!"

I slammed the cell door shut on the Hunger's gold-tooth grin. Said nothing about it to Kansas. I was going to take care of Big Hungry myself. I had no idea how. I just knew it had to be done as sure as I had known way back in fifth grade that I had to stand up to the school yard bully, Gilbert, who had chosen me one horrible week as his object of torment.

I took a beating that day from Gilbert, but he limped off minus two front teeth and an eye that would shine black and then blue for a week.

And Gilbert never fucked with me again.

As Kansas might have said: "It ain't about the banana, dawg."

You understand what I'm saying?

. . .

There are no secrets in prison.

An hour after the Great Banana Theft, Skell appeared outside our cell. As usual, he carried his favorite props to appear busy—a mop and a bucket, the faithful weapons of porters tasked with the endless assault against the steady stream of filthy toilet water spilling out from under the cell doors.

Skell hissed a few words out of the side of his mouth to Kansas while pretending to mop. Our cell was one of the blessed few with a properly working toilet and sink.

A steel shank the size of a large bass slid across the cell floor, expertly drop-kicked by Skell. Kansas made it disappear inside his mattress.

"This got nothin' to do with you, O.G.," Kansas warned before I could even register a protest. If the cops shook down our cell, we would both be charged with the shank. Prison policy is that any contraband or weapons found in a cell are considered to belong to both occupants.

Unless or until one cellie or the other cops to ownership.

"Great hiding place, Kansas. Gee, the police will never in a million years think to look *inside* a mattress. Why don't you just—"

"O.G., why don't you just shut the fuck up! This ain't your business. I got me a little Christmas tree for self-defense is all."

At the risk of sounding like a fish—again—I felt compelled to ask, "A Christmas tree?"

"Check the window, O.G."

I climbed down to play lookout. Magazine in hand, C.O. Strunk was reclining in his chair, smoking a tailor-made in the air-conditioned splendor of his office.

"The coast is clear, Kansas."

"The *coast*? What's up with that? We're fucking *pirates* or something? You're a trip, O.G."

"It's just an expression."

"Well, good lookin' out—this here's what we call a Christmas tree."

The triangular shank's base and center had been filed into a series of jagged, serrated edges, tapering gradually into an ice-pick point. I flashed to the majestic Christmas tree in the Rockefeller Center of my youth. No comparison.

Like a zealous salesman trained to stress product benefits, Kansas lovingly fondled the shank, proudly pointing out the killer applications. "See, normally when ya shove a shank deep into the gut, the motherfucker's gonna *naturally* try to pull it out. It's like a *instinct*, know what I'm sayin'? Unless the sorry-ass dawg is dead already or maybe trippin' real bad behind the pain. Now, with your Christmas tree, the punk-ass piece a shit pulls it out and big fucking *chunks* of intestine and stomach come out *with* it! It ain't *nothin'* nice, O.G. Fucking Skell makes 'em himself from the metal mop frames, know what I'm sayin'?"

I felt sick. "Yeah, Kansas, Skell uses only the freshest and finest ingredients. I want it out of the house. The last thing I need is another weapons charge—*you* understand what *I'm* saying?"

When Skell came by in the morning for the trays, Kansas gave him back the shank.

"O.G. thinks he won't need it," Kansas told him.

"That's righteous. Listen, you dawgs lookin' to buy yourselves a nice buzz? Your credit is good. I got some painkillers that are the fucking *shit*—some Vicodin. You interested, Kansas?"

"Nah, Skell, I'm good. How 'bout you, O.G.? Didn't you say you used to have some kind of pill jones?"

"No thanks. I quit."

Like an irrepressible salesman trying to make quota, Skell tries again.

"How 'bout some kick-ass pruno? A righteous drunk that won't even show up on a UA test."

Kansas declines and Skell shows me his black hole of a smile.

"No thanks, Skell. I quit that too."

As my mother might have said: *Better late than never.*

They lied about the thirty-day stay in the Fish Tank. As soon as our thirty days were up, we were told that it could be *another* thirty days until we received job assignments in the main yard.

The real reason was simple math and some institutional caution. The general-population cellblocks were already at double occupancy with two men sharing a cell designed for one. From long harsh experience the prison administration knew that attempting to stuff a third body into an eight-by-six cell could result in an outbreak of unpleasantness.

The good news was that while still confined to the Fish Tank we would ascend to nonfish status with all "limited privileges." One hour out of our cells a day for tier time or yard exercise, although it would be in the small segregated Fish Tank yard. We could now have visits once a week. If we turned in a store slip on Monday, goodies from the prison commissary would be brought into the Tank on Friday.

The actual intake processing period could have been easily completed in three days. On my second morning we were marched out through the Fish Tank gates and across the main yard to the infirmary. With five correctional officers looking on, civilian workers in white smocks took down our medical histories and drew blood to screen for AIDS, hepatitis, and other diseases common to the convict community. They stuck us in the back of our hands to see if we would test positive for tuberculosis when they checked us again in a couple of days.

An obese young medical assistant in a filthy lab coat gave us a very short speech about the unavailability of medical, dental, and vision services. Not unlike my old HMO.

"You got a toothache, too fucking bad! You should have thought about your teeth *before* you committed your crimes. If the tooth starts swelling up, getting infected, then send us a kite and we'll see about getting you some penicillin. Then we'll schedule you to see the dentist for an extraction. Just don't send us a kite whining about your fucking pain."

"Kite" is the term here for the official-looking Inmate Request Form which we were told we must fill out to obtain a medical appointment.

"Right now the average waiting time to get a pair of glasses is seventeen months. Any questions?"

One of the Group W bench dawgs from two days before raised a skinny tattooed arm. "Seventeen *months*? That's outta *line*! The cops busted my glasses when they arrested me—I can't wait no seventeen months!"

The fat medic displayed a smug little smile. "You should of thought about not committing your crime—send us a kite."

"Send a kite" is another prison version of "You got nothing coming." A written Inmate Request Form is called a kite for reasons that are clear to anyone who has ever been advised to "go fly a fucking kite."

The other big intake processing event was a highly supervised field trip to the laundry, located a few paces from the main chow hall. There we were finally relieved of the ignominious orange fish coveralls and issued blue jeans and blue cotton shirts. Naturally the laundry trustees had their own hustle. Pledge them stamps, tobacco, or coffee from your next store or be prepared to walk around in a blue circus tent. For a promise of three stamps I received a shirt and pants without holes. Two more stamps ensured they would actually fit me.

Over the first thirty-day period some fish were shipped off to other prisons. Inmates with very short sentences and no history of escape attempts or violence were sent to minimum security conservation camps.

If Nevada had a robust summer fire season, these inmates would be paid minimum wage to help fight fires. Convicts pray for devastating fires harder than farmers pray for rain.

A few lucky serial drunk drivers were released after agreeing to pay three hundred bucks a month for a "house arrest" electronic monitoring ankle bracelet. It does not comfort me to know that these guys will probably have some beer money left over after paying for the surveillance. Some of my best friends, including my daughters, are periodic pedestrians.

Kansas applauds letting the drunk drivers out. "They ain't true convicts, O.G. Won't stand up for shit, won't watch your back. They don't belong here." Kansas is very particular about who should be let into the sacred circle of Righteous Convicts. Drunks, J-Cats, youngsters, even gang-bangers dilute what Kansas considers to be the purity of the Stand-Up Convict gene pool.

It is to laugh.

A sample of Kansas's humor.

"Yogee, what do you call a woman with two black eyes?"

"I don't know. What?"

"*Nothin',* dawg! You done told the bitch *twice* already!"

Kansas has just returned from the visiting room with a balloon of speed, aka crank, nestled somewhere in his digestive track. He squats on the toilet, squeezing and grunting like he's in labor.

Now thirty-two years old, and despite having spent eight of his last eleven years locked up, Kansas nevertheless considers himself an authority on women.

"A bitch gives me any static, O.G.—tries to dis me in any way—I just kick her to the fucking curb, y'unnerstan' what I'm sayin'?"

I face the wall above my favorite upper tray. Keep my eyes fixed on the window—another dirt storm raging outside—not wanting to witness this bizarre birth of a balloon out of Kansas's butt. However, my ever-inquiring mind must know something.

"Kansas, how the hell did your girlfriend slip you drugs in visiting?"

Kansas is always happy to provide me with illustrative examples of his convict cleverness. Especially during his arduous labors on the toilet. "Hold on, O.G.—I think it's coming!"

Turns out to be false contractions, so Kansas tells of his triumph over the visiting-room guards. The visiting area is set up like a small cafeteria enclosed in a small concrete building in the main yard. Some tables and chairs, a couple of microwave ovens and vending machines dispensing delicacies ranging from microwavable burritos to Hostess Twinkies.

Experienced visitors bring little clear plastic wrappers of quarters (thirty dollars maximum) to feed the machines. Inmates may not touch the quarters or the machines. No reason has ever been given for this rule. They don't have to give us any reasons. 'Cause we got *nothin'* coming.

Visitors pass through a metal detector but are not body-searched. Three cops watch the convicts and visitors through the one-way glass wall of an enclosed office. They watch out for the most common crime in the visiting area: Excessive Physical Contact. Signs are posted everywhere warning that PROLONGED KISSING will result in IMMEDIATE TERMINATION OF THE VISIT! Unless you have already been terminated for touching a quarter. Inmates are permitted one brief kiss and hug (unprolonged) upon both the arrival and the departure of their visitors.

Kansas's "bitch," an aspiring exotic dancer named Star, had driven down from Las Vegas. She greeted Kansas with the prescribed brief kiss. Her tongue danced exotically into his mouth just long enough to transfer the balloon.

Kansas swallowed as if overwhelmed with emotion. At the end of the visit the guard ushered Kansas into a tiny holding cell where he was strip-searched and given a cavity check. *Spread those cheeks . . . now cough. Good.*

Within a few days after a visit the convict will be directed to pee into a little cup with a cop watching. If the urinalysis comes up dirty, it's bye-bye dawg. To the Shoe, to the Hole for ninety days. Where you got *nothin'* coming! New criminal charges can be filed against the inmate. No more "contact visits"—ever.

The UA test is no problem for Kansas.

"I never do drugs while I'm in the joint, O.G. I just sell them. Hold on—I think the motherfucker's poking its little rubber head out the gate." More grunts, a dainty little splash, then a moan of relief.

"The bitch done good, O.G. Gotta be at least an ounce in here."

Kansas already has his customers lined up. In my marketing class they referred to this as pre-selling. It was regarded as a good thing to do. Through the porter network Kansas has pre-sold the entire stash to his fellow woods and NLR comrades on the main yard. Kansas washes his hands with our sliver of state soap, wipes them on his huge skinned head, then finishes drying them on his dark goatee.

Visions of convict opulence dance inside his dome. When he hits the yard, he will have a Righteous House—a cell complete with a color TV, a Walkman, a fan, rugs, pounds of coffee, candy, and acres of tailors. The tailor-mades will all be Camels—unfiltered, of course. A man's smoke. A man who knows how to keep a bitch in line.

". . . y'unnerstan' what I'm sayin', O.G.? You let *your* wife get outta line and then she divorced your ass. No bitch would ever divorce *me,* dawg. If a bitch even—"

"What the fuck are you talking about, Kansas? You've never been *married*! No *bitch* will ever divorce you because no bitch will ever *marry* you. Besides, my wife didn't divorce me—it was a mutual decision and a very friendly separation."

Kansas shakes his head in mock sadness. He's busy repackaging the powdery contents of the balloon into postage-stamp-size packets using my *New York Times* Week in Review section.

"Now, that's outta line, O.G. I've had *three* fucking common-law wives." To my horror, Kansas shoves the entire drug stash into an Arts & Leisure page before securing it beneath the toilet with a piece of Skell-bought tape.

This is too much. This could add years to my sentence.

"I don't want that shit in my house, Kansas. I'm not planning to spend the rest of my life in this shit hole so you can watch *Jerry Springer* in color."

"Don't trip, dawg. Skell's making the pickup right before count. Fuck, O.G.—even if they shake us down and find it, you know I'll cop to it. I ain't lookin' to get you crossed out."

"I'm so relieved to know you're looking out for me, Kansas. And such a cunning criminal mind! The cops would never think of looking under the toilet of a *prison* cell. Hey, aren't you the one who likes to lecture *me* about not fronting people off? How righteous cons don't put their cellies out on *Front Street*? Who knows what else you—"

"Who the fuck knows who else would put up with your sideways bullshit without sticking a shank in *your* grill? You got to relax, O.G. I been down more than a few days—I know how shit works around here."

"Just get rid of it before count."

"Aiight, O.G. Don't sweat me, dawg. It's gone before count."

And it was.

Kansas is state-raised.

He's not proud of it.

"My folks kicked me to the curb when I was twelve, O.G. I went straight from juvie detention to the joint, and let me tell you, dawg, the fucking joint in Kansas ain't nothin' nice, know what I'm sayin'?"

A self-professed "straight-up, stone-cold dope fiend" (denial is not one of his issues), Kansas has a keen passion for pharmaceutical-quality drugs. Which is why he loves to rob pharmacies. After "doing a bit" in this very prison, Kansas likes to say he "caught a P.V." or "caught a new case" while on parole in Las Vegas.

He was arrested for armed robbery and attempted murder. These charges were deemed serious enough by the Department of Parole and Probation (P&P, the dawgs here call it) to warrant a parole violation. The D.A. also viewed it as an additional criminal case, worthy of some more years of Kansas's life.

Kansas had a very straightforward robbery technique. One summer night in Vegas, he simply marched up to the pharmacy counter of Drug World. To ensure he received prompt customer attention, he waved a pistol and screamed, "Give up the Dilaudid, motherfuckers!"

Dilaudid is a narcotic painkiller, highly addictive and hailed in the dope-fiend world as superior to morphine. Kansas would shoot it up and forget about all his aches and pains.

Probably because this was Kansas's seventh trip to a Vegas Drug World in seven days, the cops were waiting for him as he fled the store clutching his goodie bag of Dilaudid. He was so excited to get the drugs that he forgot to demand the cash.

Kansas is very proud that what happened next made the six o'clock news.

He fired three shots at one of the police officers, missing by inches, then his automatic jammed. It took five very pissed-off cops to put him on the ground and cuff him.

Based on these types of interactions with the criminal justice system coupled with his years of prison experience, Kansas considers himself an expert in many fields. Although he can barely read, he regularly re-

ceives in the mail such august publications as the *Aryan Sentinel,*
Supreme White Brotherhood, and *Secrets from the Bunker.*

I always end up reading them to him. His story is that his glasses
were ripped off by the cops in county jail.

He feels that these journals have mentally equipped him to make
dogmatic pronouncements in the areas of philosophy, law, theology, ge-
netic engineering, and even finance and banking. "Jews control the
fucking banks, O.G. It's like this international conspiracy."

For light reading pleasure he studies the humor page of *Reader's
Digest,* lips moving, inching toward the jokes. Then he insists on my
reading them aloud to him and gets insulted when I don't join his
laughter. He *can* "read" (from years of rote memorization) arrest war-
rants, conviction notices, and PSIs.

"Yogee! I ain't lookin' to get up in your business or nothin', but what
kind of name is *Lerner?*" This query drifts up like poison gas from the
bottom tray, where Kansas is perusing one of his rags.

Of course, I tell him it's a fine old German name, probably
German-Irish.

"Scandalous, O.G.! You're all right. So . . . *Lerner*—kind of like
Wernher, right?"

"Exactly! We were practically cousins with Wernher von Braun, the
Nazi rocket scientist."

"Straight-up business? On your skin, bro?"

"On my skin." This temporarily puts the Jewish Question to rest in
cell 47 of the Fish Tank. Swearing on one's white skin is sacred to
Kansas. Carries more credibility than swearing on a truckload of Bibles.
Or on one's mother's eyes.

"Right on, O.G. You know you gotta get yourself some stand-ups
when you hit the yard. Walking the yard by yourself could be bad for
your health. Especially with a big nigger like the Hunger wandering
around. Y'unnerstan' what I'm sayin'?"

"I'm not worried about Big Hungry," I lie.

"I hear you, dawg. All I'm sayin' to you is that when some mother-fucking two-ton toad gets up in your face, starts pressurin' you, sweatin' you, *playing* you, you're gonna want some righteous woods to stand up for you. Some good old dawgs to fuck that toad's shit up. Know what I'm sayin'? You get a punk jacket in here and you are just *meat*—y'un-nerstan'?"

Kansas also clears up the concept of "punk" for me. He hates punks almost as much as he hates snitches—but not as much as he hates toads. Or Jews, for that matter.

"A punk, O.G., is someone you make suck your dick *and* lick it clean. Over time you got yourself what we call a punk-ass bitch. He *wants* to suck dick, know what I'm sayin'?"

I indicate my preference for sexual abstinence while incarcerated.

"That only because you ain't never been down a long time . . . Fuck, in a nickel you'll be wanting to fuck the crack a dawn. In a fucking dime you'll wake up with a hard-on for some guy's hairy ass just because he's wearing lipstick."

I pray I never get that lonely.

Wednesday evening. The heat in the cell is torture.

Until we receive store in two days we depend upon the kindness of our strange neighbor, Big Bear. Big Bear is not a fish—he's being held indefinitely here "pending investigation" for assault, rape, and extor-tion. Not the kind of neighbor one would wish for.

But Big Bear has store.

And Kansas wants a cigarette—specifically a 4 Aces rollie.

He reaches up to pound on the bottom of my tray, the Kansas method of saying "Excuse me."

"What now, Kansas?" I am studying the obituary pages of the *New York Times,* comforting myself with the thought that things could be even worse for me.

"Yogee—you got a Cadillac?"

"Excuse me?"

"A *Cadillac,* bro? Ya got a fuckin' Cadillac?"

"Actually I have—*had*—a Honda Accord."

Kansas, eternally vigilant to the slightest signs of disrespect, stands up to study my face and neck for symptoms of sidewaysness. Sweat drips down and over his neck swastika, about four inches from my nose. Apparently he detects nothing but sweat leaking out of the side of my neck.

As always he's wearing only his state-issue 4XL boxer shorts. Temperatures in the cell won't drop till about one in the morning. Kansas backs off a foot.

"O.G., I keep forgetting you're just a fucking fish. I'm gonna make us a righteous Cadillac so we can score a couple of rollies from my dawg Big Bear. You play lookout."

From the comfort of my penthouse tray I look out the cell door window and watch Strunk while Kansas does God only knows what. A moan comes through the air vent. Kansas claims the real function of the central "ventilation" system is to dispense tear gas to every cell whenever the Shit Jumps Off.

"I need your shoelaces, O.G. Don't *trip*! I ain't *takin'* 'em—just borrowing." Without waiting for an answer Kansas is yanking all the laces out of both our tennis sneakers. Ties the four laces into one long string, then grabs our little bar of hotel soap. With a few jabs of the inch-long nail of his index finger (nail clippers can be bought at the store) a small hole is gouged in the soap.

"What's that punk Strunk up to, O.G.?"

"Still in the office, just chillin'."

"*Chillin'?*"

"Picked that up from you young dawgs."

"It don't sound right coming from you—but good looking out."

In seconds Kansas has a soap-on-a-rope device. He's on his stomach on the floor yelling under the door.

"Yo, Big Bear! Cadillac comin' into your house!"

From the vent: "Whatchu need, dawg?"

"Bear—hook me up with a couple of rollies."

"Aiight. Got no light, though, bro."

"It's all good. We got a working outlet."

Kansas makes a slipknot in the string, then takes a few test swings on the floor before flinging the soap in a tight arc under the door.

A second later Big Bear (whom I secretly think of as "Little Squirrel") has the soap/slipknot end of the Cadillac while Kansas still holds on to his end of the string.

Big Bear bangs on the cell wall. "Pull, dawg, *pull*!"

Kansas reels the string in slowly, landing the soap and two rollies secured in the knot. His face is lit up with the same triumphant glee that my younger daughter displayed after tying her shoes for the first time.

"Now, *that,* O.G., is a fucking Cadillac!"

I am impressed. "So why do you call it a Cadillac?"

I might as well have asked Kansas why a certain hypothesized sub-atomic particle is called a quark. He has never given any thought to this. Things in the joint just—*are.* Things have *names*—you don't question *why.*

" 'Cause, O.G."

" 'Cause why?"

" 'Cause . . . 'cause a Cadillac, you see, dawg . . . you can *drive* a Cadillac round a corner! Shit, dawg, why I gotta break everything down to you? Gotta paint a big fucking picture like we're in Hollywood."

No matches, no lighter.

No problem for Kansas.

He's back on the floor rummaging through his yellow plastic tub, where he stores his precious Nazi newsletters. Finds a paper clip, which he breaks in half.

"Gimme your pencil, O.G."

"No way—it's the only thing I have to write with."

"I ain't gonna *hurt* your little punk-ass pencil, dawg. Now, kick it down if you want to smoke."

The paper clip prongs get inserted into the outlet, set parallel, about a half inch apart. Kansas chews furiously on my punk-ass pencil, a dog on a bone. He finally spits out the prize—a one-inch-long splinter of lead, the conductor.

He lied. He hurt my pencil. I start to protest.

"Just chill, O.G. Skell will get you a nice new Bic fine-point pen— makes a great shank, y'unnerstan' what I'm sayin'?"

Kansas wraps a small piece of toilet paper around the middle of the lead and then drops the exposed ends on the paper clip prongs. A flash. Sparks! Then flaming toilet paper and two dawgs are back on their trays happily inhaling carcinogenic fumes.

"Yo, O.G. Big Bear was my cellie for a minute in Folsom—me and him did a deuce together behind them bad walls. Now, that motherfucking joint wasn't nothin' nice. Not as scandalous as the Kansas pen, though . . ."

A half hour later our lights are out. I roll against the damp cinder block wall. Close my eyes. In the joint, sleep, I am told, is a man's best friend.

"Night, Kansas—thanks for the cigarette."

"It's all good, O.G. What comes around goes around."

Outside our cell the usual screaming, laughing, and occasional sobbing from the other cells. Kansas mutters to himself from the bottom tray. "Damn, dawg—you're getting too old for this shit. You're all tore up."

Sometime in the middle of the night I wake to the sound of Kansas whispering.

". . . and forgive us our trespasses . . ."

Kansas is reciting the Lord's Prayer.

I treasure the one-hour tier time if only because it's a sixty-minute mental holiday from Kansas's nonstop war stories. Every morning Bubblecop pushes buttons, and about fifty inmates come racing out of their houses.

Whenever the small Fish Tank exercise yard is closed for sandstorms (the outside guntower cop needs a clear shot), most inmates simply procure a perch on one of the round metal stools that are attached by steel spokes to the tables.

Although a few tables host a pinochle or spades game, the chief amusement consists of "just kickin' it." You hear a lot of "Whassup, dawg?" followed by the inevitable "Just kickin' it, bro." It's a highly democratic divertissement, open to all dawgs regardless of breeding or skill sets. In fact, kicking it in prison often rises to the level of a conversational art form whereby four or five convicts shout at each other at the same time, rehashing criminal triumphs, current grudges, and future felonious schemes.

As in all discretionary activities in prison, convicts automatically self-segregate at tier time—blacks, whites, Mexicans, and Native Americans all at separate tables. Most of the convicts here are white, so they occupy most of the tables.

Even when a table usually taken by blacks is empty, no other ethnic group will sit there. "That's a toad table, O.G., you don't want to sit there," Kansas tells me. "Why don't you come kick it with the woods over here?"

I probably would have if I hadn't spotted the chess board and pieces at the vacant "toad table." I'm setting up the pieces when the Bone ap-

proaches. "Whassup, O.G.! You fittin' to play chess with yo'self?" The
Bone is sans shower cap for once, his exuberant big Afro hairdo restrained by giant pink plastic rollers.

"You want to play, Bone?"

"Nah—I ain't got no game. But here come my homeboy Big Bird.
Now, *that* old-ass muthafucka got *game*! And he love whuppin' white
boys, fo sure he love that shit."

By prison standards Big Bird is ancient, a tall thin black man with
a gray beard and a full head of bushy white hair. He's probably sixty.

"Yo, Big Bird—*Bird!* This here be the O.G. what was down with
me in that punk-ass county. Could be O.G. got hisself a little game."

Big Bird takes a seat across from me and pushes a white pawn forward two squares. "All right then, O.G. Show me some game. I be tired
of whuppin' on these ignorant niggers round here."

"I'll do my best," I tell him, countering with the Sicilian Defense
my grandfather, a chess grand master, drilled into me long ago.
Grandpa George, when he wasn't teaching me chess or algebra, drilled
the teeth of strangers. "Dentistry is a good profession," he would say
right before destroying my ten-year-old chess defense.

After a few moves Big Bird grins up at the Bone. "This here O.G.
do got game. Indeed he do!"

In seconds every seat at the toad table is taken by black youngsters
as Big Bird and I battle furiously for control of the center board. More
black Fish Tank guests surround the table kibitzing or just kickin' it
with their homies.

"White boy got no game—the Bird fittin' to fuck his shit up behind
that bishop."

"Nigger, you don't know *shit* 'bout no chess. The Bird's queen be
laying in the cut. That's what I'm talkin' about, the motherfucking
white bitch queen!"

Two moves later I trap the white bishop with a pawn.

"That O.G. got *game*—his game be *cold*!"

Big Bird brings his queen into play, lining up on my castled king.

The peanut gallery cranks up the volume. "O.G. *scared* now. Bird fittin' to bust some pawns, know what I'm sayin?"

Big Bird, perceiving an advantage, starts cackling. "I be *owning* you in two more moves, O.G." He doesn't sound anything like a bird when he cackles.

This is street chess. No chess clock, move fast and bang your pieces down to distract or intimidate your opponent. If the banging doesn't work, it's considered acceptable to taunt your opponent, his sister, his mother, whatever it takes.

I'm loving it! Reminds me of those endless sweet summers in Brooklyn when I was ten, my brother, Michael, eleven. We would buy egg cream sodas (no egg or cream in them) at Louie's candy store on Parkside Avenue. We'd read the latest DC comics—Superman and Batman—then go play baseball with the neighborhood kids in Prospect Park.

There were always these old men, black, white, and Puerto Rican, who seemed to *live* on the park benches. Sometimes one of them would set aside his brown paper bag and invite passersby to beat him in chess. For money.

For fun they would play me or Michael. And these old guys had *game*! Could also talk shit all day long.

Bird's queen starts picking off my pawns. "Watch out now, O.G. My bitch be *tearing* your shit up. Fittin' to come in the back door next!"

Bets are placed—rollies, stamps, Hershey bars.

Across the rotunda, seated in the wood section with Big Bear, Kansas and his dawgs are glaring over at the chess game. In the rigid world of the wood, hanging with toads is, to borrow a word, scandalous.

Big Bird is just figuring out that my pawns were poisoned when I sweep my rook down to the seventh row, immobilizing the white king. The Bird scratches his nappy white dome.

"That some *cold* shit right there, O.G. Motherfucking rook be layin' in the cut!"

The Bone, who seems to consider me a comrade from county jail, feels compelled to flesh out my background a bit.

"O.G. got a cold jacket. He be up wid me in county, 'cept he be chillin' with the J-Cats."

I give Bone my best Murder One stare. He backs away from the table. "It's all good, O.G. I ain't fittin' to pull yo covers. Everybody in Vegas jail be knowin' they put the cold-ass killers in with the J-Cats. Ain't no shame to your game, O.G."

"Thanks for sharing, Bone," I say, pondering the strangeness of this world where a murderer is held in higher esteem than, say, a dentist.

The Bird makes a belated defensive move. The crowd, smelling Bird blood, surges against the table, everyone shouting.

"Where yo game, Bird?"

"Whassup, Big Bird? You fittin' to let Mighty Whitey kick yo scrawny black ass?"

"Nigger got game, but got no *heart,* know what I'm sayin'? Can't handle a little pressure."

I advance my knight, forking his rook and king.

"Check." I say this softly, respectfully. It's mate in three moves. Big Bird sees it too. He tips the white king over, gently—surrender. He offers a handshake and the brothers go nuts. Rollies and candy bars fly across the table.

"That's one cold motherfuckin' white boy!"

"I tol' yo ass! The Bird got no heart, bro."

Big Bird takes exception to this comment, standing up to confront a small young brother called Little G.

"Nigger, *puh-lease*! Whatchu talkin' shit 'bout *heart* when you got no motherfuckin' *dick,* Lil G!"

Lil G dances away from the table, throwing jabs and insults at the air. "Bird, you must be trippin' behind losing to Mighty Whitey, talkin' 'bout dick and shit like you *about* something! You ain't never seen my dick 'cause it be buried up in yo momma's ass!"

"Say *what,* nigger? Say what 'bout my momma?"

And on and on until Bubblecop screams, "LOCK IT DOWN!"

In the cell Kansas is outraged. "Yo, dawg, it's your business, but I gotta tell ya, kickin' it with the fucking toads ain't cool. The woods ain't down with that shit—y'unnerstan' what I'm saying to you? Back in Kansas you'd be lucky to be standing right now. Someone woulda put a couple of padlocks in a sock and *slocked* your dome, know what I'm sayin'?"

"Slocking" is another pastime in the joint. Convicts who don't want to get crossed out behind having a shank use a slock. At the store they sell heavy padlocks for inmates to secure their plastic yellow tubs. Since most inmates have nothing worth protecting, they shove the lock in a sock and start swinging. Sometimes, to add a little flavor and heft, they toss a couple of cans of Armour chili (with beans) into the sock.

Then rock your world.

Kansas still can't shut up. ". . . or worse, O.G., and let me tell you worse ain't nothin' nice! You wanna get a fucking *wigger* jacket, dawg? That's *white nigger*—something they probably didn't teach you in college—know what I'm sayin'?"

The vein beneath the swastika is pulsing violently and this is always a bad sign.

"Kansas, it was just a chess game."

We're both standing, facing each other in the cramped cell where the temperature has to be over 100. A few inches separate our faces. Unfortunately for me, the inches are all vertical. Kansas has about six inches and at least a hundred pounds on me. All tattooed muscle. Otherwise I might feel confident.

But I'm hot, fed up, and out of patience.

"You know what, Kansas? I really don't give a rat's fuck for what your precious *woods* think. As a matter of fact, *fuck them,* and if *you* have a problem with my choice of chess partners or with how I do *my* time, then fuck you too! Y'unnerstan' what I'm sayin' to you?"

This is clearly a defining moment in our evolving relationship. For an eternal minute we are both silent, giving each other the hairy eyeball.

Kansas blinks first, then backs off before ducking down onto his tray.

"Yogee, I believe you really are one cold motherfucker." Then, for once, he is quiet, no doubt wondering how his prized pupil could stray so far from the Wood Path.

I climb up to my bunk. The last time my body was shaking this badly was when I called 911 to report that I had just killed a Monster by the name of Dwayne Hassleman.

And now I'm paying for it.

Of course, Kansas breaks the silence first. "Yogee, I didn't mean to get up in your business or disrespect you. You're right about one thing, dawg. In here, we all got to do our own time. Ain't nobody gonna do it for you. You know what I'm sayin'?"

And for once, I do.

Later Bubblecop yells, "Lights out!" Kansas has a question. "O.G., where the fuck did you come up with that business about the rat?"

I sit up in my tray and look down into the darkness. "What rat?"

"You know, whatchu was talkin' about before when I thought you was gonna bust my dome or something—you know, how you didn't give a rat's fuck or something like that."

"Oh that—I don't know, Kansas. It must be a New York thing."

"I kind of like it."

"Feel free to use it."

"Aiight, O.G. It's all good then. Good night, dawg."

"Night, dawg."

On the mornings when the dirt and sand are blowing at less than hurricane ferocity, I walk around the enclosed Fish Tank yard, a dirt rectangle surrounded by a razor-wire-topped fence. The small yard comes complete with its own hundred-foot-high stone guntower (sniper included). In one corner of the yard is a small weight pile known as the Wood Pile. It's strictly white-boy turf and Kansas's home away from the house.

There are two asphalt islands in the dirt for the basketball and handball courts. The basketball court is pure toad territory, while the handball court is a mixture of Mexican gang-bangers and woods waiting for their turn at the weights.

The less athletically inclined fish do laps, slowly circling the dirt perimeter of the yard. Fish here almost always travel in schools for protection.

The few fish that brave the yard alone are either known Shotcallers (like cellblock union bosses) or have stand-ups watching their backs.

When I tell Kansas I plan to walk some laps by myself, he trips for a few minutes before reluctantly volunteering to be my stand-up.

"A sideways fish like you won't last two laps without someone planting a Christmas tree in your chest or slocking the shit out of you. Besides, you're my cellie. Some punk jacks your shit up and it disrespects *me*—y'unnerstan'?"

I tell Kansas I appreciate his concern and friendship. And I mean it.

I follow the beaten dirt track, walking in a clockwise direction like all the other fish. No one here, except a few J-Cats, ever walks the yard counterclockwise.

Go figure.

I count my steps trying to calculate how many laps will equal a mile. It seems very important to know this. Fifty paces, pass the hand-ball court, reach the fence, turn right. Seventy paces, pass the Wood Pile, make a right at the fence. Then fifty paces alongside the basketball court, sharp right, and complete the lap with seventy paces.

Then repeat.

I catch myself compulsively counting steps, although I now have a perfectly good algorithm to compute miles. I hope I'm not coming down with one of those obsessive-compulsive disorders that will condemn me to a vigilant life of stepping over sidewalk cracks and taking six-hour showers.

Nobody sweats me except for the morning sun, which is already brutal. Kansas likes to say the weather is part of the punishment. I don't disagree.

Not wanting to appear completely antisocial, I take a strategic pause every now and then to network and hopefully build some rapport with my fellow guests. I kick it for a minute with some of the dawgs at the Wood Pile. My next-door neighbor, Big Bear, is stripped to the waist doing curls. The Bear is short and wiry (like a squirrel) with a webwork of tattoos extending from his wrists to his shoulders. *Full sleeves,* if you know what I'm saying. A piece of string from the laundry secures his ponytail.

"What's up, dawg?" he calls to me.

"Just kickin' it, Bear."

"Kicking rocks, right, O.G.?"

"Right on, Bear." I thought that "right on" was a sixties anachronism, but it's alive and kicking it here. The familiarity is a small comfort to me. I wonder if I can reintroduce "far-out" to these dawgs. Tell them it's "hip," practically "the bomb" or "the shit."

I greet the tiny Mexican with the "La Raza" tattoo on his neck with *"Buenos días."* I make sure to drop my classroom-instilled Castilian accent. In prison I suspect that lisping in Spanish would not be considered hip by a Chicano gangster.

"Buenos días, Jaime," says La Raza with a smile. It feels good to be called Jimmy again, even if it's in Spanish.

At the sidelines of the basketball court I briefly kick it with the Bone and my chess partner, Big Bird. *What's up, Bone? Bird? Aiight now, O.G. It's all good—it's all good in the hood, wood.* We all laugh and I move on, kicking rocks.

It occurs to my corporate cubicle-shaped brain that kicking it may be a primitive precursor to Networking. That perhaps all corporate Strategic Alliances and Mergers have their roots in the basic human desire either to not get hurt or to be a part of something bigger and more powerful than oneself. Because I got nothin' but time, I decide to elevate this thought to a realm even loftier than Merger and Acquisition Theory. I'm thinking about the historical attraction of organized religion and the current craze for unorganized spirituality with its attendant Higher Power. I glance up at the sun.

But such grand concepts are interfering with my counting steps—not to mention giving me a headache. I look back down at my feet. At the dirt.

There's a commotion on the basketball court. I sit down in the dirt, my back against the concrete exterior wall of the cellblock. It's a good day to watch basketball.

Big Hungry is on the court. In the sunshine he's not as huge as I had thought—maybe only six feet nine, about four hundred pounds. It must have been the gold teeth and murderous scowl that frightened me.

The Hunger can't shoot, can't run, and refuses to pass. His team wisely insists he just station himself under the hoop, which the Hunger has twisted back into a serviceable rim.

Hunger's formidable presence beneath the basket serves as a very effective deterrent to any opponent rash enough to even think of driving by him for a layup. Little G is more than rash, though, and is Hunger's chief tormentor on the court.

Lil G is very quick, very small, and absolutely fearless. In a lightning dribble around the Hunger (accompanied by a barking, mocking laugh) Lil G sinks a layup.

The Hunger immediately goes postal.

"BOTH FOOTS IS OUTTA BOUNDS, NIGGER!" Screaming, the Hunger advances on Lil G like a furious black mountain descending on a tiny black ant. "YO MUTHAFUCKIN' FOOTS BE *OUT* DA LINE!"

But *nobody* sweats Little G. Little G is from Compton. He's been there, done that. Now Lil G becomes Ice-G, standing his ground, shouting back.

"THAT'S BULLSHIT, HUNGER!—MY FEETS BE *BEHIND* THE MUTHAFUCKIN' LINE! AX THE BONE OR BIG BIRD!"

The Hunger looks down, points, and resumes screaming. "DAY AIN'T EVEN NO MUTHAFUCKIN' LINE, G—YOU SEE SOME GOTDAME LINE HERE, FOOL?"

Lil G is now jumping up and down, pointing to some imaginary demarcation in the dirt. "YO TAKES YO BIG OL' NASTY FAT ASS OUTCHO HAID, YOU BE *SEEING* THE MUTHAFUCKIN' LINE, MOTHERFUCKER!"

T-Bone sits in the dirt beside me, mourning the lack of sportsmanship with a shake of his shower cap. "Cain't a muthafucka play some basketball without everybody raising up like they all bad and shit?"

Big Hungry and Little G exchange the ritualized wolf tickets. Lots of references to ancestry, busted grapes in Napa, peeled onions, broken grills, and smashed domelights.

It's pretty much business as usual until Lil G utters the M-word and the Hunger is sweeping toward him like a molten lava flow. "Whatchu say 'bout my *momma!* Nigger, I'll put a muthafuckin' .45 to yo punk-ass dome. I'll bust a cap upside yo nappy little haid! I crack yo little peanut self!"

Little G is now in retreat but gets in the last word. "Only crack you fittin' to do be yo *pipe,* nigger! I'll stick a nine-millimeter up your big goat-smelling ass. I'll—"

"LOCK IT DOWN! PLAY FUCKING TIME IS OVER! LOCK IT DOWN—NOW!"

High above us, Guntower Cop is standing with a bullhorn and a mini-14 on his balcony. Behind us our very own Bubblecop is brandishing an M-16 from his perch in the bubble.

I take the mini-14 and M-16 as distinct cues and rush to the Fish Tank doors. We wait on our front porches for Bubblecop to open the doors. Kansas, invigorated from bench-pressing four-hundred-plus pounds for an hour, pulls the slider open.

"Fucking toads got us locked down, O.G. But ain't no big thing, dawg. Ain't no real hard time in this punk-ass prison. Fuck, today's like a day on the beach, you know what I'm sayin'?"

"LOCK IT DOWN!"

Eighty steel doors slam shut at the same time.

Thwunk!!!

It does not sound like beach music.

I think I may not be conveying the softer, artistic side of some of the woods here. My neighbor, Big Bear, for example, writes poetry. Otherwise he has impeccable wood credentials: unemployed short-order cook, needle tracks on his arms hidden by tattoos, three domestic battery convictions, and five teeth.

A pounding on the cell wall. Bear's signal to go stand by the vent for an urgent communication. Kansas doesn't stir, so I get down and put my ear to the vent.

"Yo, Kansas! O.G.!"

"What's up, Bear?"

"That you, O.G.?"

"All day, Bear—what's up?"

"Wanna hear my poem?"

"Sure."

"Aiight—hold on, I'm getting it."

This time Big Bear is back in prison for rape. A rapist is a scandalous jacket to have in the joint, but the woods here make allowances for Bear because the victim was his ex-wife. The Conventional Wood Wisdom is that "the bitch had it coming."

Bear bangs on the wall with his percussion instruments—a coffee cup and spork—and begins rapping:

> "Big-titted blond bitch
> A slut and a tease
> So I took her out to dinner
> She called me a fucking sleaze.
> Bitch drank down high-price wine
> Sucking glass after glass
> 'Til I dragged her to my house
> Rammed my cock up her ass."

Kansas is now sitting up on his tray. Bear pounds out a bizarre, atavistic bass line with the cup and spork.

> "When she started to scream
> I stuffed a rag in her hole,
> Whispered in her ear—'Bitch,
> here comes a foot-long pole.'

I fucked her all night
Did exactly as I pleased.
In the morning I untied her,
Whispered, 'Now who's the fucking sleaze.' "

Kansas loves it! Pounds on the wall. "Right on, dawg! That's the shit, bro!"

"Yogee, whatchu think?"

I think Big Bear has some *serious* issues. I try to think of something to say.

"Well, Bear . . . it has a certain rhythmic jauntiness . . . it's unique."

"You neek? That's good?"

"Ah, unique can be good."

"Aiight then—thanks, O.G."

"Always glad to lend an ear, Bear."

I remember now. It was Sartre who said "Hell is other people."

The Shit Jumps Off early in the morning of day 59. It starts off just as Kansas is announcing he needs "to drop a dookie." Before he can get over to the toilet, gunfire erupts somewhere in the main yard.

His dookie drop momentarily stalled, Kansas leaps up on my tray and tries to hog my window view. Far away, a crowd of tiny figures in state blue are battling in front of the chow hall.

More shotgun and rifle blasts from the guntowers, and now there are tiny blue and red figures sprawling in the dirt. Dozens of convicts are racing across the yard dodging bullets and birdshot, trying to make it back to the relative safety of their cellblocks.

Our toilet suddenly comes alive bubbling and gurgling. There is a giant sucking sound as the water in the bowl just vanishes. The sink hisses and groans.

The cops have shut off all the water.

We're both in our underwear, crouched on knees on the upper tray. Our domes clang together as we contest the window view.

"Fuck! It's *on*, O.G. It's coming down, dawg!" Kansas is thrilled. This is the happiest I have seen him.

"What's *on*, Kansas? You forget to pay the water bill this month?"

"That's a good one, O.G. Very fucking funny. Let's see if you're still cracking sideways when the cops got you all strained up. Yo! Check it out! Here come the motherfucking Dirt!"

"Who the hell is that?"

"That's the *Dirt*, dawg—Disciplinary Intervention and Response Team, and they ain't nothin' nice."

Marching across the yard is a phalanx of black-clad storm troopers, their visored helmets, shields, and shotguns glistening magnificently in the desert sun. If the shotguns don't kill you first, the glare from their spit-shined jackboots could blind a dawg.

Strange, fragmentary visions flood my mind, their source either tales from my great-grandmother Goldie or that great underground stream of collective racial subconsciousness. Storefront windows in Berlin shattering like crystal in the night. Farther downstream the screams of shtetl mothers and children as the riders approach for pogrom season.

"O.G.! Quit your tripping—more Dirt coming to the Fish Tank!"

Another black phalanx is marching to the Fish Tank gates. Every third cop has a crazed German shepherd straining against a short leash.

I've always been more of a cat person than a dog person, if you understand what I'm saying, so the arrival of these rabid-looking creatures is less than comforting to me.

"Yo, Kansas, where the fuck do they find these guys—and who dresses them? Hermann Göring?"

"Don't be dissin' Göring, dawg. I know everything about that dude and he was one righteous motherfucker. Hell, the Dirt here ain't shit. Buncha C.O. punk-ass wanna-be police, but too fucking dumb to pass the cop exam. They volunteer for this shit so they can dress up like Johnny Fucking Cash and get to carry guns. Motherfucking punks trying to act like they're *about* somethin'. In Kansas the Dirt there would have already dropped tear gas canisters in the vents and we'd be puking out our oatmeal."

Maybe the Dirt here ain't shit, but Kansas is frantically tearing apart his mattress, tossing all kinds of contraband on the floor.

"Watch my back, O.G."

My old military training kicks in. In 1975 I played lookout for the M.P.s' for some army buddies who were vigorously defending democracy in a brothel of a small (but ungrateful) Central American dictatorship.

I'm at the forward observer position before the cell door window, my glasses fogging from the heat. Kansas is still removing his verboten treasures from deep within the mattress. Downstairs the double doors hiss open, and the Dirt and the dogs pour through into the Fish Tank.

The barbarians have breached the gates, and Kansas is leisurely studying his contraband. He flips open a *Hustler* magazine. *Hustler* is banned in prison, considered too raunchy, I guess. *Playboy* is permitted, though, probably due to the socially redeeming articles.

Kansas places his latest implement of destruction on the cell floor. It is a toothbrush embedded with a razor blade on top. He fashioned it by stomping one of the Bic disposable razors they give out once a week. After liberating the blade he drove his Cadillac over to Bear's house and picked up a Bic disposable lighter. After heating up the end of the toothbrush he inserted the blade into the molten plastic. Kansas says it's called a "trazor."

The trazor is bad enough. What truly disturbs me are the three *New York Times*–wrapped packages of drugs.

"What the fuck is *that!* You told me you got rid of them all, that Skell picked them up!"

The dogs are howling now from the lower tier, but Kansas is smiling. "Don't trip, O.G. All the shit is going out the door now."

Using my tennis sneaker as a hockey stick, Kansas swats the trazor, the drugs, and the *Hustler* out under the cell door, across the front porch, and over the catwalk. Similar items are being launched from every cell on the upper tier.

The Dirt and the Dirtdogs are assembling in front of Strunk's office awaiting a command from their sergeant, a lean, leathery whip of a man with a jarhead crew cut and a face like a clenched fist.

Big Bear is screaming under the cell door at the cops.

"Punk-ass bitch Dirt faggots!"

Kindred sentiments spill out from other cells.

"Jo! Jo, *pen-day-ho!* Ju ain' shit, *maricón* muthafuck!" I recognize my yard acquaintance, La Raza Neck Tattoo.

Lil G is selling wolf tickets to the cops: "Yo, punk-ass Dirtboy! Put down yo gun and come on up my crib, muthafucka. We fittin' to have a par-tay. Up your butt!"

The Hunger finishes it—"And all yo punk-ass Dirt friends is *coming,* muthafucka!"

Sergeant Jarhead barks out a command to the troops—I count about thirty cops—and the German shepherds are released.

The dogs, raging and frothing, explode throughout the rotunda followed by their Dirt masters.

Big Bear begins barking—literally—under his cell door. He is quickly joined by dozens of other cells, and the Fish Tank, never exactly quiet, sounds like a dog pound in hell. Maybe louder.

The German shepherds experience minimal difficulty in sniffing out the drugs. The drugs rain down like convict confetti on their howling heads. Trazors and shanks sail through the air off the upper tier, and Jarhead shouts out "Shields!" Up go the Plexiglas shields. Out from the lower-tier cells fly Bic pen shanks, Bic trazors, pieces of burned tinfoil, steel-wool pads, more *Hustler*s, and various tattoo gun components.

Kansas is flat on his face, barking and screaming under the door, his face ablaze with a mad ecstasy. This must remind him of the good times in the Kansas pen.

"Yogee, in Kansas the fucking police gas and handcuff you *before* you can kick your contraband to the curb—y'unnerstan' what I'm sayin'? Here the stupid fucks just kill the water pressure so you can't flush your shit down. Ignorant-ass Dirt motherfuckers!

"Come on, O.G.! Bark! Come on, dawg—it gets the fucking dogs really mad."

The Dirt and dogs are climbing the stairs to our tier. Jackboots thud, doggy toenails clatter on the metal steps.

The Dirt are in front of cell 44, three down. I can hear the cell door popping open, handcuffs jangling, walkie-talkies squawking.

"O.G.! Come on—bark now!"

"Are you completely crazy, Kansas? Why do we want to get the dogs mad? They're already rabid. They'll fucking eat us!"

I have just asked another of those "Why" questions that don't compute within Kansas's dome.

" 'Cause . . . because . . ."

" 'Cause why?"

" 'Cause that's just . . . *what we do!*"

Cell 45 is cracked open, and the guests are unceremoniously hauled out and flung facedown on the catwalk and cuffed behind their backs.

"All right, Kansas. Why didn't you tell me you had such a good reason? Okay, I can't do a dog—I'm not a dog person—but I can do a hellacious cat, dawg." When my daughters were very little, I would amuse them by making cat noises and pretending there were cute little kitties hiding throughout the house. Probably under their beds and in their closets.

Kansas makes enough room on the floor for me to squeeze in beside him in front of the door.

"Aiight, O.G. A cat is cool—just do it."

I'm pressing my mouth against the opening, swallowing air. I'm ready.

"Breeoooooow!"

Kansas is so impressed he is stunned speechless. The trick is to slowly bring air up from the diaphragm, gradually building up pressure, then controlling and sustaining the release. Much easier than sex. It's a small talent of mine but one that enabled me to belch louder and longer than any of my fourth-grade classmates—no small accomplishment in P.S. 92 in Brooklyn.

I let go with another, even louder:

"BREEEEOOOOOOOOOOOW!"

There is a sudden, complete stillness throughout the Fish Tank. For one brief shining moment—my personal convict Camelot—*silence* while the Dirt, the dawgs, and the dogs contemplate the meaning of this startling newcomer to the zoo.

Then more chaos. The German shepherds are so confused and crazed they are snapping at dust motes in the air. Big Bear, no doubt emboldened and empowered by my innovation, does a cow.

"Mooooo!"

Little G down in cell 11 lets loose with a funky chicken. *"Bwuck, bwuck, bwuck,* yo punk-ass bitch po-lease fuck!"

Big Hungry seems to think one of the shepherds is female. He hisses at the dog in front of his cell.

"Clarice . . . Clarisssssse . . . yo little bitch . . . I be smelling your pussy from in here!" Another case of life imitating art.

The Bone just whines through his door—"Cain't a muthafucka just do his own time in his house?"

The Dirt has had enough. The dogs are out of control. Jarhead screams into his bullhorn:

"ON THE FLOOR IN YOUR CELLS—FACEDOWN AND HANDS ON TOP OF YOUR FUCKING HEADS. NO TALKING!"

Already facedown and in our cell, Kansas and I clasp our hands to our domes. Kansas can't stop giggling over the cat.

"Yo, O.G. One time in Kansas—"

"Will you please shut up about *Kansas*? They're right outside the door!"

The cell door is yanked violently open and a snarling German shepherd leaps over our prostrate bodies and lands on Kansas's tray. A Dirtcop handcuffs us behind our backs—*tight*. Way too tight. Kansas, of course, starts protesting in that patented convict whine he likes to use on the police.

"Excuse me, Officer, but could you loosen them cuffs a bit? I got circulation problems and a medical paper that says I got—"

The sergeant steps into the cell.

"You got *nothin'* coming, convict. That's all you got. Now shut the fuck up before I bust your dome!"

"This is outta line, C.O. These cuffs are—"

The sergeant brings a foot-long steel flashlight down on Kansas's head. Not hard enough to put out his lights but enough to momentarily shut him up. Blood spills down from his forehead and over the Nazi tattoo on his neck.

"Now get out of the fucking cell! Move! Move! Move!"

Standing up unassisted with hands cuffed behind one's back is impossible. Sergeant Jarhead yanks us to our feet by the cuffs, pulls us out to the catwalk, then slams us back down on the ground. All along the upper tier I see dawgs squirming in pain on their bellies, the cuffs cutting into flesh.

The Dirt storm into our house, tearing it up. This is what's known as a shakedown. And it ain't nothing nice. Mattresses, sheets, towels, toilet paper, state soap, and our legal paperwork are dumped on the floor then stepped on. A letter I just received from my daughters is tossed to the ground and shredded beneath the jackboots. A photo-graph of my girls, Alana and Rachel, taken at Disneyland when they were eleven and ten, is ripped off the wall. The sergeant examines it briefly before tearing it in half and tossing the pieces in the air.

Ten-year-old Rachel, smiling up at Goofy, lands a few inches from my face. I smile at her.

A photo of Kansas's girlfriend, Star—she of the balloon-laden mouth—receives identical treatment from Jarhead. Kansas is trying to struggle to his feet, enraged beyond anything I have yet seen.

"Yo! That's a picture of my *wife* you're ripping up and stomping on. Howja like it if I step on your bitches?"

The sergeant emerges from our house. His little metal nameplate identifies him as SGT. STANGER. "You got another fucking problem, convict? Facedown on the ground now or I'll throw your ass in the fucking Shoe for ninety days!"

Kansas knows there are no visiting privileges in the Hole. He clenches his teeth and presses his face to the ground. "O.G.—payback's gonna be a motherfucker. Stanger gonna find out the getback from Kansas is a bitch, know what I'm sayin'?"

I'm still looking for my other daughter, Alana, who was grinning up at Mickey in the picture. I hope she is not lost to me forever.

The Dirt, disgusted at finding no contraband *inside* any of the cells, uncuff us and shove us back inside. We are on our trays, Kansas press-ing a wad of toilet paper to his cut, clearly disappointed by the absence of any real mayhem. Still talking about Kansas.

"Yogee, in Kansas the cops pulled this shit, things would have jumped off big-time, know what I'm sayin'? C.O. there knows bet-ter than to fuck with a man's pictures. Kansas woods don't take that shit—"

"Kansas, will you shut the fuck up!" I'm drifting somewhere in Disneyland, two small hands holding mine. I don't want to come back. Not to this.

The toilet starts gurgling and the sink gushes out brown water. Kansas mounts the steel throne for his long-delayed dookie, still talking.

". . . in the Kansas pen, dawg, we'd of had something for them fucking dogs too. Would of been a few shanked shepherds for dinner, bro. You unnerstan' what I'm sayin' to you?"

I can't find Alana anywhere in the cell.

"Yo, Kansas," I begin. I'm so weary. Soul-sick. "Listen, dawg—we're not in Kansas anymore. You understand what *I'm* saying?"

Our house is a shambles. The Dirt took everything that wasn't issued to us by the state. Kansas and I take a painful inventory while the Dirt are gathering up and bagging all the contraband on the catwalk and rotunda floor. Incredibly they find a full set of handcuff keys among the shanks and drugs.

All my store is gone: two writing tablets, envelopes, stamps, Bic pens, a bag of 4 Aces tobacco with rolling papers, one Heritage Stick deodorant ("Musk"), and a can of Pacific Pearl sardines ("lightly smoked in oil").

Most devastating, though, is the loss of my comfort foods. Kansas says it's critical to make an itemized list in order to file a property claim form later on. He hands me a pencil stub and I start recording the missing-in-Dirt-action items: four Almond Joys, three bags of Digby's Jolly Ranchers (one assorted, two "fire"), a bag of Hershey's Kisses, five Reese's Peanut Butter Cups, two beef jerkies ("kipper"), three bags of Cactus Annie's pork rinds ("hot and spicy!"), one bag of licorice (cherry nibs), and seven bags of Sather's Gummi Bears.

I particularly mourn the loss of the Gummi Bears. They always put me in a frolicsome humor.

Also missing are two tattered paperback novels that Lester the Molester let me have for four stamps. The *New York Times* is gone, but I'm not sweating that—I'll get a new delivery tomorrow.

All of Kansas's stuff (except his Nazi "literature") has also gone the way of dirt. Kansas ain't trippin' because he never bought any of it. Kansas doesn't believe in *buying* store. He takes other people's store. He insists other inmates just *give* him things.

Kansas always allocates a portion of his one-hour tier time to terrorize fish into donating a percentage of their store to him. He tells them it is the standard "cell rental" charge and he is the collection agent for the landlord. Or he allows them to purchase a "life insurance" policy from him. When he spots fish who manifest sufficiently brutal tendencies, he explains that by paying "initiation dues" now they will be given top consideration for membership in his skinhead Nazi Low Rider club. And he means it.

What puzzled me at first was that some of the more seasoned cons, the so-called hard cases, were eager to also pay tribute with candy, stamps, and tobacco.

Skell tells me that Kansas is *the* Shotcaller again now that he's back in prison. He whispers this to me in the fish yard. Tells me to "keep it on the D.L." "What's the D.L., Skell?" Skell glances furtively around, which is the only way Skell ever glances around. "The D.L., dawg, is the down-low. You keep something on the D.L. and it stays with you— you down wid that?" I tell him I'm down with it.

It's the usual morning hour for tier time, and convicts are banging on cell doors to be let out.

"Tier time," they yell up at Bubblecop, who is relaxing behind the console with a *Hustler* and a bag of Gummi Bears. "Tier time!" they scream, and Bubblecop doesn't flinch.

The Dirt is gone and C.O. Strunk is compelled to leave his icy pod to make a general announcement to the Fish Tank. Lately Strunk is looking less and less like a fire hydrant and more and more like a beach ball with a bad haircut. He stands in the center of the rotunda and bellows out the one word guaranteed to engender an unhealthful amount of fear and loathing:

"LOCKDOWN!"

Lockdowns go with shakedowns like—as Kansas would say—"stank on shit." The entire prison ramps up to a supermax security mode for a few hours, days, or even months. Kansas claims they are "part of the punishment." That they are as natural "as beating your redheaded stepchild."

Strunk shouts once more before fleeing back to his office. "No tier time! You're on lockdown!"

Kansas and a hundred others react by kicking the sturdy steel cell doors. Bad for the doors. Very bad for the feet. They also scream.

"Motherfucking cocksuckers!"

"Punk-ass *po*-lease!"

"Punk-ass Strunk-ass fat muthafucka!"

"Yo, Strunk! Lock *this* down, you punk-ass bitch!"

Inmates are gathered in front of the doors, peering through the wire-mesh windows, trying to see what they can see.

There is nothing to see except the faces of other fish pressed against the windows. Unless you count watching Strunk kick back in his reclining chair with his own copy of *Hustler,* scarfing down a bag of licorice (cherry nibs).

Kansas finally gives up kung-fuing the cell door—the door won. As the heat climbs in the cellblock, the banging, clanging, pounding, and screaming gradually subside to the normal horrifying levels.

At 5 P.M. we get out for two minutes to pick up our dinner trays—liver and onions and cold mashed potatoes. The Bone registers a complaint: "Cain't a muthafucka get nothin' but no cold-ass mashed?" No one cares.

When Skell arrives on our front porch to pick up the trays (and deliver two more to Kansas), I ask him to bring me a book from Lester's library.

Skell is immediately suspicious.

"What do you mean a book?" Funny—you could ask Skell to fetch you a shank, a spear, a surface-to-air missile and he wouldn't bat a jaundiced eye. But a book?

"A novel, Skell—any kind!"

"Cost you two stamps, O.G. You down wid dat?"

"I'm down with it."

"Aiight then—later."

Kansas makes another dookie announcement. This signals me to roll over on my side and face the wall or the window to afford Kansas a small measure of privacy.

This may be more information than anyone needs, but there is a certain etiquette to taking a dookie in a prison cell. Every few seconds Kansas punches the flush button. Current convict theory holds that the continuous suction will carry the most vile odors away before they can permeate the entire cell.

This theory cries out for revisiting. An oven-hot eight-by-six concrete cell in a post-dookie environment stinks.

Too late, Kansas discovers the Dirt also took our toilet paper.

"Shit! O.G., will you holler down to the C.O. for some shit paper?"

"Aiight . . . C.O.! Cell 47!" After five minutes of shouting, C.O. Strunk deigns to put down his *Hustler* and glare up at me. To his credit he actually gets up (somewhat stiff-legged) and opens his door.

"What do you need, O.G.?"

"Toilet paper, sir." The "sir" is a syntactical appendage I am learning to overlay only when something is desperately needed.

Strunk is visibly irritated to have been separated from his coffee and newly acquired *Hustler* to deal with such a prosaic problem.

"You know the rules, O.G. You get two rolls of toilet paper per cell per week."

"But the Dirt confiscated all our toilet paper."

Strunk greets this annoying little factoid with indifference. It is clearly irrelevant. "That's on the Dirt—it ain't on me. I hand out two rolls per cell per week *per* Administrative Regulation number 22." Administrative Regulation number 22 is suspiciously cited by Strunk whenever he doesn't feel like doing his job. No one here has ever seen a copy of AR-22. And some of these dawgs have been down for more than a few days, if you know what I'm saying.

"So what are we supposed to do?" The second this whining question is out of my mouth I know I have set myself up. Strunk is already pissed off over the universal disrespect disclosed by such an abundance of contraband in "his house." The Dirt finding handcuff keys didn't help. We all know he will be hearing about the entire mess from Stanger, or possibly the warden.

"Use your fucking finger!" is Strunk's answer. Pleased with his resolution of the problem, he waddles back behind his desk, picks up the *Hustler,* and stuffs an Almond Joy in his mouth.

Apparently the big winner in the shakedown is the cops.

Still squatting, Kansas unleashes a virulent (even for him) stream of obscenities flavored with his fervent promises of "getback." It ain't gonna be nothin' nice. No sir.

There is no paper of any kind in our house except his Nazi tracts. I suggest pulling off a page or two from *Secrets from the Bunker.*

"No fuckin' way! You're talking about writings that are practically *sacred,* like them Dead Scrolls they found. What else we got?"

"*We?* You have probably over two hundred pages in your PSI and FBI reports—want me to peel off, say, ten pages of your early criminal history—age four?"

"That's way outta line, dawg. What about . . . I got it! Remember when the punk-ass chaplain give us them Bibles when we first come in? Check in my tub—see if the Dirt got that too."

Kansas snatches it from my hand, hesitates. "You figure this could be like a major sin, O.G.? 'Cause I ain't one of these fucking pagans that we got running around here, fucking Wiccans they call themselves. Buncha fucking freaks!"

"From what you've told me about yourself this will probably be recorded—if at all—as a relatively minor transgression."

"Minor? Like a misdemeanor or something?"

"Probably even less than that—more like a parking violation."

A minute later Kansas smacks the flush button, and a passage from Genesis is sucked deep down into the bowels of the Nevada prison sewage system.

Now Skell is knocking on the cell door. "I gotcha a book but it's too fat to stuff under the door. I'm gonna have to tear it in half and kick the pieces under—you down wid dat?"

"It's all good, Skell."

Skell double-drop-kicks a bifurcated copy of a novel called *The Temple of Gold* by William Goldman. I'm devouring the novel, loving it, when down in cell 7 Lester the Molester starts screaming from his wheelchair. He wants his "meds." Prescribed medications are delivered two times a day to the cells by a justifiably nervous female nurse escorted by an infirmary cop.

"C.O.—where's the fucking meds?" Lester yells under the cell door. "They're supposed to bring the meds at six!" This stirs up the J-Cats, all of whom receive psychotropic drugs, like it or not. The lower-tier J-Cat section is suddenly shrieking out requests.

"Where's my motherfucking Thorazine!"

"Yo, Strunk—I be needing my Haldol!"

"Stell-zeen! I'm supposed to get my Stell-zeen!"

"Where's the fucking Sin-nay-quan?"

The bedlam builds to an earsplitting din. C.O. Strunk finally has to put down his bag of Cactus Annie's pork rinds (hot and spicy!) to call the infirmary.

Kansas tapping on my tray.

"What's up?" I ask, eschewing the more fashionable "Whassup."

"Need to know what this word means."

"What's the word?"

"*Purge*-a-torry."

"Hmmm . . . give it to me in context."

"What contest?"

"I mean read it in the sentence."

As usual I end up reading it: *There is a special place in purgatory for Jewish sympathizers that* . . .

"Very deep stuff, Kansas. The word is 'purgatory.' "

"What's it mean?"

The J-Cat screams are bouncing off the Fish Tank walls below. From our air vent comes that mysterious sobbing sound.

"Purgatory? That's like this place."

"Straight-up business, dawg? No sideways shit?"

"On my skin, bro."

"Aiight then."

The muffled sobs amplify and become full-blown, uncontrollable weeping. Kansas and I both know it is coming from one of the teenagers' cells on our tier.

A friend of mine, a priest, once told me that the three most powerful words in the Bible are: "And Jesus wept."

The lockdown drags on for days.

The teenage fish who weeps through the air vent at night lives in cell 49, next door to Big Bear. We see him three times a day when we pick up our food trays from the lower tier. We see the bruises on his face. Sometimes we see worse things.

The kid is sixteen but looks thirteen, so thin his ribs poke out through his bony white chest. All the dawgs call him Bobby-Boy except his cellie, who calls him "punk" or "little bitch" to his face. On the fish yard he refers to Bobby-Boy as "my kid," before smiling in a grotesque mockery of paternal pride.

All the dawgs call the cellie Bruno, and he looks like one, full-sleeved with a bullet-shaped skinhead. His chest and arms reflect a decade spent between the weight piles and tattoo guns.

Bruno is anything but a fish. He's supposed to be in the Hole, doing ninety days for theft, extortion, and rape, but with the Hole at full capacity Bruno is being kept in the Fish Tank on a "temporary administrative segregation hold" until a room is found for him at the inn.

The days fall away, and September is every bit as hot and benumbing as August and July.

And the lockdown continues.

Bobby-Boy died today.

Or maybe it was yesterday—I can't be sure. In a prison lockdown, time is distorted. It bends and swirls and circles until nights dissolve into days that are perhaps Monday or Friday, but no one knows for sure and no one cares 'cause we're not going anywhere.

And we got nothing coming.

It happened when they opened the upper-tier cells for breakfast-tray pickup and we were filing out like zombies in underwear to the catwalk. It happened so fast that there was little anyone could do, presuming anyone would have been inclined to intervene.

We emerge from our houses clutching our plastic mugs with the HARD TIME logo. An inmate gets only one chance at the portable milk dispenser. If you forget your cup in your cell, you can forget about a drink. Or, as Strunk says every day, "Got no cup, you're fucking *burnt*! You got *nothin'* comin'!"

Bobby limps slowly and painfully out of cell 49. He is not carrying the obligatory cup. He is carrying a rope he has fashioned by knotting two sheets together. Bobby is holding one end of the sheet-rope. The other end is a noose and it is already around his neck.

Bobby makes it to the catwalk railing with two shuffling steps. Big Bear sees him first, shouts *"No, no, Bobby-Boy, no!"* Bobby bends over to quickly anchor his end of the sheet-rope to the rail. His white state boxers are still bright with blood.

Bubblecop gets his *Hustler* down and his shotgun up just in time to see Bobby dive headfirst over the railing. He flips once in midair before his neck snaps. It is a sound that I know will take up permanent residence in my repertoire of nightmares. Star billing alongside the Monster.

"LOCK IT DOWN—NOW!!"

Nobody is hungry anymore anyway.

In the cell Kansas offers his analysis, filtered through his customary solipsistic prism.

"Fuck! That shit was completely off the hook! Fucking Bobby-Boy should have P.C.'d up from the jump, know what I'm sayin'? Young punk like that belongs in protective custody! Bet they keep us locked down for a fucking year behind Bobby-Boy's punk-ass bullshit."

Some of the Dirt arrive and take pictures of Bobby-Boy before they take him down. They also take Bruno off to the Hole to do his belated ninety days.

Bruno actually does only seventy-eight days in the Hole. They gave him twelve days "time-served credits" for his stay in the Fish Tank.

And Jesus wept.

The lockdown grinds into a third week. No more tier time. No more visits. No phones, no showers, no store, no yard. We got nothing coming. By federal law they have to give us mail, so I continue to receive the *Times* and several magazines that my little sister, Lisa—bless her heart!—has subscribed to for me.

My "little" sister is now thirty-seven and a highly successful real estate attorney near Miami, where condominium residents think nothing of suing the condominium building owners across the street for painting the exterior pink. Or yellow. Or just for painting.

To Lisa I'll always be the big brother who, she still insists, butchered the hair of her Chatty Cathy doll when she was six years old. She has steadfastly maintained this gross calumny despite almost three decades of my denials.

For the record, I believe it was my older brother, Michael, who attacked Chatty Cathy with a scissors and a penchant for early punk hairstyles.

Michael, now a forty-eight-year-old medical doctor, claims "a one-armed man" did it.

I still think Michael did it, but sometimes my brain can no longer distinguish between things that actually happened and the way I *want* them to have happened.

Y'unnerstan' what I'm sayin' here, dawgs?

A veteran of innumerable lockdowns, Kansas decides to "fix up the cell till we're *styling*!" The first thing he does is install a Dookie Repellent System. He saves the peels from our breakfast oranges and stuffs them into the air vent. The air vent now exhales an odor of hot citrus.

Next he painstakingly unravels the nylon threads from his blanket and ties them together for a clothesline, which he runs from the metal grate of the air vent to the metal flush button above the toilet.

The excess blanket threads also make great dental floss. We can now wash our socks and shorts in the sink and hang them up to dry while we breathe in steamy citrus smells and clean our teeth. Skell fake-mops the catwalk sewage twice a day and kick-drops some tobacco wrapped in toilet paper into our cell. He apologizes to Kansas for not being able to bring any rolling papers.

We don't need no stinkin' rolling papers! We still have the Bible. Kansas extracts it—or at least the portion of it that hasn't been consigned to the crapper—tosses it to me so *I'll* get the spiritual demerit for tearing it up.

The Bible's thin rice paper is perfect for rolling up tobacco. We have already crapped and smoked our way through Genesis, Exodus, Proverbs, and parts of Ecclesiastes.

My favorite smoke so far came from Exodus, although Ecclesiastes is a strong contender by virtue of having been popularized in my youth by a Byrds song—or was that Pete Seeger? I swear I'm going senile in here, or maybe just a tad J-Cat.

When two new rolls of toilet paper are finally delivered (three weeks late), Kansas makes us a chess set. An old prison origami hand, he shapes wet toilet paper into pawns, bishops, and even the difficult knights, using state toothpaste ("SpringFresh—A Product of China") as mortar.

We save our lunchtime Kool-Aid to dye half the pieces purple. We let the toothpaste and dye dry overnight. With the pencil stub and the edge of the *Aryan Sentinel* I map out sixty-four squares on the concrete cell floor.

We play chess all day long. More accurately, I give Kansas free chess lessons all day long. To my surprise, he is an eager and adept pupil. He says Hitler played lots of chess in the bunker.

Kansas quotes Nietzsche, who has to be the patron saint of peckerwood prisoners. "O.G.—whatever does not kill me only makes me stronger, y'unnerstan' what I'm sayin'?"

"I'm down wid dat, dawg." This once-alien tongue now rolls fluently from me. I fear I may be going native.

Our next project is a deck of cards. The lunch and dinner trays often include those little restaurant-style pats of butter with the square cardboard backing. We save fifty-two of these and Kansas teaches me spades. I teach Kansas Hollywood rummy.

Before we can construct a backgammon set the lockdown ends.

We not only endured—we were *styling*!

With the lockdown over, C.O. Strunk assures us that we will shortly be "processed and classified" as workers in the main yard kitchen. Despite earlier promises, Strunk tells us we won't be permitted to buy "appliances"—TVs and radios—until we are assigned to general population in the yard.

We can expect to be transferred "at a moment's notice." We are to be ready to "roll it up!" The Fish Tank ordeal is almost over. It *will* be over the "very instant" that space is found in general population. Once there, Strunk says we can then buy our TVs, radios, cassette players, electric fans—whatever we want!

Yeah. And there will be pie in the sky when we die. By and by.

Kansas just says, "That fat punk is on my list, straight-up lying motherfucker!" And what list might that be? Kansas says never mind, if he tells me he will have to kill me. I tell him never mind. I'm used to living in ignorance.

I replenish my store with a few goodies and stamps and resume my solitary strolls in the fish yard. Big Hungry is the proud new owner of a "punk-ass bitch white boy." The Hunger, a three-time alumnus of the Nevada Prison for the Criminally Insane (J-Wing, naturally), has just been happily reunited with an old "squeeze" and fellow J-Cat alumnus called Cassandra.

Cassandra tells us that it's perfectly all right to call him Cassie. But please refer to him as *her*—or *she*. We're all down with that. No problem. Kansas refers to him as that "straight-up J-Cat faggot." Or that "toad-sucking piece a homo shit."

Cassie struts, simpers, and sashays around the yard wearing the convict counterpart to a streetwalker's hot pants—state blue jeans razored off about two inches below the crotch. The blue shirt has been shorn and tailored to display her hairy midriff.

Never out of her daddy's sight, Cassie flits around the rotunda showing off her mascara (blue pool-cue chalk from the gym), red lipstick (cherry Kool-Aid powder), and a virtual cleavage that she achieves by tightly cinching a laundry string beneath her "breasts."

The Hunger hasn't sweated me once since Cassandra disembarked from the J-Cat bus. I am happy that the Hunger now seems happy.

In fact, I wish him joy.

Every other Tuesday is laundry exchange day. It's a very big deal because this is how most of the contraband (including Cassie's mascara) gets into the Fish Tank. Strunk keeps us locked down while Skell and the other porter trustees make an unescorted road trip to retrieve the laundry carts from the main yard. They also procure anything else that they have been paid to obtain.

Rickety card tables are set up in the rotunda. The porters sort out and array a disturbingly off-white, mottled assortment of socks, underwear, sheets, and towels. This is a very slow process, as Skell and the gang first must segregate the premium garments from the rest. The superior boxer shorts are those with minimal (or no) shit stains or pecker tracks. Socks without holes command a four-stamp premium, as do un-ripped, mostly white sheets.

New fish without a porter hookup or a stand-up receive the foulest-looking, shredded, gray-brown sheets and underwear. If they have no money and no connections, then what they have is nothin' coming.

One card table is heaped with the superpremium goods. These are Private Reserve, absolutely pristine sheets and garments for a few preferred customers such as Kansas. Kansas, of course, doesn't have to pay anything. His friendship is considered payment enough.

Everything at the Private Reserve table has been freshly bleached and ironed. Skell swears this on his skin. Kansas will only participate in a laundry exchange if Skell swears this on his skin. Kansas believes that only Clorox can adequately annihilate the AIDS and hepatitis "germs." He knows this for a fact because he has shared hundreds of hypodermic needles with colleagues in less-than-perfect health and he has yet to contract any diseases. His prophylactic precaution is to dip his needle into a cup of Clorox before injecting.

When I ask him what his method is for safe sex, he tells me to shut my sideways mouth before he puts out my domelights. Skell informs me that "your hand don't call for no freebies yet," but seeing as how Kansas is my stand-up he can see his way clear to letting me shop from the Private Reserve stock for 50 percent less than plain premium. Am I down wid dat deal?

I tell him I'm down with that and pick up the beautifully bleached and ironed shorts, socks, sheets, and towel.

Bubblecop, to avert a possible riot, cracks open only five cell doors at a time during the laundry exchange period. As soon as the doors open, ten fish go racing toward the tables. They almost trample each other in their eagerness to snatch up the highest-grade items. At the Got Nothing Coming table it's chaos. Worse than a White Flower Day sale at Macy's the day after Thanksgiving. Pushing, shoving, selling wolf tickets. The only comparable spectacle that comes to my mind is when my friend Barry threw a bar mitzvah party for his son, Jason, and the buffet table started running low on free food.

Bubblecop is standing up cradling the shotgun, vastly entertained by the battle for minimally stained boxer shorts. Lester the Molester is the last convict at the tables. When he rolls up to the Premium Pay table, he withdraws a small sack from a hidden recess in his wheelchair. Skell examines it carefully before handing the Molester a bottle of narcotic pain pills and a magazine.

The magazine is entitled *Where the Boys Are!*

I don't think it is inspired by the Connie Francis song or the movie about college kids cavorting in Fort Lauderdale on spring break.

Kansas says it's scandalous but reluctantly concedes that "even Chomos got something coming if they got money." Do I understand what he's saying?

I tell him I'm down wid dat.

The prison gang war that triggered our lengthy lockdown finally spills over to the Fish Tank. Our penal institution boasts a robust and diverse variety of gangs—Mexican, black, white, and even Native American. Some of these organizations are so sensitive and savage that my Bic fine-point pen trembles (after all, I am still here) in recording some of the names: Sureños, Norteños, Border Brothers, Crips, Trey Street Deuces, Aryan Dawn, the Wood Brigade, and the Tribe. Together they make the Balkans look like the Elysian fields.

At the phone company our CEO and Human Resources V.P.'s were forever trumpeting the "accrued human capital synergies driven by our ethnically diverse, cutting-edge, globally attuned workforce." In the joint such accrued synergies sometimes drive behavior that's—well, it ain't nothin' nice.

It happens while Kansas and I are meekly waiting on the rotunda lunch line for the porters to hand us our trays and fill our Hard Time mugs with Kool-Aid. At the back of the queue my *ese* pal (with the "La Raza" neck tattoo) suddenly decides he'd rather stab someone than eat one more soybean hamburger. His target is an unreasonably tall black convict (and card-carrying Blood) who's standing peacefully in line.

The *ese,* called Niño, is only a couple of inches over five feet, but what he lacks in stature he more than compensates for in bad attitude and overall brutishness. Without a word, Niño thrusts a Bic fine-point deep into the Blood's neck, which promptly spurts out a fountain of blood. Niño keeps gouging even as the Blood slowly sinks to the concrete floor. He's still digging in with the Bic when Bubblecop looks up from his magazine and starts firing the shotgun.

Indiscriminately.

We all drop to the ground, hands clasped behind our heads—this is the standard drill. The Dirt burst into the Fish Tank in under two minutes to sort out the culprits and haul off the wounded. Five innocent fish at the back of the line are carried off to the infirmary with buckshot wounds in the back and buttocks. Niño, of course, is unscathed. Sergeant Stanger gets on the radio for a Care-Flight chopper to evacuate the now-dying Blood. No one attempts to stop the bleeding.

We are all locked down while the Dirt talk to Bubblecop and write up reports. A couple of *ese* fish are pulled out of the houses for questioning. They saw *nada* and heard less. Stanger grills a few of the homeboys. *Say what? Someone got stuck? Didn't see jack shit.*

I figure that either the Bloods are admirably upholding the Stand-up Convict Code of "no snitching," or they are simply reluctant to host a Bic penmanship contest culminating with the entire "La Raza" writing on their balls.

I expected the shakedown that followed. I did *not* expect to be dragged off to the Hole in hand and ankle shackles attached to a chain around my waist.

The Dirt first perform what is known as a skin search. They line us up outside our cells—naked. Our hands are then scrutinized for scrapes, scratches, bruises, and dried blood. On command, we bend, twirl, twist, and turn until every inch of naked flesh has been examined. We are told to do everything but curtsy and pirouette.

We are then ordered to dress and come out of the cells and face the wall—hands on our heads. The Dirt enter our houses to search, plunder, and destroy.

My downfall is not a shank or a trazor or even a Bic medium-point. It is the Sunday *New York Times*.

Stanger emerges from my cell with the "evidence."

"Lerner! Oh, *excuuuse* fucking me! O.G.! That's your homie name, right? Well, *O.G.*, what the fuck is *this*? You can come off the wall."

Stanger's smile is fixed, giving the impression of a rictal grin on a rat. He is swinging my towel back and forth like a pendulum.

Wrapped inside the towel is the *New York Times*. It represents my best effort at fashioning a pillow for myself.

"Sergeant, that's what I use for my pillow."

"A *pillow*?" Stanger affects an incredulous chuckle for the benefit of the other Dirtboys who are looking on in anticipation of some sport. Stanger swings the towel against the wall, where it makes a very impressive *whack!*

"Looks like a *weapon* to me. Sounds like one too. Pillow, my fucking ass! Let's see, *concealing* ten pounds of paper inside a state-issued towel, tying off the ends—oh yeah, definitely a dangerous fucking slock device."

Stanger takes another experimental swing at the wall as if to add validation to his weapon theory.

Whack! It almost startles me into moving my hands.

"Keep your fucking fish hands on your goddamned head! You got anything you want to tell me, O.G., *before* I throw your convict ass in the fucking Shoe?" It occurs to me that Stanger is just a larger, more twisted version of Gilbert, the fifth-grade school yard bully I vanquished long ago. Punching Stanger in the mouth, however, is not a prudent option. In here my passive aggression seems to take on a sideways shape, if you know what I'm saying.

I opt for a bit of inappropriate levity.

"Well, Sergeant, looks like I'll have to concede that the crossword puzzle is potentially dangerous to one's mental health, but the Sunday Styles section is fairly harmless." I have decided that I'm not taking any more crap from this asshole who ripped my daughters apart. Just for fun.

Now Stanger's in my face. "You talking out of the side of your fucking neck to *me*? Nobody mocks me! You think a weapons-manufacturing charge is a fucking joke?"

"In this case, yes." I know better than to even try placating a sadistic bully of this type. Mentally I have already checked into the Hole. So be it.

"Who you planning to slock with this, O.G.?" Stanger shifts into his interrogation mode. Unfortunately for me, he is one of those sibilant-challenged sadists that spray spit when they get agitated.

"I'm not planning on slocking anyone."

"Someone pressurin' you then? Looking for a little getback? This a gang thing, O.G.? The Norteños sweatin' you?"

"No one is sweating me, Sergeant."

"The Sureños? The fucking Crips?"

"No."

"You're going down anyway, O.G. Why don't you give me something—the NLR?" Kansas smothers a snicker by pressing his face against the wall.

I'm tired of the game. "Look, Sergeant, just how many guesses are you allowed?"

That does it. Stanger orders me to kiss the ground, hands on the back of my dome. He's on the radio, relaying the report back to Dirt

Headquarters that he has just smashed a major weapons-manufacturing facility—possibly "gang-related."

Stanger is so pleased with having uncovered the concealed slocking device that he halts the search and destruction of our house. My Gummi Bears will go unmolested.

So will Kansas's latest trazor, *Hustler,* and Bic fine-point that he diabolically conceals right under his mattress.

Once again I'm shuffling like a shackled coolie, this time across the Fish Tank yard to the gate. The guntower cop punches a button and Stanger pushes open the gate. Hands and ankles cuffed and shackled, belly chains jingling, I am led out through the main yard.

The sun is a desert broiler, and gusts of sand and dirt sting my face. It feels great to finally be out of the Fish Tank—free at last! Well, except for the "free" part, it feels wonderful. I receive my first guided tour of the general population yard. It seems huge. We pass the P.I. (prison industry) buildings: furniture repair, auto shop, vinyl, and dry cleaning.

Dozens of convicts in state blue are sauntering everywhere and anywhere—like they are freemen. Every now and then Stanger prods me forward by giving my little harness bells a shake. We pass the chow hall, the commissary, a small law library, and the chapel. Now I know where to buy more Gummi Bears and get more Bibles.

We proceed past a series of identical one-story cellblock buildings and the main administrative offices. The cons pause to scope out this little drama, many of them having taken the journey to the Hole themselves. They shout encouragement at me and insults at Stanger.

"Yo, wood! Don't sweat it, dawg. The Hole ain't shit!"

"Hey, Stanger! Yo, *Stanger*! Wanna smell yo wife's pussy? Then *suck my dick!*" This witticism produces raucous howls of laughter from the yard dawgs. Stanger halts us to yell back.

"You assholes want to join this fish in the Shoe?"

"Join *this,* motherfucker!" The dust storm makes identification of his tormentors (not to mention accurate guntower support) impossible, so Stanger gives me another ungentle shove forward.

At the end of the asphalt path is another gate leading to the two-story concrete and steel box formally known as the Security Housing Unit—the Shoe.

The inside of the Hole is arranged just like the Fish Tank, with two welcome exceptions: no foul toilet water spills out from under the cell doors, and the fluorescent ceiling lights actually work. There's the usual generic Bubblecop in his glass-enclosed office above the second tier. The same C.O. staff office in the center of the rotunda downstairs.

Stanger uncuffs my hands and ankles and jerks off the belly chain. He flashes me the sugar-sweet smile of a crew-cutted ferret with painful flatulence problems.

"Have a *nice* day, O.G. See you at the disciplinary hearing when they burn your sideways ass. Oh, *excuuuuse* me, O.G., did I say *burn?* I know how sensitive you people get about that. I think I even read it in the *JEW York Times*—ha!"

Stanger hands me over to the custody of the Hole C.O. before executing a crisp and bizarre about-face and marching back through the double steel doors, his black-clad body stiff from the broomstick up his ass.

C.O. Leach, overseer of the Hole, is a scrawny twenty-something with a five-day growth of beard whose mouthwash reeks strongly of Johnnie Walker Scotch. He directs me behind the red line while he consults the electronic console on his desk for a cell vacancy.

"Motherfucking piece a shit!" Leach pounds his fist on the console, screams some more, then beats at the console with a heavy leather boot.

"Is there a problem, C.O.?" I strive for a courteous and helpful tone, a legacy of my years as a corporate cubicle slave and not infrequent ass-kisser extraordinaire.

"Fuckin' Dirt! They roll you fish up without checking to see if I got cells. Dick-licking dirtbag Dirtboys! Fucking Stanger thinks he can do whatever the fuck he wants—coming here into *my* house like he's *about* something!" Leach collapses into the Salvation Army cast-off chair behind his desk.

"We got a real problem here, Lerner."

This is the first time (not the last) I have heard one C.O. "bad-rap" another to an inmate, and I am instantly favorably disposed toward Leach. I almost volunteer some advice bequeathed to me by a soon-to-be-downsized marketing V.P.: "Problems are merely opportunities in disguise."

I squelch my helpful impulse.

"The fucking Shoe is full! I don't got a cell for you—you gotta go back to the Fish Tank." Leach resumes beating the console with his fist while I wonder if I'm supposed to call a cab or what.

Leach is now drinking deeply from a coffee thermos, which seems to be the source of the Johnnie Walker aroma. "They act like this is a fucking *hotel* or something! That I just check fucked-up convicts in and out of here like some faggot-ass desk clerk!"

Leach motions me across the forbidden red zone and into his small air-conditioned office. Another taboo broken. Cops here never invite inmates into *their* houses. I take the one chair in front of the desk. My first chair-sitting session since I went to court. The electronic panel displays two rows of lights corresponding to the upper- and lower-tier cell numbers. I assume the lighted bulbs indicate "occupancies."

On the floor is an opened box of Domino's pizza. The one remaining half-chewed piece (with decaying mushrooms) exudes a putrid stench that mingles unpleasantly with Leach's whiskey breath.

We are both leaning over the console.

"What's up with cells 1 to 5, C.O.?" Those lights are unlit.

"No good—they're reserved for the J-Cats. The infirmary C.O. wants 'em all together so the nurse bitch doesn't have to walk around the entire fucking Shoe shoving Thorazine suppositories up psycho assholes—you know what I'm sayin'?"

All the cells in the Hole are single occupancy—one steel tray per house. I find this very appealing.

"Put me in a J-Cat cell," I tell Leach, who now studies me with intense interest. He opens the top drawer of his desk, roots around through a pile of soggy french fries, and extracts a tiny airline bottle of Old Smuggler. Sucks it down with one quick swallow and tosses the empty into the Domino's box.

"You a fucking J-Cat? Your jacket don't say nothing about that. This having to deal with all these J-Cats in a fucking prison is some scandalous shit, I'll tell you that—y'unnerstan' what I'm sayin'?"

I find myself reflecting on just how much the C.O.'s sound like the convicts. Must be some kind of reverse Stockholm syndrome.

The private cell is calling to me. "I *could* be a J-Cat. I even have some county jail experience at it. Wouldn't that solve the problem?"

"You was a J-Cat in county? Straight-up business?"

I almost say, "On my skin, bro." Instead I say, "I shit you not, C.O."

Leach leans over the desk and hawks a lunger smack into the center of the pizza box. I silently vow to never again order a mushroom pizza.

Rejuvenated with that Old Smuggler spirit, Leach makes a painful executive decision. He finally hands me two sheets, a towel, and a blanket.

"Aiight, Lerner—you're a J-Cat now. Take cell 1." He punches the button on the console and the door of cell 1 opens a few inches. Leach assures me that all my property, all my store, will be safely kept in the Property Office until after a Disciplinary Committee hearing.

"I'm supposed to do a cavity search, but fuck me if I get paid enough to put my nose up anybody's asshole—know what I'm sayin'?"

"I thought the same thing when I was your age."

"Aiight then. Go lock it down."

"I'm down wid dat, C.O."

After having to share an eight-by-six cage with the state of Kansas, this eight-by-six cell seems palatial. Even better, it's quiet. I have the toilet and sink to myself, a generous chunk of state soap (by way of China), and not one, but *two* rolls of toilet paper. Nothing else.

And nothing coming.

There is a mutilated Bible stuffed under the mattress—a *Biblia* actually, it's in Spanish. No *problema*. Before being allowed to defend democracy in the Panamanian dictatorship, I was treated to a six-month Spanish lesson at the Defense Language Institute in Monterey, California. I'm grateful now that I paid attention.

My *Biblia* is more than a little "tore up." It is missing certain pages from the Gospels. All reference by the disciples to Jesus' last moments have been torn out. Perhaps the previous guest here objected to the story's unhappy ending and selected those passages for rollie or dookie duty.

I'm kicking it now, just chilling. Basking in the cathedral silence of my private suite. They call it solitary confinement, but I consider it solitary freedom—from Kansas and his interminable rants and dookie sessions.

I amuse myself by speculating on the possible confusion of the next *ese* con who picks up this strangely excised *Biblia*. Does Jesus die? Or merely sustain some non-life-threatening puncture wounds? Such is the nature of my spiritual musings as somewhere in the free world the sun must be setting.

The overhead fluorescents flicker on. There is no light switch in the cell like in the Fish Tank. I figure it must be part of the punishment. Stanger stripped me of my watch back in the Fish Tank, so I can only guess at the time. Nevada prisons, like their casinos, never put wall clocks in public places.

Nobody leaves till they've paid in full.

Unlike the J-Cat cell in county, I do have a window in the cell door but no outside window. It's all good. The Shoe utilizes the same food-tray-flying-through-the-slot method as the county jail. We never leave our cells except for a ten-minute shower (absolutely no phones!) every other night.

Hey, been there, done that.

After three days of isolation I am climbing the walls, desperate for some conversation, even if it's about the "Jewish sympathizers in purgatory." I'm still not clear on just who these people were—sensitive Jews or sympathetic Nazis?

On the evening of the fourth day I am awakened by the telltale rumbling of the food cart. I watch through the little wire-reinforced window as Leach staggers around the food cart attempting to supervise the meal porter—*Skell!* Leach is accompanying Skell and the cart from cell to cell as trays are shoved through the slots.

The slot cracks open and my tray comes careening through—baked

ham. Of course it's not real ham. No pork products can be served here.
The ham is really some species of processed turkey sprayed pink to sim-
ulate pork.

Next to my virtual ham are two pieces of white bread with the little paper-backed butters, a slot containing lettuce, cucumber slices, and
a slice of tomato all smothered in Italian dressing. Dessert is chocolate
pudding and it's delicious.

The only dawgs that gripe about the food in here have never been
in the army. I have no complaints about the meals.

After fifteen minutes Leach slurs out the order to push our empty
trays back through the slots. Skell's face is at my window. He is hissing,
"Whachu need, O.G.?"

I tell him I need a small rock hammer and a large poster of Rita
Hayworth but would settle for something to read. Skell goes hysterical
with laughter, ripping wildly at a scab on his head, alternately hissing
and shrieking while displaying the blackened stumps of his remaining
teeth.

"Fucking O.G.! Hold on, dawg—Kansas told me to hook you up,
no charge." When Skell bends down to pick up the tray, the slot opens
and a bag of Gummi Bears drops through, followed by two Almond Joy
bars, a writing tablet, three pencils, and a bag of 4 Aces.

"Got no lighter, O.G. You need a stinger?"

"Please."

Skell flips a paper clip through the slot and straightens up with the
tray just as Leach totters up behind him.

"Wanna join him, Skell?" Skell comes out as "Shell."

"No, sir, boss, just picking up the trays, boss." Skell oozes out
the words in his most obsequious, state-raised style—our very own
Uriah Heep.

"Then get *moving*, you skank-ass, scab-domed piece a shit!"
Peeshashith.

"Right away, boss, coming right now," and Skell is wheeling the cart down to cell 6, hissing "Whachu need?" through the food slots. When appropriate, he substitutes "Whachu need, *ese?*" or "Whachu need, *homes?*" for "Whachu need, dawg?" At the phone company we referred to this technique as Target Marketing or Customer-Driven Differentiation.

I spend the evening reading the unripped Old Testament in Spanish, an endlessly depressing cycle of the Divine Shotcaller hooking up his Chosen Dawgs only to be continually dissed to the point where He finally finds it necessary to actually *kill* a few of these ungrateful, "stiff-necked" dawgs, sometimes entire cities of them at a time. Even after death they got *nothing* coming.

Always seemed a bit overreactive to me.

But go figure the ways of God.

I fall asleep thinking of the riddle, probably Jewish:

How do you make God laugh?

Give up?

Just tell him your plans.

I wake up in the Hole from my usual nightmare of the
Monster rushing at me with the knife. I wake up blind. Not deaf, because I can clearly hear Leach screaming at someone near my front porch. I remember to take off the night shades—two giant wads of wet toilet paper I stick over my eyes as a shield against the fluorescents.

I have a perfect window view.

Leach is trying to drag the latest arrival into cell 2, next door.

"Get your nasty faggot ass in the fucking cell, Rosenbloom! Don't you *dare* slow-play me, you cocksucker!" Our new guest is prostrate and crying in front of the cell door.

Her name is Cassandra and she's weeping like, well . . . like a punk-ass bitch. Cassie's shoulder-length hair is now two-toned, splotches of blond on black. She's not dressed for the Shoe. Same tight blue hot pants, Kool-Aid lipstick, and pool-cue mascara. To complete her casual day outfit, Cassie has strategically sliced out little sections of her hot pants in order to dazzle the world with horrifying flashes of hairy butt and thighs.

Cassandra is clutching the steel handle of the cell door, refusing to enter her new house. Leach finally backs away, looking up to Bubble-cop for armed assistance.

"*Shoot* this piece a shit! She's refusing a direct order to lock it down!"

Bubblecop removes his state-trooper-style sunglasses and peers through the rifle slot in the Plexiglas, his weapon on his desk.

"Can't do it unless she attacks you or something. I ain't looking to get crossed out behind no J-Cat faggot. Why don't you just *bitch-slap* her into the house?" And Bubblecop sits back down, rejoining his coffee and *National Enquirer.*

Leach yells up at the bubble, "Well, thank you very much, part-ner—good looking out!" He whirls back on the kneeling, whimpering Cassie.

"Let go of the fucking door and get on your faggot feet, you cum-sucking maggot!"

Cassie reluctantly releases the door handle. I can't see the handle but I suspect there are claw marks on it. Blue tears streak down her face.

"But I didn't do *anything,*" she wails. "Big Hungry's the one who should be here, not me!"

Leach is disgusted beyond all reason.

"No? I hear you *did* every toad in the Fish Tank!" This remark in-stantly produces violent protests from the Shoe's resident toads, who start kung-fuing the cell doors.

"Yo, Leach! That's way outta line, you drunk-ass sorry peckawood muthafucka!"

"Leach! Come on up to my crib and start talking that 'toad' shit! I'll peel your muthafuckin' drunk onion!"

While Leach gets into a screaming match, Cassie seizes the opportunity to wander around the lower tier looking through windows.

"O.G.? Is that you?" Cassie's face pressing against my window, tears and pool chalk streaking the glass.

"What are you here for, Cassie?"

"They say they're going to charge me with 'altering state property.' " Cassie attempts a brave smile, tears drying on her cheeks.

"You mean ripping up the state shirt and pants?"

"That, and for getting a tattoo." And she loses it again, blubbering against the glass. "That fat bastard Hunger said he'd do a nice butterfly on my back—he *swore* it was a butterfly, but instead he—"

"GET IN YOUR FUCKING CELL!" Leach grabs Cassie by the hair and drags her off. *Thwunk* goes cell door number 2. Leach retreats wearily to the tranquillity of his office, where he starts throwing sodden french fries against the wall.

I'm working my way through the *Biblia*, skimming Kings—too many names getting in the way of the plot. When is Skell coming back with some books?

"O.G.? O.G.? You in there?" Cassie's disembodied voice whines through the air vent above the sink. I put my face to the grate.

"No, Cassandra, I'm laying on the beach in San Juan sipping a piña colada."

A girlish giggle comes through the vent. "That's a good one, O.G. Say, what's your real name?"

I hesitate before answering. If the Hunger finds out I even *talked* to his "be-yatch," he'll bust a grape for sure. Word!

Then again, I didn't get to where I am today by being cautious. "It's Jimmy. Jimmy Lerner. Now give me *your* real name and don't insist on that 'Cassandra' business."

"Rosenbloom. *Cary* Rosenbloom. My mother was a *huge* Cary Grant fan. Personally he's not my type. I'm more of—"

"This is more information than I need," I interrupt. "What did the Hunger do? I take it he was fresh out of butterfly patterns."

"Oh God, it's just so *vile,* absolutely *sick!*" And Cassandra/ Cassie/Cary Rosenbloom is sobbing into the vent.

"All right, calm down. You don't have to talk about it if you don't want to."

"Thanks." Cassie's tone resumes its artificial brightness once more. "Are there any *phones* in this hole? I have to call my mother."

"Sorry—no phones in the Shoe, Cary."

"*Please*—it's *Cassandra.* Or Cassie."

"That still won't change my answer."

"Oh, now you're being *cruel.* I bet you could be *very* cruel to a girl. I bet you would—"

"Will you shut up! I'm hanging up now—"

"No! Wait . . . sorry. Listen: what about my meds? They have to give me my meds in here, don't they?"

"Trust me—they come twice a day and I can't imagine them over-looking you."

"You really can be very sweet, Jimmy. If you like, I could talk dirty into the vent while you touch yourself or—"

"Good-bye, Cassie."

"Bye, Jimmy."

Please, God, don't ever let me get that lonely.

Throughout the day Cassie chatters happily through the air vent. She's a twenty-two-year-old "street hustler" from L.A. who had the misfortune of getting arrested for peddling her hairy ass to a male undercover cop in Reno. When they took her down for booking, the cops found a condom stuffed with crank—speed—in her pocket.

The judge gave her eighteen to thirty months for the crank and dismissed the soliciting charges. This is her first time in a regular prison—she's used to the J-Cat ward prison "where it's more like a hospital."

After dinner—spinach lasagna, which is great—Leach shouts out, "Shower time, gentlemen—and *ladies*!" Leach giggles at his little joke. So do the Hole dawgs behind their doors.

"You all know the fucking drill! Two cells at a time. You will exit your houses fully dressed and holding *only* your towel and your soap!"

The doors open and Cassie and I head for the six-man communal shower stalls at the end of the lower tier.

"I'll show you the tattoo in the shower," Cassie whispers.

"NO TALKING, YOU FUCKING FREAK!" Bubblecop shows us his shotgun.

There is a metal bench bolted to the floor outside the showers for our clothes and towels. I quickly strip and step into the stall, finding a showerhead as distant as possible from Cassie.

Cassie, her back to me, takes her time removing her "altered state property." Inmates' bodies are also considered to be the property of the state. Get a tattoo and you can be charged with "altering and defacing state property."

Cassie is whispering urgently.

"Look at what that black bastard did to me."

Tattooed in large block letters on Cassie's lower back is the Hunger's "butterfly." Three words and a downward-pointing arrow below them. The thin arrow points straight down, the tip perfectly aligned with the crack of Cassie's ass.

Tattooed above the arrow is the instruction:

INSERT DICK HERE

And Jesus wept.

Leach is on my front porch, tapping courteously against the window.

"Rise and shine, O.G.! You got the Disciplinary Board in twenty minutes." All of a sudden I am "O.G.?" I wonder whassup wid dat?

The cell door slides open and Leach gives me a conspiratorial grin. "Hey, O.G. Why didn't you tell me you was down with Kansas? Me and that old boy go back a little ways, y'unnerstan' what I'm sayin' to you?"

Leach looks like he spent the night curled up in a Dumpster behind Domino's Pizza. His rumpled khaki uniform is stained with tomato sauce and reeks of cheese. The cheese is not fresh. Today's mouthwash selection is very fresh, however—I would guess Eau de Thunderbird Wine.

Leach's peckerwood-issue ponytail, usually tucked in behind his collar, is now unfurled and waving in unwashed glory. He tosses a cleaned, *starched* state blue shirt on my tray.

"You wanna look *stract* for the Disciplinary Committee. Appearances count a lot with the warden—you wanna shave?" Leach enters the cell and hands me a Bic disposable and a small square of polished metal.

"J-Cat cells don't normally get razors, so I gotta watch you."

It's been a long time since I've looked into a mirror, and I'm shocked to see some specks of white in the beard I've let grow since county jail. Actually the specks are more like broad swaths of white with a few brown specks. Sometimes, at first consideration, my brain cannot tell the difference between how I imagine things to be and how they really are.

Not that that's such a bad thing.

Leach is sitting on my bunk smoking a tailor-made while I take care of business at the sink. I keep the beard full, just trimming around it. No one could mistake it for a badass goatee. More like an O.G.— Old Goat.

"Wanna tailor, O.G.? I know you got a stinger in here. I see the flashes at night."

I accept a Marlboro from his crumpled pack and start tying my state sneaker, waiting for Leach's other shoe to drop. When it does, it's more with a whimper than a bang.

"Ah . . . O.G. . . . ya know there's no need to tell the Disciplinary Committee about the *occupancy* problem in here, know what I'm saying? Not that they'd *ask,* but you wasn't in no J-Cat cell, y'unnerstan'? Them fucking Dirtboys supposed to be keeping better track, know what I'm sayin'?"

"I got your back, Leach—*what* J-Cat cell?"

"Aiight. It's all good then. Come on up to the office when you're ready."

Sergeant Stanger is waiting in the office to fully acces-sorize me with the cuffs and waist chain. He seems very excited to see me again.

"You're going *down,* motherfucker! The board don't like weapons possession charges. Not to mention the conspiracy charge I threw into the mix when they told me to change the 'manufacturing' to 'possession.' "

"I appreciate your flexibility. I'm sure the board won't appreciate having their time wasted by some trumped-up Mickey Mouse charges, C.O."

In response Stanger ratchets up the pressure on my wrists. "Oh *nooo*, O.G. Nothing 'Mickey Mouse' about these charges. We're talking *major* violations of the Code of Penal Discipline. You're looking at two to five more years, and that's *Sergeant*, asshole! A *C.O.* got mosquito wings like this piece of drunken shit Leach here."

Leach objects. "Come on, Sarge—that's *way* outta line!" Stanger ignores him and yanks my chain. Behind us Cassie is yelling from her cell, "Good luck, O.G.!"

Once again out into the sandstorm and the sun, Stanger ranting nonstop while he sprays me with his saliva.

"Heard through the wire you been coming on to the Hunger's bitch. The Hunger ain't gonna like that when I tell him . . . oh *noooo*, Big Hungry is gonna be Big Jealous!" We halt in front of the electronic gate that protects the administration building from uninvited guests bearing grudges. Guntower Cop stares down before hitting his remote to let us in.

"Yeah, you going *down*! Going down *hard*! Talking outta the side of your neck to *me*!" I am still trying to decide if Stanger is doing a Rocky Balboa ("Yo—I ain't goin' down no more, Apollo") or a Travis Bickle ("You talking ta *me*?") when he shoves me down into a bench outside the hearing room.

Stanger unchains me and then we are in the conference room, three men seated at a long table and an empty chair placed behind a red line painted on the floor about six feet from the table. My second chair in a week!

"Lerner? Jimmy?" says the spokesman in the center. He is a very tall, very thin stick of a man with a thick white head of hair.

"Yes, sir."

"Back number?"

"Six-one-six-three-four." I know it now better than my Social Security number.

"I'm Assistant Warden Noble and with us today are Caseworkers Joe Ringer and Wally Sykes." The caseworkers—civil servants in short-sleeved white shirts—don't bother to look up. They are perusing my "full jacket"—the file containing my life history up to and including any "disciplinary problems" while incarcerated.

"Mr. Lerner, you are charged with two major violations of the Code of Penal Discipline: MJ21, possession of a weapon, and MJ22, conspiracy to possess a weapon."

Behind me Stanger emits a somewhat insane giggle. Noble is not pleased with the interruption.

"Sergeant Stanger, this is a formal disciplinary hearing and you will kindly remain silent unless and until you are asked to testify. Is that understood?"

"Yes, sir. Sorry, sir."

Joe and Wally are still studying the folder before them, shaking their heads in obvious puzzlement. Caseworkers can be a prisoner's best friend or worst nightmare. They are not cops, often have some background in psychology or social work and can serve to slightly offset the overwhelming power of the guards.

If they want to.

Assistant Warden Noble places a small tape recorder on the table. "Mr. Lerner, you have a right to be represented by an inmate-counsel substitute—a law clerk. Private attorneys are not permitted at these proceedings. Do you now wish inmate-counsel representation at this time?"

"No, sir, I believe I can adequately defend myself against these charges."

"Do you understand that if found guilty of these charges the

Disciplinary Committee may refer your case to the State Attorney General's Office, where new criminal charges may be filed against you?"

"I understand that, sir."

"Let's proceed then. Mr. Sykes, would you turn on the tape recorder? Thank you. Mr. Ringer, you have examined the write-up from Sergeant Stanger. What weapon is involved here? A shank? A trazor? A Bic?"

Ringer smirks and smooths his thick black hair, which is greased severely back from a massive shiny forehead. His bird-black eyes seem to be smiling above a hooked proboscis.

"Mr. Noble, according to the Notice of Charges, 'pursuant to a routine cell search for contraband, Mr. Lerner was found to be in possession of . . .' "

"Well? Come on, Mr. Ringer—we have six more disciplinaries to get through today."

"Sorry, sir—'found to be in possession of a Sunday issue of the *New York Times,* folded and concealed within a state-issue towel.' "

Caseworker Sykes, a small man with tiny hands that tend to flutter involuntarily in the air, has suddenly discovered some object of fascination on the ceiling. One fluttering hand descends to arrange the four strands of gray hair he has painstakingly pasted across his bald dome.

The assistant warden's voice is rich with disbelief. "The Sunday *New York Times*? What section?"—as if possession of, say, the Week in Review section would constitute a mitigating circumstance.

"It doesn't specify, sir," Ringer answers.

Little Wally Sykes now decides he wants to participate. "Sir, uh . . . I'm not precisely certain as to the particular relevance of any one section."

Noble releases the issue. "Oh well, the wife and I subscribe to the Sunday *Times.* Lerner, why did you conceal the paper in the state towel?"

His expression, to my relief, is one of benign and fatherly be-musement.

"Sir, I didn't conceal it. I used it to make a pillow."

"A pillow?"

"Yes, sir. And that took *all* the sections of the paper."

"Including the *Book Review*?"

"Yes, sir. Also the Money & Business section."

"Do you work the crossword puzzle?"

"No, sir—much too difficult for me." Noble is positively beaming now at my humble admission of ignorance. I'm beginning to feel it's all going to be good—in the hood.

"Too tough for me too," says the assistant warden, not without a trace of sadness. "My wife does, though—in *pen!*" He is smiling with obvious pride.

"She must be a remarkable woman, sir," I say, always alert to rapport-building opportunities with my new masters.

Noble ignores this ass-kissing overture and returns to reading Stanger's fiction. "Okay . . . Mr. Lerner, what about the Conspiracy to Possess a Weapon?"

"Sir, I have no idea. Unless I *conspired* with the United States Postal Service to deliver the paper to me."

"Hmmm . . . your point is well taken. I think we can now conclude these proceedings with—"

Stanger can no longer keep a lid on it. "Sir! We're talking about a ten-pound *slocking* device—*concealed* and *affixed* to a state towel!"

Noble is not convinced. "And the conspiracy?"

"Sir, we believe the O.G.—*Lerner*—did not act alone. He's a new fish, never been down before. He *had* to have some help. Some old con, probably that hard case Kansas, must of conspired with him."

The assistant warden slowly lets out a world-weary sigh. Sykes and Ringer are now captivated by their shoes.

"Can you produce a co-conspirator at this time, Sergeant?"

Stanger reverts to the comfortable territory of Copspeak. "Sir, we are still in the preliminary stages of an *ongoing* investigation."

"I'll take that as a no, Sergeant."

Ringer is quietly humming the theme to the old *Mickey Mouse Club.*

Noble has heard enough. "Sergeant, exactly what kind of . . . trumped-up *Mickey Mouse* charges are these?"

The assistant warden cuts off Stanger's stuttering response with a curt wave of his hand. "That was a rhetorical question. These charges are found to be without substance and without . . ." Noble pauses to enlist Wally's input. "Wally, do you perceive any merit to these allegations?"

This time Wally is quick. "Merit? I most assuredly think not."

"Mr. Ringer?"

"No substance and no merit."

"Then this case is dismissed." The assistant warden turns off the tape recorder.

I'm *loving* this guy! This is not going to be one of those hackneyed prison tales starring an Evil Warden.

"Next case, Sergeant, and if it turns out to be even remotely similar to this piece of claptrap, don't waste the committee's time." *Claptrap*— the man actually uses that word. "In fact, Wally, why is *my* presence even necessary at these proceedings? Surely a single caseworker can handle the disciplinary process."

Wally is paging through a battered copy of *The Nevada Code of Penal Discipline.* "I think not, sir. The code states that a committee should consist of at least three members to hear major disciplinary charges."

The assistant warden picks up on the word "should." As well he should. "Wally, that sounds like a *suggestion* to me. Is there anything in AR-22 that relates to this?"

Wally doesn't bother to look for the reference. "Administrative Regulation 22 also stipulates a three-member committee—*except* in the event of staff shortages." Wally and Noble are grinning at each other.

"Well, that covers it, wouldn't you say? We have *chronic* staff shortages. Mr. Ringer, going forward you will now be the Disciplinary Committee."

Ringer tilts his beak at him. "No problem, sir."

Noble is digging through my jacket. "Mr. Lerner, it says here that you have an M.B.A. What school did you attend?"

"Golden Gate University in San Francisco." Noble frowns slightly. What is he expecting? A Harvard M.B.A.?

The assistant warden has an agenda. "Lerner, we'll have an opening shortly in the law library for a clerk. Do you have any legal background or experience at all?"

"No, sir." And the entire committee looks pleased. Correct answer, I guess.

"Are you currently appealing your sentence or do you have a habeas corpus petition filed in federal court?"

"Sir—I can't even spell 'habeas corpus.' " Now all three of them are grinning and nodding in approval. I have just had a successful job interview. The phone company had a similar screening process for top management.

"All right then. I want you in general population—out of the Shoe, out of the Fish Tank—as of now. You'll be required to put in your time as a kitchen worker first—we can't have any favoritism in here, bad for inmate morale. Then you'll be working as our new law clerk."

"Thanks for the opportunity, sir."

Stanger and another Dirt member enter the room with the next defendant—it's La Raza Boy himself, Niño. He looks around the room, bewildered. I stand up and motion to the chair. *"Gracias, Jaime."* I tell him *"De nada."*

Stanger leaves his Dirt partner in charge so he can escort me back through the yard, this time without chains and cuffs. I'm so happy I don't know whether to shit or go blind.

"Dick-licker," snarls Stanger.

"Excuse me, Sergeant?" I am all innocence and light now.

"You heard me, asshole. M.B.A., huh—what's that? Master of Bullshit and Ass-Kissing?" Stanger's comment is actually quite accurate, but I remain silent, the better to appreciate the unrelenting flow of insults.

"On-the-leg piece a shit!" A slight saliva spray on my neck.

"Warden-jeffing suck-ass!" A mild shower.

"Punk-ass stanky-on-the-hang-low bitch motherfucker!"

It's pouring.

But it's all good now. I love the smell of Stanger's spit in the morning.

It smells like . . . *Victory!*

C.O. Strunk looks up from his copy of *Prison Times* and tells me to roll it the fuck up. My property and tub are back in cell 47. I'm *moving!*

Kansas is sitting in his underwear on his tray, trying to compose a personal ad he plans on placing in a local paper. He has decided a female pen pal would enrich his life.

"What happened to Star?" I ask.

"Had to kick that bitch to the curb."

"Let me guess—a lover's quarrel?"

"Let me guess what kind of noise you will make when I stuff your head in the toilet. Star got busted behind messing around with a slot machine in one of the big casinos. She'll be down for a few days, dawg."

"Messing around? That's a crime?"

"Well, she was messing around with like, *tools*. Trying to encourage the Megabucks machine to pay off." In Nevada, tampering with a casino's slot machine can get you more time than kidnapping a busload of schoolchildren.

Having passed fairly quickly through the grief and mourning stages, Kansas is now admirably reaching out for a new relationship, preferably one that can be consummated by a balloon ceremony.

I look over his shoulder. So far he has managed to write his name. I understand the writer's block. What is he going to say? *Wanted, one young female with big lips and a fondness for giant skinheaded Nazis who reside in prison?* This will have to be a very special girl.

I decide to help out. "How about a concise, simple ad, say, 'Have swastika—can't travel'?"

"Come on, O.G. This is serious business here—I need your help." Kansas always sounds sad and sincere when he has to write anything. Or when he wants something.

"O.G., you know I can't write worth a shit. You gotta help me before you roll it up. I already put it on the wire that you're hitting the yard so my dawgs can watch your back. You know what I'm saying here?"

I'm counting my candy bars and stamps. It's all there. I stuff the sheets and towel into the yellow plastic tub and sit down next to Kansas.

"I appreciate your putting out the word for me, dawg. Look, why don't you put down some of your hobbies—try to appear multidimensional."

"*Hobbies?* What the fuck I gotta put them down for?"

"You don't have to, but trust me on this—I was married for fifteen years. Women tend to be more interested in men who are interested in something other than themselves." Kansas sighs and I already know that I will end up writing his personal ad.

"Don't have no hobbies."

"Sure you do. Everybody has hobbies—just think of the things you enjoy, the things you like to do."

Kansas is meditating quietly. He suddenly brightens.

"*Aiight!* I enjoy going into drugstores at night with my best friends, Smith and Wesson, and taking all the drugs."

I try to be supportive. At our Goal-Setting and Calibration training they stressed "aligning with your subordinate's objectives." Say what you want about me as a manager, I was always aligned and frequently calibrated.

"All right, Kansas. It's great you're clear on your objectives, but you might want to hold off on sharing that with your prospective pen pals. At least until your relationship has evolved a little bit."

Kansas flings his Bic pen against the cinder-block wall and starts manipulating in earnest. "See, that's what I'm talking about. Your way with the words, dawg. Me, I'm more of a people person, know what I'm saying? O.G., you gotta write this for me—cellies are supposed to be *down* for each other."

"I'll do it, but give me a few days to think of something. Look, I better roll it up before Strunk goes nuts."

"Don't sweat that fat-ass punk! I think I got it—how about tattooing? I like getting tattoos. Is that a hobby?"

"I think you're onto something. We'll put down that you appreciate art."

"Art?" Then Kansas is pounding my back, positively aglow with a childish delight. "That's what I'm talking about! What else?"

"Well, I notice you love reading about the Nazis and the Third Reich. Let's put down you love reading. In fact, let's say that you love European history!" I'm into it now, on a roll.

"Nah, O.G., I don't know nothin' about European history. I just like reading about how the Germans crushed all them punk-ass countries like little grapes, y'unnerstan' what I'm saying?"

"That's close enough."

"So it's all good then?"

"Hey—it's all good in the hood, wood."

Strunk is smashing his fist against the cell door. "Roll it the fuck up *now*, O.G.! You're going to cellblock 1—the kitchen workers' unit. You can finish sucking your cellie's two-inch dick when *he* hits the yard."

I hit the yard carrying my yellow tub, unescorted for the first time since I've been down. The fall sunshine is golden on my face and I feel free and easy, practically skipping down the yellow brick road.

I'm not in Kansas anymore.

PART TWO
THE INFERNO

This is not the place of burning,
it is the place of waiting,
the gray warehouse of regret . . .
—IT'S ALL PART OF THE PUNISHMENT:
THE PRISON POEMS OF THE O.G.

The main yard is about the size of two football fields, a huge rectangle of dirt with a crumbling asphalt walkway. After the claustrophobic Fish Tank and the Shoe, I feel like I've finally reached the Promised Land. I'm as excited as a virgin at her first sacrificial altar.

Six guntowers are strategically spaced just outside the dual razor-wire-topped fences so that virtually every section of the yard can be sprayed with bullets.

Even if a dawg could somehow make it over or through one fence, he would then be stuck in a six-foot no-man's-land, confronted by a second fifty-foot fence—a fish in a razor-wire-wrapped barrel. Make it past the second fence (by flying, maybe) and there is nothing but miles of desert, no vegetation of any kind to conceal oneself. An easy target for the guntowers.

To complete this Big Brother experience, surveillance cameras are mounted on top of the inner fence at twenty-five-foot intervals.

It comforts me somewhat to know that subsequent to my being shanked forty or fifty times, the perpetrator might eventually be identified on video. Unless Stanger and the Dirt investigate, in which case my aerated corpse would be charged with possessing and concealing multiple chest wounds. And conspiring.

Later I will learn of the "blind spots" in the yard—the narrow alleys between cellblock structures that are out of the sight lines of the guntowers and cameras. The blind spots are the preferred real estate for drug deals, slockings, shankings, or just good old general gang war mayhem.

Despite what you see in the movies—convicts getting gang-raped in the showers and everywhere else in prison—in this particular, convicts are much like the rest of us, favoring a modicum of privacy for their more intimate encounters. The dawgs here regard rape as an indoor, enclosed recreation and thus pursue this interest in the safety and security of the cells.

When the yard isn't on lockdown, it is open to pedestrian traffic from 7 A.M. till sunset. The walkways bustle like Times Square: convicts (and patrolling Dirt) on their way to work assignments, the handball court, the weight pile, the store, the chapel, the law library, or just to their houses for a nap. Most cons just cluster in little ethnic groups, watching, waiting, kicking it. These are the Yard Rats. And Kansas is King Rat. Or will be once he's out of the Fish Tank.

A new fish schlepping his yellow tub through the yard is always an event of great interest, one invariably heralded by a "wire" from the intake clerks or porters to alert the Yard Rats just who is coming out, their gang affiliations, if any, their jacket details, and their stand-ups. It's like having your résumé posted on the Internet. Without the monthly fee.

Thanks to Kansas's wire, every few steps I am greeted by some strange wood or even packs of these dawgs.

"What's up, O.G.!" they shout. "When's Kansas gonna come out and kick rocks wid us?" they all want to know.

"Aiight, O.G.," they call out, and give me a friendly nod. I am thinking of running for yard mayor, but I suspect Kansas already has that job. He's like Napoleon in exile right now.

I answer all the dawgs with "What's up, dawg!" or with the other Convict Correct response: "Same ol' same ol'." I imagine I deliver these snappy retorts with such nonchalance, such panache, that they cannot help but regard me as a dawg who's down wid it—a Righteous Con!

Of course I get into it. "Kansas will be kickin' it witchu soon,

dawg!" I reassure the Peckerwood Tribe, the members easily distin-
guishable from the skinheads by their long, greasy hair and the puzzling
absence of light when they open their mouths to smile at me. All the
dawgs walk around bare-chested. The Peckerwoods prefer the non-
political tattoos: "Linda," "Sue," or "Amy" on their chests, their arms,
their necks. A family-values bunch of guys with fresh tattoos that will
only fade long after they have faded from the memories of girlfriends
who have already faded into the arms of Jody or Sancho.

Many of the woods are down with traditional decorations—
tattooed dragons, serpents, crosses, swords, big-titted half-naked Ama-
zons. They are walking billboards advertising everything but their
native habitat—a trashed-out trailer park with the rusted shells of
Camaros up on blocks surrounded by crushed beer cans and broken syringes, their trailer treasures fiercely guarded by pet rottweilers.

The skinheads like to sport their political and racial views on their
literal sleeves. Lots of "SWP"—Supreme White Power—or "White"
(back of left arm) "Pride" (back of right arm). The "NLR" tattoos are
abundant, as are an astonishingly diverse variety of swastikas.

Neither the peckerwoods nor the skinheads are the much-ridiculed
rednecks with gun racks in their pickup trucks. The only guns or trucks
these dawgs ever get to touch are the ones they steal, usually from their
redneck acquaintances.

These dawgs here are the people who are never invited to focus
groups to share their views about the relative attributes of cellular versus
PCS technologies. They are the castoffs, the undesirables of the Old
Economy and the wretched dwellers in the crevice of the New Economy.
They are the sunken-cheeked shadow people, the ungreat unwashed
who silently seethe with a thousand ineffable resentments until, fueled
by drink and drugs, they lash out blindly at their imagined oppressors,
who often turn out to be their girlfriends or "common-laws."

They end up in here, of course. And here, kicking it with their
friends on the yard, is the only true and stable home they have ever

known. A home they will return to again and again, as surely as the
swallows fly south in flocks.

And here I am. With them. Living among an alien and savage tribe
that I once regarded as no more than a troublesome curiosity, safely
distant.

My lawyer, Shapiro, insists that I will serve no more than two years.
That I am the perfect candidate for early parole. That I shouldn't worry.

Shapiro was wrong.

To my everlasting sorrow.

I report to a very young, generously pimpled C.O. in unit 1
who conducts a perfunctory search of my tub before assigning me to a
bunk in B wing. Unit 1, home to cooks, bakers, dishwashers, floor
sweepers, floor moppers, and food servers, is misleadingly referred to by
the prison as having "dormitory-style" housing.

I have a news flash for them: I have lived in college dormitories, and
with the exception of the pervasive odor of infrequently washed bodies,
there is no resemblance. Instead of two-man cells with upper and lower
tiers, unit 1 (and don't call it a "cellblock" either) is a single-story concrete mausoleum containing several separate twelve-man barracks
spread through three "wings."

There is no Bubblecop. Just a C.O.'s small office in the center of a
rotunda that boasts three phones, a small library, and an office for the
unit caseworker. Instead of the double sliding steel doors of the Fish
Tank, massive "crash gates" can be deployed by the console in the office
to seal off each wing from the rotunda. In the event the Shit Jumps Off,
we are free to maim, rape, and kill each other behind the locked gate.
The C.O. locks the gate at nine each evening and keeps it open all day
so the kitchen workers can get in and out.

Each "dorm" area has its own communal shower and bathroom reached through a swinging door at the back of the dorm. The trays are not bolted to the wall. They are heavy metal slabs with four legs on the floor. Bedsprings are unheard-of here. Given what a creative convict can do with a pen or a toothbrush, just imagine the lethal potential of a bunch of bedsprings. This deprivation forces everyone to make his own shank out of metal supplied by the welding or auto shop.

I schlepp my tub through the open crash gate of B wing, down a long dark corridor with twelve-man barracks on both sides. I use the tub to push open the door of my assigned dorm. The only doorknob in prison is rumored to belong to the warden's office. Status symbols are strange here (as they often are elsewhere: I recall once having counted the ceiling tiles in a new vice president's office to try to determine square footage and thereby quickly ascertain his importance in the executive officer hierarchy of the corporation).

In my own cubicle I had a personalized stapler which I made sure was prominently displayed on my desk. It helped to let the new guys know who was who around there.

Inside my new dorm, I am immediately assaulted by a bedlam of competing sounds—boom boxes blasting, TV talk show hosts inciting their guests to riot, radios blaring, and convicts yelling and jumping around. It was probably more peaceful in Dante's Inferno.

Most of my new "roommates" have thirteen-inch color TVs on top of their tubs. Today everybody is tuned—at full volume—to *The Jerry Springer Show*. They are all yelling at the TVs, urging the guests on to even greater violence.

I slide my tub under my bunk and arrange my sheets and blanket over the ridiculously thin vinyl "mattress." My new cellies are mostly woods and skinheads, with three blacks and a token *ese* sprinkled in to achieve some sort of diversity goal.

They are all staring at me. I already long for the relative privacy and peace of my two-man Fish Tank home.

On the bunk to my immediate right is a familiar lanky figure wearing an oversize plastic shower cap to cover his bush of a head. He is one of the few dawgs bothering to wear headphones as he gyrates and gestures to a rap song from his Walkman.

T-Bone gives me a friendly welcoming smile and then shares the song with me by shouting out the lyrics, complete with the requisite gangsta hand gestures:

"Busted a cap on yo bitch ass—
You been down wid da white boyz
Be tryin' ta pass—
So now bitch
Mutha-fuck yo dead nigger ass!"

Content aside, I would say the Bone delivered this with a lot of feeling.

"Whassup, O.G.!" The Bone and I exchange the cute little prison handshake that Kansas taught me. We clench our right fists, tap knuckles against each other, followed by three quick taps of one fist on top of the other. This ritual possibly has its origins in the playground game of "Rock, paper, scissor, match," where both guys are the Rock. Sometimes I feel like a social anthropologist on Mars.

"Whassup, Bone—when did you get out of the Fish Tank?"

"Ain't been here but two days. Ain't no black fish come on out with y'all?"

"I don't think so, but I was strained up in the Shoe for a few days, so I'm not sure."

"Heard 'bout dat, O.G." The Bone is glancing around, assuring himself that all the dawgs are still entranced by their TVs and boom boxes. He whispers something that sends a chill rocketing up my spine.

"Best watch yo back, O.G. Big Hungry say you be up on his bitch in the muthafuckin' Shoe. The Hunger be layin' in the cut fo you—fo *sho*! Talkin' 'bout peelin' yo onion."

"Who told you that?"

The Bone hesitates, adjusting his shower cap. "Check it out, O.G. I ain't lookin' to catch nothin' but pa-*role*, know what I'm sayin'? We all just be *knowin'*, dass all."

A TV commercial break is the signal for some of the dawgs to come over and greet me. The Bone puts his headphones back on and retreats to his bunk.

A skinhead who seems to be held together by sinew and spit is standing at the foot of my bed.

"You gotta be the O.G.—Kansas says you're a Righteous Con. I'm Snake." Snake extends a clenched fist and we do the little knuckle dance thing.

Snake has a spiderweb tattoo, which is not particularly unusual in here. What is unusual—and alarming—is that this spiderweb is tattooed on the Snake's *face*. The web begins at the top of his forehead and spins down over and around both eyes, giving a raccoon impression.

It's a bit disconcerting until you get used to it.

"When's Kansas hitting the yard? I hear that punk Stranger got him strained up in the Fish Tank pending some bullshit Dirt investigation."

I tell Snake everything I know, which is nothing. Jerry Springer comes back and Snake turns to cheer on the berserking guests. The show's theme is "When Sons and Mothers Are Lovers." It is a big hit in the dorm, where everyone calls everyone else a motherfucker.

I notice something on the back of Snake's shaved head that completely disorients me for a moment—two golf ball–size tattoos, inches apart. They are eyeballs. The Snake literally has eyes in the back of his head!

And they are staring at me. This is almost as creepy as contemplating the Hunger laying in the cut for me somewhere.

And peeling my poor onion.

The ice broken, a few of the other woods kick it with me, all of them asking about Kansas before racing back to Jerry, who is interviewing one of the mothers. Mom is wearing a tight black miniskirt, legs splayed in her chair, apparently striving for a Sharon Stone effect.

"Fucking slut!" Snake screams.

"Scandalous bitch!" yell the dawgs.

T-Bone strolls down to the end of the dorm to join the two black youngsters who are also screaming at the TV.

"Tore-up old ho!" they shout.

"Nasty-ass be-*yatch*!" they scream at the TV.

"She be nasty but that bitch got *ass*!"

The woods are urging Jerry to "kick the bitch to the curb!" A couple of boom boxes are cranked up to drown out the TVs. In retaliation the TVs are turned up even higher.

Our resident *ese*, a quiet young man with intense dark eyes, is trying in vain to read a book. He turns a page and shakes his head in dismay, aghast by the depraved, incestuous depths this gringo trash can sink to. The *ese*'s name is tattooed on his neck—Loco.

"*Qué putas!*" Loco murmurs before putting his own headphones on for protection. It is obvious to me that I will have to go to the store and buy a radio and headphones just to keep from going insane in here.

I have an hour before I have to report to the kitchen, and the yard is open. Workers can come and go as they please. Like they're *about* something, if you know what I'm saying.

The crash gate at the end of the corridor is open. So is the double front door of the unit. The adolescent-looking C.O. is studying his *Hustler.* I can just push the front door open. Amazing to me. I feel free.

Then I'm on the yard, on my way to the store. Just like your average Joe Six-Pack on the streets who decides to pull into 7-Eleven for some chips and a brew or two. Or so I try to convince myself as I cross the yard, watching out for a certain Big Hungry Bastard layin' in the cut for me.

I'm not completely clear on the concept of having one's onion peeled.

But I suspect it ain't *nothin'* nice.

I do ninety days in the kitchen, mostly scooping clumps of green Jell-O or mashed potatoes onto plastic trays for patently ungrateful customers. It is the not-so-secret dream of almost every kitchen worker to find another job on the yard. Not because the kitchen work is particularly onerous—the Bone says "it ain't no thang"—but because escaping from the kitchen means also escaping from the Inferno of unit 1. Unit 1 is the only cellblock—excuse me, "housing unit"—without the cozy eight-by-six cells that most convicts prefer. Cell living, as opposed to "dormitory-style" life, is considered "preferred housing" by both the prison administrators and the cons.

All fish are required to do a minimum of ninety days in the kitchen before being free to seek other prison employment. The phone company called it "pursuing outside opportunities" whenever someone was forced out or fired. The official company announcement was always the same, except for the names and the job title:

"Marvin Finkelbinder, Vice President of Human Resources Quality Reengineering, has elected, effective January 1, to pursue outside opportunities." Marvin would be calling us in a week boasting about the plethora of profitable outside opportunities inundating his home fax before casually inquiring if we knew of any inside opportunities for an outside "consultant." Of course, he had nothing coming from us.

The instant that news of Marvin's demise was announced, all the

still cushily employed corporate dawgs would snicker at the water coolers. "Hear about old Marv? You mean the *Finkster*? What happened?
He's *history*! Outside opportunities? You got it." And we'd all feel pretty
good and smug about ourselves to have survived the latest downsizing,
right-sizing, streamlining, restructuring, or the highly feared "market
repositioning."

Oh how we strutted about the corporate corridors like we were
about something! I often obtain the same empowering sensation by
reading the obituary columns. Particularly the death notices of my bet-
ters—who are seemingly legion. I am convinced it's only a matter of
time and some unfocused scientific research until all situationally depressed people are taken off Prozac prescriptions and given subscriptions to the obituary sections of their local papers.

I like to get my exercise and entertainment by walking in
endless circles around the yard, counting my steps. It's no longer op-
pressively hot and it beats kicking it in the Inferno with the Jerry
Springer Fan Club.

There is a bank of phones just outside the chow hall where the Yard
Rats love to swarm around the young fish trying to call home. The Yard
Rats here are either the weight-pile pumped-up skinheads or their first
cousins, the woods. Most woods are just a haircut and a tattoo or two
removed from a state of skinheadedness.

This is how the Pressure works.

A fish fresh from the Tank named Timmy finally gets his pale and
trembling hand on a free phone. This is after he has paid a "toll" to the
Yard Rats for the privilege of walking in *their* yard. He also has to pay
the skinhead Phone Posse first if he wants to actually *use* the phone.

It's the same economic principle we employed at the phone company by charging customers for both "access" (dial tone) and "usage" (toll). Except we called it "market bundling." A few of our detractors (mostly nutcase "consumer" groups) called it "predatory and monopolistic practices." Sometimes the phone lines of these public interest "guardians" would mysteriously stop working. Then they would frantically call 611 demanding instant restoral of service.

You can bet they were high on our priority repair list! Ha! They had nothing coming! Go whine to the Public Utilities Commission. *Punkass bitches!*

But I digress. The Phone Posse would pretend to wait on line behind Little Timmy so they could overhear each tremulous word to Mommy. As instructed, Little Timmy beseeches Mommy to send him some more money. He tells her it's for store items like stamps and envelopes so he can write her more often.

He doesn't tell her the money is really for his daily yard toll. (A monthly fee can be negotiated at an attractive discount.) He also doesn't tell her it's for his cell or bunk rental or for his seat in the chow hall or his "life insurance policy."

If Mommy questions why Little Timmy needs five hundred dollars *a week* for some stamped envelopes, if Mommy appears to be balking, one of Timmy's new friends might get on the line. He would politely explain to Mom that if she desires to have Timmy returned to her one day without an asshole the size of Texas, she should seriously consider contributing to his health and welfare.

Sometimes—*lots* of times—this works. Unless this happens to be one of the calls randomly monitored by the prison. All calls are recorded but few are monitored. Or Mommy might take it into her head to call up the prison. She tells the whole shabby story to an assistant warden, who has only heard the music of these violins about five thousand times before. The A.W. assures Mommy he will immediately handle this outrageous incident and eventually refers it to the Dirt for investigation.

The crack investigators of the Dirt review all of the phone tapes for the date and time in question. About two months later, decisive Dirt action is taken.

Little Timmy is summoned to Dirt Headquarters, a wing in the administrative building. Timmy's visit is instant public knowledge in the yard. Sergeant Stanger sits a highly agitated Timmy down. He then delivers a friendly, fatherly lecture, a "tough love" kind of talk, which is overheard by the ubiquitous Skell mopping the office next door.

"What *are* you?" Stanger says. "Some little punk-ass *bitch*? A snitch-ass punk whining and *puling* on his mommy's titty!"

After a few minutes of tough love, Timmy breaks down, sobs like a self-fulfilling prophecy, and finally snitches out the Phone Posse and the Yard Rats.

Stanger pats him on the back and offers a few final words of advice. "Be a fucking *man*! You did the crime, now do the time! Stand up for your little punk-ass self! Now get the fuck out of my office, you little *snitch* piece a shit!"

Nobody likes snitches in prison.

Timmy's "friends" visit him that evening at his bunk in C wing of the Inferno. *Didja snitch?* the dawgs want to know. *Didja rat us out?* Timmy swears up and down and sideways that he didn't snitch on anyone, would *never* try to get nobody crossed out and yada, yada, yada until the boys get completely nauseated and start slocking the crap out of him.

A couple of the sickest dawgs then help Little Timmy into bed. They join him.

Later they will brag about having administered a "snitch inoculation"—a series of penile injections up Little Timmy's already battered butt. No one in C wing saw nothing. Heard nothing. It wasn't their lookout, y'unnerstand?

In the morning the unit C.O. makes his rounds through the wings doing the six o'clock head count. He notices that Little Timmy can't get out of bed. He is less than responsive to simple sentences such as "What's your name and back number?" Timmy, his grill busted and dome dented, gets to visit the infirmary for a two-week vacation.

Upon his release the Dirt make sure he P.C.'s up for the duration of his two-year sentence. The protective custody cellblock, adjacent to the Shoe, is nothing more than a twenty-four-seven solitary confinement lockdown unit. It is populated by Chomos, serial rapists, snitches, rape victims, and some of the more irritating J-Cats whose symptoms are not sufficiently smothered by Thorazine.

Timmy's mom will receive an official-looking form letter assuring her of the "intensive and ongoing investigation," that "swift and certain measures" have already been taken to ensure Timmy's safety and reha- bilitative progress.

The yard swims with Timmys—fish food for the sharks. And more arrive every day even smaller and younger than Timmy, courtesy of the current fashion of trying and sentencing children as adults.

In all fairness to the investigative prowess of the Dirt, there *are* cases where the phone-taping system has yielded some fruitful results. Just a year ago the Bone made his famous escape. Shortly after being sent from this prison to a minimum security conservation camp, the Bone just walked away from his duties as a firefighter. He figured he didn't *start* the muthafucka and, besides, it wasn't his lookout.

An hour following T-Bone's abrupt departure, the Dirt reviewed hours of his recorded phone conversations with his girlfriend, Lu- cindreth, in Las Vegas. The Bone was indiscreet enough to confide his escape plan to her, including the address of his favorite crack house in Vegas "where I fittin' to lay up." The Bone says he only enjoyed a cou- ple of hours of freedom, chillin' with Lucindreth and a pipe in the crack house before he was taken back into custody.

He insists he *did* have time for sex with Lucindreth. He smiles shyly when he tells us he "got some stanky on the hang-low."

The Bone is convinced the police violated his free speech rights. He spends all his free time in the law library, where he stares at the covers of big, intimidating books about the First Amendment and applicable case law.

He tells anyone who will listen that it's all about "a muthafuckin' 'spiracy to silence the blap man."

No one listens.

'Cause the Bone got caught.

And now he got *nothin'* comin'!

Sooner or later all new fish receive a "Heart Check" from the Yard Rats. It is a test of the inmate's willingness to physically fight back. It is considered a test of courage here.

Timmy flunked his Heart Check. Stanger's tough-love speech to him was actually very much in alignment with the Code of the Stand-up Con. The fish who resist threats and extortion, who valiantly fight back and don't snitch when they are beaten down, are granted that all-important Respect on the yard. Having survived the Heart Check, they are frequently inducted into one of the many social clubs where they can proudly participate in the infliction of organized misery on fish with heart problems.

Some fish that flunk the Heart Check and have no money are permitted to work off their rental and insurance overhead by serving as "Yard Tricks." They look out for the police or rival gangs. They keister balloons or even tattoo guns up their obliging assholes. They are employed to gather market intelligence on incoming vans of fish and J-Cats. Yard Tricks can be seen hustling across the yard carrying some righteous stand-up dawg's dirty clothes to the laundry or sweeping and scrubbing out the cells of the Shotcallers.

In the corporation we called these guys gofers, or worse. You could identify them on the organization chart by their own little boxes just below some Executive Shotcaller. They would have titles like "Executive Assistant."

My latest home, the Inferno, and the rest of the prison are run by a loose coalition of woods and skinheads known collectively as the Car. They even have an organizational mission statement of sorts: "If you're not in the Car, then you're out of the Car." The statement could use a bit of wordsmithing (a skill for which I was legendary at the phone company), but it essentially conveys the underlying threat of being kicked to the curb. To pursue outside opportunities.

If Kansas is the chairman and CEO of the Car, then Snake is his chief operating officer. The Snake allocates, monitors, and controls the revenue-producing market segments—the phones, the store thefts, laundry, prison industry scams, and the very lifeblood of the Car, the drug trade.

In Kansas's absence the Snake forges strategic alliances with the Toads, *Eses,* and the Tribe. The overarching goal is market stability and equilibrium. And that's something I'm down with. What former monopolist wouldn't be? Kansas has even worked out a generous revenue-sharing plan to preempt any emerging or presumptive competitors.

The laundry here is an *Ese*-run subsidiary of the Car. Want your nasty underwear and socks machine-washed? No *problema.* Just haul your shit down to Luis at the window counter. Kick down some stamps, a few full decks of tailors, or even a store can of jalapeño peppers. You can buy yourself a month's worth of laundry services, including sewing and repairs.

For a negligible charge, the *eses* will even throw some bleach in with your whites. Need your blue state shirt pressed and ironed? *Por supuesto* you do! Luis will hook you up, dawg, Luis will handle everything 'cause he knows his customers, he *knows* that your girlfriend, your *novia,* your *esposa,* is coming to visit and you need to be stylin' in a starched and pressed state shirt.

Say what? You got . . . nothing? No *estampillas*? No tailors? *No tienes jalapeños*? Then you're burnt—whatchu got, *amigo,* is *exactamente nada*! Nothin' coming! Whatchu got is *lost* laundry, shredded laundry, *wet* laundry returned to you because your hand don't call for no dry cycle. Whatchu got is some quality time with your state soap and sink—*hand*-scrubbing your shit.

" 'Cause," proclaims Luis, "ju ga notheen comin'—*motherfooka*!"

Luis and his ilk may even be responsible for all these middle-class white kids kickin' it in the malls with their pants fashionably falling down below their underwear. When new fish are marched down to exchange their orange coveralls for blue jeans and shirts, Luis likes to flash a serious clipboard and make an elaborate pretense of recording requested sizes.

He'll let the fish wait fifteen minutes at the window while he disappears back into the supply room. He invariably returns with a stack of triple-X-wide waists and shirts that could dwarf a circus tent.

Since the state doesn't provide belts, the convicts do the best they can with pieces of laundry string that Luis will sell to them. Unless, of course, you can kick something down or pledge something from a future store. Then Luis will see to it that you're stylin'.

The end fashion statement is called "jailing it"—a five-to-eight-inch revelation of white boxer tops precariously embraced by the string-tightened pants below. So who says convicts don't contribute to popular culture?

I'm inordinately proud of the fact that I have a belt. I purchased it for twenty-five bucks' worth of stamps from a lifer with a precious "hobby-craft card." The prison issues only a handful of these cards each year and only to lifers who are permitted to purchase leather supplies and use the tools in the cramped hobby-craft office in the gym.

My belt is my personalized stapler. It's hand-tooled leather. Just try to find a fish with a belt like this!

Sometimes it is good to feel like you're *about* something.

My immediate supervisor in the chow hall is a convict, and fellow Inferno resident, named Scud. His official title is "Food Server Leadman."

There are leadman cooks, leadman bakers, and leadman moppers. It's a seniority thing. The leadmen in the kitchen report to the Freemen—civilian supervisors, most of them aging free woods. Correctional officers are also posted in the kitchen, where they are nominally in charge. They rarely leave the comfort of their cluttered little staff office, located—out of sight—behind the bakery.

The cops also know better than to interfere with the lucrative trade between the leadmen and Freemen. The only reason Kansas would bother to have drugs smuggled in through visiting is that he loves the drama of it all. Most of the contraband on the yard floods in through the Freemen, facilitated by a few entrepreneurial guards. Outside gangs provide the cash and occasional motivation.

Scud is another template wood in his late twenties—full sleeves, empty mouth, and a filthy ponytail secured by an even filthier black rubber band.

"O.G.—all you gotta do is scoop the motherfucking Jell-O into the left slot on the tray." This completes my orientation and training from Scud.

"Is that it?" I ask, eyeing the giant metal vat quivering with green Jell-O, an ice cream scooper buried deep in the undulating mass. Sort of erotic, I'm thinking.

"No, that ain't it," Scud sighs, clearly overburdened by the prospect of having to "train" yet another fish in the art of Jell-O dispensing. All this *responsibility* thrust upon his bony, amphetamine-attrited shoulders for the princely prison sum of ten dollars a month.

My job as food server pays nothing. I do it for love.

"Ya gotta wear gloves and a hair net when you're working near food," Scud says, yanking these items out of a large cardboard box labeled CHICKEN BREASTS—UNFIT FOR HUMAN CONSUMPTION.

"It's a sanitation thing," Scud explains, turning his head in a well-practiced maneuver to blow his nose. His nose-blowing technique is crude but effective. It involves placing one nicotine-stained thumb over his left nostril while vigorously expelling a tsunami of snot out the right nostril.

It ain't nothin' nice.

Splat! A green projectile explodes against the wall and hovers indecisively above a steaming vat of vegetable soup. Scud then completes the process, thumbing his right nostril and turning his head away from us and toward the salad, which rests limply in a metal canister the size of Cuba.

Ping! The missile impacts the side of the metal container. My fellow servers, woods and toads alike, blaze hotly with righteous indignation.

"That's outta line, dawg!"

"*Way* the fuck outta line!"

And it's pandemonium in the serving area! Moral outrage! *Righteous fucking resentment!*

"Muthafuckin' *nasty*-ass white boy!" screams our salad server, a chubby black teenager called Tooshay. Tooshay tells anyone who cares that "you best be pronouncing it Two-*Shay*!" It must be a Francophile thing.

"That's some fucked-up shit, Scud!" contributes C-Note, whose role on the team is to put two pats of butter on each tray—when he's not busy fussing with the tight cornrows under the hair net.

Snake and the other dawgs down the serving line are also howling in rage at Scud, who just looks confused.

T-Bone, who is on the cleanup crew out in the chow hall, pokes his shower cap through the small opening in the window. To our relief, we are sealed off from the chow hall and our customers by a railroad car metal partition. When we see hands through the window, we push out the trays. The back of the serving area is open to the grills, ovens, and bakery of the main kitchen.

"Cain't a muthafucka get nothin' but a rollie?" The Bone wants a real cigarette, a tailor. C-Note taps a long ash off his half-smoked tailor—*into* a vat of mashed potatoes—offers it to the Bone.

"Here be a short, bro."

The Bone studies the "short" with clinical interest. He has the melancholy suspicion of a man who senses disease and disaster everywhere. The Bone declines the short.

"I ain't lookin' to catch *nothin'* but pa-*role*!" And the shower cap disappears back into the chow hall.

All eyes are again on the moist green creature pulsing ominously above the vegetable soup. The freeman boss walks into the serving area.

"What the fuck are you convicts doing?" Freeman Marshall is a beer-gutted, fiftyish wood with faded sleeves. He's been working in the prison system, in the kitchen, for twenty-seven years. The years have not been kind to him, but in an alternate universe he could have been an unemployed short-order cook in here, with us. Everybody likes Marshall because he wears a "house arrest" electronic bracelet around his ankle, courtesy of his second domestic battery offense. He's sort of a wood role model.

"What the fuck are you dickwads looking at! We got three hundred cocksucking cons to feed tonight!"

Tooshay, who's doing a dime behind a crack sale gone bad, extends a chubby black finger, pointing to a spot on the wall above the vat of soup.

Where, like some hideous extraterrestrial spider, the green body of Scud's booger is slowly detaching itself, one slick strand at a time, from the wall. Next stop—Vegetable Soup World.

We all just stand there—frozen. A group of hardened cons, one cubicle refugee, and a serial wife-batterer paralyzed by the spectacle of a *Living, Moving, Sentient Booger from Beyond* as it slides inexorably down the wall.

And into the soup. It says *plop!*

Outside the metal partition, starving convicts beat their fists against the railroad car walls. The Bone sticks his head through the slot.

"Cain't a muthafucka get some nasty-ass chow trays out here? People's be *trippin'*!"

And it's on! A classic assembly-line process (with none of the efficiencies) unfolds, each server adding his small increment of value as we slide, spin, and spill trays along the long metal counter. The trays come at me so fast that half the time I end up scooping the Jell-O on top of the mashed potatoes, which in turn have been hastily scooped on top of the peas and carrots instead of the soybean patties. A few Jell-O slabs find their way into the bowls of vegetable soup, perhaps seeking a union with their lone, green extraterrestrial brother.

Scud and Freeman Marshall take turns shoving the trays through the slot, where they disappear instantly. All I can see are grasping hands. We can all hear the shouts, the wolf tickets being sold outside.

"Fucking fish servers be puttin' Jell-O on the muthafuckin' *mashed*!"

"C-Note! I know that's you back there—you best not be giving us no melted-ass butter!"

"Who the fuck be slammin' *Jell-O* upside the bowl!"

To drown out the shouts and threats, Tooshay leads us in a group sing-along. We warm up with "I Heard It Through the Grapevine," hit a solid harmonious stride with Little Anthony and the Imperials' "Tears on My Pillow," and as the last tray is snatched away, an absolutely rousing rendition of that old prison standard "Working on the Chain Gang."

"Servers fucking rule!" yells Scud, politely averting his head as he violently dispels yet another alien from his nose.

"Break it down!" screams the Freeman, the signal to start cleaning up. We all grab an assortment of soiled black rags and swipe energetically and ineffectually at the mess on the counter, basically just *pushing* the detritus around until we have sculpted one huge soggy mountain of gravy, Jell-O, and mashed potatoes.

Scud puts on his plastic gloves and shoves the monstrosity, or most of it, onto the cement floor, turns on a spigot, and floods most of the mess down a metal drainage grate in the cement. Some of it even goes down. The rest will harden nicely overnight so T-Bone and the cleanup crew can sweep it away in the morning.

Freeman Marshall leads us out back through the bakery area. The bakery smells like a brewery. That's because it *is* a brewery. In addition to making bread, rolls, and cakes, the bakers also mass-produce "pruno," a potent alcoholic brew available in such fruity flavors as orange, apple, and peach.

The bakers simply appropriate some spare fifty-gallon soup drums, fill them with the fruit of the day, add water, sugar, and yeast, and *voilà!* In a few days the concoction has fermented sufficiently to permit pruno product launch and associated marketing activities to ensue.

The pruno is surreptitiously bottled under the brand name Pert Plus (available at the local store), since the green plastic bottles hold a convenient 15.2 ounces and retail on the yard for the equivalent of eight dollars a bottle.

Of course, the thrifty (read "indigent"), self-sufficient inmate simply brews his own, using a Ziploc bag and oranges, adding sugar and substituting bread for yeast.

Freeman Marshall herds us to the locked exit doors in the back of the kitchen where an elderly C.O. waits with the keys. The C.O.'s white hair smells like it has just been shampooed in pruno. He fishes a key off the ring attached to his webbed belt and tells us to line up for the pat-down.

C.O. Pert ignores the small bulges in our pants pockets. Stealing food is practically a built-in job perk. Stealing butcher knives or metal objects is a no-no.

The servers never steal knives. They don't have to. They design and make their own shanks with metal obtained from the cons in the auto and welding shops.

Outside, the sun is setting behind the vast desert wasteland. With winter not long off, temperatures drop sharply in the evenings and the air is brisk and cool. A strong breeze brushes my face as I look up, past the fences, over the razor wire and the guntowers.

I am glad—no, I am enormously grateful at this moment to be alive. The Bone stands beside me, fretting over the wind and the possibility of another sandstorm.

"Cain't a muthafucka get nothin' but a dirt storm? Shit!" The Bone clutches the shower cap tighter over his head.

The Bone knows you can never be too prepared in prison for a shitstorm.

We all take turns sweeping and mopping the Inferno. T-Bone, generally acknowledged to be the mop master (and rumored candidate for cleanup crew leadman), gives me some one-on-one tutoring.

"White boys cain't do nothin' but *push* a muthafuckin' mop! The blap man, he be *glidin'* wiff da mop, blap man be styling!" So I adjust my awkward task-oriented focus to incorporate the Bone's suggestions about rhythm, fluidity, and grace. Under the Bone's tutelage I gradually surrender to the process until one evening the Bone confers the ultimate accolade on my sorry white ass.

"The O.G. be *stylin'* now!" the Bone announces proudly to anyone in the barracks who cares.

No one does. "Bone, why don't y'all *style* that muthafuckin' mop up yo ignorant nigger ass!" says C-Note. C-Note is sitting on his end bunk by the bathroom where Tooshay is styling C's cornrows into Rastafarian dreadlocks.

I continue happily mopping while the Bone and C-Note begin their nightly jab, dance, jab, duck, and jab ritual without ever actually hitting each other. I glide with the mop between the beds recalling a Future Leaders Management Team-Building workshop. Our five-hundred-dollar-an-hour training consultant stressed the importance of focusing on the *moment,* on the task right in front of us. We were to clear our minds of aberrant thoughts about lunch and learn to just "be in the moment." To learn to be effective communicators, effective *leaders,* we had to first learn how to "be here now."

We called it Be Here Now training. And now I finally have some use for it, melding with the mop, giving myself over to the awe and mystery of living in the moment. I finally lay the mop down and face the room. I am transformed, like an est novitiate who finally "gets it."

"Bone . . . I *be* the mop!" I exult to anyone who cares.

No one does. Except the Bone.

"You be *somethin',* O.G., but I doan be knowin' zackly *what.*"

The Inferno is the only "housing unit" in the prison where a parochial convict can experience the rich benefits of ethnically diverse living. The C.O.'s assign cellies to the two-man cells strictly on the basis of race, with a total disregard for any subtle geographic distinctions. This can lead to convict carping.

"Yo, See-Oh! I'm *Filipino*—why the fuck you celling me up with some motherfucking punk-ass *Micronesian* that don't even know what fucking *island* he's from?"

The C.O. tells him to shut the fuck up. "We got a shortage of flip cases this year," he explains.

In the Inferno the woods and skinheads hang together, the toads "kick it with mines," Loco, our sole Hispanic, keeps to himself, and I usually isolate on my bunk with my headphones and radio, pen and writing tablet.

After the 6 P.M. standing count, it is "mail call" in front of the C.O.'s office in the rotunda. The cop yells out a back number and tosses letters, magazines, and newspapers into the air. It reminds me of the time I took my then little girls to Marine World to watch the porpoises leap for those little doomed fish.

The Bone is perched on his bunk, trying to read Lucindreth's latest letter. Some convicts view letter reading as a communal activity, so C-Note and Tooshay look over the Bone's shoulder.

"Cain't a muthafucka get some *privacy*?" the Bone says as C-Note sits beside him. "C-Note, you're sweatin' my spot! I'm fittin' to read my bitch's letter here."

"Da-*yam*, Bone! That be-yatch Lucindreth ain't nothin' but a crack ho!"

"Doan be *dissin' mines*, C!" The Bone is removing his shower cap—always a danger signal.

C-Note, untrained by the phone company in discerning "minimal environmental cues," snatches the letter from Bone's hand.

"Ain't dissin' *shit*, Bone. I just be tellin' you Lucindreth suck a cock for a rock! All the brothers in Vegas be knowin' that."

The Bone's fist moves so fast that by the time C-Note sees it he's flying backward off the Bone's tray, wondering what kind of freight train just crushed his once-lovely nose.

C-Note's Rasta dreadlocks hit the concrete floor—hard.

Kind of a crunching sound, like an egg meeting a baseball bat in midswing. "My bad," says the Bone.

Very bad for C-Note, who is sprawled on his back unconscious, his nose pumping out a blood geyser that would have impressed the captain of the *Exxon Valdez*.

We all scramble off our bunks, crowding around the fallen C-Note, careful not to get blood on our state-issue white tennis sneakers—bad for the sneakers.

"Fucking Bone! Ya peeled his fucking *onion*!" exclaims the Snake, who is shaking his shaved head in admiration, the eyeballs in *back* of his head watching the door for the Man, his spiderwebbed eyeballs in front surveying the puddle of blood around C-Note's head.

Tooshay is backing away in horror. "You cracked his *dome*, T! You kilt his ass, fo sho!"

"Nah," drawls a highly relaxed Bone. "That nigger got hisself a *hard* haid—y'all know how he is."

Scud comes over and prods C-Note in the grill with his foot. Actually it's more like a kick in the ribs. "Fuck—he ain't breathing, dawgs. Now we got the fucking heat coming down on *all* our asses."

Loco takes a quick look at C-Note and pronounces him *muerto*.

The Bone differs. "Nah, Loco, that nigger be too *ignorant* to even *find* his way to dead. Nigger got up in *mines*! I tol' C not to be gettin' up in mines when I gots a letter from my bitch."

Every cellblock has a Shotcaller, and Snake is ours. We now all defer to his proven leadership skills and experience.

Snake looks down at the flattened C-Note, who is starting to resemble a bloody black Gumby. Snake kicks C's grill. No response.

"Fuck him!" decides our leader. "He was way outta line, dissin' the Bone's bitch. Motherfucker got nothing coming from us—it's C.O.P.!"

The standard "convict operating procedure" for a fight inside the cellblock is to strip the loser, toss him in the shower, turn on the water, and *then* start yelling for C.O. assistance. *Just an accident . . . motherfucker musta slipped in the shower—clumsy-ass fool!*

In a splendid display of interracial teamwork, C-Note is swiftly reduced to bare-butt essentials. Most of the dawgs here are not completely unfamiliar with this exercise, having stripped cars, homes, and bodies many times before.

"Damn! Nasty-ass C-Note got no muthafuckin' *shorts*," observes Tooshay.

"Motherfucker got no *dick* either," says Snake.

"That's 'cause he's dead," says Scud as he half lifts C-Note under the arms and starts dragging him to the shower. "Your dick shrivels when you die—I saw that on Discovery once."

"Then you be *born* dead, Scud," says the Bone, who is still sitting serenely on his bunk, refusing to go anywhere near all that potentially infectious blood.

"C'mon, Bone, give us a hand—this is your lookout," Snake says.

The Bone is unmoved and unmoving. "Nigger probably got the muthafuckin' *AIDS*! And I ain't lookin' to catch nothin' but pa-*role*, y'unnerstan' what I'm sayin'?"

"Aiight, Bone. O.G., give me a hand here." Somehow we manage to drag C-Note into the shower. Snake turns on the cold water, directing the showerhead so C-Note receives a steady blast right on his busted nose.

C-Note doesn't stir.

Scud starts tripping. "Fuck, fuck, fuck, *fuck*! He's fuckin' dead and we're all going down!" Scud considerately tilts his head away from the body, does that disgusting thing with his thumb over one nostril, and expels a booger against the shower wall.

"You *nasty*, Scud—you one real nasty white boy," Tooshay informs him, not for the first time. The jet stream is carrying C-Note's blood down the drain as we all crowd around the shower praying for the res-urrection of C-Note.

"Anybody know first aid? CPR? We gotta get him breathing." Scud also learned this from Discovery. T-Bone has finally decided to join us at the shower to admire his artwork: *Still Life Taking Shower.*

"Scud," the Bone says, "you fittin' to put *yo* mouf on that nigger's nasty lips?" The prospect of this actually happening before his eyes so appalls the germ-crazy Bone that he rushes back to the safety of his bunk.

Snake is unscrewing the lid off a bottle of bleach. He kneels just outside the jet spray, studying C-Note.

Scud is intrigued. "What the fuck you gonna do, dawg? Gonna *bleach* him awake?"

"The Snake fittin' to bleach him *white* back to life," puns Tooshay, and we all crack up as Snake pours the bleach (which he later insists was ammonia) directly onto C-Note's mashed face.

C-Note twitches awake like Lazarus rising. "Muthafucka!" he screams. "You be burning my *eyes!*" C-Note is scuttling ass-backward away from the deluge of bleach, tries to stand, makes it halfway to his feet before falling facedown on the hard concrete of the shower floor.

This time it sounds more like an egg meeting a hammer in midswing as C-Note's front teeth shatter and are swept away by the bleached water and down the drain. I am reminded of my grandpa George's reflection: "Whether the hammer hits the egg or the egg hits the hammer, it's *always* bad for the egg."

We all race down the corridor to the locked crash gates.

"Man down! Man down!" we scream at the pimply young cop in the office, who eventually puts down his *Soldier of Fortune* and coffee and comes to investigate this latest affront to his correctional routine.

C-Note returns from the infirmary three days later after explaining to a skeptical nurse how a Clorox bottle *tripped* him in the shower, thereby knocking out his front teeth and bleaching his Rasta locks peckerwood white.

'Cause C-Note ain't no snitch, he ain't no punk, and he sure ain't fittin' to catch *nothin' but parole*!

The D-word.

Ask any convict who has been down a few days for his definition of a "man" and the concept of "disrespect" will surface quicker than stank on shit. Let's use Kansas's definition of a man, since it's illustrative of the prison's general population.

"A man," Kansas might say, "is someone who tolerates no disrespect! A real man, a *stand-up* man, seeks out disrespect and destroys it!" Not surprisingly, this Manly Mission Statement keeps all the Real Men in prison very busy, prison being such a fertile incubator for disrespect.

It also keeps them coming back here. Until the parole system succeeds in obliterating all traces, all minute suggestions, of disrespect on the outside, I suspect the recidivism rate here will remain at over 80 percent.

What makes the Big D such a formidable foe for the nearly extinct forces of rehabilitation is not so much its pervasiveness as its utter absence of gradation.

There is no *little* disrespect. There is no "somewhat" or "mildly" disrespectful, no inadvertent slights, no concept of being *accidentally* jostled by some dawg in the chow line.

Many of the dawgs here do not make a distinction between an enemy who tries to "bitch-slap" him and a friend who simply forgets to say "What's up, dawg?" as a yard greeting. It's all disrespect.

When necessary, the Real Man, the Stand-up Righteous Con, *will* offer a distinction should someone be foolish enough (never happens) to suggest that "sinking a dick in Timmy's tight little ass" could be construed as "faggot" behavior. The Righteous Dawg would simply laugh at such ignorance because *he* is a *"pitcher,"* y'unnerstan', not a *"catcher."*

And every Righteous Con in the joint knows a catcher ain't nothin' but a *punk-ass bitch*!

Of course, these manly assertions require a temporary suspension of belief in other convict adages: "Today's pitcher, tomorrow's catcher," or "Today's punk, tomorrow's rapist."

But as Emerson explained: "A foolish consistency is the hobgoblin of little minds . . ."

So when some wood suggests I stop bird-dogging his conversation (*eavesdropping*—one of my many character flaws) or Mr. Toad advises me not to be "getting up in mines" ("mines" in this instance referring to *mines bidness*—y'unnerstan'?), I *respect* their wishes.

Do your own time . . . or someone
will make you do theirs.
—OLD HEAD SAYING

The Old Heads are lifers and other convicts who have been down for decades. Sometimes I stop counting my steps in the yard to sit down in the dirt and play chess with them.

The Old Heads like to talk about the good old days in the joint—the late sixties and the seventies—when the guards ("the pigs!") were the true enemy instead of fellow convicts. When a Convict Code of Honor prevailed because back then, a Real Convict was a "Straight-up, Stand-up Con!"

The Old Heads have seen everything. *Done* everything. Just ask them.

"*Attica?* Fucking A, dawg! I was doing a double nickel in that fucking joint back in '71 when the Shit Jumped Off—and I'm talkin' about some *serious* shit, you know what I'm saying? Some *serious* fucking shit! None of this punk-ass bullshit you see today with faggots and J-Cats and wanna-be gangsta boys getting in the Car and rolling up to some snitch's crib to slock and cock 'im, know what I'm sayin'?"

All the Old Heads tell you how they did time at Attica when the Shit Jumped Off, making Attica prison the convict equivalent of

Woodstock, which was attended by all 50 million or so of my fellow baby boomers.

Just ask any boomer.

If the Attica riot was the Old Heads' Woodstock, then they had to have traveled there not by some Day-Glo VW microbus, but by horseback. Because the dream they dwelled in back then, when the Code of the Stand-up Con held sway, when Convict Righteousness ruled, was nothing less than a bright and shining concrete and barbed-wire Camelot of the imagination.

So I sit in the dirt playing chess with the Old Heads, listening to the stories. Respectfully. Listen as they continually reinvent and refresh the decades of hard time until the past glimmers, if only in their hearts.

I listen. Because I, too, need a Camelot of the heart.

Big Hungry comes for me in broad daylight. Right in the center of the yard where every guntower cop can see us. He bears down on me like an enraged bull elephant, roaring.

"O.G.! You been up in *mines*!" The Hunger is stylin' today, his black silk do-rag covering his tiny head and the gold teeth sparkling in the desert sun.

Five yards away now. "O.G.! You been sweatin' my bitch! Been up on my Cassie!" Then a mountainous shadow falls over me as the Hunger reaches down to crush my dome. Or onion.

But I'm not there.

Smooth and slick as my mop gliding across the Inferno floor, I evade the black tree limb about to crash down on my head. The Hunger is crushing nothing but air.

Knowing it is suicidal, hopeless, and probably even stupid, I drive my right fist into the Hunger's face, connecting with a gold tooth or two. Very bad for my hand. It has no more effect on Big Hungry than a bee sting on a grizzly. Except to make him even madder.

The Hunger is lifting me right off my feet—by my neck. A massive right paw pulls back to center a killing shot to my domelights.

There is a soft, wet, sucking sound. The sound of a muted rattle. It comes from the spot on the back of the Hunger's head where the Snake and Scud have just double-slocked him with a dozen or so C batteries.

The Hunger melts in slow motion to the dirt, an incredibly poignant reenactment of King Kong toppling slo-mo from the Empire State Building.

By the time the beast kisses the earth, the Snake is already shoving my petrified ass forward, Scud playing lookout. "Just move, O.G. Gotta get into the Inferno—*don't look back!*"

"Fuck, Snake, you killed him! You killed Big Hungry!" Scud wails as we pass through the open gate of the Inferno.

"You mean *we* fucking killed him," Snake answers. "You always fucking whine about the same shit, ya know that, Scud? Look at C-Note over here, kicking it with the Bone—wasn't he dead too?"

The Bone, playing spades with C-Note, removes his shower cap. "Whassup, Snake, O.G.? Who be dead *today?*"

In answer, the Inferno C.O. starts shouting "LOCK IT DOWN!" and pushes the button that slides the gate shut. We can hear the cop radios in the yard sputtering "MAN DOWN!"

Because the Hunger is thoughtful enough not to die, we are only locked down for two days.

The Code of the Stand-up Con holds firm. So far, anyway.
None of the dozen or so dawgs who witnessed the Hunger's meltdown have snitched. The guntower cops are too high up to identify anyone.

The Dirt, led by Sergeant Stanger, once again revel in the opportunity to skin-search us, then tear apart our personal belongings. During the lockdown the Freemen and cops load bag lunches—peanut butter and jelly mostly—onto food carts, which are wheeled to every cellblock.

The Inferno dawgs view it as a nice vacation from kitchen labor. They spend their free time watching Jerry, Ricki, Montel, and WWF. Convicts are required to wear their headphones when watching TV or listening to music. It is a "housing regulation" that is universally ignored. Headphones would interfere with the communal bonding experience of dissecting the anatomies of the female talk show guests.

A lot of heated debate takes place over whether a particular female guest "got ass" or don't got ass. Or if she's a "straight-up ho" or just a potential whore.

"That bitch be all tore up!"

"She be tore up, Tooshay, but she got some *ass*!"

"But the bitch got a nasty ol' *leather* crotch!"

"Yo, Scud, check it out! Yo momma be on the TV!"

"Nah, ain't my momma, Bone—my momma works at the methadone clinic handing out drugs to *your* momma!"

"Damn, that's some cold-ass shit, Scud!"

I get out my little radio and headphones. The radios have clear plastic cases to deter their use as crank or crack stashes. The TVs are also transparent. The vinyl mattresses are not, however, and most convicts keep their drugs and Pert bottles tucked inside them. Shanks are taped under the beds.

I find a station playing gold—James Taylor, Bob Dylan, Joni Mitchell, the Beach Boys, my kind of music. I crank the volume up, tighten the headphones, and go time-traveling while pushing my Bic against the lined paper.

The Bone looks up for a moment from an examination of one of the ho's.

"Yogee! Always be *writing*! You the *writinest* muthafucka I been knowin' . . . Why you always be writin'?"

I remove the headphones.

"Because Bone . . . because I can't fly."

Big Hungry recovers from the dent in his dome in the in-firmary. He refuses to take his J-Cat medication—Haldol—which is supposed to diminish his delusion that everything he desires in life "be mines!" He is shackled and cuffed and shipped back to the Nevada Prison for the Criminally Insane—J wing.

If tears were shed on the yard, I didn't hear about it.

Stanger is waiting for me when I come out of the chow hall after a four-hundred green Jell-O scoop session. He's looking all stract in his black Darth Vader costume, although the jarhead crew cut ruins the Darth effect.

"O.G.! Front and center, asshole!" Stanger growls this greeting in his best "command voice," which C.O.'s are trained to affect. An old infantry sergeant myself, albeit twenty years removed, I can recognize a fellow graduate of Command Voice 101.

"Good morning, Sergeant," I say—pleasantly. My mother always said that "good manners cost nothing."

Stanger is leaning with his back against the chow hall wall, methodically hand-rolling a cigarette from a Bugler can. His state trooper–style shades went out of fashion around the same time that *Dragnet* went off the air.

"Just wondering if you got any extra *batteries*, O.G." Stanger's billy club steel flashlight is out and he's shaking it with exaggerated distress. "Yeah, I heard you sometimes carry a few extra batteries. Oh, but those would be size C, and this baby takes D." Stanger fires up his rollie and gives me that sweet, sadistic smile.

"Sorry, Sarge, I'm fresh out. I didn't know you were going to have a light show so soon after lunch."

The rollie is instantly ground out beneath a polished black jackboot. In the army I wouldn't have trusted this guy to carry my backpack. In the corporation he couldn't have carried my briefcase.

"Still talking shit outta the side of your fucking neck!" The Inferno dawgs have all paused, ready to bear witness or take my back should Stanger go postal.

"I'm watching you, asshole—*nobody* fronts me off with the assistant warden. Somebody's gonna roll on your lying ass. Now go roll it the fuck up!"

This is a shock. "Roll it up?" This could mean going to the Hole, getting released, or just moving cellblocks. I'm voting for door number 2.

"Are you fucking *retarded*?" Stanger screams, spraying me with flecks of spit-soaked Bugler. "Roll it the fuck up! Take your sorry-ass shit over to cellblock 4, then report to the law library—your little dick-licking, on-the-leg bullshit got over on the assistant warden."

O happy day! Free from the kitchen, from the Inferno, from Jerry and Ricki and Montel and whores that may or may not have ass! Back to the sweet peace of a two-man cell.

Stanger dismisses me on his usual ominous note. "Yeah, got a couple of witnesses, couple of punk-ass bitch dawgs who were kickin' it in front of the store when the Shit Jumped Off and bashed the Hunger's head in . . . oh yeah, just a matter of tracking the Energizer Bunny back to the slock. A little squeezing, a little pressure—y'unnerstan'?—and one of these punks will roll on you. You understand what I'm saying to you, *convict*?"

But I'm already moving, moving fast, back to the Inferno for what I pray is the last time. Things are definitely looking up.

'Cause I'm *rolling it up*!

. . .

On my way back to the Inferno to roll up my stuff, I stop
to watch the latest county jail van disgorge a new batch of fish. This being a great prison spectator sport, I am soon surrounded by a crowd of
convicts checking out "the meat." The fish are being marched across the
yard by three Security and Escort cops to the Fish Tank.

The new fish, yet to experience the delights of Luis's laundry service, are dressed in street clothes. They pass through the gauntlet of
hard cases who are already taking inventory. Shoes, shirts, pants,
rings—all are instantly and expertly appraised by the Yard Rats, who
live for these moments.

Representatives from the various social and fraternal organizations
are also here, scouting for new gang members—or fresh victims, potential "renters" of cells or a seat in the chow hall. Or just punks crying
out for a "daddy."

Some fish are warmly greeted. Fish with full sleeves (the badge of
the recidivist) or acceptable gang tattoos are hailed like returning war
heroes. These dawgs are not true fish. These dawgs have all been down
before, and most of them are known quantities on the yard. The Yard
Rats award big points to the fish with swastika tattoos, and the teardrop
tattoos—said to denote a cop-killer—always win the grand prize of
Respect.

"Yo, dawg! Whatchu down for?"

"Life *Without*!" says Teardrop Tattoo to an admiring audience. Life
With the possibility of parole is considered a sentence worthy of respect,
but Life Without demands adulation.

The real interest of the Yard Rats is in the *fresh* fish, the first-time
guest, untainted, untarnished, and uninitiated into How Things Really
Work Around Here. Today's special focus is on a very young fish whose

case has been in the newspapers and on television for the past few
months.

He is thirteen years old and could easily pass for eleven. Food-stamp
thin, barely five feet tall with a baby face bursting with freckles, topped
by an unruly shock of red hair. The kid's ears stick out from his head at
an almost right angle.

I find myself staring at this child in his Nike sneakers (kiss *them*
good-bye) and 'N Sync T-shirt. He does his best to walk with dignity,
despite the shackles and waist chains. He is holding himself straight,
head up, ears flaring out, not flinching from the catcalls of the Yard
Rats. He keeps his moist brown eyes—just drying now from county?—
fixed on Teardrop Tattoo's back. If he's alarmed by all the *par-tay* invitations, he does not show it.

"Yo, *Bob,* come to *Daddy*! Your daddy's been waiting on you!" Back
in the world, "Bob" is the nickname for "Robert." In here it's an
acronym for "bend over backwards."

"Hey! His name ain't *Bob*—look at them fucking *ears*! It's *Dumbo*!"
The Yard Rats squeal with laughter—Dumbo! That's a good one—until the next convict tops it.

"Nah, he ain't Dumbo—Dumbo would *fly* over the fucking fences!
With them fuckin' ears he's a *teacup* head!" *Teacup!* That one hits an 8.0
on the Rat Richter scale.

And "Teacup" will be his name for at least the next forty years because this kid, this *meat,* is looking at two Life Withs, running wild.

His trial was covered in lurid detail. At the age of twelve, weary beyond reason of his stepfather's nightly visits to his bed (and emboldened
by a six-pack of beer stolen from a neighbor's garage), Teacup decided
to pay Stepdad a visit one night.

With a twelve-inch kitchen carving knife.

The county medical examiner testified at the trial to forty-seven
stab wounds. Had Teacup just called it a night at that point, just gone
back to his room, maybe called 911 before booting up a computer

game and an 'N Sync CD, he *might* have been all right. A jury might have looked at the "mitigating factors."

But, as Stanger is fond of saying, *Nooooooo!* After dispatching the evil stepdad, Teacup decides his sixteen-year-old sister, Trisha, also has something coming. Because she knew about Stepdad. Knew about the rapes, the beatings, 'cause Teacup had *told* her, begged her for help when Mom, too drugged and drunk, did nothing, telling Teacup to "just work it out with him."

So now Trisha's got something coming because she didn't help, didn't even say anything to a soul. Now Teacup's going to work it out.

So Teacup pays a little visit to Trisha's room, after first fitting his face with a Jason-style hockey mask left over from his Halloween adventures. "Showing clear premeditation," intoned the D.A. at the trial.

The six-pack of beer apparently slowed Teacup down somewhat because after only thirteen whacks with the cleaver to Trisha's chest and neck, he passed out from exhaustion by the side of her bed.

Before he could decide whether to return to Stepdad's bedroom and do his passed-out mother.

Nine-one-one didn't get the call till the next morning when Mom, unable to find her "wake-up"—a shot of speed—went wandering around the house in search of her stash.

Two hours later, still screaming, she got her shot from an E.R. doctor—a sedative to shut her up.

Now Teacup, toothpick wrists shackled, belly chains rattling, is our latest and youngest guest. Something about him—maybe it's the moist brown eyes—reminds me of my younger daughter, Rachel. And I just know that Teacup's bridal reception party in the Fish Tank will make the stepdad look like a saint by comparison.

As Teacup shuffles by me, I step through the mob and whisper in one of his Dumbo ears.

"Just listen! When you get to the Tank, ask for *Kansas*—cell 47, upper tier. You got that? Hook up with Kansas—tell him the O.G. sent you."

Teacup is startled, but he makes eye contact and nods before they march him away.

The Bone touches my elbow. "O.G. fittin' to be a *daddy*?"

And all the Yard Rats rock with laughter.

Cellblock 4 is considered a "preferred housing unit" by the prison. It's a one-story structure with three blocks—A, B, and C. In this age of euphemism, the prison's official designation is not "A block" or "B block," but "A wing," "B wing."

I'm relieved to be in a single-tier "housing unit." No worrying about taking an involuntary dive off the upper tier because some J-Cat is struggling with a burning curiosity about *exactly* what kind of sound my head would make when it splattered on the concrete floor of the lower tier.

There is also no Bubblecop with a big gun. Just a kiosk-like staff office in the central rotunda. It's like a Fotomat booth encased in steel; wire-mesh and Plexiglas windows with an open counter for the C.O. to hand out mail, toilet paper, or just some verbal abuse.

In the not unlikely event that the Shit Jumps Off, the guard can simply seal himself in and microwave popcorn and listen to news of the riot over his radio. Waiting for rescue.

Not that there's anything wrong with that.

The rotunda has the same setup as the Inferno: a staff office for the caseworker, a closet-size "library," two wall telephones, and a bathroom. A crude, hand-lettered sign reading STAFF ONLY is taped to the bathroom door. Another paper sign beneath it reads "After taking your shit, please proceed directly to the Hole!"

Sounds like an honor system to me.

The cop in the kiosk is an aging cowboy with a full head of white hair and a tanned, weather-beaten face. A network of burst capillaries on his face suggests his off-duty hobby. He's also refreshingly courteous.

"Mr. Lerner," he drawls, consulting the "Movement Sheet." "You'll be in 17 cell, A wing. See the porter for your bedding issue. You can leave your tub right here for now." His nametag reads SCO FALLON. He has two stripes—a *senior* correctional officer, which is a big deal for these cops.

Fallon points to a supply room adjacent to the caseworker's office. "Mr. Lerner, if you have anything in your tub, *anything* at all that you're not supposed to have, I'll give you a couple of minutes now to dispose of it."

"No, sir, nothing at all." Fallon studies me for a moment, taking in the mostly white beard, the absence of tattoos, and the still semibewildered look of a fish out of water.

He seems to reach some sort of decision. "Excellent—I think we'll get along just fine. I understand your friend Kansas will be joining us soon from the Fish Tank."

I don't know if this is some kind of test.

"Well, I can use all the friends I can get around here," I say, and push open the door to the supply room.

I find the porter in the back of the supply room, crouching behind a five-foot-high stack of mattresses, sucking greedily on a Pert Plus shampoo bottle—Skell!

"What's up, dawg?" Skell greets me, shoving the Pert inside a stack of towels. His bloodshot eyes manage to focus for a moment. "*O.G.! Aiight!* Heard you heading over . . . yeah, was on the wire, bro. You the new *Lawdog* and all."

"I haven't even started in the law library yet."

"Well, whatchu need, dawg?" Skell whispers in that intimate conspiratorial hiss of his—"Wash shoe need"—that renders even the most commonplace English expression somehow obscene. Skell still has the same four rotting yellow teeth he had back in the Fish Tank, but his shaved head now sports a bright red scab the size of a giant squid, shaped curiously like an old map of North Vietnam.

A few baby squids decorate his sunken, unshaved cheeks. I tell him I need bedding, soap, and toothpaste.

"No, dawg—what I'm sayin' is I can hook you up! Y'unnerstan'? I got a *Hilton* Hotel towel for ya, dawg. I got sheets—*real* sheets, donated from Saint Mary's Hospice—you think them nuns is gonna let some poor, dying sonofabitch check out on top of some fucked-up rag? Nah, dawg, I'm talkin' *cotton!*"

Skell's on a pruno roll now, excited by the prospect of some rollies and stamps. He gives the Mother of All Squids a vicious scratch, unleashing a river of blood that travels down his forehead and links up with a baby squid on his cheek—the Ho Chi Minh Trail?

"Aiight. I'll take the Hilton, pass on the Saint Mary."

"Ten stamps, dawg."

"Five—and give me a mattress without a rat's nest inside."

"Done deal, dawg," and Skell extends a clenched fist. I tap knuckles, making a mental note to *boil* my hand later—if Skell will sell me a hot stove.

"What about a rug, dawg? I got one of them sand-nigger prayer rugs the Muslims gotta use when they beg Allah for another oil well or missile or whatever the fuck those sand toads pray for."

"No thanks. Figuring out which way is east *and* praying to Mecca is more than I can handle right now."

"That's all good then. What cell did Fallon put you in?"

"Seventeen cell, A wing." Skell grabs a clipboard and looks at the housing roster. "*Scandalous!* That cell's empty right now. I'll put you in the bottom bunk."

"Thanks—how much is that?"

"Seeing as how you Kansas's dawg, it's on me." Overwhelmed by his own generosity, Skell takes a swig of Pert and another swipe at Mother Squid. This time a brigade of Red Chinese troops floods down the Ho Chi Minh Trail toward the Calamari Pass.

I decide not to wait around for the fall of Saigon. I grab my purchases and head toward my new house. It's the familiar eight-by-six of the Fish Tank except it has a window that I can open and close with a heavy steel lever. The window is some sort of thick plastic, reinforced with heavy metal mesh. But it's a real window with a view of the yard.

And, until I get a cellie, it's *mines*!

The law clerk job is a piece of cake, mostly consisting of delivering lawbooks or NSF (nonsufficient funds) packages of writing paper and stamped envelopes to "indigents" in the lockdown units. As I suspected, it requires absolutely zero knowledge of the law. There are plenty of jailhouse lawyers on the yard who charge hundreds of dollars to handle an appeal or a habeas corpus petition to the feds.

Just when I am falling into a complacent routine, the *eses* decide to beat the hell out of someone right in front of cellblock 4 when I'm coming back from the law library. Five or six Mexicans—Sureños—surrounding a solitary victim, also Mexican, on the dirt lawn. Punching him in the stomach and kicking him in the face when he falls.

"*Maricón sucio!*" they scream. Then they kick him some more.

"*Cabrón!*" And a final vicious kick to the head.

The *ese* collapses and then sprawls facedown in the dirt while the Sureños calmly stroll off. So casual, just doing a synchronized convict strut. Another walk in the park on a sunny day. *Qué paso, ese!*

The sirens go off all over the yard, loudspeakers crackle, then announce, LOCK IT DOWN! CLEAR THE YARD! Convicts scurry from every corner of the yard, streaming like rats back to their cell-blocks, the sirens a continuous earsplitting wail.

It is a surreal scene out of H. G. Wells's *The Time Machine,* the movie with Rod Taylor where the Morlocks sound an "air raid" siren to summon the innocent (but tasty) Eloi to their dark cannibalistic caves. Once the Morlocks have assembled sufficient Eloi ingredients for their feast (and maybe a midnight snack as well), they sound the siren again—this time the *good* siren sound signifying "all clear."

I retreat to my still private suite in cellblock 4. If the Morlocks want me, they will have to come for me. I'm ready for a long lockdown—plenty of store and a stack of novels.

For the next five days my good and great companions are Joyce, Hemingway, and Irwin Shaw. At 5 P.M. I turn on my thirteen-inch TV to watch whatever prison movie is being shown from the central VCR.

Tonight they are showing *Chained Heat—Penitentiary Girls III.*

I like it—not too much plot getting in the way of the action. The kind of movie my wife and girls would never have let me rent at home.

In prison it's a good mental health habit to focus on the positive. Because the Morlocks can come for you at any time.

And it ain't nothin' nice.

I take advantage of the lockdown to do some interior cell decoration, relying on the Kansas approach, as opposed to, say, Martha Stewart. I even fashion a monthly calendar, drawing the little squares and pasting it to the cell wall with state toothpaste. Christmas is rapidly approaching and I still haven't shopped.

I study the calendar on the wall and count the days till my Parole Board hearing and then my release. I come up with 520 days. Not so bad. I can do this, I think. My first hearing is in five months; the next, and final one, a year after that.

I wonder how to populate the little blank days on the calendar. At home, before the wife elected to become the former wife, we had a "daily organizer" posted on the refrigerator. I would fill it up with items like "Pick up Alana from soccer practice." "Drive Rachel to Girl Scout meeting." "Chinese food?" "Recital—7 P.M."

Another life—pre-O.G. Too much time to think in these cells. Avoid self-pity at all costs. That is the dubious luxury of freemen. I stare at the calendar.

Sorry I missed your soccer finals, Alana.

Sorry I missed your choir recital, Rachel.

I turn my face to the cell wall and, not for the first time, sob quietly against the cinder blocks.

Not unlike some punk-ass bitch.

The law library is a madhouse of ancient, chattering typewriters and lifers researching "post-conviction relief." The typewriters are the latest in 1950s high tech—electric, but before someone added value with the lift-off correction-tape feature. Welcome to Wite-Out. Fortunately I am of an age when carbon paper was regarded as a major advance toward the office of the future. It was the spearhead of what we would now call a "paradigm shift."

Legal books are crammed floor-to-ceiling, some of them on shelves, most of them piled on the floor. Convicts wander in and out yelling questions, answers, insults, and wolf tickets.

"Who's Bogarting the fucking Wite-Out?"

My old Fish Tank chess partner, Big Bird, is guilty. He also has—as they like to say around here—"priors." Big Bird lifts his nappy white head up from a volume of *Shepard's U.S. Citations* to confront his accuser, a lifer wood.

"If you could *type,* you wouldn't be trippin' behind no Wite-Out shit, you ignorant muthafucka!"

"Big Fucking Bird, how 'bout I type some 'post-conviction' *respect* into your goat-smelling old ass?"

The Bird adjusts his state-issue black horn-rimmed glasses to assess the viability of this latest wolf ticket.

"Whatchu fittin' to do, Mighty Whitey Lifer Boy? You fittin' to raise up like you *about* something? I'll hit you so hard make yo toenail flip like a muthafuckin' poe-*tater* chip!" Wolf ticket receipted for and resold! Everyone laughs—lifer typists, jailhouse lawyers looking for business, my fellow Lawdogs, and our Freeman supervisor, Mr. Arbuster.

Arbuster, a long-suffering civil servant for the Department of Prisons, favors generous quantities of Brylcreem on his thinning gray hair and Hawaiian shirts over an enormous beer gut. He, like us, is just doing his time.

I was not his pick for this job. He motions me to take a seat in the steel folding chair at the side of his desk. My three fellow Lawdogs—law clerks—momentarily stop pawing at their electrics to better sniff the scent of every word.

"Sergeant Stanger tells me you chumped him off in front of the assistant warden. Says you were way up *on the leg*! So tell me, O.G.—how did you get this job? Did you suck Noble's dick like Stanger says?" The Lawdogs titter appreciatively from behind their typewriters.

"Just the tip," I answer.

"Say what?"

"Just the *tip*—I tried, but I couldn't get the entire cock down my throat, which was still sore from sucking Stanger's dick the night before."

Arbuster's eyes bug out before he bursts into a violent giggling attack, his face turning purple.

"Oh, that's off the hook! You really *are* one sideways-talking *twisted dawg!*" Arbuster dabs at the tears running down his cheeks, unconscious of his own convict-flavored language. Like the C.O.'s, most Freemen, over time, start talking like the asylum inmates instead of the keepers.

Arbuster's delighted response is the cue for my fellow Lawdogs to howl in approval. On-the-leg sycophants is my perhaps uncharitable judgment. Mighty Whitey Bogart and Big Bird, having made up, laughingly replay it.

"Just the *tip*," they repeat. " 'Cause his throat be *sore*—from the night *before!*" cries the Bird.

Arbuster, whom we all call the Bluster behind his back, tells me to memorize a copy of *The Nevada Code of Penal Discipline*—it will be my sole job aid. As the new "fish" in the law library, I am assigned the most distasteful tasks—attending disciplinary hearings in the lockdown units.

"You'll work the Fish Tank, the Hole, the P.C. punks, and the fucking Moo."

"The Moo?" I used to know this one, but the acronyms here are worse than in the army, or even the phone company.

"The MHU—Medical Housing Unit, the fucking retards and J-Cats too fucked-up to even wipe themselves. You got a *problem* with that?"

"No sir, no problem."

"Good, 'cause if you got a problem, the kitchen has an opening for Jell-O scoopers, you understand what I'm saying?" More titters from the Lawdog Gallery.

A former business associate, good friend, and occasional mentor once gave me this piece of advice: *"Never* underestimate the power of ass-kissing." Mr. Mentor—let's call him Mr. Brown (since that's his name)—rose through the mid-corporate ranks largely on the consistent, massive, and creative application of this principle. In all fairness, he was also brilliant and conversationally adept at *any* topic of interest to his superiors—fly-fishing, the 49ers ("Hey, how about those Niners!"), metaphysics, duck hunting, nonlinear correlation and regression techniques, you name it. He knew how to Build Rapport—instantly!

I decide that now would be a good time to apply Brown's Axiom. Don't want the Bluster sweating me every day. You Lawdogs think you know On The Leg? I'll show you some pure, unabashed, unrestrained Corporate Obsequiousness!

"Mr. Arbuster, I sure appreciate this overview." I smile—appreciatively. "You're not a *lawyer* by any chance? I guess you'd *have* to be one to do your job, having to know all those case histories and all." Brown's Ass-Kissing Corollary to Ass-Kissing Axiom 1 is "Transparency doesn't matter."

Of course it works. The Bluster is puffing up self-importantly, his chest inflating like a hot-air balloon. His face shineth upon me. Finally—a Lawdog who appreciates him, a rare simpatico soul refreshingly attuned to the unjust burdens he single-handedly, *heroically* carries every day.

"Well, O.G. . . . er, actually I *do* have a bit of a legal background—also some sociology and psychology. You need it if you're going to deal with cons all day."

"I can *tell.*" I nod admiringly, nodding to the Great Gods of Unction, cementing our rapport, as the Lawdogs howl and moan in sickened disbelief.

Mr. Brown, wherever in the corporate crevices you are now, thank you.

The store here is not one where you can walk inside and look at the merchandise. It is a warehouse with a "service" window. You

enter an opened gate on the yard and hand your order slip to the convict clerk, who, depending on how much store you kick back to him,
will fill your order in minutes, days, or never.

Skell likes snuff. We agree on six cans of Skoal Wintergreen in exchange for his continuing to falsify the "housing roster" to indicate my
cell has *two* guests. After bickering like an Arab rug merchant, he also
agrees to throw in two pairs of boxer shorts, which he swears on his skin
are not from Saint Mary's Hospice.

"Ain't no pecker tracks on these, dawg!" he assures me before disappearing behind his mattress fortress where he can inject himself with his
daily dose of crank—while safely supervising the helicopter evacuation
of the American Embassy in Saigon.

Every morning I report to the law library, read the kites from the
"lockdowns," and load up my handcart with the requested lawbooks.
Then I'm ready to roll the wheels of justice to a convict population that
prison surveys reveal to be 70 percent "functionally illiterate." Which
means they cannot read or understand the disciplinary write-ups that
they collect faster than Skell collects stamps and snuff.

Most of the kites reveal some confusion.

"To: Law Liberyen—How they got a warent for me back in
Tennessee? I never messed with no incense! Ken you pleese help me before they exerdite me to Memfus."

Having once paid my dues in the Market Research, Assessment and
Customer-Driven Analytics Divison, I am especially qualified to add
value here. I remove *Black's Law Dictionary* from a shelf, flip to the definition of "incest," copy it on the kite for delivery under the cell door.
Then a quick exit.

"To: Law Clerk—Kansas says you can help me. The judge reca-
mendit me to a house rest program but my PO says I got nothin coming. Is there any legal remorse avalebul to me?"

This time, because it's one of Kansas's dawgs, I attach a copy of the
house arrest criteria to the kite. I also enlist Mr. Webster's help in pro-

viding definitions for both "remorse" and "recourse." The phone company, which loved to talk about our "unparalleled record of customer responsiveness," would have been proud.

When necessary I would read the kites to the Bluster, who really did know a thing or two about the law. He would listen to the question and then refer me to the appropriate reference.

"*Shepard's U.S. Citations,* volume 3," Bluster yells. "*Pacific Reporter . . . Corpus Juris Secundum . . . Federal Supplement,* volume 27 . . . Nevada Revised Statutes* 209 point 17 paragraph B . . . *Supreme Court Reporter . . .* Ineffective counsel? Let's see—get *Hill versus Lockhart.*"

With my vision and his track record we made a hell of a team. Definitely consultative and collaborative, as we used to say in the phone company.

I hate visiting clients in the Moo. The Moo C.O. strip-searches me, then checks the contents of my box, holding each lawbook up by one flap and shaking it. He's always disappointed when no contraband falls out—no nail files, no plastic packets of crank, no decomposed body of Jimmy Hoffa.

The J-Cats are all in solitary confinement cells, and the ones not too sedated leap to their feet the moment they hear the squeal of the handcart's rubber wheels on the floor—Pavlov's Dawgs: The Next Generation. These are the J-Cats deemed too dangerous to be in general population and too numerous to try to send back to the state nuthouse prison, which is at full capacity.

I am supposed to "counsel" them about their disciplinary charges before they appear before the Disciplinary Committee, which now consists of one caseworker, Mr. Ringer. My client is on the upper tier in cell

63. The Bubblecop, just a few feet above us, cracks open the cell door. I wait, penal code in hand, until the J-Cat slides it open.

Most of the J-Cats here are black and my client is no exception. After sliding the door he does the Thorazine shuffle back to his tray, sits. His face is crisscrossed with old razor scars, his eyes blank, unseeing. He wears the standard J-Cat Moo uniform, a white paper coverall. The J-Cat's crotch area is soaked with urine. Give a guy enough psychotropics and he'll easily confuse paper pants with a toilet bowl. The smell ain't nothin' nice.

"What's your write-up for, bro?" I ask this slowly to match his movements. I keep my voice soft and low. A string of saliva is descending from the J-Cat's mouth.

I consult my new clipboard, a welcome-on-board gift from the Bluster and, I'm convinced, an object of yard envy. Or possibly contempt.

"Demetrius," I try again. "Do you know why you're here?"

Maybe it was the use of his name that did it, but something stirs and spins inside his defective hard drive, his head jerking side to side in little spasms while his mouth gasps open and closed soundlessly. I can practically feel the heat of a billion neurons misfiring in his brain.

My first J-Cat "case," and my client is not just a sandwich short of a picnic, he's a *picnic* short of a picnic.

"What medications do they have you on, Demetrius?"

His lips convulse and produce some garbled words. ". . . icks nin . . . zeen . . . nay nay nay . . . quan." But hey, at least we're *communicating.*

I'm guessing he's on—or has been on—Prolixin, Thorazine, and Sinequan. *The Physician's Desk Reference* in the law library lists them all as having a "sedative" effect. I'm wondering why they didn't sedate his bladder along with his brain.

I start reading from the Notice of Charges, hoping this might jar his two or three still functioning synapses into action. I stand between the

open cell door and the closed door of Demetrius's dome. The Bubblecop is at his open slot, shotgun ready. The write-up is in pure Copspeak:

"... that on December 3 at approximately 7:04 A.M. I, Sergeant
Stanger, while making routine rounds in the chow hall, did observe inmate Demetrius Johnson, back number 31458, stuffing an unidentified
round object down the front of his pants in a manner suggesting con-
cealment or an attempt to conceal."

The faintest glimmer of recognition comes to the J-Cat's glazed
eyes. He is even managing to wipe the dribble off his mouth.
Encouraged, I continue with the Copspeak:

"... thereupon said inmate did attempt to exit the chow hall in a
hurried and stealthy manner ... when I confronted inmate Johnson
and ordered him to drop his pants, inmate Johnson became irate, waving his arms in a threatening manner and yelling obscenities. Inmate
Johnson demanded to know why he couldn't get himself a 'motherfucking apple.' "

Just the tiniest hint of an insane smile is starting to spread across
Demetrius's slack face. Half a sandwich, or at least a pickle, has just arrived at the Thorazine picnic.

"... loud and abusive language combined with the threatening arm
movements led me to conclude the inmate was attempting to incite a
riot in the chow hall to cover up the smuggling of contraband ..."

Another page or two of Copspeak and finally the bottom line:
"After subduing and placing inmate Johnson in hand and ankle re-
straints I was then able to confiscate and secure the contraband in question—one partially eaten apple, probably McIntosh in manner, which
I immediately sealed in a plastic evidence bag. The Dirt investigation is
still ongoing at this time. Inmate Demetrius Johnson, back number
31458, is hereby charged with the following violations of the Nevada
Code of Penal Discipline: MJ-27, a major violation, rioting or inciting
others to riot; MJ-21, a major violation, theft or possession of contraband; MJ-25, a major violation, issuing a threat, either verbally or by

gesture, to a correctional officer; and G-9, a general violation, using profane or abusive language to a correctional officer. In addition we are charging inmate Johnson with a violation of M-7, a minor violation, unauthorized use of institutional equipment, machinery, tools, or food."

The Bubblecop a few feet above us snorts in derision. "Felonious fucking *apple* smuggling—what a crock!" The cop suddenly remembers he's wearing a prison uniform and decides to try to clean it up. "Of course, you was outta line, Demetrius—can't have convicts running around with apples beneath their johnsons!" And Bubblecop is cackling crazily over his bad pun, which I find pretty funny as well.

But Demetrius isn't smiling. No, the man is far beyond amusement. As a matter of fact he's peeling off his piss-soaked paper jumpsuit until he's sitting butt-naked on his tray, one hand clutching his johnson.

Waving it at Bubblecop.

"Ain't no motherfucking zip-locked apples in here, boss!"

This is one of those phone company "minimal cues." I exit the cell ass-backward, crashing into the Moo cop who has run up the tier in response to Bubblecop's shouts.

I'm halfway across the catwalk when Bubblecop raises radio backup from the Dirt.

And Johnson and johnson are waving good-bye.

Kansas gleams like a steel shank in the sun, bench-pressing four-hundred-plus pounds before an admiring pack of spotter dawgs. The weight pile in the Aryan Woods is segregated from the rest of the yard by a razor-wire-topped fence. A steel gate in the fence is remotely controlled by a guntower cop high above the Wood Pile.

Every hour, on the hour, the gate cracks open, unleashing a bi-directional flow of skinheads and their philosophical cousins and often comrades-in-tattooed-arms, the woods.

The institutional idea behind the sixty-minute lockdowns is to "contain" the Wood Pile whenever the Shit Jumps Off. This happens at least once a week in the Wood Pile when twenty-pound free weights wing through the air like Frisbees out of hell.

To qualify for the Frisbee Olympics, a convict needs to supply only an attitude and a target—weights are included, free. The Old Heads tell me that past gold medal winners were able to embed a Frisbee in some-one's dome from twenty yards away. These punks today ain't shit. Then they tell me about Attica.

Kansas spots me across the yard, wheeling my Lawdog handcart.

"*Yogee!*" he shouts. "*Yogee!*" The guntower cop (unkindly called the "Tower Pig" by the Old Heads) watches my progress toward the weight pile with binoculars. He spots Kansas and cracks the gate open long be-fore the hour.

As they say here, "Kansas got *juice!*"

"What's up, dawg?" Kansas greets me like a long-lost brother as we tap clenched fists.

We kick it for a few minutes, catching up. Kansas beat Stanger's investigation into extortion and drug dealing. The Dirt couldn't pro-duce any witnesses. Kansas denies the yard rumor that an assistant warden may have intervened after noticing a dramatic increase in Nazi Low Riders casually circling around his daughter's preschool playground.

Kansas did just three days in the kitchen, and not scooping Jell-O. He was the "veg prep dawg," chopping and slicing celery and carrots with one hand, accepting crank and heroin packets from the Freeman with the other.

"Small-time shit, O.G." Kansas shakes his huge skinhead, eyes now filling with the familiar nostalgia that always augurs a long riff back to

". . . the Kansas pen, O.G., where I was running a fucking *meth* lab right out of the bakery—none of this pussy pruno shit these punks got going here, y'unnerstan' what I'm sayin'? Fuck, dawg, I remember one time I was doing a little deuce in Marianna—that's *fed* time, bro, down in Florida, a real stand-up joint . . ."

And on and on down what has to be the partially imagined memory lane of a dozen prisons. I have added up all the time Kansas claims to have done and the total is 547 years. He's been down, done time in Sing Sing, Arizona State Prison, Rahway, Marianna, and in Louisiana. He rattles off these credentials the same way a new candidate for our Corporate Fast Track program used to underwhelm me with his Fulbright, Harvard M.B.A., and Yale Law background.

I guess we all want our ticket punched and admired.

"And with you being the new Lawdog and all, you can do me a favor, y'unnerstan' what I'm sayin', O.G.?" So here it comes at last—conversational foreplay over, Kansas is turning over his hole card. And I just know it ain't nothin' nice.

"What kind of favor, Kansas?"

"Some of my dawgs in lockdown got *things* coming—y'unnerstan'? Maybe a few items could kind of *fall* into the bindings of them lawbooks, know what I'm saying?" I understand I'm receiving *another* Heart Check from Kansas. I decide to flunk. Use a little Bonespeak.

"Yeah, Kansas, I understand perfectly—you're fittin' ta put me in a muthafuckin' *trick bag,* dawg. And the only *hole* in that bag is *Hole time*—y'unnerstan' what I'm sayin'? Well, fuck you very much for the opportunity to do you a favor, but the only thing I'm fittin' to catch is pa-*role!*"

Kansas, astounded, speechless, looking down at me like I just crash-landed my spacecraft and need directions back to Alpha Centauri. I sense that this is one of those "be here now" moments that will define the quality of the rest of my stay on this strange planet.

Kansas backs off a step and wraps a blue bandana around his dome to keep the sweat from smearing his swastika tattoo.

"Trick bag? . . . fittin' ta catch pa-role?" And Kansas's six-foot-six incredibly muscled frame is rocking with laughter. He laughs so hard he starts *crying*. Wipes away the tears with the bandana.

"Yogee—you've gone from *sideways* talk to fucking *toad* talk! Where'd you pick *up* this shit?" he splutters, holding on to the Aryan Woods fence for support. His spotter dawgs come rushing over to see what's up.

Kansas introduces me to the Carful of skinheads, some of whom I have been greeted by in the yard. Their names are a blur to me: Shank, Big Nasty, Chug, Little Feeb, Snake, Shakey, Dizzy, Sandman, Roach, Lurch . . .

Confused at first by Kansas's formal introduction, they take turns smacking my knuckles with their SWP- or NLR-tattooed fingers. "What's up, O.G.?" they say.

"What's up, dawgs!" I exclaim. "Where's Dopey and Grumpy today?" Which sends Kansas into a fresh paroxysm of hysterics. This lets the dawgs know that I am just a sideways-talking kind of guy and *they* are not being Disrespected. "Aiight, O.G.—later, dawg," they call, and return to the Wood Pile.

Kansas is sober now. "Listen, O.G.—forget all that shit about the lockdown and the lawbooks an' all. I'll just use the porters or the guards, but ya gotta help with the letters I been getting from all kinds of crazy bitches behind that ad you put in the paper."

"That's the kind of favor I'd be happy to help you with." And I mean it.

"Scandalous! I'll bring 'em down to your house tonight."

"Have you read them yet?" I ask, forgetting that Kansas can barely read. Unless it's a summons, a warrant, or his FBI file.

"Uh . . . yeah, you know, a little bit, but I need you to write them back."

"What house you in now?"

"I'm over in your cellblock. Same wing, cell 26, Lifer's Row. It's quieter there, know what I'm sayin'? I stopped by your house earlier but no one home except some new fish sleeping on the top bunk—guess you got a new cellie." Skell said he couldn't keep up the scam much longer, so I'm not surprised.

"All right, Kansas, then I'll see you later." We do the fist tap, Nazi Low Rider knuckle meets Once Nice Jewish Boy knuckle. I'm not that nice boy anymore. Maybe I never was.

Whatever it is I am, or am becoming in here, I suspect it ain't nothin' nice.

C.O. Fallon calls me over to hand me an "unauthorized mail" notification from the prison. My magazine has been confiscated due to "the depiction of weaponry and gang violence" in one of the articles. The magazine is *Newsweek*.

Tonight the prison movie is another showing of a soft-porn "western." I've only seen it three times now. It has at least twelve murders, three rapes, one sodomy (by a dwarf), torture by branding iron, and a great deal of gratuitous mutilation.

Pretty good movie—I give it three stars.

My new cellie is asleep on the top bunk, his face pressed against the graffiti-covered wall (FUCK THE POLICE and other forms of misplaced hostility). His shaved head is visible. On the right side of his neck is a beautifully scripted tattoo—"Mandy." The little skinhead seems too young to be a Barry Manilow fan, so I know when he wakes up and tells me his life story (the youngsters here always do that), Mandy will play a starring role in his particular psychodrama.

He's going to tell me Mandy's his "fiancée"—prison translation: He dated her one time and got lucky before she threw up. She's waiting faithfully (by the phone, of course) for him to complete his bid so they can get married and ascend to Trailer-Trash Heaven together.

After she gets out of drug rehab.

My less than charitable musings are interrupted by Mr. Mandy's sneezing fit. He rolls over to face me. Young, maybe eighteen, with handsome features in a smooth face trying desperately to sprout a badass prison goatee.

"What's up, dawg?" He smiles, extending a fist. He still has his teeth, suggesting the crank has yet to catch up with him.

"I'm Jimmy—pleased to meet you."

"Shawn, but all my road dogs call me Spoony. You're the O.G., right? I heard about you in the Fish Tank—making a killer slock out of a *newspaper*! That's the *shit*, dawg!"

"Do me a favor, Spoony, since we're celling together. Call me Jimmy, Jim, or O.G., but don't call me dawg."

"Aiight, O.G."

Both prison etiquette and convict common sense ("Today's road dog—tomorrow's snitch") counsel against inquiring about one's cellie's "crime." Unfortunately this unwritten restriction has resulted in the rise and concomitant shaping and honing of the Convict Song of Self—an endless, self-serving soliloquy utterly devoid of any real wrongdoing, always ending in the Fall, the convict term for his arrest.

So Spoony sings the song, clearly in awe of a cellie capable of assault with the *New York Times*. I wonder what I could have done with that *Newsweek*. I lie down on my bunk to better appreciate the cadences and rhythm of a ruptured life.

I half-nap through Spoony's early dysfunctional years shuttling between CPS (Child Protective Services), juvie hall, and his dope-fiend mom. I awaken fully to "so then Mandy's mom kicked us out of the trailer when Mandy got pregnant—said her SSI check didn't cover *two* more dope fiends, with a baby dope fiend in the making—even though we was planning to get *married* as soon as we got off the crank, y'un-nerstan' what I'm sayin', O.G.?" This is my minimal cue to fake some Active Listening skills.

"Yeah, Spoony, you were planning to get married and Mom still wanted you out of her trailer—that's *scandalous,* dawg."

"For real," says Spoony, retrieving the threads of his Me Melody while I attempt to nap.

"Then when Mandy got kicked out of the drug rehab, the CPS just *took* the baby . . . so we had to move back to her mom's, but I had my eye on our own place—this awesome double-wide with like phone, ca-ble, water hookup, *everything,* even had a built-in microwave—when I fell behind some crank sales I had to get involved in 'cause Kmart fired me. All the employees was stealing them blind, but they fucking fire *me.*" I always like the part where they are the victim.

The Fall is a good part too. Convicts don't get busted or arrested—they *fall.* They fall behind dope, behind a woman, behind a snitch. *They* had nothing to do with it! The rationale system is staggering in its self-enclosed logic, in its utter absence of volition.

Anybody can Fall. It's like *gravity* or something sucks us all down. The earth itself sucks—sucks a righteous dawg like Spoony down.

The Fall is the convict version of the Slip—a favorite twelve-step term for a drinking or drug relapse. Between gravity and banana peels how can a recovering righteous dawg *not* Slip and Fall?

Spoony, all of eighteen, is doing four to ten behind a drug traffick-ing conviction, measuring out his life with collect calls to Mandy's (mom's) trailer, wondering if Mandy will answer, wondering if she's high, worrying if she's *been* with someone, if she *is* with someone at this very moment—and who is it? Jody? Sancho? And wondering just where Mandy is on the long waiting list for the Salvation Army's drug rehab program.

Spoony's doing "hard time."

. . .

In the movies, convicts in prison always get a special
meal for Christmas. In here it's the same ol' same ol'—we were served
soybean patties with mashed potatoes on top, green Jell-O on top of the
mashed potatoes, purple Kool-Aid.

Events of interest to the denizens of the free world, such as New
Year's Eve—the Millennium 2000 Edition—passed unremarked. I
watched the ball drop in Times Square. People screamed and danced
drunkenly in the streets. Predictions of Armageddon triggered by "non-
compliant Y2K" computer chips failed to materialize. If anything unusual happened on Groundhog Day, Dan Rather chose not to report it.

It stays desert hot in the days, cold now at nights. The dirt and sand
continue to sting our faces every day.

While I am delivering books and attending disciplinary hearings,
Spoony attends GED preparation classes in a converted cellblock used
as a school. Instead of a hall monitor, there is a Bubblecop with an AK-
47 to ensure a rich learning environment.

Spoony doesn't mind. Says it reminds him of the public schools he
briefly attended.

Spoony, state-raised and institutionally savvy, is a Yard Trick. I
arranged the job interview for him (with Kansas) when it appeared that
he was in danger of being utilized as a sperm bank depository for some
of the more bestial members of the Car.

I was wrong about Spoony having teeth—he has a full set of den-
tures, compliments of a juvie prison dentist who first pulled all of
Spoony's crank-rotted teeth. The dental plates don't fit properly, and
Spoony only wears them for special occasions—like eating.

When he's not struggling with the mysteries of converting GED fractions to percents and decimals (sometimes they tell him to reverse the process), he can be seen snipe-hunting in the yard—collecting the discarded shorts of rollies. He puts the butts in a Bugler can and rerolls the preowned tobacco in the cell, selling full rollies to new fish.

He takes care of the Car's laundry and runs contraband from one cellblock to another. I tell him I don't care what he does outside the cell (that's *his* lookout) as long as he doesn't bring anything into the house that will attract heat. "Y'unnerstan' what I'm sayin' to you, Spoony?" "It's all good, O.G.," he says.

Sometimes, after he's done an especially thorough job of sweeping and mopping our house, I toss a Hershey's Kiss or a Digby's Jolly Rancher ("fire"-flavored) up to the top bunk.

The GED fractions are driving Spoony crazy. He was kicked out of school in the seventh grade and never returned. He had trouble sitting still, trouble concentrating. He's a member of the Ritalin Generation and they won't give him any speed in prison. He has to barter for his crank on the yard.

"The teachers said I was *dyslepnic*," Spoony confides in me one chilly evening. "They said I got ADD too." Spoony shares these diagnoses with me with the quiet pride of someone whose life challenges have been dignified by an official-sounding disease label.

I assure him he doesn't suffer from dyslepnic disorders or even dyslexia. I have observed that he can read, comprehend, and concentrate like a Rhodes scholar when given incentives like candy or drugs.

Spoony just has a different "learning strategy" from most students. After a few evenings of M.B.A. brainstorming with myself, I arrive (as I usually do) at a Breakthrough Learning Paradigm.

I address the metal bottom of the upper bunk. "Spoony—what do you do when you buy an ounce of crank?"

"What do ya mean what do I *do*? I *snort* some, *shoot* some, maybe sell the rest. What do ya think I do?"

"I mean what do you do *before* you sell it, assuming you and Mandy don't snort and shoot all of it?"

"We cut it with Ex-Lax," Spoony answers without hesitation, finally in a familiar classroom where *he* is an A student.

"Why Ex-Lax?" I'm genuinely curious. Is this another new applications-driven stock I should purchase, assuming I have any cash left after buying up blocks of Bic?

" 'Cause it's water-soluble so the customer don't get no impurities when he shoots it." Spoony is energized now, practically twitching on his bunk with amphetamine longing.

"So you just sell the whole ounce, or what's left, to make your profit?" Give Spoony a minimal cue, a lead-in to Fun With Fractions.

"Fuck no, O.G.! I thought you grew up in the *sixties*! We cut it, break it down, and bag it, you know what I'm saying, dawg—*sorry*, I meant 'O.G.' "

"Spoony, trust me when I tell you that I have probably *spilled* more drugs on the floor than you have taken in your entire life, but what I'm asking is just *how* do you break the stuff down?" My Inner Teacher can be relentless!

"You know, like . . . into quarters, teeners, eight balls, whatever the customer wants."

"Spoony, I rest my case—you're down with fractions."

Later I turn off the overhead light. "Night, Spoony."

Outside the relatively safe cocoon of our locked cell (we can lock ourselves in), the ghetto blasters blare out their themes of murder, robbery, and rape while predators—white, black, brown—roam the corridors.

In prison the Morlocks always come out at night.

Spoony's squeaky adolescent voice drifts down in the darkness.

"Yogee—you still awake?"

"Yeah, Spoony, I'm enjoying the music from the street fair."

"Listen . . . uh . . . thanks for helping me with the GED stuff and all. Hey! We got biscuits and gravy tomorrow. You want I should bring a biscuit back for you?"

"No thanks, just an apple or orange would be fine."

"I'm down with that."

"Then it's all good."

"Night, O.G."

"Night, Spoony."

Every Friday I join Caseworker Ringer for the disciplinary hearings. They are held in his office in the administrative building, down the hall from Dirt Headquarters. Sergeant Stanger drags in up to thirty accused convicts during the course of a long day.

Ringer looks like a refugee from a production of *Grease,* his thick black pompadour slicked into shape by a gallon of gel. His hooked nose would not be out of place on some birdlike, prehistoric creature.

Ringer is all bark and no bite. I like and respect him.

"Your job," Ringer likes to explain to me, "is to shut the fuck up and write down the punishments imposed—the *sanction*—after I find these fuckups guilty. They had plenty of time to send you a kite and *consult* with you before the hearing. Anything you don't understand about the process?"

Caseworker Ringer is firm but fair. I know this because of the hand-lettered sign taped to the front of his desk: SENIOR CASEWORKER RINGER—FIRM BUT FAIR!

A veteran of Quality Improvement Process meetings, I thank him for the role clarification. He tells me to knock off the sideways shit. We get along fine. Ringer is ready.

"Sergeant Stanger, send in the meat!"

And here comes the meat! One shackled, cuffed, cowering victim after another is hauled in by Stanger, who then exits the room to guard the remaining meat on the Group W bench in the hall. Busy as he is, Stanger always makes some time to glare at me and spray threats. "I hear your little bitch Spoony is running drugs for you and the Car, O.G. You're going down *real* soon, asshole." Then Ringer orders him out of the hearing room. Senior caseworkers outrank Dirt sergeants around here.

"How do you plead?" Ringer asks the first victim, a confused black teenager charged with "M-5, a minor violation: failure to keep one's person or assigned area neat and clean." The kid slumps in the chair, bewildered, as Ringer reads the Notice of Charges aloud, omitting the Copspeak narrative.

"Guilty . . . I guess," he whispers to his state sneakers.

"You *guess*—you can't fucking GUESS!" Ringer roars. He tosses aside the write-up and tilts his beak down at Kid Guess. His tone is suddenly calm, reasonable.

"Why don't you just tell me what this is all about—you didn't clean your cell? Scared of dropping the soap in the shower?"

"No . . . nothin' like dat," Guess murmurs to his feet. "I takes my showers, keeps myself clean . . . I ain't be havin' no nasty-ass crib neither . . . but I was in the *holding* cell by the intake waiting, you know what I'm sayin', all day I be up in that muthafucka . . . den I axed the C.O. to use the bathroom, you . . ." Kid Guess hunches further down in his chair, acutely embarrassed.

"And the C.O. told you to *hold* it—right?" finishes the suddenly helpful Ringer.

"Yes, sir . . . Sergeant Stanger, he say 'hold it' or piss myself because he be too busy to come to the holding cell right then." Kid Guess is now trying to disappear through the floor.

Ringer senses a confession. "So you did, in fact, proceed to piss yourself!"

"Yes, sir, Mr. Ringer . . . so I guess I be pleadin' guilty."

"Plead *not* guilty," orders Ringer.

"Sir?" Kid Guess glances at me, his silent advocate. I give the kid my best legalistic shrug. Ringer is writing on his disposition form.

"I'm entering your plea of not guilty to the charge of M-5. I have considered all the available evidence in this case and I find you"—Ringer pauses for dramatic effect—"*not* guilty!"

Ringer is ripping up another of Stanger's write-ups. "Now get the fuck out of here! Your charge is *dismissed*! No man should have to piss himself—you've been punished enough."

Over the next five hours, Ringer judges twenty-three more cases, often advising convicts how to plead when it is in their best interest. Final score: eleven guilty, seven charges reduced from major to general or minor violations, and six not guilty.

Senior Caseworker Ringer: firm but fair!

As a Lawdog I am permitted to review various Department of Prisons guidelines if they are relevant to an inmate's disciplinary charges. Among my favorites are the UA Drug Testing Guidelines. In addition to random urinalysis tests (usually administered to convicts the cops hate), inmates may also be tested if they meet any of the following criteria:

1. The inmate exhibits an "inexplicably cheerful demeanor."
2. The inmate "appears depressed."
3. The inmate "exhibits mood swings."
4. The inmate "isolates" in his cell.
5. The inmate "is excessively sociable or garrulous."

6. The inmate is in "a state of denial" characterized by refusals to attend A.A. or N.A. meetings.
7. The inmate "exhibits impaired motor skills."
8. The inmate engages in "confrontational behavior toward others."
9. The inmate has a "criminal history involving drug abuse."
10. The inmate "protests a pat-down or strip search."

The cops do a lot of urine sampling around here. Successful test candidates make it to the final interview stage with Mr. Ringer on Fridays. I have already "counseled" (in a collaborative or consultative way) most of these guys during my daily rounds to the lockdowns. My value-added counsel consists primarily of advising these dawgs of the sanctions that they will be subjected to after Caseworker Ringer finds them guilty.

And he will. Ringer never dismisses dirty UAs, never reduces them, and always imposes the harshest penalties. It's a political issue right now. Federal agents have just arrested one of our very own correctional officers for dealing drugs to inmates. The federal investigation, as Stanger would say, is ongoing.

"Mr. Narducci," intones Ringer, reading from the Notice of Charges, "you are charged with MJ-45, a major violation: possession, introduction, sales or use of any narcotics, drugs, alcohol or other intoxicants, or possession of materials suitable for such manufacture." Ringer adjusts his head-beak unit to better scrutinize Narducci, a real hard case doing Life on the Installment Plan. His full sleeves are his résumé from various prisons and gangs.

"How do you plead, Mr. Narducci?"

Narducci, well seasoned in these little chats, has never copped to anything in his unillustrious life and isn't going to start now.

"Not guilty, sir. I ain't lookin' to get crossed out behind no drugs. I don't do drugs. There can't be no speed in my piss unless the cops put it there, trying to get me crossed out and off the yard, you know what I'm sayin'?" Narducci leans back in his chair, convict-cool, fiddling with the rubber band around his ponytail.

Ringer absolutely *hates* not guilty pleas on dirty UAs—he has the lab results and that's all he needs. A not guilty plea not only wastes his time, it is Disrespectful! It insults his intelligence, which is not inconsiderable.

"Mr. Narducci, after reviewing the available evidence, I find you guilty of MJ-45 and impose the following sanctions: 180 days in disciplinary segregation, loss of all visiting, phones, commissary." Narducci snickers. This ain't *shit*. He's been down and done all that.

Ringer is saving the silver bullet for the end, though. He smiles and resumes. "In addition, Mr. Narducci, you will immediately forfeit all category A stat time."

At the mention of stat-time loss, Narducci is on his feet, chains rattling in outrage. This sanction is clearly *outta line!*

"That's *bullshit!* I know the fucking code! You can't take no more than 120 days of good time for a dirty UA!" Narducci is just about to share some additional insights into the code when Stanger races into the office and clamps a choke hold around his neck. Stanger squeezes hard, grinding this outta-line con back down into the chair.

"Thank you, Sergeant," says Ringer. "I believe that will be enough." But Stanger's bloodlust has been roused. He increases the pressure on Narducci's trachea until blood vessels promise to burst from the cuffed and chained convict's eyes.

"Sergeant *Stanger!* I said that's *enough!*" Stanger reluctantly lets go of Narducci's throat but not before jabbing two kung-fu stiffened fingers into his larynx.

Stanger saunters out of the office, making sure to flash me his bright sociopathic smile, a smile that promises me future pain, great suffering, and *lots* of it. I smile back sweetly.

Narducci is now massaging his throat with cuffed hands, his hard-case act in temporary deep storage, along with the patented convict smirk. He starts whining and puling.

"Please don't take my good time, Mr. Ringer," he croaks through his abused throat. Good time, time off a sentence for "good behavior," is computed at the rate of ten days off for every thirty days served. Narducci, almost six years now into an eight bid, is eligible to hit the front gate in a month.

Was eligible. The drugs that he doesn't do 'cause he ain't looking to get crossed out just cost him two years of accrued good time. Two years crossed out. He now knows he should have taken my advice to plead guilty. Also shouldn't have dissed the caseworker, throwing the code in his face.

Shoulda, woulda, coulda.

"Get the fuck outta my office," says Ringer, already studying the next write-up.

'Cause Narducci got *nothin'* comin'!

One of the least stressful jobs on the yard is the grounds maintenance worker's, since there is nothing to maintain. For "security reasons" the prison prefers steel, concrete, and asphalt. Between the asphalt path on the yard and the cellblocks are flattened wastelands of dirt. The maintenance crews rake the dirt every morning. The purpose of raking dirt is to discourage inmates from secreting their shanks and hypodermic needles in dirt crevices on the yard.

For this reason, as well as a love of proximity, cons keep their shanks and drug paraphernalia in their cells or in their yellow plastic tubs. They are confident of the efficacy of the grapevine, "The Wire," to provide them with ample opportunity to move the contraband in case of a shakedown.

As a former telecommunications manager, I can confidently state that The Wire is the convict analog to the World Wide Web, ubiquitous, accessible, instantaneous. Who needs packet switching? The Wire is capable of quickly disseminating news ranging from a stabbing in the San Quentin yard to the quality of this week's pruno in the bakery.

Kansas used his juice card to get a job as a raker. This enables him to keep an eye on all yard commerce, human and otherwise. His raking system consists of slinging four rakes behind him, two over each massive tattooed shoulder, while he plows unevenly across the dirt fields, his Walkman delivering his favorite country music.

Country music captivates many of the woods here with its suspenseful narratives. Will that cheating, lying slut come back seeking forgiveness from her man? And will he forgive her or just kick her to the curb? Where she got nothin' comin'. Will the righteous dawg's dog die as a consequence of him drunkenly backing his pickup over Old Yella? A tragedy caused by that lyin', cheating be-yatch Sue-Ellen.

Kansas adjusts his headphones, sweat streaming down over the tattooed mural of his chest. The rakes churn dirt, discouraging any green grass conspiracies. Nothing grows on the yard.

Except where the Witches kick it. Excuse me, the *Wiccans*—a recognized (by the Supreme Court and reluctantly by the prison) religion. The warden, a man of transcendent tolerance, has even bequeathed (following a court order) a small, miserable patch of dirt for Wiccan gatherings.

To cultivate and do with as the Wiccans wilt. The Wiccans never tell you what their religion is all about, other than some vague references to the seasons, nature, the moon, and a goddess. They *will* tell you what they are not—not devil-worshipers, not sacrificers of babies and children, not casters of bad spells (only good ones), and *definitely* not Christians.

"Not that there's anything wrong with *that*," the Wiccans insist. It is not clear if "that" refers to devil-worshipers, baby-killers, or Christians. How do I describe the members here without sounding disrespectful of a recognized religious group? Picture your prototypical pimpled (from excessive masturbation) white teenage *Star Trek* aficionado. Now picture him in prison for robbery, rape, murder, whatever. Finally he's usually high on crank. Of course, I am looking at a highly biased statistical sampling of the Wiccan population. I am sure that the free Wiccans are nothing like the creatures in here.

Things *grow* in the Wiccan patch of dirt. Brown things. Like desert-baked mesquite, they don't grow so much as *spread*, cancerlike—stunted, twisted little branches rising in tortured chaos from the Wiccans' sacred soil.

The Wiccan World is fenced off from the rest of us in a special enclosure at the end of the yard. Wiccan ground zero is a pentacle planted in their sacred patch of dirt—a flat piece of contraband metal inscribed with pentagrams. The pentacle is just the right size for a squalling infant.

Ever the intrepid observer of human diversity, I secrete myself in a blind spot on the yard—a narrow dirt alley between cellblocks 7 and 8. Metal prongs drag on the dirt behind me. I whirl, startled, to face Kansas, who has also succumbed to a voyeuristic spell. Nothing goes down on this yard without Kansas's full knowledge, if not approval.

"What are these punk-ass Witches up to now?" he asks, removing the headphones.

"Shhhh . . . ," I warn him—the Witches are chanting softly now, gathered in a circle around the pentacle. We fasten ourselves deep in the shadows of the walls, straining to make out the words—the Secret Spell of the Wiccans! Their chant is a frightening familiar melody—Iron Butterfly's "In-A-Gadda" something or other.

The actual words, the Wiccan Coven's Chant, are less than terror-inspiring:

I am rubber
You are glue.
Whatever you say
Bounces back on you!

It was not until a week later that Hector, one of the Wiccan "Elders," told me the chant was an ongoing practical joke. Whenever the Wiccans suspected any convicts were bird-dogging their ceremony, they simply substituted this child's rhyme for the real thing. Which he would reveal to me for three cans of Bugler.

Those crazy Witches! You gotta love 'em!

For a Lawdog, wolf tickets come with the territory. Every morning, making my rounds through the Fish Tank, the Hole, and the Moo, I am besieged by shouts, screams, and threats from behind the steel doors. Stopping to chat with any of these dawgs (unless they are on the authorized list for the day) can get me crossed out.

"Yo, Lawdog! *Lawdog!* Give me a rollie!" A black face pressed against the cell window. I roll on down the catwalk, mindful of Bubblecop, who watches my every step.

"Lawdog . . . take this over to Snake's house, cellblock 1—you know the Snake!" A white wood face against the glass, a white envelope kicked out from under his door. The pale goateed face is brightened by two blue teardrop tattoos. A very scary-looking dawg, definitely not a fish. I roll on ignoring the envelope and the wood, conscious of the implied disrespect to this dawggie at the window. He screams through the cell door. "Good looking out, dawg! I'll see you on the yard, you punk motherfucker!"

"Yo, homie—*homes!* Ju gotta lie?" A brown face framed in the glass, gesturing frantically for me to slide a *light* under his door. I roll on.

"Maricón!" he shouts. *"La chocha de tu madre es sucia!"* I don't recall this phrase from my Spanish lessons at the Defense Language Institute, but I suspect it ain't nothing nice.

I stop to deliver the most popular legal forms—appeals, divorces, and bankruptcies—sliding them under the doors without kicking it. If it's a book, Bubblecop will crack the cell door open. I place it on the cell floor. Most of the lockdowns sleep sixteen to twenty hours a day and rarely stir off their trays except to eat or take a dookie, some of the J-Cats not even bothering with the latter.

Two-Tears has been in the Fish Tank for quite a while. I can expect to see him on the yard at any time. So why am I not excited about this?

Inspired by Kansas's example in the Fish Tank, I exercise every day in my cell. Back in the world I was a weekend racquetball warrior and indifferent golfer. My weight-training program consisted of slinging cases of Costco cabernet, chips, cola, and cigarette cartons into a shopping cart.

Times change.

This morning, with an unawed Spoony looking down from his crib, I knocked out fifty push-ups (hands close-in to work the chest), 150 sit-ups, took a five-minute break, then repeated. I filled the four-gallon plastic wastebasket (Skell only charged me a bag of Gummis) with water. Did a few sets of curls, fingers grasping the plastic lip.

I'm not going to scare anybody in here, but my soft fish underbelly is gone. Somebody wants to stick me, they're going to have to push that shank—at least a little bit. I conveniently forget my grandfather's wisdom about the hammer striking the egg. Besides, this is about a shank striking a belly, and mixing metaphors could be disempowering for me.

It's a week later and Two-Tears Tattoo is on the yard, heading toward the Wood Pile. He spots me and is coming on fast, one hand beneath his shirt. I don't think he's grasping for a metaphor.

"Lawdog!" he yells, crossing one of Kansas's freshly raked dirt lawns. I study the dirt, pretend not to hear him, and simply pick up my pace, ever so slightly. Then I'm back in my cell, steel door locked tight.

Kansas and a few of the Car dawgs—Sleepy, Dopey, and Grumpy, I think (I can never remember these tattooed skinheads' names)—are on my front porch. I slide the door open.

Kansas looks down at me. "Yogee, who were you running from in the yard?"

I look up at him like he is completely J-Cat.

"I wasn't *running* from anything, dawg—I was walking briskly, getting my aerobics in."

"He was *running*," Sleepy volunteers.

"The O.G. was fuckin' *sprinting* across the yard, Kansas." This from Dopey, who really is a dwarf—a toothless, tattooed, inbred homunculus, but built like a small stack of bricks.

Kansas just grins. "Come on down to my house later—we'll kick it." And Kansas is leading his retinue—extras from the cast of *Deliverance*—back to the Wood Pile.

Kansas's house, cell 26, marks the informal beginning of Lifer's Row—a section of ten cells at the end of my wing. I can look out my cell door window and see Kansas's face at the windows during our 6 P.M. stand-up count. Two doors down from Kansas, in cell 24, is the local prostitute's house. He/she—her name is Cheekie—always has a line of customers on her front porch. The customers, woods and skinheads, have their wallets ready—full decks of tailors, little plastic packets with white powder, long strips of dollar stamps. Between Cheekie and Kansas are the Bone and his cellie, Big Bird, in cell 25.

Cheekie, a young, slender blond, has her own door monitor, a former pimp and current vassal in the Kingdom of Kansas, called Big Tiny.

Tiny, as you would expect, is the wood facsimile of Big Hungry—huge, fat, and attitudinally challenged.

You pay at the door. Big Tiny frisks everyone first. No drugs or shanks are allowed in Cheekie's house unless it's Tiny who needs to bring them in for the periodic motivation session with Cheekie. Big Tiny gets to keep a third of the bounty. Kansas is given the rest.

Cheekie gets the best drugs on the yard and also gets to live to turn another trick tomorrow. Altogether, Kansas considers it a righteous arrangement. Y'unnerstan'?

Kansas lives in Lifer's Row by choice. Even though he is only doing a four-to-ten bid, he prefers the company of the Old Heads and hard cases. For they are the last, dying vestiges of the True Stand-up, defenders of the Righteous Convict Code.

Step into Kansas's private cell and you momentarily forget you are in prison. Brightly colored Muslim prayer rugs carpet the concrete floor and camouflage the cinder block walls. A dark blue Saint Mary's Hospice blanket has been transformed into window drapes. A real mattress (maybe not a Sealy Posturepedic, but at least not a vinyl pallet) cushions the lower steel bunk. More Saint Mary's blue, beige, and red blankets and throw pillows complete this cozy nest.

Kansas is styling!

He tells me not to worry about Two-Tears. "That punk who's looking to stick you is a piece a shit—used to be a road dog of Snake's. Went J-Cat down in Folsom—thinks he's a fucking cowboy now."

"A cowboy?" I am trying to contour my cheeks to the toilet seat.

"Yeah, the J-Cat don't run with nobody. The Car kicked him to the curb. Don't trip behind this piece a shit—the Car got your back, you know that. Better see Skell, though—he'll hook you up with a Christmas tree or something."

Translation—I'm in deep shit. The Car has my back, but they are not exactly a proactive organization. I do not derive any comfort from knowing the Car will run over Two-Tears *after* I'm dead.

Kansas is pulling a letter from his tub. He pretends to read it until he remembers I know he can hardly read.

"Whatchu think of this bitch, dawg? She loved your ad." Kansas hands me the letter to read to him, and we glide easily into the familiar dance, two old Fish Tank partners. I read the careful, old-fashioned handwriting.

"Well, O.G.?" Kansas is squirming on his bunk.

"Good news and bad news, dawg."

"What? You gonna tell me she's a fat, fuckin' bull dyke or something?" Kansas stands up, expecting the worst, which is his general worldview.

"No . . . nothing like that. Actually she sounds like a lovely person. Describes herself as young, well read, and . . ." I pause, just because I can—it's good for Kansas to sweat a little.

"And what, O.G.? Don't fuck with me—and *what?*"

"She says she's well proportioned."

"Well portioned? Is that good?"

"It could be good, depending upon your tastes or how the portions are spread around, if you know what I'm saying."

"Yeah, I'm down with that. So that's the good news?"

"Nope. The really good news is she's not an ex-felon or a criminal like Star."

"Star," Kansas sighs. "*That* bitch could cram a *kilo* of coke up her snatch and still shimmy across the Mexican border."

Kansas sits back down and leans back to savor this romantic image. Which I shatter.

"Yeah, well, *this* bitch sounds like she could smuggle a kilo of Bibles in her well-proportioned underwear across the border."

"Whatchu sayin', O.G.? She like a religious freak or something?" Kansas is on his feet again, alarmed.

"No, I don't think so. As a matter of fact, Mary—that's her name—

sounds like the perfect girl for you. Likes European history and art—
and likes working out."

"So what's up with the Bible shit, O.G.? Or is that just your usual
side-a-the-neck shit?"

"Well . . . it's just that Mary sort of belongs to a *group* . . . like a
church . . . and would like to know, before she will write again, if you
have accepted Jesus Christ as your personal savior. Why don't you let
me read some of the other letters?"

"Christ!" he says, rubbing his smooth dome.

"Exactly! So how do you want me to answer?"

Kansas is squirming like a third grader who has just been called to
the blackboard to spell out a really tough word—like "chrysanthemum."

"Fuck, O.G. Whaddya think's a good answer here? I like the 'working out' part and the 'well portioned.' "

"How about the truth?" I offer. "It's not a trick question."

Kansas is pouting. I reach deep into my Personnel Development
tool bag and come up with a framework for Goal Clarity.

"Look, what do you really want from this girl—a pen pal, a priest-
ess, or just someone to visit you?"

Kansas considers a quick lie, always his first instinct, then, surprisingly, tells me the truth. "Let me break it down for you, O.G. You
know the state of Kansas got a parole hold on me. The minute I finish
this chump-ass bid in Nevada they'll be coming to take me back to finish out my time in the Kansas pen."

"And?"

"And then I'm fucked! Unless . . . unless I had what they call 'roots
in the community' here—like a *wife,* f'rinstance."

Ah, the sordid, *scandalous* plot is unveiled at last. Now, at least, my
fictional letters to Mary will have some focus.

"Sounds like you're seeking a long-term relationship."

"Nah, O.G.—just a marriage."

"In that case, I recommend an emphatic 'yes' answer to the Jesus question. Hey, it can't be that much of a stretch—I used to hear you saying your prayers at night in the Fish Tank."

"That ain't the same thing. Prayers is like, *personal*—y'unnerstan' what I'm sayin'?"

"So what's it going to be? Jesus yes, Satan no?"

Kansas, who I thought loved the Kansas penitentiary with its snitchless, J-Cat-free, Stand-up ambience, is hesitating.

"Aiight, O.G. Do it . . . and make sure you tell her I can bench-press 440 pounds of Bibles. Ha!"

"You sure, dawg? 'Yes' to accepting Jesus Christ as your personal savior? This is a big step, you know."

"Jesus," Kansas moans. A moment later, *"Mary,* huh?" Then the epiphany.

"Yes—tell her yes."

I start writing, assuring Mary of Kansas's profound love of Jesus and his weight-lifting devotions.

Poor Mary.

And Jesus wept.

Skell's doing his supply room inventory when I come in for my "hookup." A shipment of crack—"toad food," Skell calls it—arrived this morning, and Skell is doing a brisk Brillo business. Homemade crack pipes of Vantage cola cans require a metal screen, and Brillo does the job nicely. I wonder how Brillo is listed on the NASDAQ.

He says, "Whatchu need, O.G.?" but Skell's already reaching behind his mattress palace to display a lethal assortment of shanks, pieces of pipe, and trazors. He arrays them like a jewelry salesman on his display case—a cardboard box of SpringFresh toothpaste. Dopey, the inbred dwarf, is playing lookout for the Dirt. C.O. Fallon, who usually takes care of lookout duties, is fast asleep in his pod.

Skell launches into a well-practiced sales pitch, extolling the relative benefits and features of the weaponry.

". . . then ya got your basic shank here, double-edged blade, good for all-round self-defense, conceals perfect under your shirt . . . course, your Christmas tree, top-of-the-line . . ."

Skell pulls out a length of hollow pipe that has been flattened and sharpened like a spear. "Good for your Zulu uprising, dawg, know what I'm sayin'?" Another piece of pipe bristles with razor blades. "Dat one's five full decks, dawg."

And on and on as I fade away, fall almost two decades back to the jewelry salesman at Zale's in San Francisco. Diamond engagement rings on an immaculate glass display case. Glittering with the promise of Forever, like long-term debt hidden in the footnotes of the annual report. The salesman explaining the four Cs of diamond purchasing to me. I can only remember one.

". . . *cuts* clean, dawg, and when the punk pulls the fucking Christmas tree *out,* he gets a stocking stuffer full of *guts* in his lap! You down wid dat, O.G.?"

No sale. "Do you have anything in, say, a nine-millimeter—basic black?" Skell considers this customer request with such gravity that he is compelled to scratch his scabbed head, producing a bloody topograph of the Iberian Peninsula. (I can't be sure. I had high school geography in the sixties—I wasn't there. But watching Iberia taking shape on Skell's skull, my stressed-out synapses summon forth a fragment of a biology lecture from Mr. Horn, my ninth-grade teacher: "Ontogeny recapitulates phylogeny.")

"Just kidding, Skell," I tell him. "Listen, forget all this stuff. What kind of sandwiches you have today?"

Skell snaps out of his nine-millimeter reverie and pulls a giant Styrofoam cooler from behind a stack of Saint Mary's Hospice blankets.

"Whatchu need, O.G.? Got ham and cheese—*real* ham, none a dat sand toad substitute."

"What else you got?"

Skell pokes through the cooler. "How 'bout pastrami, dawg? Got mustard too." His broken bloody fingernails are clawing through the ice.

"On rye?" One can always hope.

"What the fuck you think this is—fucking *Nathan's* hot dogs? We got Wonder bread." My father once said that Wonder bread was "manna for the goyim," but it beats getting shanked in the chow hall by Two-Tears.

"Sold, Skell." The ritual tapping of fists and knuckles.

"Six stamps," says Skell.

"Only if I get to make the sandwich."

"I'm down wid dat, dawg."

My dad took me and my brother, Mikey, to Nathan's in Coney Island—the "original" Nathan's. I am six years old and Daddy says Nathan's has the best hot dogs and fries in the world. If I'm a good boy, I can get a candy apple too. Maybe even a cotton candy. Mikey got a cotton candy last year—he told me.

And Mikey might take me up on the rollacoaster 'cause I'm big now. If I'm good. If I'm a good boy.

We scream on the rollacoaster, the *cyclome,* Mikey's breath warm and sweet with cotton candy on my face, an endless New York summer soft and sweet with promise. When magic soared and danced and delighted me. Not yet dimmed, not yet denied.

Later I get sick. No one sees me throw the candy apple at the feet of the Fat Lady, who once sang to me, the apple still red and rich with promise.

In my concrete cell I bite into the pastrami on white. My dad was a physician, one of the last of a dying breed of general practitioners who made house calls, day or night.

My dad had an emergency house call on that Sunday we were supposed to go to Nathan's in Coney Island. Daddy never did take us to Coney Island that summer, but I remember it anyway—the crunchy sound the french fries made in my mouth and Mikey screaming in delight on the Cyclone.

Sometimes my mind can no longer tell the difference between things that happened and things I just *wanted* to happen.

My dad died while I was locked up in the county jail—Suicide Watch Cell No. 3. If there is anyone on this troubled earth that loved him more than me, I haven't met him yet.

I miss my dad.

I miss Mikey.

Inventing new pseudo-gang hand signals is one of my favorite pastimes. It began as an innocuous amusement in the semi-privacy of my cell but has now progressed to a full-blown obsessive-compulsive disorder with a unique etiological basis.

With so many different gangs flashing hand signs on the yard, all of which I find incomprehensible, I have felt driven to develop my own to facilitate my safe passage around the yard. My role model is the sixties rock performer Joe Cocker, who would writhe in contorted agonies while singing. Of particular interest to me were Joe's strenuous spasmodic clenchings of his hands, a spastic display of finger convulsions that I found—well—compelling.

I walk the yard daily for exercise, counting steps. A dirt-blown rectangle, no curves. The Old Heads say that "a freeman sees a curve—the convict sees an angle." I stride with the demented determination of the born New Yorker, bouncing on my heels, head swiveling to scope out would-be muggers lurking behind parked cars or loitering dangerously in alleyways.

Whenever I pass the Wood Pile, Kansas and his Mutant Warriors flash me the crossed-finger-on-chest sign for Wood Solidarity. I instantly form an inverted "V" with the fingers of my right hand, gnarl it up Joe Cocker style, and thump it against my chest.

"Right on!" the dawgs yell, and this pleases me.

There is a new dawg today, a youngster. I notice two enormous ears jutting out from a red-haired jug of a head. Teacup is now a proud member of the Dawg Pound, courtesy of Kansas, who had his back in the Fish Tank.

Thanks to Kansas's recommendation (unsolicited) and good word-of-mouth, I am now doing a brisk barter business, reading and writing letters in exchange for civilian clothes, tailors, Gummi Bears, and Hershey's Kisses for Spoony. For two full decks of tailor I'll even write a "love poem" to a dawg's "fiancée." I bundle this service with my legal consultant business, which involves nothing more complex than filling out boilerplate appeal, divorce, and bankruptcy forms.

I'm not exactly styling during my yard strolls, but there's no state issue on me. I'm wearing new Nikes, blue Dickies jeans, a solid blue T-shirt, and soft paisley socks. Only fish walk around in state issue. It doesn't inspire respect.

Cassie sashays by in her hot pants. "*Nice* socks, O.G.!"

I ignore her. I have no desire to be introduced to her latest "daddy." The Bone has also advised me to never stop and talk to a "he/she" on the yard unless I'm "fittin' to get some stanky on the hang-low."

Which I ain't.

"Whassup, O.G.?" A couple of black gangstas that I helped beat their disciplinary write-ups. I favor them with a specially modified Black Power salute from the sixties, because if you live long enough, all old things shall be made as new. My hand signs are now as spontaneous as an outburst of Tourette's.

I just wish I didn't have to pause every few steps to wipe the dirt off my spectacles. Ruins the image of purposeful menace I am trying to project. Never know when some J-Cat or Two-Tears Tattoo might turn the corner of the yard.

In my right pants pocket, twenty AA batteries shake, rattle, and roll. In my left pocket rests a large thermal sock. In the event of a surprise greeting from Two-Tears, I'm fittin' to pull an Energizer Bunny out of my slock. Fittin' to *bitch-slock* the muthafuckin' J-Cat!

In short, I'm in role. Kansas says I have gone J-Cat.

Snake and Scud are coming down the path. "What's up, dawg?" Snake says. Scud just twists his head, thumbs a nostril, and blows his nose. Some of it lands in the dirt. For these old Inferno dawgs I flash the Larry Fine sign, a Three Stooges–inspired gangsta greeting. I place my upraised hand, palm in, under my chin, vigorously wiggling three fingers.

When Spoony leaves the house to check the contents of the cell-block garbage can—nothing gets thrown away in prison, just endlessly recycled—I practice rapidly assembling my battery slock. I stand, gun-slinger style, facing the cell wall, which I imagine supports a full-length mirror. Right hand moves like lightning to the pants pocket, snatching up the AAs, left hand a blur of speed withdrawing the thermal sock. The Energizer cartridges are loaded into the sock cylinder, then secured with a tight slock knot.

In the imagined mirror I accomplish all this in nanoseconds. I do not dwell on the possibility that a nonvirtual mirror might have re-flected a fifteen-minute sequence of fumbling on the cell floor for rolling batteries.

I face the cinder block mirror, both hands dangling casually but with deadly potential at my sides, slock ready in the right-hand pocket.

"Yo, *punk*!" I snarl. "You tawkin' ta *me*?" I shift my slock hand slightly toward the pocket. Two-Tears Tattoo glares back at me, hesitates. I can smell his fear.

"Bring it on *down,* punk! C'mon—whatchu fittin' to do, *Frog*-Boy? You fittin' to *jump,* you punk-ass teardrop muthafucka!"

Two-Tears squints back from the mirror, his hand—too slow—moving for the shank beneath his shirt.

"Make my *day,* punk!" I scream at the bare cinder block wall while my energized slock busts out his domelights. Drops him like a bad habit. I study the punk's prostrate body at my feet. My voice is thick with contempt.

"Next time you're fittin' to bust an omelet, you best be bringing an *egg*—Home *Skillet!*" Then I kick in his grill.

To give credit where it's due, I picked this technique up at a phone company seminar titled "Visualizing Success in the Marketplace." If you *think* it, you can do it!

I paid attention.

A cat is a priceless treasure in prison, and my friend Chico, doing Life Without, owns an ancient, half-blind gray tabby he calls Belinda. Chico and Belinda have been doing time together for the last twelve years on Lifer's Row. Chico, a short, dark Chicano, fell twenty years ago behind a gang-banger drive-by that left two dead on the streets of Reno.

Chico, then nineteen, was the designated driver that day. Since there is no Designated Driver Defense in criminal law, Chico went down just as hard as if he had been the shooter. Never rolled, never ratted out his homie. Homie, less honorable, copped to Murder Two, got a Life *With,* after testifying Chico was the mastermind behind the hit—was, in fact, the shooter.

This is Chico's version anyway. I don't care if he's telling me the truth or not as long as he can bring a colorful narrative to the table— y'unnerstan'?

Homie never got to the "With" part of his sentence. What he got was a visit to his protective custody cell by some of the "La Raza" boys. Homie got a two-foot-long ice pick shoved through his right eye and out the back of his snitch skull. This injury resulted in partial blindness, followed by brain death—in quick succession.

Doing Life Without, Chico got nothing coming from the judicial system except his cherished Belinda, a legacy from a kinder, gentler era of penology. Belinda, like many of the items in Chico's private cell, is "grandfathered." A decade ago inmates here could receive packages containing books, art supplies, radios, and clothes from relatives or friends. Then the Department of Prisons, possibly in response to the prevailing punitive winds, banned all future care packages, including Book-of-the-Month memberships. Books, boom boxes, and art supplies are brought in the same way the drugs are—illegally.

Belinda's an anachronism—and she's dying of old age. The store still carries Tender Vittles Gourmet ($2.03) for upscale felines or Purina Cat Chow (18 oz., $1.88) for the Belindas with budgetarily constrained owners like Chico. Johnny Cat pet litter is also available ($1.38) at the store, but Skell provides a generic substitute in exchange for one caramel Twix bar ($.48). It's a good deal for Belinda.

Since I get store, I handle the candy and cat litter transactions with Skell. In exchange, Chico lets me pet Belinda and use his grandfathered dictionary and other reference books.

We play chess every Saturday afternoon in Chico's cell, Belinda faithfully attending from the nest of state blankets we have built for her on the upper bunk.

The score so far in this ongoing chess Olympics: La Raza 3, the Jews 94. The three "losses" I found it prudent to engineer whenever I detected a significant flattening in Chico's learning curve.

When I worked in the Revenue Forecasting Department, I once produced a statistically solid annual sales forecast for the marketing V.P. My data, bolstered and bursting with "validations of significance," proved disappointing to the professionally sanguine veep. He suggested that my forecast simply did not conform to the "market opportunity," which he viewed as limitless.

The fact that *his* boss, our wannabe visionary CEO, had just handed him a very aggressive, "tops-down" sales quota may have considerably broadened the veep's opportunity horizon.

"I don't like the *slope*" was his comment after pretending to glance at the supporting data behind the graph.

I had only worked on this report for twelve straight sixteen-hour days. You might say I was emotionally vested in its acceptance.

"Then you don't like our sales history," I replied, possibly out of the side of my neck. Even then this sinister sideways malignancy had taken up residence—silently, inexorably metastasizing me off the fast track, out of the Future Leaders inner circle.

The marketing V.P., universally referred to as the Empty Suit by his legions of resentful underlings, gave me a killer stare that was anything but empty. I didn't recognize the look then, but now I would characterize it as the "you got nothin' comin' in my corporation" look.

"What's *in* the history?" Empty Suit demanded. Perhaps I had tainted the data by including actual and accurate sales numbers. I was guilty.

"There are 120 data points—twelve years of monthly *actuals*," I told him, already knowing where this was leading.

"Then that's *it*!" he cried, smacking a hand down sharply on his desk, which, by its size, could qualify for its own zip code. "The first four years the economy was in a goddamn *recession*! Did you adjust for that? They were poor performance years."

"Actually, sir, we were in an *inflationary* period and I adjusted for that by normalizing the cash flow statements." Empty Suit was unimpressed by my due diligence.

"Take out years one to four," he commanded. "If it makes *you* happy, stick a footnote at the bottom. Say the data's *non*normalized for illustrative purposes, or you removed the outer years of the history to, you know, *smooth* them, or whatever you bean counters call it."

"Smoothing the outliers?" I asked.

"Exactly! That's the ticket, son—smooth those goddamn *outliers* right out of my revenue forecast. *Now* we're on the same page. Just *do* it!"

"Sir, I can run a revised forecast in a couple of days. When do you need this by?" Stupid, *stupid* question.

"Yesterday," Empty Suit said. Like he always did.

In prison my three chess losses to Chico represent my failure to smooth out the outliers. In here, such failures are rewarded with quality petting time with Belinda.

Breeeoooooow.

Chico's cell walls blaze with color. Every square inch of dirty cinder block is covered with painted canvas portraying birds in flight—eagles, falcons, hawks, all soaring majestically over oceans of infinite blue, purple mountains, or golden beaches bordering lush green jungles.

The art, like Belinda the cat, is grandfathered. When art supplies, along with cats, books, and music tapes, were declared contraband, Chico mastered the highly lucrative prison art form of pencil portraits. Bring Chico paper, pencil, and a photograph of your loved one and he will return a wondrous, slightly idealized portrait to your cell in a week.

Chico has a backlog of fifteen to twenty customers at all times and a cell overflowing with old grandfathered books. I've seen Chico turn down two hundred dollars to do some tat work on someone's back or chest. He will, however, create a penciled blueprint for your favorite prison tat gun jockey.

Big Bird is tapping gently on Chico's cell door. We look up from our chess game to the cell door window where a gray-stubbled beard pokes out of a face so black that it seems blue when the sun hits it at a certain angle.

"'Scuse me," says Bird, sliding the door open only after Chico nods an okay. In prison you *never* enter a man's house without permission. Unless you intend him some harm.

Chico brightens at the sight of Big Bird, who is a fellow resident of the Row and a Comrade-for-Life.

Bird is holding out a tattered color photograph of a young black man smiling in his high school cap and gown. "This here's my son, Albert. Figured maybe you could do one of them stipplin' drawings of him. Hey now, O.G.—you still got game?"

Chico nods sadly, accepts the photo with the grace and solemnity of a deity of old receiving a burnt offering. Belinda is purring down at Bird from her perch.

"It was on the wire, Pops," Chico says softly. "Fucking Crips capped him behind some bogus rocks. I'm sorry, Pops."

"Yeah, well, it weren't nothin' nice. Look . . . I got no store, but a Freeman I know can bring in some colored pencils, maybe some of that charcoal you used to get. Course, I ain't tryin' to put you in no trick bag."

Chico considers this offer from his bunk while I adjust my aching cheeks on the steel toilet, the chess set on the cardboard box between us forgotten for the moment.

"Thanks, Pops, good looking out. But they come down harder now on art than they do on crank or shanks. If you can just lawdog the Pardons Board for me this year, we'll be square."

"You know I be doing that for you anyway, Chico," Bird says, slightly affronted at the implied quid pro quo. Big Bird is a jailhouse lawyer who is also doing Life on the Installment Plan. He comes through the Fish Tank every few years, each time with a new two-to-five-year sentence.

"It's all good then, Pops—leave the photo with me and give me a few days."

" 'Preciate that. The Pardons Board be meeting again next month—your package be ready."

The Pardons Board is the sole remaining hope of the Life Withouts. They are essentially a clemency board, convening annually to dispense mercy to an infinitesimal number of supplicants. Unless you are over eighty *and* dying of cancer or the governor's brother, you got nothing coming. The odds don't stop the Life Withouts from submitting a package every year. It only takes some time to put together, and they got nothing but time.

Chico is fully aware that his chances of "action" by the board are even less than the chance of being struck in the ass by a meteor while piloting the *Nautilus* beneath the Arctic ice.

But the Pardons Board is all Chico has, so he dutifully dispatches his pleas every year, having progressed through all of the other phases of doing life. His first phase, two decades ago, was the dream of early release through some legal miracle—a new trial, a successful appeal, a writ, a petition, a pardon, *something.* This fantasy is common to all fish facing Without.

Till they learn they got nothing coming.

Chico spent his first five years trying, then discarding, other prison lifestyles: sleeping eighteen hours a day, doing drugs, trying religion, pumping iron with the *eses,* kicking it and jailing it with the homeboys, constant pruno consumption, a suicide attempt followed by a J-Cat stretch with psychotropics, and two horrendously botched escape attempts.

The painting, then the books and writing poetry, saved him.

Now he's determined to master chess, and his strategy seems to be to compile as many defeats as fast as possible in order to learn something from each game. So far, the first part of this strategy is enjoying a spectacular success.

Chico's upper bunk, in addition to nesting Belinda, houses a small library of grandfathered books sent in years ago by his large and still supportive family. Philosophy, religion, sociology, psychology, and anatomy texts rise to the ceiling along with mounds of novels. The library is the refreshingly eclectic selection of the self-educated. Chico has taught himself to read Latin, French, German, and Italian but refuses to help me refresh my fluency in Spanish. He claims he can't tolerate the sound of my fake Castilian "accent." Can I help it if my Spanish instructors at the Defense Language Institute in Monterey all had lisps? So what if I say *"thita"* instead of the Chicano-sanctioned *"cita."* It's all good—isn't it?

Chico says it's not all good. *"Maricón* shit" is what he says. "Why did the U.S. government train you guys in faggot Spanish? Were they planning to conquer Central America by sucking cock? *Drain* the guerrillas of resistance?" So I just keep my pleasant tour of duty in Panama and war stories to my *maricón* self, just another misunderstood veteran. Hey, *I* didn't give back the Panama Canal.

"Check!" Chico slams his queen down. My white bishop, lurking in the corner, just laying in the cut for this blunder, takes black queen.

"Fuck! Took my *bitch*!"

"Nah—your bitch committed suicide," I clarify. This leads to five minutes of talking shit and selling wolf tickets, the most entertaining part of prison chess games.

"Checkmate." I do not slam my piece down. It's a respect thing.

"Chingada!" But Chico is never discouraged, convinced his long-term strategy will inevitably yield dividends. Perhaps I will die of old age or just sink into premature senility.

Chico earned a B.A. degree in prison five years ago. That was the year the prison college program was terminated here. In 1995 the U.S. Congress voted to eliminate prisoner eligibility for Pell grants, which once enabled inmates to pursue a postsecondary education. When the Pell grants were repealed, no college or university had any economic incentive to continue inmate education programs.

This makes sense to my M.B.A. mentality. But I had harbored the naive notion that an A.A. or B.A. degree could reduce the recidivism rate. That this might be a public policy goal, in fact. I asked Ringer about this.

"Fuck no," Ringer explained. "The idea now is *punishment*—nobody can even spell 'rehabilitation' anymore. There's only one public policy now."

Together, we chanted the mantra:

"Convicts got nothin' comin'!"

There is a mob in front of the bulletin board outside the caseworker's office in the rotunda. It happens every month when the Parole Board issues the following month's list of "applicants." My heart is pounding. I push through the crowd in what I would consider to be an assertive, rather than disrespectful, manner.

PAROLE BOARD HEARING AGENDA

I appreciate the big, 24-point bold title. Having an agenda is also a good thing. I learned this in a Quality Improvement workshop. "An agenda provides purposeful focus and direction to the value-added input stream." And *this* fish is now fittin' to upstream and outsource, having been refocused and restructured. Right-sized dawgs will understand what I'm saying.

THE FOLLOWING APPLICANTS WILL BE CONSIDERED
FOR POSSIBLE RELEASE TO THE COMMUNITY OR TO A
CONSECUTIVE SENTENCE

The crowd around me is young, black, and highly pissed off. They yell, threaten, push, pull, and slap each other while scanning the list. Just your Average Urban Nightmare struggling for ruh-*lease* to the community.

The Bone is inflaming the crowd by pointing out the absence of black inmates' names.

"Ain't nothin' but white boys on dis month's list—ain't *no* toads in the Wood Pile." The Bone is working the throng beautifully, playing the race card, the only card the Man has dealt him.

"*Tooshay* be on da lists." Little G, ever the captious Crip, challenges the Bone.

"Tooshay ain't fittin' ta catch nothin' but a *dump*!" says the Bone, who is wise beyond his years in the ways of the Man. The Parole Board can approve the applicant, can deny ("dump") parole for a year or more, and in the worst-case scenario they can dump a convict "to expiration." (See you again when your sentence is completely over—*expired*—'cause you got nothin' comin' from the board!)

Eighteen names and numbers down: LERNER—61634. My relief is physical, a five-hundred-pound boulder off my chest. I would weep with joy, weep like a bitch-slapped punk, if such a public display of unmanliness wasn't considered so unseemly.

Not that there's anything wrong with that. Just the wrong demographics at the moment.

With my county jail time "credits," I have been down almost a year now.

"The O.G. fittin' ta roll over to the wild leg!" The Bone, self-appointed interpreter of this madhouse, is correct. The board will approve me ("It's a slam-dunk," insists Shapiro) for parole to my next sentence, a one-to-six, the last leg.

I will be *free* in twelve months!

In my cell I study the calendar, count the days. Aside from counting steps in the yard, this is my primary passion here. I deduct the jail credits and come up with *362* days! The same answer I have gotten two or three hundred times before, but it never hurts to check. My father, whose hobby was carpentry, used to say, "Measure twice—cut once."

I measure again—*361* days and four hours!

Spoony is tweaking behind Mandy's trailer phone being cut off. He now has no way to reach her and confirm his worst fears about Jody or Sancho. "Probably was a little late on the bill," Spoony surmises.

I have no sympathy for Spoony on this issue. I began my career in the phone company's Collection Services Division (later rechristened the Revenue Fulfillment Center). After talking to thousands of deadbeats with insulting excuses for late payments—"My mother died and forgot to go to the mailbox first"—I had concluded these late- or nonpaying customers had nothing coming. You had money for Mom's *funeral,* didn't you? Better rethink your priorities—until then, enjoy dead dial tone!

Collection work can make an otherwise sensitive man a bit callous.

Sergeant Stanger decides to have some fun with Spoony on the yard.

"EAT DIRT, ASSHOLE!" This is Stanglish for "Drop to the ground, facedown, hands clasped behind your head."

Spoony, who has just finished making his crank deliveries for the Car, isn't holding. He drops, facedown, while Stanger approaches bran-

dishing the cattle-prod-size flashlight. Six Dirt members fan out, form-
ing a security perimeter around Stanger and Spoony as the Yard Rats
scurry over to scope out the score on the latest installment of *Cops versus Cons.*

Last time I checked, the cops were leading by something like 5,000
to nothing.

Spoony's little shaved bean is bobbing up and down in fear. Stanger
has to scream again. "I said eat *dirt*! Don't move your head!" And
Spoony makes the mistake of looking up to see just who is screaming
at him. And why.

Stanger knows the penal code, although he is rarely restrained by
it. "Failure to immediately obey a correctional officer's order" can be
construed as "resisting or threatening" behavior. So Stanger steps
forward and slams the flashlight down, connecting with a sickening
thud against the "M" in the "Mandy" neck tattoo. Very bad for
Mandy.

The Wood Pile, led by Kansas, is racing over. "That's outta line!"
Kansas yells at the Dirt. The Yard Rats and Wood Pile press forward,
carrying me—a reluctant spectator—with them. The Shit is about to
Jump Off.

I was wondering just which way it was going to roll when Guntower
Cop starts blasting in the general direction of the surging crowd of
convicts.

All of the convicts and a few of the more experienced Dirt hit the
dirt. Kansas knocks me flat on my face, and my glasses shatter on the
ground. Two of the Dirt, last men standing, catch shotgun pellets in
their asses and legs.

Final score before they lock us down: convicts still nothing (with
nothing coming), but the cops are minus two—O happy day!

Except I am minus my only pair of eyeglasses, which is going to be
a problem (and not "an opportunity in disguise") unless they send me
to Braille classes *and* require Two-Tears Tattoo to telegraph his visit

with a bullhorn from across the yard: "You're dead! You disrespectful Lawdog motherfucker!"

The DOP's Department of Internal Affairs and Investigations concludes that the "unfortunate friendly fire" that cut down two of the Dirt's Finest "highlights a training and development opportunity." This is my kind of bureaucratic language. They also recommend a budgetary solution. I *love* these guys!

We are locked down for three days, which is how long it takes Spoony to stop croaking like a frog. Stanger and the boys drop by my house, tear it up and leave before I can even offer them a cup of instant coffee. C.O. Fallon gave us plenty of advance notice, so Skell's private stock was moved long before the Dirt arrived.

I'm still searching for some fish who will sell me his glasses for a bag or two of 4 Aces tobacco. There is no way I can survive the fourteen-month waiting list.

Besides watching out for Two-Tears, the Bone reminds me that some of the Hunger's gangster homeboys might still be seeking a little getback against me.

"Bone," I plead, "can't you just tell me who they are? I'm blind now and I'll never see it coming."

"Sorry, O.G., but I ain't tryin' to catch nothin' from snitch city, know what I'm sayin'?"

"All right, I understand. How about you just sort of *sing* out a name or two, like it's part of a rap song or something. That wouldn't be snitching."

The Bone adjusts his shower cap and considers the idea. After a few moments he shakes his head.

"Nah, O.G. That would be a *dry* snitch."

· · ·

Caseworker Sykes ("Call me Wally") summons me to his office in the rotunda a few days before my Parole Board. As assistant director of inmate programming he is required to make sure I am appropriately programmed. Of course, all prison rehabilitative "programs" were eliminated years ago. Probably a budgetary issue. Somebody smoothing out the expense outliers.

Mr. Sykes is not deterred one whit by the almost total absence of "programming" in the prison. His job is to *slot* us into the proper (for our particular crimes) programs. The fact that these programs do not exist has not diminished his enthusiasm for his job.

Wally looks up from what I know to be my I-file. The same four gray hairs that were pasted across his shiny dome back when I made slocks of newspapers have not been disturbed. Wally is a very small man with some big ideas.

"Good morning, Mr. Lerner. Your back number, please?"

"Six-one-six-three-four."

Wally seems immensely pleased with my answer to the back number query and beams at me behind his black institutional horn-rims. No wonder there's more than a year wait for glasses. The employees are sucking up all the perks. I'm still hunting for that myopic fish.

"Let's talk *programming*!" he exclaims, a tiny hand snatching at something in the air. Possibly a memory of programming.

"Mr. Sykes—"

"Call me Wally."

"Well, Wally, it's my understanding that there is no longer any programming available in this prison."

Wally frowns. This is distasteful. He has heard this before.

"No programming? I think not. We have many programs, a diverse offering, solid programs. They are simply temporarily abeyed pending funding approval."

"Oh—thanks for clearing that up. I thought they were all canceled over five years ago."

"Canceled? Don't believe that. Abeyed, perhaps, even *delayed,* but hardly canceled." Wally wants some compassion on this issue. "Look, Mr. Lerner, I've read your I-file—you're an educated man. Surely you encountered these types of budgeting problems during your years with a corporation."

A former corporate spin doctor, I allow that I do.

"Good—we're on the same team, you know. Now let's proceed *irregardless* of the funding issues."

"Yes," I agree, anxious to get this charade over with. "Let's proceed, *regardless.*"

Wally is turning the pages in my file. "Hmmm . . . let's see . . . voluntary manslaughter . . . use of a deadly weapon . . . oh *yes,* yes . . . good—this is *very* good." Wally is licking his upper lip with an unreasonably long tongue.

"Wally?"

"Just checking for appropriate programs."

I'm getting worried. "Wally—uh, why is voluntary manslaughter, uh, *good*? I mean from the Parole Board's perspective."

"From a *parole* perspective? *Good?* Oh no, I think not." Wally shakes his head sadly.

Now I'm totally confused. "You think not . . . not good? But you just said *very* good."

"Very good from a *programming* perspective, so to speak. You see, Mr. Lerner, you are a *violent* offender and we have a *program* for violent offenders—a wonderful Anger Management workshop called 'Cage Yo Rage.' The Parole Board, since you are so concerned with *their* perspective, looks very favorably on applicants with Anger Management Certification. Oh yes, it's practically *de rigueur* these days."

"Well, that's good—so you'll sign me up for the next workshop?"

"I think not."

"But you just said—"

"I said we have Anger Management, so to speak, when it's being *of-*

fered—it's temporarily abeyed, awaiting a fresh infusion of budget funding. And when it is offered again, you *will* be placed on the list—an abeyance list, so to speak."

"And when might that be, Wally? I'm scheduled to see the Parole Board in a few days, so to speak."

"I think not." I think if Wally says this again I will kill him, and his programming successor can program me for Extreme Rage Management.

"You think that I'm *not* scheduled for the Parole Board?" My voice is calm, my mind seeking out the mantra I paid thirty-five dollars for at a T.M. class in 1972.

"No—you are going to the board," Wally reassures me. "You'll just have to go *sans* Anger Management Certification. However, the board will take note, so to speak, of the fact that I have put you on the *program track* for the class."

Oh, this little pedantic, punk-ass twit! Must not let him see I'm just a tad irritated, so to speak. Oh no.

"Tell me, Jimmy—may I call you Jimmy?—does this unfortunate hiatus in programming perturb you? Perhaps it even *angers* you a bit, so to speak. Mayhap just a bit?"

"Mayhap not a bit, Wally. In fact, I'm quite appreciative of your efforts to guide me along the appropriate program path." When in doubt, never underestimate the power of Brown's Ass-Kissing Axioms. Mayhap toss in a bit of the old Mirroring and Echoing Sales Training techniques in my mangled ninth-grade French.

Wally is smiling now. "Tell me about sex," he says.

"Sex? What about sex? You have programs for it or something?"

"Most assuredly—more like sexual *deprogramming,* so to speak." Wally is sniffing now in my I-file for the scent of sex. "Hmm . . . that's regrettable—no programming opportunities in here. And we have a very comprehensive Sexual Offender Program."

"Well, maybe my next trip."

Wally scratches out "Managing Sexual Compulsions" from his list of abeyed programs. Returns to my life history file in search of other programming opportunities.

"Hmm . . . I see that this is your first arrest—most unusual. Absolutely no criminal history to work with, so to speak."

"And isn't *that* good? Doesn't the Parole Board look favorably upon first offenders?" (My lawyer, Freddy Shapiro, assures me that my limited résumé of depravity will guarantee early parole.)

Wally is annoyed by my continual references to nonprogramming events. "I think the Parole Board is *more* impressed by appropriately scheduled programming." Wally has finally reached my PSI and police report.

"What was the deadly weapon?"

"Isn't that right there in the police report in front of you?"

"Indeed . . . indeed . . . but programming works best when the inmate *participates* in the process. Never mind—mayhap we can mine out some programming material from the reports."

Wally pushes his state-issue glasses against the bridge of his nose and reads aloud.

"When the defendant, Jimmy A. Lerner, was attacked by one Dwayne Hassleman—the deceased—in the living room area of the Diamond Executive suite of the Excelsior Hotel in Las Vegas where Mr. Lerner . . ." Wally's little lizard of a tongue leaps out at the mention of Excelsior. "Hmmm . . . isn't that the hotel that hosts the Dot-Comdex conventions? Is that what you were doing in Vegas? A little *jaunt* from the San Francisco Bay area, a bit of fun? Hmmm . . . Comdex *sounds* like some kind of naughtiness for the techie set. Were you—"

"No, Wally, I wasn't there for any naughty conventions."

Unconvinced, Wally resumes his mining expedition. ". . . whereupon the defendant, Jimmy Lerner, called 911 . . ."

Wally has apparently found a programming nugget. "Calling 911 was good, Jimmy. Very good."

I'm down now with the programming program. "Thank you, Wally, but is it programmable?"

"I'm afraid not. There are no elements of *denial* present. You made a full statement—a *confession*, actually—even waived your rights to remain silent and to have an attorney present."

"So denial is good—from a programming perspective?"

"Well, let's just say it's better than the truth—from a purely programming perspective, of course."

"Of course."

Wally is now digging down through the medical examiner's report. "Hmmm . . . we may have something here . . . oh indeed . . . Hassleman's autopsy shows 'extraordinarily high levels' of methamphetamine, cocaine, morphine, codeine, barbiturates, not to mention an alcohol level of . . ." Wally trades this report for a copy of the preliminary hearing.

"Let's see . . . this Hassleman was described as a 'veritable fruit salad of narcotics' . . . interesting turn of phrase . . . and *you*, Mr. Lerner, admitted to having been *drinking* and playing blackjack *all day.* The *witnesses* say you threatened to *kill* the defendant, threatened to kill him just shortly before you took a taxi back to the hotel, and Mr. Hassleman burst into the room with the knife, and . . ." Wally's hand flutters above us, searching for the correct words. "And you shortly found it somehow necessary to *prematurely* dispatch Mr. Hassleman's soul, to cleave it, so to speak, from the flesh." Wally looks at me for agreement. *"N'est-ce pas?"*

"C'est vrai, Wal-*lee*, except for the cleaving business. So where's the programming jackpot?"

"It's right there in the report—drinking all day at the tables! *This* is programmable. Alcoholism is the *best*! Drugs are good too. We have a BADA class here—Bureau of Alcohol and Drug Abuse—a wonderful program, especially when overlaid with Anger Management!"

I don't know why I ask, but I have to. "Can you enroll me in BADA then?"

"I think not. Funding cuts. Most regrettable. But I'm putting you at the *top* of the waiting list. In the meantime, you can go to an A.A. meeting. They cost the state nothing—even the books are donated. The Twelve Steps are most cost-effective."

"But I understand they've been suspended as well."

"Not at all. A bit of an A.A. programming hiatus, perhaps, while Sergeant Stanger sleuthed down the source of a certain Pert shampoo bottle—most regrettable. However, the Brotherhood of Bill will be re-assembling—sober, let us hope—imminently."

"And the Parole Board looks favorably upon A.A. attendance?"

Wally, dismayed by my exclusive focus on getting out of prison, actually responds out of the side of his neck.

"Well, certainly *more* favorably than they do on people who decide to top off a day of blackjack and drinking by *killing* someone."

"*Touché,* Wally. When do they meet?"

Wally consults his desk calendar. "Sunday at noon—you *are* an alcoholic, right?"

"A card-carrying member, Wally. I even have the chips to prove it. You're *sure* that alcoholism is good—from a programming perspective?"

"Most assuredly."

"I'll be at the next meeting then."

"Good luck with the board, Jimmy."

"Thanks. I hope luck doesn't enter into the decision."

"I would think not. Remember to tell them you and I have met and decided upon a full programming schedule, so to speak."

I think not. But I bury this thought beneath the rubble of my new-found programming potential.

So to speak.

.   .   .

In the rotunda the Phone Posse is collecting toll charges
from the new fish. C.O. Fallon looks on with quiet resignation from his
sealed-in kiosk. I would characterize Fallon's managerial style as somewhere between "hands off" and "not present or accounted for."

He waves me over to his office. "Where's your glasses, Mr. Lerner?"
Fallon is opening the steel door so I won't have to talk through the slot
at the counter.

"They were a casualty of the last great Dirt wars."

"Sorry to hear that. Listen, do you know a lot about divorce in
Nevada? I heard you filed the paperwork for C.O. Leach and it all went
smoothly." He motions me into the tiny kiosk.

Inside his tiny domain I can detect the distinct odor of opportunity. "I might be able to help you with that," I tell him. "A couple of
questions."

"Shoot."

"Is it going to be uncontested?"

Fallon tilts back in his chair, runs a hand through his gray hair.
"Well, I'm not going to fight it, if that's what you mean. She's the one
who filed, though, so I got to do something and the lawyers are all
wanting four or five hundred dollars."

"I'm sorry about your troubles. Are there any custody issues?"
Fallon looks far too old to have minor children, but hey, this is
Nevada—you never know.

"No . . . she's never been in custody—well, maybe one time behind
a drunk driving beef. But she beat it in court. Why?"

"No, I mean do you have any dependent children, *child custody*
issues?"

"No. We have three kids, but they're all grown up and gone from
the house now." The scent of opportunity is crystallizing, and despite
my myopia I can now make out the shape of glass.

"I need new glasses," I tell him.

A few minutes later Fallon has the name of my optometrist in

Danville and I have most of the information I need to fill out the simple forms. I love community property laws.

I emerge from the office to the barking of the dawgs by the phones. "O.G. is on the *leg*!" "He *way* up on the Man!" But this is all good—just good-natured barking. Sometimes a convict can spend just a minute in the office and come out with a snitch jacket that will smother him later in his cell—literally.

But Kansas and the Car, the Bone, and the others yelling all know that the O.G. is a Stand-up Con.

So to speak.

A day before the Parole Board I'm styling in the yard with my new glasses on my way to get my A.A. program ticket punched. It's still early, so the temperature is only about 105 degrees, with occasional gusts of sand and dirt stinging my face.

I never see Two-Tears Tattoo coming.

He stabs me in the chest while I'm wiping grime off my glasses. The shank is a piece of paper from the Parole Board.

"Whatchu dodging me for, Lawdog?" Two-Tears asks, quite reasonably. "I ain't lookin' ta sweatchu. I want to appeal this punk-ass Parole Board bullshit."

I read the notice, pleased that there is not the slightest tremor in my hand—not so anyone would notice anyway. All this time, all this fear, and all Two-Tears wanted was legal advice. I'm trying to remember which phone company seminar trainer distributed a handout explaining that "FEAR" was an acronym for "false expectations appearing real."

"I'll be glad to help you out, dawg," I say, shaking the sand from the document. "Parole is denied . . ." An inauspicious beginning.

It turns out Two-Tears recently spun the parole Wheel of Misfortune and came up with the worst-case scenario—a "dump until expiration of sentence." His sentence structure is the same as mine—two one-to-sixes, bowlegged. The "denial" notice essentially says, "Come back and see us in three more years, convict, after you've done every day, every minute of your sentence. Don't call, don't write, 'cause you got nothing coming!" The board does not have to provide a reason and it doesn't.

And when Two-Tears is granted parole on the first one-to-six, he will probably be required to serve out his next sentence in full, about four more years, assuming he accrues good-time credits. The parole commissioners' vote, listed at the bottom of the notice, was unanimous. Two-Tears would have a better chance of appealing global warming.

"What is it you think I can do?" The Parole Board decision is an "administrative" one, not a court action.

Two-Tears, beneath his carefully cultivated badass goatee, actually has an open, not-unpleasant face, perpetually weeping two blue tears.

"I know I got nothin' comin', Lawdog—I just want to know how they figure the good-time and work credits toward the expiration." I break the math down for him, we knuckle-dance, and once again, for O.G. it's all good in the prison hood.

Until I get slocked by the next set of false expectations.

I am no stranger to A.A. meetings.

Years before I would voluntarily show up in the church basements, I dated a girl in college who first introduced me to A.A. She was a strikingly beautiful girl with a penchant for Sylvia Plath's poetry and Wild Turkey. I shared her fondness for the Wild Turkey. Her name was

Crystal, a name she gave to herself because she said it was a "good hippie name." I told her it was a good hooker name.

We had communications issues.

Whenever Crystal wasn't working on her Dylan Thomas term paper or recuperating in the university hospital from a suicide attempt (always halfhearted), she would insist I accompany her to her A.A.
meetings. She was convinced that I was also an alcoholic. That, unlike
her, I was in denial. I denied this but would accompany her to her
meetings. From her perspective it was a "bonding" opportunity for our
relationship. Long before it became fashionable, Crystal wanted me to
"feel her pain."

The A.A. meetings in prison are just like the ones back in the
world—except for the wolf tickets and the violence. *The 12-Step Guide
to Meeting Etiquette* (still awaiting a publisher) contains strict admoni-
tions against "cross-talk"—interrupting someone who is "sharing," or
worse, directing one's own comments *at* someone else in the meeting,
usually with a nonspiritual intent.

Cross-talk is the very lifeblood of prison A.A. meetings. Screaming,
shouting, and death threats are perfectly acceptable. Share something
considered outta line—say, how you got really shit-faced behind a quart
of tequila one night and went to bed with a similarly shit-faced (but
lovely) twenty-three-year-old woman, and then share that when you
awoke to the harsh, sober nontequila sunrise, your drunken sex partner
from the night before had inexplicably shed ten years in her sleep and
woke up next to you as a thirteen-year-old with big tits: this sort of con-
fessional sharing, while preferable to acknowledging she barely had *any*
tits, that, in fact, she had sprouted a big *dick* while you slept, usually
elicits some cross-talk.

"That's outta line, dawg!"

"You be one child-molesting muthafucka!"

"I got something for you on the yard, Chomo!"

In prison the discreetly recovering inmate quickly learns to subdue his tendency toward rigorous honesty. Instead, he eventually develops a politically correct narrative in which all past misdeeds and errors in judgment can be attributed to the evils of John Barleycorn. *The devil made me do it!*

Seven of us Wally-programmed convicts sit in a small circle on metal folding chairs in the GED classroom. Taped to the walls are the Twelve Steps and Twelve Traditions. No cops, unless you count Bubblecop down the corridor. There is a sign-up sheet passed around by our group "secretary," Ace—a Life Without but with a major attitude. Ace looks like Charlie Manson on a bad hair day. Crankster thin, muddy dark eyes set in a stygian stare, hair and beard one continuous, furious tangle.

The strange thing about the sign-up sheet is the one hundred or so "signatures" with back numbers, despite the presence of only seven of us. One of Ace's secretarial perks is signing in phantom members of the fellowship who need "programming credit" (the lists are turned in to Wally) but have scheduling conflicts. Ace's sign-up services can be obtained for a full deck. I decline the service. Teacup and Tooshay also decline.

Somewhere Bill Wilson and Dr. Bob spin in their graves.

After welcoming the new "members" by explaining that he, Ace, has been "running these meetings" for the last six years, he opens the meeting. "Today's topic is acceptance," Ace directs. He tells us to confine our comments to one minute or less or "get the fuck out of my meeting."

I read the wall poster. A.A. Tradition Two states, in part: "Our leaders are but trusted servants; they do not govern." Perhaps Ace's copy of the Big Book is missing that page.

Ace is reading from the book. ". . . and acceptance is the answer to *all* my problems today . . . Nothing, absolutely nothing happens in God's world by mistake." Ace looks up and glares at us, flashing two fanglike crank survivors. Teacup and Tooshay give me horrified glances.

"Who's gonna share first!" Ace demands. He points to Teacup. "You—*fish!* What have you got to say about what I just read?"

Teacup, who just celebrated his fourteenth birthday, lets loose with a small moan and turns his redheaded mop and handles toward the posters on the wall. This enrages Ace, who starts pounding on his Big Book.

"The answer isn't on the *fucking wall*! The answer—*all* the fucking answers are contained in the first 164 pages of the Big Book of Alcoholics Anonymous!" Ace emphasizes each word of "Big Book of Alcoholics Anonymous" with a savage hand smash against the book's cover. The back of Ace's right hand bears a common prison tattoo: "H-A-T-E," one letter on each knuckle. I glance at the back of his other hand expecting to see "L-O-V-E." Instead, his other hand also reads "H-A-T-E."

Guess Ace missed that movie with Robert Mitchum and Gregory Peck. Or was that Robert De Niro?

"I haven't read the book yet," Teacup mumbles into his state sneakers.

"Then shut the fuck up!" our trusted servant rages.

Teacup's freckled face compresses with the promise of tears. *Please don't let him make the kid cry,* I pray to whatever Higher Power might be paying attention. Ace, smelling the fear, escalates the verbal assault.

"Maybe if you'd fucking *read* this book you wouldn't of had that six-pack and decided to take a fucking meat cleaver to your *sister*!"

Teacup starts crying.

"You are *way* the fuck out of line, Ace," I say.

Ace springs out of his chair and is in my face with three quick steps. Or he would be in my face if I hadn't stood up the moment I saw him tense. The top of his rat's nest comes up to my chin. Ace is talking shit.

"Just who the *fuck* are you! Acting like you're *about* something! Telling *me* I'm outta line!" The sound of steel folding chairs scraping on concrete as all the A.A. dawgs scamper to shelter against the wall. When the Shit Jumps Off, unless you want to be up in the mix, it's best to find a hole and pull it over you.

Ace is ranting and raving two inches from my face—definitely a violation of my personal space. But so far, no foul. Just wolf tickets.

". . . you the punk's *daddy* or something, think you're the motherfucking *Red Cross*? You ain't jack *shit*!"

I remain silent. I don't have to do anything unless Ace crosses the line and puts his hate-hate hands on me.

Ace puts his hands on me.

His finger, to be precise. The one with the "H." Jabs it against my chest.

I back up two steps, ostensibly to signal Ace my cowardice. This creates the necessary slack for my right hand to fly out of my pocket like a jackhammer on steroids. I haven't been curling four-gallon garbage cans in my cell every morning to impress the babes on the beach one day.

I opt for the clenched-fist, backhanded bitch-slap. For a couple of reasons: it won't kill Ace and, perhaps more important, a prison bitch-slap brings the added burden of humiliation to the recipient. Sends a message much more powerful than physical pain: *You ain't nothing but a punk-ass bitch, so this time you're getting a little bitch-slap. Dis me again, motherfucker, and you're dead!*

My fist crashes into Ace's mouth. There is a sharp snapping sound as his upper fangs shatter, followed by a satisfying thud as he hits the floor, ass-first. Blood is pouring from his fang hole onto a hate hand, which he is pressing against his now completely toothless mouth.

"You fucking *crazy*, dawg!" The bark has been transformed into a whine. He doesn't try to get up. "I was just trying to get a fucking *discussion* started! *Fuck,* dawg, you busted my teeth." Ace is moaning in pain now.

Tooshay, who's been playing lookout for Bubblecop, approaches the stricken Ace with the care of a man inspecting a rattlesnake that's wounded but still writhing and hissing.

"*Damn,* O.G.! You be one *cold* muthafucka!"

I decide not to wait for the closing Lord's Prayer. I'm the first out the door and on the yard. I don't unclench my fist until I'm halfway to my house.

Four bloody AA batteries drop into the raked brown dirt.

Three Parole Board members, representing the full board of seven, travel from prison to prison in Nevada like the itinerant judges in the old western territories. Once a month they encamp in a conference room in the visiting building, where they plot out the future career paths of thirty to fifty applicants.

C.O. Leach, wearing plastic gloves and Jack Daniel's aftershave, strip-searches me in a small holding cell before sending me into the conference room. At Chico's suggestion, I am wearing only my state-issue blues and sneakers. Chico's only other counsel was to "check your sideways shit at the door."

Leach escorts me past all the dawgs waiting on the benches and into the hearing room. He guides me into the chair in front of the conference table and manages to stagger off without falling down once.

The Parole Board—three tired suits encasing three middle-aged, sunbaked white guys, all wearing those little string tie contraptions with ornamental buckle clasps. No pictures on the wall, no furniture, no rugs, not even the state flag of Nevada. Which I believe depicts Bugsy Siegel shooting craps at the Flamingo Hotel.

Center String speaks first. "Please state your back number."

"Six-one-six-three-four," I answer, and they all nod—approvingly? I think so. I am absurdly, childishly delighted to get their first question right. My Inner Nerd, that ass-licking, favor-currying, chronic A student, that unfailingly neat and Nice Jewish Boy from Brooklyn, scholar and scourge of imprecision, is *resonating*. My parents didn't spend good money on my SAT prep classes for nothing.

Center String makes the introductions. "I'm Chairman Griffin, and joining us today are Commissioners Shelton and Carruth. Mr. Lerner, we have reviewed your I-file and Caseworker Sykes's program progress report. Your file is complete."

My file is complete? Like omniscient archangels perusing the Book of Deeds, they have my entire life in front of them. My file is *complete*. Could they possibly know about the time, aged eleven or so, I (allegedly) disfigured my little sister Lisa's Chatty Cathy doll? Or was it Barbie? My brother, Michael, would know—he did it. Or the one-armed man.

Does the complete I-file disclose the time I liberated a copy of *Playboy* from beneath the mattress of my older cousin, Billy? Strictly for the article about setting up the new "Stereo" sound system.

Of course, they know I killed the Monster. But does the I-file also enumerate all my sins of omission? The time I was too lazy and self-centered to visit Crystal once again at the University Hospital. The phone calls and the letters not returned from old friends who had moved away. The smiles withheld from strangers on the street. The gifts forgotten or never given.

I took the Monster's life. Does the I-file reflect the life I once *saved*? A five-year-old girl I pulled from the bottom of a swimming pool and breathed life back into.

Griffin looks up from the complete file and smiles—a good sign I think.

"I must say, Mr. Lerner, after reviewing your file, I—*we*"—he nods to the second and third strings, who now also smile—"are quite favorably impressed. Your military service, your education, your career at the phone company, and your unblemished record while incarcerated here. In addition, Caseworker Sykes's report indicates you are on a solid programming track."

"Thank you, sir." Mental note to self: put Wally on my Hanukkah card list. Which I will compile—one day.

"Mr. Lerner, we only have a few minutes per applicant, and there are a few dozen *difficult* cases waiting outside. So let me just say now that our staff has computed your 'risk assessment factors' and the numbers fall squarely on the matrix for the earliest possible release . . ."

I *love* this matrix! At the phone company I was a master of the multidimensional matrix. After a consultant suggested we copy American Airlines's Frequent Flier concept, I developed a matrix to distinguish the dial-tone dogs from our high-toll, enhanced-services "Gold" customers. I know from matrixes and I have rarely met one I didn't like.

". . . so unless you have any questions, we must move on to our more . . . *problematical* candidates."

I'm down with that, but I don't tell him that. I also have no questions. My mentor, Mr. Brown, once told me to *never,* "never sell past the close."

In what is probably a departure from the usual script, I rise to clasp the hands of the three String Ties. Warm smiles and handshakes all around. Definitely some Major Rapport here.

Chairman Griffin dismisses me on a comforting note. "I think you already know our decision, but of course our formal, written decision will be sent to Caseworker Sykes in about two weeks, who will then call you in for the results."

"Thank you again, sir."

Leach enters—unsteadily—with the next petitioner. I can't wait to get back to my house and study my calendar, to count and recount my dwindling days here on Planet Wood.

I think I finally got *something* coming!

. . .

Back in cellblock 4, C.O. Fallon unlocks the small library room for me. Spoony's been spreading it through the wire that "O.G. is down with fractions, dawgs—his English is good too." What started as an infrequent, hesitant teenage knock on my cell door at night— "Yogee, can you check my numbers?"—cascaded swiftly to a virtual school of felonious fish seeking my help in unraveling the mysteries of double multiplication and sentence structure.

Rather than deal with this nightly deluge, I obtained permission from Wally to just conduct a math and English class twice a week in the library. Open-door policy and I don't record "tardies." I used to be a *liberal* arts kind of guy. Before I became an M.B.A. kind of guy, a cubicle kind of guy, then a killer kind of guy.

Definitely a different drum beating out my karma. Go figure.

Chico, although not a Fun with Fractions fan, takes advantage of the unlocked library door to slip in to search for any new Saint Mary's donated paperbacks. Deathrow Dom is right behind him.

Deathrow Dominic Carlucci acts like he and I are soulmates because he is also from New York, originally. He is forever asking me about possible mutual acquaintances. "Yo, O.G. Didja know Lenny da Hump that usta hang out on Flatbush?" No, sorry, Dom. "How 'bout dis guy Phil, probably went witchu to Erasmus High School?" Sorry, Dom. Deathrow Dom is a compact bull of a man in his sixties. His death sentence was converted to Life Without back in the seventies when the Supreme Court invalidated existing state death penalty laws.

"Any new poetry come in, O.G.?" Chico asks, already sifting through the boxes on the floor.

"Who are you looking for?" The dawgs here just assume I'm the cellblock librarian because I'm in here so often.

"This one looks good," Chico says. He holds a thick paperback up for my inspection: *The Best of T. S. Eliot and Dylan Thomas.* The best of? What's next—a Walt Whitman sampler?

"Did you read this one yet?" Chico flips open the tattered cover, which falls promptly to the floor.

"No, but I think I may have caught the movie: *Alfred Prufrock Goes Ungently into the Night, Trousers Unrolled.*"

"That's pretty good. Did you share that one with the Parole Board?"

"Wrong demographics, Chico." Deathrow Dom, after asking if I know a Vinnie somebody from Canarsie, scoops up Stephen King's *The Green Mile* and takes off.

Chico spots my students coming across the rotunda. "Uh-oh . . . here comes the Sesame Swastika Street Gang. Spoony, Looney, Teacup, et al."

"Who ate Al?" I want to know.

"Your *madre*, O.G. Gonna stop by later for a chess lesson? I feel like busting some pawns."

"I'll be by after the count."

"Later, bro." We tap clenched fists.

At eighteen, Spoony is the oldest member of my "class." He's also the only one of the skinhead teens not doing life. Teacup has just succumbed to the siren call of the Aryan Tribes. The wild mop of red hair is gone, his dome gleaming beneath the library fluorescents, his neck swollen from his first tattoo—a small swastika. They are all the rage since Kansas reclaimed his throne as Chief Shotcaller.

Kansas also encourages his cattle to brand themselves while they are in the pen. Might need to round up a stray one day.

There are eight baby Nazis in all, aged fourteen to eighteen, seated solemnly around a small conference table Wally acquired from the DMV. The GED test is scheduled for next month.

"How about some geography today, dawgs?" I take my place in front of the blackboard, where I tape a map of Europe. Baby skinheads

shine with suspicion. If they want to stay "classified" to education status (thereby avoiding being a kitchen worker and living in the Inferno),
they must either pass the GED or at least be able to demonstrate a
strong effort on the test.

"Let's say you live *here*," I instruct, placing my fingertip pointer on
the black dot representing Berlin. "And one morning, oh, let's say one
morning in 1939, you wake up with an overpowering urge to goose-
step straight through Poland. Which way do you go?"

Spoony raises a hand—I insist on a modicum of classroom discipline. "Whatchu mean which way? Ya mean like up or down? Or
across?"

"Good question! Would you and your like-minded buddies march
north, east, south, or west?"

Eight white cue balls are bobbing in concentration, calling out the
answers.

"North!"

"East!"

"Both!"

"Who said both?" These white cue balls all look alike to me.
Probably some unconscious racism on my part.

"Me!" Looney, a fifteen-year-old apprentice Aryan (Kansas is with-
holding his swastika until "he shows some heart"), raises his hand. "It's
both because you gotta *surround* them, ya know, like cut off their escape, like." Looney, a straight-up J-Cat, is in this class only because he
was expelled from his regular high school in Reno after bringing two
unauthorized guests to school with him—Messieurs Smith and
Wesson.

Smith and Wesson must not have liked the geometry class because
in the thick of a lecture on the Pythagorean theorem, S and W went
ballistic, spraying federal 125-grain Magnums at the blackboard. Bad
for the blackboard.

Very bad for the geometry teacher standing in front of it.

During the sentencing phase of the murder trial, Looney's lawyer was able to introduce psychiatric testimony to the effect that Looney had been conversing, since the age of five, with tiny, yogurt-fleshed creatures that lived in his refrigerator. Sometimes they told him to do bad things.

The inmates here dubbed it the Dannon Defense. The judge gave Looney a Life With, and Looney spent his first six months here in the Moo, eating Haldol.

Now he's my star pupil—a future conqueror of Poland, a closet irredentist.

" 'Both' is a *good* answer," I assure Looney, conscious I am standing between him and a blackboard. "But *east* is more precise."

An hour later I'm wrapping the session up with some applied mathematics, inspired by my surprising encounter with Two-Tears.

"Okay, Teacup, let's say you're down for a double dime, running wild. You get good-time and work credit for *half* the first leg. The rest of the time you're strained up in the Shoe. How long to expire the first sentence?"

Teacup scribbles furiously on his pad, adding, subtracting, calculating his way to mathematical freedom.

"Anyone? Anyone can answer." I'm a collaborative kind of pedagogue. Teacup, calculations complete, raises his hand.

"Well, you have to subtract out twenty months good time for the first nickel—but you add *back* twenty months work credits, sooo . . . you're looking at another three and a half years till you roll over to the wild leg."

It's moments like this that make teaching a rewarding avocation.

Almost.

"Class dismissed."

. . .

"Who's up first, O.G.?" Ringer is already tired, anxious to get home for the Fourth of July holiday.

I consult my clipboard with today's roster of reprobates.

"Cheslewick, Walter. Six-two-one-three-nine. A fish. General violation G-2: unauthorized or unwanted contact with a private citizen."

Ringer yells out to Stanger, who is keeping order on the bench. "Send in *Cheesedick!*"

"Cheesedick! On your feet!" Stanger slams this skinny white boy down in the chair and races back out to the bench.

The kid gazes first at Ringer, then me, his lawyer. His green eyes are glowing not with anger or even apprehension, but with the fire of the True Believer.

"That's *Cheslewick,* sir," he says. Ringer glances at me to confirm this assertion. Convicts will lie about anything.

"That's correct—*Cheslewick,* Walter." I didn't survive years of downsizing, restructuring, streamlining, and market repositioning without adding value to whatever process I was involved in. Ringer picks up a copy of the write-up.

". . . and are charged with a violation of the Nevada Code of Penal Discipline, G-2, in that, despite previous verbal warnings, you persisted in attempting to establish unwanted contact via a series of letters with a private citizen, one Jodie Foster, said repeated attempts constituting harassment. How do you plead?"

I counseled him to plead guilty.

"Not guilty," he says with the serenity of the full-blown fanatic. "It's my First Amendment right to correspond with anyone I want."

Ringer sighs the universal sigh of the Beleaguered Civil Servant. We have twenty-three more hearings to go today.

"Before I pronounce you guilty, is there anything you want to tell me?"

Cheesedick shakes his head, empowered with First Amendment righteousness.

"Inmate substitute counsel Lerner—any factors in mitigation you wish to present?"

The best I can do here is preserve my client's good time—no way to keep him out of the Hole. I check my notes.

Cheesedick is down behind a "stalking" charge—an ex-girlfriend dropped a dime on him. Nothing mitigating there.

"I think not," I say. "Mr. Cheslewick would respectfully request that any sanctions imposed do not include the loss of category A stat time." I give Cheesedick a cautionary look—*please don't say anything.*

Cheesedick decides to make a speech.

"*Fuck!* The prison, *this* fucking prison, showed us her movie, *Contact*! All I did was write her telling her how great she was in the movie and asking for her photograph. How the fuck is that *harassment?*" Cheesedick, who has never heard of a movie called *Taxi Driver* or of a fellow True Believer named John Hinckley, is about to be buried beneath the weight of some sordid history.

"Mr. Cheesedick, six-two-one-three-nine, I find you guilty of G-2. I find that eighty-three letters requesting photos, including fifty-seven specific requests to 'show me your titties,' constitutes harassment. Sanctions imposed are 180 days of disciplinary segregation and loss of all stat time."

Cheesedick just sits there smiling, convinced that somehow news of his martyrdom will reach Jodie Foster.

"What the fuck are you grinning at?" Ringer demands, anxious to get home in time for the fireworks.

"Well, I can still write letters—that's a First Amendment right." Cheesedick is already mentally composing his letter to Jodie, telling her of his latest sacrifice for love.

"Sure," says Ringer, "but you'll have to write your fan letters without pen, pencil, or paper for 180 days. Sergeant Stanger—*next!*"

Stanger storms in, yanking Cheesedick up by his belly chains. Cheesedick screams out his last words.

"THEN I'LL WRITE IT IN MY OWN FUCKING BLOOD ON THE CELL WALLS!" Ringer is not saddened by this threat.

"Christ, I hate this fucking job, O.G. Don't we have any *normal* shit going down on the yard? A good old-fashioned slock and cock or something? Happy fucking Fourth of July!"

"Happy Fourth, Mr. Ringer."

Prison stories—that is, convict war stories—tend to have a common culprit. Behind almost every Fall—and most Slips—lurks the Bitch Who Snitched Me Out. The odious Oz girl behind the curtain goes by several names—girlfriend, fiancée, old lady, main squeeze, ho, slut, common-law, even wife, although I have yet to meet anyone here who is legally married.

The preferred epithet, of course, is "bitch," pronounced with two syllables: be-*yaaatch*, accent on the drawn-out second syllable. It is invariably preceded by "the fucking." The Fucking Be-*Yatch* is blamed by convicts for a wide range of societal afflictions that the Stand-up Man must endure—domestic battery laws, child support, rape and kidnapping allegations. Even AIDS—"The Fucking Be-*Yatch* gave me the *nasty* stanky on the hang-low." Sometimes "nasty" can be a very bad thing.

Spoony finally cops to Mandy being a Fucking Be-*Yatch*. (She's still a Be-Yatch without dial tone.)

"She snitched me out, O.G.," Spoony confesses one night. I toss a Hershey's Kiss up to the top bunk. Good for encouraging some catharsis. Chickenshit for the soul.

"Sorry to hear about that, Spoony," I say, not sorry at all but simply preoccupied. Kansas and the Car are selling wolf tickets about Stanger—"Smackin' Spoony was *way* outta line!" With my Parole

Board decision due soon, the last thing I need is a bogus write-up behind the Shit Jumping Off.

And, as Richard Nixon loved to say, *Make No Mistake.* The Shit is definitely about to Jump Off. Stanger and the Dirt have crossed the Righteous Con line one too many times. It's more than Kansas and his outraged dawgs will tolerate.

And "getback," Kansas says, "is going to be a motherfucker!"

Spoony is dribbling out his tale of Be-Yatch treachery. It seems the police and the D.A. pressured Mandy to rat out Spoony's little crank-dealing enterprise at the trailer park. Promised to drop charges against her if she would cooperate. A no-brainer for Mandy, whose modest career aspirations never included becoming some Cellblock Be-Yatch for the bull dyke contingent at the Nevada Women's Detention Center.

". . . but I forgive her, O.G. She just did what she had to do." (Don't we all, Spoony?) "And I still love her." My mother would tell Spoony that "love fades." She might also add that "beauty fades." Or that "this too shall pass." Good advice.

I roll over and go to sleep.

And have my nightmare about the Monster.

Waiting for the Parole Board decision, I analyze things too much now, a by-product of having "nothin' but time," of having added "prisoner" to my once-pristine (well, *slightly* besmirched) and glittering résumé. With any luck the current ruling brigades of Political Correctitude will shortly add "ex-felon" to its ever-expanding list of oppressed species. The phone company, always sensitive to accusations of "nondiverse hiring practices" (and potential EEO-based lawsuits), will be forced to give me a job in the mail room.

Deep in the basement.

Where I will charge for xeroxing services. A rollie per page. Got an urgent memo? Need fifty copies? Kick me down three stamps! You got nothing? Then you got *nothin'* comin', you punk-ass corporate bitch!

And if anyone whispers about the strange creature hoarding toilet paper and tobacco and pieces of soap and string in the basement mail room, if anyone *points* at me, then it's *on*!

Want to know the quickest way to get maimed or killed in the joint? A very simple recipe—I'll share it: point at someone. *What? Whatchu talkin' 'bout, O.G.?*

Pointing at someone?

Let's say (since this happened to me) you're just walking along in the yard, kicking rocks and kickin' it with your road dog, who happens to be Chico. Some skinheaded FNG ("fucking new guy") is pumping iron behind the Wood Pile's gated community. He's watching us.

"I know that fucking J-Cat from somewhere," Chico says, his Old Head never looking in the direction of the weight pile. Fish that I still am, I point a finger in J-Cat's direction, ask "Who? That guy with the horns tattooed on his head?" Chico's hand flashes up to seize mine, yanking it back down to my side just as we pass the horned J-Cat.

"Yo, dawg, you got a problem?" J-Cat yells through the gate. "You got a problem wid *me*?" Is he talking to me? Ta *me*?

Yes and yes.

"I *said* you got a fucking problem or something!" J-Cat drops the weight to the ground and puffs up his already impressive chest. A horned rooster on PCP, all puffed up and pissed off.

Chico saves my life.

"It's cool, dawg," he soothes J-Cat, "no disrespect intended—my homie here is still shaking off the Fish Tank." J-Cat considers this for a moment—only a fish would actually *point* at someone on the yard— and decides to let this bit of disrespect pass.

"Aiight—it's all good, dawgs." J-Cat tilts his horns back down to his weights, content to wait and watch for the next sliver of imagined disrespect to be slung in his direction.

Why this curious sensitivity behind pointing?

"Your Honor, at this time I would like permission to approach the witness."

"Permission granted—proceed."

"Thank you, Your Honor. Now, Miss . . . uh . . . Jennings, at this time I want you to identify your assailant, whom you have indicated is presently seated in this courtroom at the defendant's table." Miss Jennings starts to shake, then weep.

"Miss Jennings, would you please identify your assailant by pointing to him."

Miss Jennings points a trembling finger.

Case closed.

Point a finger at someone in the chow hall or the yard and you're fittin' to have it broke off and shoved up your ass.

I don't point anymore. E.T. could land in the middle of this yard with a flotilla of flying saucers and I still wouldn't point. I might remark, in passing, "Yo, dawgs, check out the extraterrestrial fish!" And as sure as God made little green apples and aliens, some dawg, tracking E.T.'s descent from the spaceship's portal, will say, "*Scandalous,* dawg! A green *punk-ass* alien!"

Without nobody pointing at nothin'.

And E.T. got *nothin'* comin'!

The Dirt came for Spoony in the middle of the night. Stanger ordered me out of the cell, facing the wall, hands on my head. Been there, done that, I thought. After handing Spoony the Notice of

Charges detailing the presence of unauthorized chemicals in his last
UA—crank and pot—they trussed him up as snugly as Hannibal
Lecter, while Spoony gobbled out the usual protestations of innocence.

"No way I tested dirty! You fuckers *planted* that shit in the UA. I
don't do no crank no more and I ain't smoked no pot since I fell!"

Stanger jerks Spoony to his feet and propels him face-forward into
the cell wall. *Craaack!* Bad for the wall.

Very bad for Spoony's dome.

The Dirt lead the semiconscious Spoony away, Stanger pausing to
sell me a quick wolf ticket. "You're *next,* O Fuckin' Gee!" he snarls.

Cell doors opening in A wing. The convict wolf tickets go on sale.

"Hey, Stanger!—you're the motherfucker that's *next!*"

"The Car be layin' in the muthafuckin' cut for yo' Dirt ass!"

"BACK IN YOUR FUCKING HOUSES!" Stanger screams. A
dozen steel sliders slam shut. No one wants to join Spoony in the Hole.

I have the cell to myself and it feels wonderful. Spoony will also
have a cell to himself.

My Old Head dawgs, Chico and Deathrow Dom, drop by my
house in the morning. No one has any real sympathy for Spoony. "If
you play, you pay!" Deathrow proclaims. Chico also knows it is the job
of the convict to break the rules and the job of the cops to catch
them—as long as the cops don't get out of line in the performance of
their duties.

"Spoony got what his hand called for," Chico says. The Old Heads
despise Yard Tricks like Spoony—they bring heat down on everyone.
Lifers have a vested interest in peace and stability. When you got nothing coming for life, you don't need any extra shit coming down on you.

I work out a deal with C.O. Fallon to indefinitely delay assigning
me another cellmate. Fallon has no problem with that. It seems he now
needs assistance with the not-uncommon second phase of divorce—
bankruptcy. I'm down with the forms.

I am now able to watch the local news without Spoony whining about Mandy, her dial-tone-dead phone, her (recently forgiven) Be-Yatch treachery.

O blessed silence!

I just try to Be Here Now, embracing the blessed privacy, the *serenity* of a cell of my own.

Bye-bye Spoony.

If you play, you pay.

Chico drops by after count and suggests I turn on the local TV news. What I see chills me. The big story concerns an ex-convict, a parolee from this prison. After three short weeks on parole in Las Vegas our former comrade decided he needed a car. He found the process of buying one to be an obstacle course of unfair and outrageous hurdles. The people who had the cars wanted money or credit or even a valid driver's license. No way he was going to put up with that kind of petty-ass bullshit after being down for six years. A righteous man does that kind of time and he's . . . well, he's *Entitled* to things!

He carjacked a Chevy Blazer that had stopped for a red light. After robbing and evicting the driver he drove the female passenger to a secluded construction site, where he raped and robbed her. That evening, drunk, stoned, and buying drinks for the crowd at his favorite biker bar, he bragged about his earlier adventures. The bar was a gathering place for ex-felons, practicing felons, and future ex-felons, some of whom saw an opportunity to solve their own legal problems by giving up this very unrighteous rapist.

The proverbial dime was dropped. Several of them. From the pay phone in the bar, the Chinese take-out next door, the phone at the gas station across the street.

After taking our erstwhile colleague into custody the police attributed the quick arrest to relentless police work and investigative prowess. The police, unlike Fitzgerald's rich, are just like the rest of us. They want to feel good about themselves too.

My stomach churns as the talking TV head describes the public outrage. The absolute shock and disgust that the Parole Board could release a "repeat violent offender," after he had served only the minimum four years on a four-to-ten voluntary manslaughter charge. State senators are clamoring for an investigation. The governor might get involved. Heads are expected to roll. Downhill.

"This is bad, Chico, very bad."

Chico, doing Life Without, is unconcerned.

"It's beyond bad, O.G. Wait till you see what happens next—it ain't gonna be nothin' nice. You feel like busting some pawns? It'll distract you from the sound of ten tons of shit rolling downhill."

"Sure, as long as you don't bust my grape."

It's been ten days since I built Major Rapport with the String Ties. When I thought I maybe had something coming.

As the bumper sticker says, SHIT HAPPENS.

I'm kicking it with Kansas in his cell, reading Mary's third letter to him (me). She is deeply moved by Kansas's letters, their tone of humility, kindness, tolerance, and love for all of God's children. (I may have gotten a bit carried away with this pen-pal project.)

"So break it on down to me, O.G. She lookin' to visit? I'm tired of all this letter shit."

The ingratitude! I can't let this slide. "Hey, dawg, *I'm* the one reading and answering these letters. It's exhausting to have to churn out lie after lie about how intelligent and sensitive you are."

"Fuck all that, O.G. Is she tryin' to visit me or not?" (In Conspeak, "trying" is synonymous with "wanting.")

"She'll be here in two weeks."

"*Aiight!* That's what I'm talkin' about!"

"We're going to have to have some coaching sessions first. I shared a few minor details about myself—*you*—that may not be entirely accurate."

"Whatchu sayin', O.G.?" Kansas is off the bunk and pacing.

I adjust my sore buns on the toilet seat. "Don't trip. A few tiny things you'll need to clean up—like you having a tattoo of a cross on your neck instead of a swastika."

Before Kansas can decide whether to bust my grape or peel my onion, C.O. Fallon is on the front porch.

"Lerner, you in there? You need to go see Wally—he got your Parole Board results."

Kansas gets back on his bunk so I can get to the door. He's wolfing.

"You better pray you catch some parole action, O.G. How the fuck am I supposed to show up at a visit with a goddamned *cross* on my neck?"

"Look . . . you just tell her it was a bad tattoo job—that you asked for a cross but it came out a bit, uh, twisted . . . and you're going to have it straightened out, like laser treatments or something. But that's not really a big deal. There's a few other sort of *major* things we have to go over."

And I'm out of the cell before Kansas can eviscerate me.

I sit in the steel folding chair and watch Wally searching for my file from the pile on his desk.

"Hmmm . . . I know I put it right over here with the other Parole Board results."

I feel myself aging five years in a minute.

Wally finally produces a pink sheet of paper. Frowns.

"Hmmm . . . this is unusual. In fact, quite irregular."

I don't know whether to shit, die, go blind, or just kill Wally.

"What? What is it? What's *irregular*?"

Still studying what I can only surmise is the wreckage of my future, Wally leans back in his chair and adjusts two errant gray strands on his head. An eternity passes before he hands me the paper.

YOUR APPLICATION FOR PAROLE IS DENIED. . . .

I didn't—*couldn't*—read past those first six words. It was like reading a death sentence. *Denied.* So at least another year *just on this first sentence alone*! Then what? Two, three, or even four years on the next sentence?

I can't breathe.

I'm looking at a minimum of two *more* years and that's assuming I can hang on to all my good-time and work credits. If I can't, then they can just keep denying me and I could end up doing the entire twelve years.

My M.B.A. brain runs the scenarios over and over. Best case: two more years. Probable case: three or four? Worst case: eight to eleven more.

I can't seem to get air—need to get a deep breath. There is a terrible pounding in my ears. So this is how a heart attack starts.

"Lerner, you all right?"

Wally is standing, looking alarmed. If I die in his office, he will have to fill out all sorts of complicated forms.

"I'm okay, Wally, just couldn't get my breath for a minute."

I was not unaware of the harsh political winds that had been blowing since our infamous "parolee" made the evening news. I somehow, deep down, did not believe that it could affect me. After all, I'm not a criminal. Not a *convict*. Maybe on paper but not where it counts—not in my heart or in my mind.

I force some air deep into my lungs. The same technique I use for making my cat noises.

"Wally, there has to be a mistake—I've never even been *down* before. I meet all the criteria for parole! I have a perfect work record, no disciplinary actions. Did they get my I-file mixed up with someone else's?"

Wally removes the pink form letter from my trembling fingers.

"Sorry, Jimmy, but I think not. But look at the upside. Next time you go back to the board you'll be armed with some *programming* certifications. We expect new funding shortly for our Anger Management Program, and we will most assuredly propound some new programs as well."

"Wally, I'm afraid that by the time you get funded, the benefits of Anger Management will be wasted on me."

Wally is relentlessly upbeat. "We'll probably be offering all kinds of new programs or bring back some of the old ones like Correcting Criminal Thinking Errors and maybe even . . ."

But the words don't reach me through the fog, don't even register, because I'm sinking down, down into the abyss. I can hear the roar of blood in my ears. I suddenly feel so exhausted, so utterly drained of life, that I must appear comatose.

". . . Jimmy, *Jimmy*! Are you all right?" Wally's voice filters down through the mist, a curtain so dense and dark that I can feel my soul disappearing.

"I think not, Wally. Thanks for the readout."

I fall asleep the moment my head touches the comfort of the Saint Mary's Hospice blanket that serves as my pillow.

O Mary, Sweet Mother of Mercy, succor this poor Jew in this, the hour of his need.

. . .

I slept for three days straight, not showing up at the law library or the chow hall or anywhere else. Every now and then, C.O. Fallon or one of my dawgs—Chico, Kansas, or Deathrow Dom— would tap gently on my cell door to awaken me. I would open my eyes and, seeing nothing worth waking for, go back to sleep, drinking deeply of the dark narcotic waters of Lethe. At 6 P.M. each day, I would rise, zombielike, for the institutional count.

Then fall back into the abyss.

I ate nothing, dreamed of nothing, and hoped for less.

PART THREE

THE FALL

He who fights with monsters might take care
lest he thereby become a monster.
And if you gaze for long into an abyss,
the abyss gazes also into you.
—FRIEDRICH WILHELM NIETZSCHE

The man takes a drink.
Then the drink takes a drink . . .
then the drink takes the man.
—OVERHEARD AT AN A.A. MEETING

Late at night in my cell the dreams always come. In my dreams there is a very bad place it seems I am required to visit nightly. It is a place of fear and darkness, a place of pain and death. I have come to think of it as the Killing Place.

Of course, there is also a Monster. What makes the Monster especially terrifying is the fact that he has a name.

The Monster's name is Dwayne Hassleman.

I met the Monster in church a year before I killed him.

He showed up at an A.A. meeting in Danville. I had been the speaker that night, and after the meeting he approached me and asked me to be his "sponsor." I had never "sponsored" anyone before, but I wasn't troubled by the prospect. In fact, I looked forward to it. It seemed like an opportunity for me to practice psychotherapy (without all the hard work of obtaining a degree), and I had always been adept at identifying the character defects and shortcomings of my fellows.

And I wasn't shy about helping others to recognize their faults.

In regard to myself I was far less rigorous in my judgments—infinitely charitable and forgiving. Consistency was not my strong point. Again, Emerson's "hobgoblin of little minds." My A.A. friends said I suffered from Denial. Big-time, Capital *D*.

I would respond with the standard recovery joke. "Denial? Isn't that a river in Egypt?" No one would laugh. Some of them would whisper (thinking I didn't hear) that I suffered from "spiritual bankruptcy." This is one of the worst things an A.A. member can suffer from. Almost as bad as drinking again. Some say it's worse. A contentious group, A.A. members rarely agree on anything.

A.A. "sponsorship" is not to be confused with sponsoring someone for membership into an exclusive country club. There isn't even a job description of "sponsor" in the A.A. "Big Book." If there was a formal description, I suspect most members would have ignored it. After first debating it for days.

Drunks, even the recovering variety, generally don't like to be told what to do.

That's one of the things I loved about the folks I met at A.A. meetings. A highly autonomous bunch. Bad for corporate team-building exercises, but fun to hang out with. I especially liked the "meeting after the meeting"—going to a coffee shop after the meeting and sharing vicious gossip about some of the people we were just hugging and smiling at.

You mean Jerry? Doesn't he have, like, fourteen years of sobriety?

Yeah, if smoking pot every day doesn't count.

No! You telling us Jerry's on the marijuana maintenance program?

Hey, I'm not taking the guy's moral inventory. That's between him and his Higher Power.

Hey, I hear Mark is working on his Thirteenth Step."

Again? Who's he fucking now?

You know that new girl, Tina, who just got out of the twenty-eight-day spin dry?

The role of sponsor, as I understood it, was to guide the newcomer through the Twelve Steps—the program of recovery. In practice, A.A. sponsorship often consists of simply listening to the newcomer's questions and concerns and taking their frantic (and often bizarre) middle-of-the-night phone calls:

"Joe, sorry to wake you—listen, I had another of those horrible dreams."

"Marvin? Is that you? What? A drinking dream? Don't worry about it. They are normal in your first few months of recovery. Go back to sleep."

"Nah, Joe. Not drinking or using. I dreamt my Higher Power was in my bedroom—he came up through the floorboards or something."

"Did he have a white beard and robe?"

"I wish. He had horns and a friggin' *tail*! Does this mean I'm going to drink?"

"No—it means you're going to hell! For chrissakes, it's four in the fucking morning!"

Sponsorship involves sharing one's own experience with drinking and recovery. Preaching, pedagogy, and moralizing are frowned upon, although plenty of it takes place.

I had recently been presented with a two-year "birthday chip" (a plastic "coin"), so when the scheduled speaker didn't show up (a not uncommon event in A.A. circles), I was asked by the group secretary, Doris, to substitute. To spend about fifteen minutes sharing my "experience, strength, and hope."

It was a small meeting, a Monday night. One of the few remaining "smoking meetings" in Danville, which is why I attended that particular meeting once a week. I had no intention of giving up all my vices at once. It had taken years of effort to cultivate them. That night, there were about twenty men and women sitting on the hard metal folding chairs, most of them grimly chain-smoking and guzzling coffee that was one-third sugar and cream. A box of chocolate chip cookies (homemade by Doris) and another box containing doughnuts (store-bought) were being circulated.

No one passed on either the cookies or the doughnuts. Recovery is hard work and requires lots of sugar-based calories.

Before turning the meeting over to me for my fifteen minutes of infamy, Doris (a frighteningly obese woman who insisted on greeting every arriving member at the door with a savagely prolonged hug) read the A.A. preamble and a section from the Big Book called "How It Works."

Doris then studied the faces in the room.

"Do we have any new members—anyone in their first, second, or third A.A. meeting?"

No one raised a hand or moved.

Doris continued. "Do we have anyone in their first thirty days of sobriety who would like to identify yourself by standing or raising your hand?" Doris tried an encouraging smile. Cracks appeared in all three chins. The effect was grotesque.

Again, no response. A few of the regular members were nervously studying the poster on the wall containing the Twelve Traditions. In the revolving door, endlessly recycling circle that characterizes the journey of so many A.A. members, publicly identifying oneself as having less than thirty days (after achieving thirty, sixty, or ninety days—or even thirty years—of sobriety) is tantamount to a public humiliation.

I personally had no problem with it. The public humiliation, that is. In my garage at home I had a whole coffee can full of thirty-, sixty-, and ninety-day chips. I even had a few six-month and three one-year chips.

Raising one's hand to announce one is (again) new to sobriety is a treasured A.A. meeting ritual. It's a public confession of backsliding. Of *sin*!

And A.A. loves nothing more than the public confession of sins. The more sordid, degenerate, and twisted, the better. Followed, of course, by displays of contrition. The contrition is preferably preceded by a "moment of clarity," which leads to the requisite "spiritual awakening." It's an old formula, right out of the tent-revival meetings, with a strong evangelical flavor. Just substitute sin for drunkenness and redemption for recovery (and even the Big Book for the Bible) and you've got the theological background Muzak for many A.A. meetings. In fact, the most popular A.A. speakers, the ones who make the rounds from city to city on the speaker circuit, all adhere to this boilerplate presentation:

A. *I drank too much and did terrible things* (describe in elaborate and shocking detail the illicit drunken sex, the violence, depravity, godless debauchery and criminality—it's best if you fell from great heights) *and finally I hit bottom and prayed for help, which is when . . .*

B. *I found God* (a Burning Bush experience goes over great), *quit drinking, and made amends to those I had hurt and . . .*

C. *Now I help other people, spreading the Good News to other alcoholics, praying only for the power to do His will.* (And *grateful* to be doing it. It's essential to work in the concept of gratitude—repeatedly.)

Given my cynicism about much of what went on, no one in A.A. was surprised that it took me almost ten years of intermittent A.A. meetings to acquire two years of continuous sobriety. I went through sponsors, the Twelve Steps, and myriad Higher Powers faster than a detoxing junkie goes through a box of Kleenex.

Given A.A.'s roots in a religious society (the Oxford Group), it's no coincidence that some A.A. meetings are filled with the same people who go to Bible study classes together. And people who like to preach. A.A. members insist (protesting too much, methinks) that the A.A. program is "spiritual," not "religious." But sometimes it sure waddles and quacks like a duck.

But I digress. I meant to tell you about the Monster.

When no one stood or raised a hand to identify himself as a new arrival (or wet recycle) to Planet Clean and Sober, Doris tried some gentle prodding, reading from a sheet of paper titled "A.A. Meeting Format":

"This is not to embarrass you but so that we may get to *know* you."
Doris looked up and beamed at the back row of chairs where newcomers always tried to hide. In her mid-thirties, with just eighteen months of sobriety, Doris had the grimly determined cheerfulness of the new convert.

She scared the hell out of me.

There were some muffled coughs and nervous shuffling of chairs. Then the Monster raised his hand and showed us a brave smile.

"I'm Dwayne—this is my first A.A. meeting." He didn't look like a monster. A handsome guy in his early forties, he looked like an ex-linebacker who got lost in an army surplus store. With his massive frame, combat boots (jungle green), and tiger-striped fatigue pants, Dwayne looked like he was determined to march and shoot his way toward sobriety.

Everyone clapped and a few of the old-timers yelled out "Welcome."

Dwayne settled his bulk back into the uncomfortable chair with an embarrassed smile. I had a few qualms about some of the less than attractive aspects of A.A. meetings (Big Book Thumpers and Twelve-Step Nazis headed my list), but I found most of the members to be warm, welcoming, and sincere in their desire to help each other and especially assist the newcomers. A few of the old-timers had spent a lot of (mostly futile) time trying to help me, and I loved them for it.

I guess you could say I was attracted to the fellowship and the principles of A.A. (such as tolerance of others) but often repelled by the behavior of some of the members. A stance not dissimilar to de Tocqueville's admiration of the *concept* of early American democracy but distrust of its practitioners.

Doris was making the usual announcements, reading from a memo. "On Friday night, there will be an A.A. young people's dance at the Veterans Hall . . . Johnny S., from Los Angeles, will be the speaker Saturday night at the Community Presbyterian Church—get there by seven if you want to get a parking spot . . . A weekend spiritual retreat in Carmel—the cost is three hundred dollars . . . Ray K. is in the V.A. Hospital with liver failure and would love some visitors . . ."

Ten minutes of announcements later, Doris motioned me to the speaker's podium at the front of the room. "Keep it short and simple, Jimmy," she said.

I had every intention of keeping my talk brief. My goal was to tell my story with as much honesty and humility as I could muster, trying to focus mostly on the benefits of being sober. I didn't find anything interesting or glamorous or instructive in my own drinking history, and I presumed my audience already knew about getting drunk. I always cringed inside when an A.A. speaker embarked on an endless "drunka-log," seeming to revel (and thereby glorify) in episodes from his or her drunken past. I often suspected that the speaker's colorful and passionate description of his drunken escapades revealed a deep and abiding thirst, a longing that could not be quenched by any number of meetings or "Big Book studies."

It was no surprise to me when I would hear that one of these circuit speakers had "slipped" and was drinking again.

I felt that my own story lacked sufficient drama. No vehicular manslaughter, no string of lost jobs, no drunken adultery (or even *sober* adultery) or wife-beating or prison sentences. Nor did my tale have the stuff of a Greek tragedy—no fall from great career or financial heights (although plenty of hubris was present) followed by years of rolling around in the gutter (preferably a gutter in the *Bowery*) in my own vomit. I still had my wife and kids, my house, a good job, two cars in the garage, and even a shirt or two without vomit stains.

To some A.A. members—particularly the hard-core old-timers— my good fortune simply meant that I hadn't yet "hit bottom." They would (and often did) say the *really* bad things just hadn't happened to me *yet*. They claimed that YET was an acronym for "you're eligible too." They had acronyms for everything.

I swear these people just made stuff up sometimes.

I often got the impression from some of the old-timers (who *had* lost everything) that they would love to see me hit bottom. To collect some YETs. To lose everything. For my own good, of course. So I would be more open and humble. Be ready to finally allow God to enter my life. To *surrender*.

Sort of a "misery loves company" kind of thing.

Since the only story I had to tell was my own, I told it. I forgot about being brief and to the point. I rambled and raved for the next forty minutes.

I told how the origin of my alcoholism was a mystery to me. No one in my family had a drinking or drug problem. So I couldn't blame it on genetics. My parents were both loving and supportive, and if they had any *dysfunctions* I never noticed or heard about them. My brother and sister went straight from college to medical school and law school, respectively, without any breaks for drugs or madness. They were both successful and well-adjusted professionals today.

"I was happy growing up," I told the A.A. meeting. "A great childhood."

Many blank faces, like stone, looked back at me. Some looked annoyed. A few were glaring at me. This was not the usual script.

Many A.A. members don't want to hear someone share about family unless that family was alcoholic, physically abusive, or, preferably, both. If you say you had a *happy childhood,* you are clearly in denial. You have more work to do to unearth your miserable inner child. You need to get *honest*!

I talked a little about the sixties. The little that I remember.

I've been thinking about who made that observation about the sixties. Maybe it wasn't Abbie Hoffman. Maybe it was Wavy Gravy, that quintessential sixties hippie, who had that great line about "the only people who remember the sixties weren't there." I don't remember much of the sixties, but friends of mine who do tell me that I missed a lot. That I may have lingered a bit too long around the communal bong, pondering Jefferson Airplane lyrics (and later, the suicidally depressing "Songs of Leonard Cohen"). That my inquisitive and intrepid spirit compelled me to try every mind-altering drug at least once.

My basic research on Quaaludes alone demanded my attention for close to an inattentive year of my young life. (At the mention of drugs, Luther, a dyspeptic old-timer, started scowling at me from across the room.) Even as a teenager, in addition to a fondness for pot and hash and pills (the ones that make you larger—or smaller), I was open-minded about booze. Unlike some of my post-Beat buddies who looked down on alcohol as the province of parents, politicians, and "juiceheads," I had no such elitist pretensions.

I was a longhaired teenage hippie desperately trying to conform to the freethinking hippie herds around me. Part of my job description was to be open to all potential mind-altering experiences.

As an equal-opportunity abuser of mind-altering substances, in college I developed a fondness for Andre's Cold Duck champagne as well as the occasional (or frequent) glass of Boone's Farm apple "wine." And forget the glass—wrecks the bouquet. On my college campus a goatskin flask was the only way to imbibe. Then pass the flask. That was when I was still a "social drinker."

Protected from Vietnam by a high number in the lottery, I took a semester off from Brooklyn College to drive a cab. In the early seventies it was a New York hippie rite of passage. We would eat Black Beauties (amphetamines) and pick up fares without a break for hours.

Later we'd drink and take 'Ludes to come down. I would pick up my cab from the garage at Flatbush and Nostrand Avenue every day at 3 P.M. I'd work the Manhattan streets (harder work but more lucrative than the airports or hotels) until about two in the morning, pocketing as much cash as I could. The cab company provided the cab, the gas, and the insurance. In return they were entitled to 50 percent of the meter.

On my first night as a cabdriver my union rep (an old-time Teamster) instructed me in how to steal.

"Ya don't wanna book too much. Makes the rest of us look bad. Ya book maybe seventy, eighty bucks on the meter and that's it. The rest you leave the flag down. No fucking meter. Just make up the trips on the sheet. The customers don't mind as long as you give them a good discount on the fare. Fuck, they're *New Yorkers.* Above eighty bucks you keep the money. Here's your pancake so you can control the meter and the off-duty lights."

The "pancake" was a simple coil of wires wrapped in electrical tape and attached to two stereo jacks, which could be plugged into both the meter and the overhead medallion lights. I could work both the meter and the off-duty light with a toggle switch. The union dispatcher also made sure I knew how to steal before letting me have the keys to the cab.

After bringing the cab back to Brooklyn and handing in my fictitious "trip" sheet I would join my fellow thieves at a bar, where we would down boilermakers and swap tall cabbie stories till dawn.

My cabdriving career came to an abrupt end when (a bit confused after miscalculating a combination of 'Ludes and Beauties) I crashed the cab into a fire hydrant on East 57th Street. Lots of property damage. And water.

I spent that night in the Manhattan jail known as the Tombs, down on Centre Street. The cops had found Black Beauties and 'Ludes in the cab. There was talk of felony charges. Plus fines. Fire hydrant medical bills, I guess.

The U.S. Army saved me. With the Vietnam War requiring a monthly infusion of new bodies, all sorts of legal problems could be forgiven. I was given the option of facing a criminal trial (and a probable prison sentence) or "enlisting" for a four-year stretch in the infantry. Charges would be dismissed. The record expunged.

I opted for the four-year enlistment and never regretted it.

I never made it to Vietnam. After basic training at Fort Jackson, South Carolina (and advanced infantry training at Fort Polk, Louisiana), I did well on some aptitude tests and was selected to attend the Defense Language Institute in Monterey, California. I studied Spanish there for six months before being sent to Panama.

Political control of the Canal Zone was becoming a major issue in U.S. foreign policy, and the army wanted trained personnel there ("onsite specialists") who were also fluent in Spanish. I was assigned to *Escuela de las Américas*—School of the Americas. We were a training center for military units from Central and South American countries. Courses were offered in everything from infantry tactics to psy-ops— psychological operations. A lot of people would later charge that it was a U.S. "spy school"—a center for electronic intercept warfare and many other clandestine activities.

I wouldn't know. I was an NCO in the administration center. I filled out supply requisition forms during the day and drank at night. Every night. (This got approving nods from the A.A. old-timers. Even sour old Luther beamed.)

It was in Panama, in my twenties, while defending democracy from a barstool, that I developed a deep friendship with guys with macho names like Jack Daniel's and Johnnie Walker. I once (I've been told) leaped off a second-floor Panama City hotel balcony and into the swimming pool. I thought I was interviewing for a test pilot position with Jack Daniel's. (Laughs from the room.)

Catholic in my tastes, I made room in that circle of friends for Comrade Smirnoff and Señor Cuervo. Beer and wine went down just fine too, but I preferred the hard stuff because it worked faster.

I began to drink for the effect, not to be social. On more occasions

than I cared to remember, I went into the NCO club at 5 P.M. intend-
ing to have no more than two drinks and ended up closing the place
down at 2 A.M. Drunk beyond belief and all reason.

And sometimes not remembering anything after the fourth or fifth
drink.

The blackouts were the scary part. Friends (fellow alcoholics) at the
NCO club would assure me the next day that I was a happy, peaceful
drunk, although very silly. Not to worry, Jimmy-boy! Besides, there's
nothing else to do in this godforsaken country.

Not remembering terrified me. The blackouts were what finally
convinced me I had a real problem and couldn't drink at all. I began my
twenty-year war with John Barleycorn.

I would gather up all my willpower, all the considerable strength of
my (presumed) rationality, and quit drinking. For a month. Or a year.
Then I would drink as if I had to make up for lost time. Drink insanely
for two or three days or even a month before invariably coming to my
senses and again quitting for months, or even two years.

This pattern had gone on for a long time. For many years. The wife
was pretty sick of it. I would come home from work at 6 P.M. and
steadily drink Scotch in front of the TV until it was time for bed (which
meant passing out). My little girls (especially as they got older) were
both mystified by it and afraid of the transformation from Rational
Dad to Babbling, Incoherent Dad.

"Jimmy, why don't you go to bed?" the wife would plead.

"Sure, yesssh, shune's this show's over."

"Dad, puh-lease go to bed," the older girl would beg.

Not a pretty picture—a very painful one and one I was determined
never to present again to my family. Or to anyone else.

If I had a bottom, it was the image of my older daughter's horrified
face when I interrupted her slumber party one night by stumbling
drunkenly around the living room looking for God only knows what.

I had humiliated her in front of her friends, and my own subsequent humiliation and remorse and guilt were overwhelming.

Pitiful and incomprehensible demoralization is the apt A.A. description.

I could rationalize the harm I was doing to myself, but I could not excuse the pain I was inflicting on my loved ones. My demoralization and self-hatred were complete. I had reached what A.A. calls the "jumping-off point."

So welcome to A.A., Jimmy. A.A. had a healthy chapter in Danville, lots of meetings every day of the week. Twelve-step recovery programs were in suburban vogue in the nineties, and, having experienced the sixties zeitgeist of excess, I was not about to miss out on the abstinence and spirituality trip of the nineties. Know what I'm saying?

Of course, I had good reasons to drink (unlike "real" alcoholics who drank because of character weakness and moral depravity). Unique reasons. I had job pressures. Bills to pay. Financial concerns—the uncertain direction of my 401(k). My girls were going to need orthodontia. Probably college as well. The fed might cut interest rates and then I'd have to refinance the mortgage again. A nerve-racking ordeal! There were worries about guns in school, the environment, and the deteriorating (isn't it always?) geopolitical situation.

My reasons for drinking were valid and endless.

When concerned friends earnestly asked why I drank so much, why I got drunk, I had no answer. No answer that made any sense. I was baffled (and sickened) by my drinking behavior. The standard A.A. response to the question is a simple one, although not particularly explanatory: "I drink too much because I'm an alcoholic." This would be expressed in the same way that a diabetic might explain why he used insulin.

I had no answers. I had the ability to forget the discomfiture of one day's horrible hangover by 5 P.M. the next day. In the meetings they say

alcohol is cunning, baffling, and powerful. That it is also the only disease that tells you that you don't have a disease.

I did know that I *deserved* a drink. I worked hard, made good
money, and paid the mortgage. I was, in the peculiar Jewish jargon of
Flatbush Avenue in the 1950s, a *Good Provider.* A Good Provider is entitled to get shit-faced every now and then. A bit of well-deserved relaxation.

And yet, despite my elaborate denial system, I didn't want any more
YETs. I didn't want to lose my family, the love and affection (what still
remained) of my wife and children. Didn't want to lose my job or have
to get on a list for a liver transplant (which they won't give you if you
are an alcoholic—unless you are Mickey Mantle, which I wasn't) or get
drunk and kill someone while driving.

I never wanted to hurt anyone.

I certainly didn't want to kill anyone.

I stood at the podium in the church basement and (heed-
ing Doris's urgent whispers) finished talking about my drinking history—what A.A. calls "qualifying." Of course, despite my best
intentions, I had just delivered a lengthy drunkalog. I then launched
into my uneven experience with the program, the steps, and sponsorship. My ongoing struggle to find a Higher Power that made sense to
me. My skepticism about the whole process. The lack of role models in
A.A. The strong scent of religion in A.A. not quite masked by the
vanilla language of "spirituality."

By this time the old-timers were shaking their heads in consterna-
tion. I had been babbling and rambling for almost forty minutes. Doris
made an elaborate display of checking her watch and waving at me. She
held up two plump fingers. But I was on a roll and *hey, Doris, I didn't*

volunteer to speak. I plunged on, or, as the A.A. expression goes, having hit rock bottom, I started to drill.

In the remaining two minutes I managed to work in the choice tidbit that the A.A. founder, Bill Wilson, had been fond of LSD. That the leader of the Oxford Group (which Bill Wilson and Dr. Bob belonged to) was a Nazi supporter. I may have said something to the effect that even the A.A. gods, Bill and Dr. Bob, had clay feet.

With seconds remaining I quickly (and pompously) delivered a lecture on the benefits of getting psychiatric treatment and mood-altering drugs. My own shrink, Dr. Shekelman, had me on Prozac and Trazodone for depression, Xanax for anxiety and panic attacks, and Restoril for insomnia. I shared his philosophy—A.A. heresy!—with the group that alcoholism is not a "disease," but a symptom of other underlying disorders.

A stunned silence in the room.

Doris's face was a red balloon of outrage. Strangled noises were coming from her mouth. Most of the old-timers just stared at me, slack-jawed and benumbed. I figured it was time for a strong close.

Always leave them laughing. So I ended my little talk with a joke.

"What," I addressed the group through a thick haze of smoke, "do you call a dyslexic, agnostic alcoholic with insomnia?"

Since no one would play straight man for me, I provided the punch line without help.

"Someone who lies awake at night wondering if there really is a Dog! Ha! I love that joke!" Since I was the only one laughing, I turned the meeting back to Doris. "Thank you all for listening, and thank you, Doris, for asking me to speak."

"Thank you, Jimmy." Doris favored me with a horrified look. "Keep coming back." She then took her place back at the podium and began reading more A.A.-related announcements from an A.A. Central Office flyer before addressing the group.

"Does anyone have a topic for the meeting tonight?"

Everyone must have been energized by my little speech, because hands were going up and people were all talking and shouting at once.

"How about *gratitude,* Doris—that's always a good topic." Luther, the old-timer, always suggested gratitude. Luther was in his late sixties, with twenty-three years of sobriety, a full head of white hair, and two spare truck tires rolling around his midsection. He had a hacking smoker's cough and a bright red pizza face of burst capillaries. Luther was also awaiting trial for soliciting a prostitute (who turned out to be an undercover policewoman) in San Francisco.

Luther had been my first A.A. sponsor (for about a month) before I fired him. He claimed he couldn't be fired because the job paid nothing, so he continued to act as if he were my sponsor, giving me unsolicited advice (including marriage, career, and financial counseling). Luther's favorite theme was my "denial." In addition to being a self-appointed A.A. guru, Luther attended Overeaters Anonymous, Narcotics Anonymous, Smokers Anonymous, and now, at his lawyer's suggestion, Sex Addicts Anonymous.

Luther liked to say that "a man can quit drinking but the disease just moves on to some other addiction—it's like squeezing a balloon."

Paul, a starved-looking teenager wearing all black (including eyeliner and leather gloves with the fingers cut off), objected to the topic. Paul was court-ordered to A.A. as part of a plea bargain. He and his Goth-boy buddies had been caught attempting an (unauthorized) exhumation of a body from the local cemetery. Alcohol and drugs were said to be involved. (We all hoped so.) A.A. picks up a lot of new members this way. It doesn't have to recruit.

Paul shook a gloved fist at the Twelve Steps on the wall and snarled.

"*Fuck* gratitude! That's been the topic for the last ten meetings! I'm fucking sick of it!"

Doris, grateful to have me away from the podium, went into her "trusted servant" mode attempting to facilitate. "Well, Paul, would you like to suggest a different topic?"

Paul glared at Luther, then smiled sweetly at Doris.

"Yeah, how 'bout *resentment*! That's a *real* topic!"

Then all the hands went up and the room filled with shouted suggestions.

"Letting go and letting God!"

"Acceptance! That's always a good topic!"

"Fuck *that* bullshit too! *Resentment!* How about it, Doris?"

"Hey, you know we got a newcomer here. We should have a topic about the First Step. Or the Serenity Prayer."

"Or powerlessness! That's a good newcomer topic."

"*Surrender!* That's the best newcomer topic!"

The newcomer, Dwayne Hassleman, just sat there bewildered, trying to disappear into his chair, clearly mortified to suddenly be the center of attention.

"No, we did 'surrender' last month at the Lutheran Church—how about 'making amends'?"

"Fuck your bullshit amends. The topic should be fucking *resentment*!"

And on and on until Doris called for a "group conscience"—a vote.

The topic of gratitude won for the eleventh consecutive meeting. Doris shared how she was grateful to God for providing everything she needed, "although not everything I want—but thank God that today I know the difference." She had recently been having car problems and she was currently praying to God for a new transmission.

This comment pissed Paul off, who felt compelled to violate the (unwritten) A.A. rule against cross-talk.

"Yo, Doris," he sneered. "Hey, you think God gives a fuck about your *car*? Why don't you just wait until you're hungry, then lock yourself in a closet and pray for a hot dog?"

Luther came to Doris's aid. "No cross-talk in this meeting, Paul."

"Fuck that bullshit! What are you supposed to be? The fucking Red Cross?"

And on and on till Doris wisely ended the meeting with the Lord's Prayer and the hand-holding-in-a-circle ritual.

"Jimmy, will you please lead us out?"

"Thank you, Doris. Let this circle represent . . . that we no longer have to stand . . . in a *square*—ha!" Sometimes I wish there was an Assholes Anonymous because that group might be my true spiritual home. When no one chuckled at my intro to the prayer, I bowed my head, said "Our Father . . ." and everyone, including some of our court-ordered alcoholic atheists, joined in the chorus.

It was a bonding thing.

Doris closed out the meeting with the usual advisory about anonymity. "Who you see here and what you hear in these rooms *stays* in these rooms."

We all nodded solemnly. In ten minutes some of us would be at Denny's (which had the last smoking section in Danville) "taking the inventory" (see "bad-rapping") of some of our fellows. Recovery is said to be all about "progress, not perfection." We were proof of that.

After the meeting I stayed around to dump out ashtrays and help stack and put away the chairs. Doris hugged me and thanked me for speaking.

"Jimmy, thanks for your chair—it was very, uh . . . *unusual*."

"Thanks, Doris. Sorry if I got off track there a little bit." I was struggling to extricate myself from her iron embrace.

In the linguistic subculture of A.A., people are thanked for their "chairs." I was tempted to thank Doris for her couch or dining room table, but I stifled this impulse (which I now recognize as a Sideways Dysfunction) and just thanked her. Somewhere in the Big

Book it is suggested that "restraint of tongue" is occasionally a good idea.

Occasionally I could follow a suggestion.

The church parking lot was dark with a soft summer breeze rustling the trees. The newcomer, Dwayne, stepped out from the shadows and intercepted me as I walked to my car.

"You're Jimmy, right? Listen, I really liked your chair tonight and I was wondering if you would be my sponsor." I immediately liked the guy. He was the first person to say he liked my chair. You had to respect someone with such discernment.

Hand extended, smiling, there were no external clues to suggest a monster might lurk within. A lot of guys walked around in camouflage pants and army boots. Taller than me, about six-three, Dwayne was about my age, with brown hair clipped short, practically military style. There was nothing but warmth and apparent good humor in his green eyes. Easily over two hundred pounds, mostly muscle, Dwayne was clearly not a stranger to the gym.

His handshake was something else. Forget firm—it was an Attempted Assault on my delicate, frustrated pianist's fingers. Excessive pressure, held excessively long.

It should have been my first real clue.

Dwayne followed me in his car to Denny's, where the nose-ringed teenage "hostess" snapped her gum (showing us a stud through her tongue) and snickered when I asked for the smoking room.

"Your other A.A. friends are already there."

So much for anonymity. Small towns are like that. "Thanks, Cindy, but we'll get our own table."

Dwayne and I took a table out of earshot of Luther, Doris, Don, Johnny, and some of the others. Their table was already piled with chocolate cake and bowls of ice cream.

Dwayne smoked, drank black coffee loaded with sugar, and told me his story.

I smoked, drank Cherry Coke (with a maraschino cherry in it), and listened. Did my best to appear sponsorlike. Nodded slowly and seriously. Occasionally uttered a "hmmm" or "yes." Like a guru. Like Yoda from *Star Wars.*

Dwayne was forty-three. He had an ex-wife and three kids back east. He wasn't on speaking terms with any of them. He'd moved to the Bay Area after his divorce almost ten years ago. He was currently on some kind of physical disability from a corporate sales job in San Francisco.

"What company, Dwayne?"

The eyes flickered to the ceiling.

"Well, actually I worked for quite a few different Fortune 500 companies—sort of a roving troubleshooter, you know, sales quality issues." My bullshit detector was going off. I didn't know you could *rove* that easily from one company to another and still get medical benefits, but I had nothing to do with sales—or quality.

I was in marketing. The long-term planning district. We viewed ourselves as a giant step above sales. We were *strategists,* deep thinkers. Visionaries.

After a little more small talk, Dwayne launched into his lengthy drug history.

". . . and then I got into this whole scene where I was shooting an eight ball every day and got hurt on the job and had to go on disability . . ."

I listened, wondering why Dwayne had showed up at an A.A. meeting.

There was no alcohol in Dwayne's story. Not that there's anything wrong with that. Dwayne's tale was all cocaine and speed, barbiturates and morphine and heroin. Lots of needles, lots of drama—but no alcohol. If it hadn't been for my own fear of needles, I'm sure I would have made a passionately committed heroin addict.

However, I was not a drug counselor. I had pretty much abandoned drugs (the *illegal* kind) years ago, replacing them with alcohol. (I didn't consider my Xanax or Prozac or sleeping pills to be *drugs*—they were *prescribed medications*. Oh, and what is the name of that river in Egypt?) I was not an alcohol counselor either. I was just some guy who had been fortunate enough to stay away from the booze for a couple of years.

A guy who didn't know it then but who still had some major YETs.

But Dwayne was on a roll. My wife and kids would all be in bed, probably asleep by the time I got home. There was no rush. I didn't need to be in my phone company cubicle until eight o'clock tomorrow morning. We had some "emergency" meeting later in the morning with the network planning and engineering lobs. Something about the country running out of area codes. The 800 numbers were almost all used up. The way some of the techno-geeks were whining you'd think it was like an oil crisis or something.

Sure wasn't a *marketing* problem—I knew that much. There were also rumors that the phone company was a takeover target by an even bigger Baby Bell. Now, *that* was a marketing concern—a paycheck issue. Dwayne was still rolling while I wondered if there might not be some marketing opportunity lurking in the number-shortage crisis. As I've said, I had been specifically trained to fashion opportunities (or the appearance of them) from apparent problems.

". . . so right now, I got about twenty days clean, no using anything, but—"

"Excuse me, Dwayne. But what brought you to an A.A. meeting? It doesn't sound like you have any alcohol problems. Not that that's anything to be ashamed of."

Dwayne exhaled some smoke and nodded sadly, almost guiltily. You know the whole twelve-step movement has gotten out of hand when people feel bad about *not* having a certain addiction. Like it's something that will keep them from fitting in.

"Yeah, Jimmy . . . I know. I don't drink much—I like a few beers now and then but I don't go crazy with it. You see, I've been going to Narcotics Anonymous, and . . . I just don't like the people there—I don't know, it's like the quality of sobriety in those meetings isn't very good. I like A.A. much better."

"How do you know? I thought tonight was your first meeting."

Dwayne's eyes again searched the ceiling. They were a startling shade of green—preternaturally green. Colored contacts?

"It *was* my first meeting. I just meant that the people seem friend-lier at A.A., more helpful. I grew up in New York so I'm always amazed when complete strangers, like you, Jimmy, are friendly."

This got my attention. Not the false flattery.

"Where in New York are you from, Dwayne?"

"Brooklyn. Like you. That's one of the things I really identified with when you told your story. I left when I got divorced almost ten years ago."

I left Brooklyn over twenty years ago. When I received an offer from Uncle Sam that I couldn't refuse. In all that time in the Bay Area I had met a few transplanted New Yorkers but no one from Brooklyn. I was stoked.

"Whereabouts in Brooklyn?"

"Park Slope, but before the yuppies gentrified all the fun and dan-ger out of it."

I laughed so hard some Cherry Coke sprayed out through my nose. I hate when that happens. For the next hour we forgot about A.A. and the steps and recovery and just swapped Brooklyn memories. Or our rose-colored reinventions.

"Jimmy, did you know Barbra Streisand when you went to Erasmus?"

"Nope—she was before my time."

"How about Neil Diamond—didn't he go there too?"

"I don't know—didn't he go to a yeshiva or something?"

Dwayne took a deep drag on his Marlboro and considered. "I don't know about that. I went to parochial school."

"That's all right—we all have something to be ashamed of."

We laughed so hard Luther and the others looked up from their table, spoonfuls of ice cream cake frozen in midair.

We compared Brooklyn to San Francisco, New York to California, and in the delusional tradition of native New Yorkers declared all things New York to be the winner. Of course, it was not exactly an apples-to-apples comparison. We were comparing the New York of our youth to the San Francisco of today. Contrasting the soft golden myth that memory can make of youth to harsh grown-up realities.

By this yardstick, everything in New York was superior—especially the prices of food. (We didn't bother to adjust for twenty years of inflation.) Pizza was better (crispier crust); Chinese food was better (*real* wonton soup with meat inside the wonton, plus they gave you those crispy noodles for the soup for *free*). Hot dogs? French fries? No comparison. One word covered it all—*Nathan's!* We discussed pickles and pastrami and corned beef, Ebinger's bakery and New York cheesecake (not this New York–*style* heavy-crusted crud that they sold "out here").

We ignored all the reasons we were glad to leave New York, all the reasons we *preferred* California, especially the San Francisco Bay Area—the great weather, the beautiful scenery, the nicer, friendlier people. Left unsaid was our relief at escaping the crime-ridden, graffitied cesspool that New York was becoming in the mid-seventies.

"Californians *are* nice," Dwayne said, "but I don't know, they're *too* nice—they don't seem *real* somehow. No, that's not right—they're just not direct and *honest* like New Yorkers."

"New Yorkers are *authentic*!" I concluded, smacking my glass down for emphasis.

Dwayne slammed a hand the size of my old Yogi Berra's catcher's mitt on the table, spilling half his coffee.

"*Authentic!* That's what I'm talking about. A New Yorker will tell you exactly what he thinks—to your *face*—none of this 'Have a nice smiley day' bullshit and then stab you in the back."

"Precisely. New Yorkers are authentically *rude*."

"*Brutally* honest—more brutal than honest, come to think of it."

And we were laughing again because we didn't miss the rudeness or the crowded subways or the cold and winter snow that temporarily concealed acres of dog turds.

What we missed were the innocence and boundless possibilities of youth.

"Jimmy, did you ever play skelly back in Brooklyn?" The question came out as *didjaver play . . .* We were both automatically regressing to the rhythms and contractions of the native New Yawker.

"Sure, we usta get the bottle caps from the machine at Lenny's deli."

"The one on Parkside? Up the block from Louie's? Where you could get an egg cream or a Dr. Brown's and read Superman comics all day?"

"That's the one, Dwayne."

"Ged-*adda*-here!"

"How 'bout stoopball? You need the front stoop and a great eye."

"And you gotta have that special ball—what was the name of that?"

"A penny pinkie?"

"No—a *pensy* pinkie!"

"That's it!"

"And stickball—with a sawed-off broomstick for your bat."

"And home plate was a manhole cover on the street."

It was about eleven when we finally left, with Luther giving me strange agitated looks from his table. In the parking lot Dwayne and I swapped phone numbers. I promised to call him by the end of the week. We would get together and figure out the best way for Dwayne to get a sponsor. Even if it wasn't an A.A. sponsor.

"It probably won't be me, though, Dwayne. I don't think I'm qualified."

"That's cool, Jimmy, 'cause I feel like we're friends now and I think a sponsor, at least at first, should not be a good friend. He needs to be objective, you know, tough love and all."

As soon as I started my car, the phone chirped. It was Luther, self-appointed guardian of the A.A. Traditions.

"Jimmy, glad I caught you. Listen, I hope you're not thinking of sponsoring that guy Dwayne."

"Why not? I thought A.A. was in the business of helping others."

"It is. Other *alcoholics*. This guy—look, you know I don't normally talk about people behind their backs, don't take nobody's inventory, but this guy just isn't—"

"Luther, come off it! Talking about people behind their backs is what you do best! Gossip and coffee are your lifeblood!"

"That's funny, Jimmy. Look, smart-ass, I'm just looking out for you here. This guy Dwayne—well, Shelly has seen him at A.A. meetings in Pleasanton. Johnny's seen him before at the Sunday morning step study in Walnut Creek. He always identifies himself as a newcomer, says it's his first meeting."

"So? This is a crime?"

"So, look, I'm not one to blow anybody's anonymity, but *I've* seen him at my Sex Addicts Anonymous meetings and Doris saw him at her N.A. meetings in San Ramon. Doris says he got disruptive at a meeting and they had to ask him to leave."

"Luther, it sounds to me like this guy is just trying to get some help from wherever he can. Anyway, I already told him I'm not qualified to sponsor him." I pulled into my driveway, pressing the garage door opener. The wife (soon to be former wife) had left the outside flood-lights on for me. All the upstairs bedrooms were dark.

"You're right about that, Jimmy. Hey, this Dwayne sounds like a nutcase to me. Besides, from what I've heard, he's a druggie, not an alkie. A.A. is not for him. If you ever paid attention to the Traditions, you would know that. The Third Tradition states: 'The only requirement for A.A. membership is a desire to stop drinking.' If he doesn't have a drinking problem, then he can't be an A.A. member."

"Luther," I whispered, "I'm in the house now and don't want to wake up the girls. I'll talk to you tomorrow."

"All right then. Good night. You might want to think about your chair. Work on gratitude. And God. And humility. Get on your knees every morning and say the Third Step prayer and the Seventh Step prayer—"

"Good night, Luther."

Luther wasn't my sponsor. I had fired him. He just refused to get the message.

Our pivotal disagreement was over the Fifth Step and my psychiatrist. The Fourth Step states that "we made a searching and fearless moral inventory of ourselves," and the Fifth Step is the confession step: "We admitted to God, to ourselves, and to another human being the exact nature of our wrongs."

When it came time to do my Fifth Step, I had no problem admitting things to myself or God. I had resigned from the atheist and agnostic debating societies long ago. I had seen too many "coincidences" and had come (with the speed of a glacier) to agree with Einstein that "God doesn't play dice with the universe."

In terms of management style, I perceived God to be a very hands-off kind of guy. Supremely indifferent to the state of our auto transmissions.

As for the "other human being," no way was I going to bare the intimate, highly embarrassing details of my life to the obscenely indiscreet Luther. Instead, I made an appointment with my psychiatrist, Dr. Shekelman, the same one who over the last two years had prescribed a variety of antidepressants, tranquilizers, and sleeping pills. Shekelman explained he was treating my *underlying* disorders, extirpating the roots, confident the alcoholic branches would then wither and disappear. Shekelman's theory (which I had just inflicted upon an infuriated A.A. meeting) was that excessive drinking was a *behavior*—an undesirable one—*not a disease, but a symptom.* It was a theory and a treatment approach I very much wanted to believe in.

It seems that shortly after I quit drinking I contracted depression, panic attacks, and insomnia. It was astonishing to me. I had never had a panic attack when I was drinking. Suddenly, at certain unexpected times, I would become deathly afraid of heights, of driving on the highway, or of just being in a room full of people. Not just afraid. This was the full-fledged terror of a racing heart and ragged breath, the white-knuckled knowledge that death was imminent.

Astounding. I had thought that with sobriety everything would get better, not worse.

Dr. Shekelman reluctantly agreed to hear my Fifth Step. After listening patiently to my heartfelt confession for almost forty-five minutes, he studied his watch and reached for a prescription pad. Chemical absolution.

"Well," he said, "I hope it helped you to get all that off your chest. I think we should increase your Prozac dosage." Shekelman was not a fan of Freud.

"That's all you've got to say? More *Prozac*? I just spilled my guts out to you! Revealed my inner demons! What about all the terrible things I've done?"

"I've heard worse. Don't take yourself so seriously."

When I informed Luther I'd already done the Fifth Step with a "human being" other than himself, he was hurt, then angry.

"You're supposed to do that step with your sponsor!" Luther yelled at me over his plate of chocolate cake and ice cream at Denny's.

"Where is *that* rule written, Luther?"

"Not everything in A.A. is *written,* smart-ass! Some things are just *understood.* You do your Fifth Step with your sponsor. I did mine with my sponsor, he did his with his sponsor—it's what sponsors are for. What—what is it? You don't trust me—is that it?"

"No."

We agreed to part ways as sponsor and "sponsee." It's like breaking off a romance and agreeing to be "just friends."

Now Luther just viewed himself as "concerned about" my recovery (as well as the recoveries of a dozen other people in A.A.) and called me almost every day. Sometimes with gossip, sometimes with well-intentioned advice.

Like staying clear of Dwayne Hassleman.

Good advice, Luther.

I first encountered the Monster over the phone.

The night after the A.A. meeting, Dwayne called me at home—at three in the morning. I managed to catch it on the second ring, but the future ex-wife was already sitting up, looking alarmed. If expressions were literal, hers would read: *Who died?*

Dwayne sounded unusually energetic for the middle of the night. Music was blasting in the background. He either had his stereo on at full blast or he was calling from one of those Ecstasy raves in San Francisco. (Which I would have dearly loved to attend if I wasn't too old and burdened by bourgeois respectability.)

Dwayne was shouting over a pounding bass line.

"Hey, pal, I thought you were going to call me! What's going on?"

"Dwayne, what do you mean what's going on? It's three in the morning."

"Oh, sorry if I woke you. I was just wondering when we were going to get together. I'm excited about you sponsoring me and all."

I was waking up now. I found my glasses on the nightstand and put them on. I hear better when I can see. Something I have never understood.

"Look, Dwayne, I never said I was sponsoring you. In fact, the opposite. Anyway, let's talk about it tomorrow."

In the background I heard a crash. Like something brittle flung against a wall.

"Dwayne, where the hell are you calling from?"

"I'm at home. Hold on, I'm turning down the music."

Then blessed silence except for the Monster's labored breathing over the phone. The wife mouthing, "Who is it?"

"It's okay, honey, just a guy from A.A. Go back to bed."

"All right. Remember to take the girls to the dentist after you pick them up from school."

"I won't forget."

"Jimmy, can you hear me now? Who you talking to?"

"My wife, Dwayne. Look, I have to be up at five in the morning. I'll call you from work, tomorrow."

"Fuck *that,* pal! You were supposed to call me *today*! How can you be my sponsor if you don't even keep your word about calling?" Here was the Monster. The Monster clearly on speed. There was no trace of Dwayne from last night—the funny, calm, intelligent guy who once played stoopball and skelly in Park Slope.

"Dwayne, listen to me. I'm not going to talk to you when you're high. I'll call you tomorrow when—"

"Don't you fucking dare hang up on *me,* cocksucker! You have no idea who—"

I hung up.

A few seconds later it rang again.

"NOBODY HANGS UP ON ME, YOU COCKSUCKER! I OUGHT TO COME OVER THERE AND BURN YOUR MOTH-ERFUCKING HOUSE DOWN, YOU PIECE—"

I hung up and decided to leave the phone off the hook.

It was a long time before I could fall back to sleep.

The Monster apologized the next afternoon—by way of voice mail. I didn't retrieve the message until the following day. I never answered the phone at work. It was part of an efficiency system I had developed over the years. Let all calls go to voice mail. Then let the messages—especially the "urgent" ones—age at least twenty-four hours before even thinking about responding or taking any action.

My experience was that 90 percent of the questions or requests would simply evaporate within twenty-four hours. Most issues and problems at work tended to resolve themselves just fine without my assistance. I was a scarred survivor of countless office wars. I had pretty much had all the proactive problem-solving propensities beaten out of me. It would not be unfair to say that after eighteen years I was a tad burned-out.

I had been working on the computer the entire day. In the morning I played eighteen exhausting (but exhilarating) rounds of virtual golf. The game was called Mean Green, scoring a 63 at Pebble Beach—no mean feat. I was now battling the dealer in a marathon session of blackjack. The game, called Dr. Blackjack, helped the player learn counting tactics and strategies, and I was determined to master them before again confronting the live dealers at Las Vegas.

In the cubicle facing mine, separated by a five-foot-high partition divider, an intelligent and pleasant young man (although a distinctly nonmarketing type of person) named Scott was drawing a cartoon and on the phone trying to get some newspapers to carry it. He had sat (mostly unseen) a few feet from me for years. Hidden behind the soft gray barrier. Cubicle life is like that.

The name of the cartoon was *Dilbert*. He eventually got it syndicated.

Across the aisle, cocooned in an extra-large cubicle, a few of the market research people were fleshing out the financial projections for their own planned research and consulting company.

I loved the Dr. Blackjack program. Every year I would go with three or four phone company buddies (all marketing types) to Las Vegas for a weekend. Sort of an extended boys night out. Our wives were glad to get rid of us. We all fancied ourselves expert blackjack players (the casino's dream customer), and we would do other manly things—eat vast quantities of prime rib (rare) and steak and belch extravagantly after each meal.

The casino loved to comp us meals and drinks as long as we made donations at the blackjack tables. Those of us not on the wagon (in recent years, everyone but me) would guzzle down prodigious quantities of comped casino whiskey and beer. We liked going to any comedy show that featured foul and sexually explicit language, racial and misogynistic slurs, and scatological references. Occasionally one or two of our group might later find himself in a club featuring loud canned music and scantily clad women dancers who were always very friendly. The women were so friendly to tourists that they were happy to demonstrate their dancing abilities by gyrating directly on one's lap.

An underappreciated art form.

I instructed the computer dealer to hit me on a soft 17 (Dr. Blackjack was showing a king—I have to assume he's sitting pretty with 20). I busted. I was determined on the next Las Vegas trip to break the casino with my new computer-enhanced skills. Impress the boys. Maybe even get banned from the casino for counting—the ultimate respect.

By three in the afternoon it was almost time to pick up the girls from school (our company prided itself on offering "flex-time" to all managers). I did about ten minutes of work, which consisted of deleting all of my new e-mails without reading them. My theory was that if an issue was truly important, the person would send me an urgent voice mail (which I could let age), page me, or, God forbid, pay an actual visit to my gaming cubicle.

I then listened to yesterday's voice mails. The first message was from Dwayne. There was no hint of the 3 A.M. Monster in his tone.

"Hey, pal, look . . . I just want to apologize for calling you last night and acting like a total jerk. I don't remember much of it but I feel like a total asshole, really sorry. I'll understand it if you don't ever want to speak to me again . . . It's just that I felt we really got along great the other night and I could sure use some help . . . Anyway, whatever you decide, I understand. Tell your wife I apologize for calling so late, probably woke everybody up . . . Well, that's it."

I have had my own mortifying experiences with calling people on the phone when I was drunk. There was nothing more embarrassing to me than having that person bring up my phone call at a later date. Usually I remembered nothing of the conversation. Sometimes I didn't even remember making the call.

I called Dwayne and he picked up on the first ring.

"Jimmy, thanks for calling—I was afraid you'd never speak to me again."

"You ever call me again all fucked-up at three in the morning and I won't."

"Damn, I'm so sorry, pal. I probably woke up your wife and kids. Please apologize to them for me. I don't know what gets into me—not working, I don't know, just too much time on my hands."

We agreed to meet again at Denny's on Monday night after the meeting.

"All right, pal! So you're officially my sponsor?"

"No, but I'll try to help you until we can get someone more qualified."

"Listen, if there's an issue because you think I don't really belong in A.A., well, I *used* to drink too much and I *do* have a desire to stop drinking."

Bingo! The magic words were spoken. Dwayne had done some research on the "only requirement for A.A. membership."

"That's not what you told me the other night."

"I was so nervous—I was going to get into it but we got off on the whole New York trip. So you will sponsor me?"

"I'll be your *temporary* sponsor. Just show up clean and sober Monday night and we'll talk after the meeting."

"No homework assignment?" Dwayne had clearly had sponsors before.

I told Dwayne the same thing I had been told, many times. "Yeah, go to as many meetings as you can and don't drink or use in between meetings. Read the chapter on Step One. We'll discuss it at Denny's."

"Jimmy, just promise me you're not going to pull the whole Higher Power *God as I Understand Him* trip on me—I already put in my time at Saint John's in Brooklyn. I've still got the scars on my knuckles from crazed, ruler-wielding nuns. I have no problem with God—I'm just scared shitless of some of His earthly representatives."

I laughed. "I feel the same way. Besides, you're talking to a recovering agnostic. You should have gone to Erasmus—no nuns, Jewish guilt instead of the Catholic variety, and we all know there are no Jewish alcoholics or drug addicts."

"I've heard that myth. So what happened to you?"

"I guess nature just abhors a vacuum. Or a myth."

"Speaking of whores, did you ever go to this after-hours club down on Atlantic Avenue . . ."

We were friends again.

As we used to say back in Brooklyn: "Everything is everything."

. . .

The Monster resurfaced about a month later. Right after
Dwayne did his Fifth Step with me.

We had been talking on the phone a few times a week and meeting
at Denny's every Monday night after the meeting. Dwayne was working his way quickly through the Twelve Steps of A.A.

"Might as well, Jimmy. I still have four more months of full disability pay, so now's a good time for me to focus on my recovery."

I never really understood either Dwayne's work situation or his disability status. Once he told me that while working as a corporate consultant in sales quality, he had slipped in the lobby of a client's building
and injured his back. ("I'm suing their asses off—they had just mopped
and waxed the floor and there were no warning signs"). Another time
he said he was a "senior account executive" for a San Francisco–based
computer company. He had been at the warehouse, overseeing the delivery of some new high-end workstations, when a piece of loading
equipment smashed into his shoulder.

I figured if and when he was ready to tell me the truth, he would.

Whatever the real story, he must have made a full and complete recovery because Dwayne never seemed to have any back or shoulder
problems.

For his Fifth Step, we took a table all the way in the back of the
smoking section of Denny's. Luther, Doris, and the gang had gone to
get pizza, so the entire section was deserted that night. Cindy, our gra-
cious teenage hostess, brought us black coffee and my Cherry Coke and
then abandoned us, after what passed for her as a pleasant greeting:
"Where's the rest of you drunks tonight?"

Privacy and confidentiality are essential for the Fifth Step. To me, it
was so important that I chose to do mine with my psychiatrist rather

than with Luther (or any other of my half dozen former sponsors). To help Dwayne feel comfortable and safe, I had offered to drive over to his house to listen to this step.

"Why don't you give me directions to your place—you live near downtown, right?"

"Yeah, on Maple Street, but that's okay, Jimmy. My place is a disaster area—my cleaning boy didn't show up this week. Denny's will be just fine—there's never anyone in smoking anymore other than recovering junkies and drunks."

Once again we faced each other through a haze of cigarette smoke. Dwayne had brought his written Fourth Step—his "moral inventory"—and started reading it like a laundry list. He delivered his litany of misdeeds, his moral missteps, with the practiced nonchalance of a mischievous Brooklyn kid once again in the confession booth.

Dwayne's Fifth Step contained no dramatic confessions, nothing even particularly unusual (unless, of course, you're not a drug addict or an alcoholic—in that case, it might seem shocking). Lots of lying, cheating, stealing, manipulating, and petty criminality. In the same perfunctory tone, Dwayne related a dozen or so incidents "where I caused pain to others."

I took a leaf from Dr. Shekelman's book, saying nothing. Just nodding, making eye contact, and muttering the occasional "right" and "I see." The phone company called it "Active Listening." I just wanted Dwayne to know I wasn't making any judgments. Or was about to interrupt with advice. For a sponsor, the Fifth Step is mostly about listening. I had no prescription pad I could reach for, no magic pill for the pain.

". . . and there's probably a lot more, but I was pretty stoned so much of the time that this is all I can remember right now." Dwayne put down his laundry list and took a mighty drag on his cigarette, staring into the black pit of his coffee cup. He was waiting for something. Penance? Absolution? Understanding?

Probably the same thing we're all waiting for.

"Dwayne, I think you did a great job. This step takes a lot of courage and I can also understand your not remembering things. Forgive the program cliché, which I believe they borrowed from the Bible, but they say 'More will be revealed.' Practically every week I remember something else that I did or said that I didn't remember when I did my Fifth Step. Even a few things that I'm still ashamed of."

Dwayne's body suddenly tensed slightly and his head cocked, like when you hear one of those high-pitched sounds that no one else around you seems to hear. For the first time that evening I noticed that his previously green eyes were an intense shade of blue. He wore his usual fatigue pants and jungle boots but had on one of those khaki long-sleeved survivalist shirts with all the cute little pockets and epaulets.

"Jimmy, this moral inventory—is it supposed to include those things we are *ashamed* of? I thought it was just the things we did wrong."

"I'm no expert here, Dwayne. I did this step with my shrink, and all he said was to take some more Prozac. All I can tell you is that I was told—by every one of my six ex-sponsors—that if it's something that *bothers* us we should include it in the Fifth Step. The prevailing A.A. wisdom seems to be that if we don't—if we keep it to ourselves—it could be something that we get drunk about later. The A.A. cliché is that 'we're only as sick as our secrets.' "

Dwayne nodded solemnly, considering this.

"That makes sense."

"Is there something else you want to talk about?"

Dwayne stubbed out his cigarette and immediately lit another. He glanced nervously around the room. We still had the smoking section to ourselves.

"Well, maybe . . . Once when I was pretty young, not even out of high school, I got pretty fucked-up at this party thrown by this older guy in the neighborhood, and I ended up . . ." Dwayne looked up, exhaling smoke painfully. He took another survey of the empty room.

"Look, Dwayne, you don't have to talk about anything you don't want to, and you sure don't have to tell it to me. You can do like I did—see a professional counselor—or you could even talk to a priest if you wanted to. A lot of A.A. guys do the Fifth Step with their priest—"

"No, Jimmy"—Dwayne waved the smoke away between us—"I trust you. I know you'd never repeat this to anyone . . . never betray me."

Betray? This was starting to get very—what was that sixties word? *Heavy. Too* heavy.

Dwayne looked down, studying his hands, squeezing the coffee cup like it was a life preserver.

"Like I said, I was pretty wasted, taking downers—reds, I think—chasing them with one-five-one rum." Dwayne tightened his grip on the cup, knuckles going white. I was afraid he was going to have a stroke or something—a bluish vein surfaced on his forehead and it was beating and pulsing like a tiny troubled heart.

"Dwayne, listen, whatever this is, you don't have to talk about it now. You—"

"No, Jimmy, I do . . . I don't know how I got there, but when I woke up the next morning, I was in this older guy's bed. Naked. Next to him. I guess we had done some things. It took me a week of brushing my teeth to get that horrible taste out of my mouth, to . . ."

Dwayne released the coffee cup and finally looked up. He lit another cigarette, hand shaking, then just looked at me. Intense blue eyes. Waiting. For what? My judgment?

All I could think was *big deal.* I didn't care, and even if I did it wasn't relevant.

I told him so.

"Dwayne—this is a big *so what*! You're telling me you got really high at a party when you were a kid and went to bed with some guy. I don't see how that comes under the category of a Fourth Step 'moral inventory.' If you could see some of the creatures I woke up next to when—"

"But were any of those creatures men?"

"No, but a few may not have even been human, so—"

Dwayne smacked his cup down on the table. He was not going to let himself wriggle off of whatever hook he had fashioned for himself long ago.

"Jimmy, that was only the first time. It only happened when I got really stoned, though. I went back to the guy, Dale's house, the next weekend. For the drugs. He had the best drugs. The same thing happened . . . and maybe one or two times after that. Once in college. At New York University. And then never again."

I had no idea what to say. I knew I wasn't qualified to do this. If Dwayne was scratching at some locked closet door, I was not the one with the key.

"Dwayne, so far all I'm hearing comes under the category of youthful—and stoned—sexual experimentation. It's hardly a *moral* failing, you know. It's—"

"IT'S AN ABOMINATION!" Dwayne smashed the coffee cup down on the Formica and glared at me. The forehead vein was now beating like a wild beast. I looked around, hoping someone would come into the smoking section. I was in way over my head. Clearly Dwayne had some significant emotional issues that the A.A. tool kit was never designed to repair.

This was what the old-timers referred to as an *Outside Issue*.

I avoided Dwayne's gaze and bought some time by pretending to thoroughly extinguish my cigarette. Dwayne's too-blue eyes pinned me to my seat like a bug.

I reached into the Coke and extracted the cherry, popping it into my mouth. I've been told by friends that I have a talent for saying the wrong thing at precisely the worst possible time. This was one of those times.

"Dwayne, you know, there are A.A. meetings in San Francisco for all kinds of specialized . . . uh, *interests*. They even have—"

"What the *fuck* are you saying, pal?" The question was a coiled hiss. Another minimal clue I missed.

"I'm just saying that they have lots of gay A.A. meetings and you would probably find a sponsor there who could help you to—"

Crash!

With a savage swipe of one huge forearm the Monster cleared the table. Glasses, ashtrays, cups, silverware, salt and sugar dispensers flew to the floor.

The Monster was on his feet, backing away toward the emergency fire exit.

"You ignorant *asshole*! I try to tell you one fucking thing, confide in you a . . . *mistake* and you advise me to go to *Faggots* Anonymous? Who the fuck do you think you are? Judging *me*. Do I look like some kind of *cocksucker* to you? I was fucking married for twelve years! I got three kids!"

The Monster was loose again, backing up against the fire exit door, still shouting, index finger stabbing the air between us, more veins throbbing darkly on his face.

Too late, I tried to clean it up. "Dwayne, I never meant—"

"Shut the fuck up! You're *fired*, motherfucker! Sponsor, my *ass*! I must have been crazy to tell you about . . . You say one word, one fucking word, to anyone about what I said here and you've got a war, motherfucker, a war with *me*!"

The fire exit door slammed shut as Cindy came in to investigate the noise. She looked at the mess of sugar on the floor.

"What are you drunks doing back here? Tearing up the place? Everything all right, Jimmy?"

"Fine, Cindy. Sorry about the mess. I'll clean it up."

"No, that's okay. Where's your big friend?"

"He just left—he doesn't feel very well."

Cindy thoughtfully assessed the clutter on the floor and snapped her gum.

"Yeah, well . . . who does?"

The phone calls from the Monster started the following night—at two in the morning.

Dwayne was always high. Sometimes his words were slow and slurring, at other times they would rocket out in a frenzied torrent, usually incomprehensible. The content and tone would alternate from weepy and apologetic to abusive and threatening.

Sometimes the phone would just ring once or twice, but the Monster's number was displayed on our caller ID.

This middle-of-the-night pattern continued until the wife, both exhausted and worried, insisted I resolve the problem. After unsuccessfully trying to reach Dwayne at home all week, I finally turned to Ma Bell. The phone company (for three dollars a month—no employee discount) set up a call-blocking service so the Monster could not call us from his home phone number.

Over the next month I received at least three voice mails from Dwayne. Apologizing for his behavior, for the phone calls. His voice was sober and apparently sincere.

I didn't return the calls.

It was almost a year until I ran into Dwayne again.

Maybe a day or two longer until I was reacquainted with the Monster.

. . .

In the stock nightmares of my childhood the always un-named monster would either get me or almost get me (the usual case), but I would always wake up with enormous relief. Just a nightmare. There really are no monsters.

Once the monster has a name, there is no real waking, just a slight shift in mental and physiological states. I killed the Monster in real life just once, but he has since killed me a hundred times in my dreams.

I naively believed that I had banished the nocturnal demons of my childhood, built grown-up fortifications and buttressed them with the impenetrable armor of middle-class respectability—the wife, the kids, the job, the house, the cars. Even the cubicle and the computers; the house with an electronic keypad to beep out the burglars and the other bad guys.

To keep out the Monster.

But the Monster is only amused by these pathetically flimsy fortifi-cations, the high-tech cocoons of cell phones, voice mail, pagers, bur-glar alarms, and bloated 401(k) plans.

Better get busy. Busy is the best defense against the Monster. Take the wife and the kids to Disneyland. Then Disney World. To Maui—wowee! Build a redwood deck in the backyard. Make it big, I told the landscaping contractor. Less grass that way. I do not wish to be intimate with the lawn mower in the garage. Give the Vietnamese kids thirty bucks to grapple with that thing. And the electric lawn trimmer—whatever the hell that really does.

I honestly don't know. Growing up in Brooklyn, I didn't know any-one who had a lawn, or if they did, it didn't warrant machine care.

When Brooklyn Jews of my generation wanted to know about such things, they simply married outside of the faith—shiksas often know about these home maintenance issues. They know about cars too.

I married a shiksa, and coming from a pastoral background (the suburbs of New Jersey), she brought to our marriage a knowledge of snail bait and weed killer and how to change fuses in that mysterious box in the garage. In phone company jargon we had "complementary skill sets." She would alert me to things like having to periodically add air to the car tires while I helped her with Lotus spreadsheets.

The wife also had what I regarded to be, early in the marriage, bizarre and extreme ideas about recreation ("Camping is *fun,* Jimmy"), health ("Smoking is bad for you"), exercise (she would, unforced, *shvitz* like a galley slave in a "gym" three times a week), and child-rearing ("Don't give the baby a Gummi Bear").

I loved my wife.

I loved my two little girls, my house in the beautiful Bay Area suburbs, my computer, my diversified equity portfolio. I especially loved the white baby grand piano in the living room. By the time the girls grew to be eleven and twelve they simultaneously lost interest in becoming world-class pianists, so I had to fill the vacuum of a soundless parlor.

My parents didn't waste their money on *my* piano lessons. I could pound out a dozen versions of "Heart and Soul," handling the bass and treble all by myself—I didn't need no stinking duets! And pound it out I would—punishment, payback for the girls not appreciating the *privilege* of piano lessons.

"*Da-ad!* Could you *puh-lease* not play that now? I'm trying to study." Daughter #1 was a very conscientious student, but not of my music.

"Sorry, honey, I was just experimenting with some improvisational jazz." Good dads give good culture. Girl #2 yells down from the top of the spiral (faux oak) stairway, "Dad, it sounds like 'Heart and Soul' again—*everything* you play sounds like 'Heart and Soul.' "

Everyone's a critic.

We lived in the idyllic town of Danville, California, located about thirty miles east of San Francisco, in the protective shadow of nearby Mount Diablo. Having lived in big cities my entire life with their crime, noise, dirt, frenzied congestion, and uninspired subway graffiti, Danville seemed like paradise to me. Immaculately kept public streets and buildings in the old western-style (calculated but charming) five-block downtown area, virtually no serious crime, lush green hidden gems of parks and playgrounds for children, secret creeks and the unconvincing artificial "lakes" in front of the newer upscale housing developments.

Farms, cows, horses, and deer coexist with the sprawling gated communities of golf courses, tennis courts, and health clubs. The business parks in nearby San Ramon and Pleasanton—the high-tech I-680 corridor—allow for a pleasant 10- or 15-minute commute from most of the homes. A welcome reprieve from the traffic horrors of the Bay Bridge leading to San Francisco. The phone company moved its headquarters from San Francisco to the business park in San Ramon in the early eighties. We could now plot rate increases in the isolated splendor of the suburbs and feel safer doing it.

The public schools are the kind where parents stay enthusiastically involved in all aspects of education, generously contributing their time and dollars with a zeal normally associated with the alumni of private colleges. The public high schools consistently pump out adolescent grist for the polishing mills of U.C. Berkeley and Stanford.

There are still large patches of woods, tree-laden walking paths, scenic bike trails, and even a shrine for the local literati, the Tao House, where Eugene O'Neill is said to have written *The Iceman Cometh*.

Downtown Hartz Avenue is dotted with antique stores and art galleries, boutiques striving to be chic and quaint and charming all at once and often succeeding, elegant restaurants and European-style alfresco cafés where the young, the old, or just the weary can sip exotic coffees or a glass of chardonnay. Young mothers in bright summer dresses push baby carriages and window-shop, stopping to chat and laugh with friends and neighbors they encounter on the street.

With its almost all-white demographics and high concentration of professionals, Danville is an easy target for satire by our friends in San Francisco, a bridge and a universe away. To them it is a privileged enclave of Republicans and smug materialism. To them I would say, "So sue me!" I felt I had paid my urban dues.

For me, a survivor of a thousand nightmarish D train subway rides in New York's stifling summer heat, Danville was a place of such surpassing beauty and mountain-shadowed serenity that if it didn't exist I might have invented a place in my heart for it.

Danville, with its sheltering canopy of majestic old oaks, with an old-fashioned downtown soda fountain and an independent bookstore (where the friendly owners not only knew my name but would send me postcards to let me know when books they thought might be of interest to me had arrived), was to me a refugee from Flatbush Avenue, the American Dream.

With its own Monster, Dwayne Hassleman, lurking behind his curtains in a small house on Maple Street, just a few blocks from the Danville Players theater group. Just waiting. Waiting almost a year to come back into my life.

Was he really waiting for me? Waiting for me to get divorced and move in across the street from him with my girls helping me to schlepp boxes of books and blankets and towels and photo albums and old vinyl LPs? Was he watching us even then as the former wife gave me decorating suggestions and the piano movers wrestled with my piano so later I could pound out the music of pain and loss and despair?

Was it the sharp scent of my pain that roused the Monster, that was once again to make me the target of his obsessive interest? Or just my bad luck?

Or maybe it was just someone playing dice with my universe.

I was unpacking boxes that the former wife had considerately labeled "dishes," "books," "bathroom," "bedroom." I had taken a one-year lease on a small house on Maple Street in Danville. For $1,500 a month I was rewarded with a washer and dryer, two bedrooms (one for the girls on weekends and Wednesday nights), a small living room with hardwood floors, two bathrooms, and a beautiful backyard with preinstalled flowers, Japanese maples, and lots of bushes and plants. (Is there a difference?)

For an extra $150 a month the homeowners' association provided an Olympic-size swimming pool, tennis and basketball courts, and a health club. The pool even had a diving board and a lifeguard on duty. It was my deluded hope that the girls would love having the use of a diving board (no diving boards at the former wife's pool) so much it would mitigate some of the fresh pain of the divorce.

Best of all was my view of Mount Diablo, which dominates the San Ramon and Diablo Valleys.

I was removing some books when the doorbell rang.

Assuming the former wife (for brevity's sake I'll call her the F.W.) or the girls had forgotten to give me some last-minute box, I opened the door.

Dwayne Hassleman stood there.

"Welcome to the neighborhood, Jimmy. I thought I recognized you. My house is the one with the green roof just across the street and three down. Need some help with those boxes?"

We shook hands. There was no sign of the Monster I had last seen at Denny's. Or that had made the late phone calls and threats. Dwayne appeared to be calm and healthy, muscles straining against a white T-shirt over his camouflage pants. Same jungle combat boots. Intense green eyes.

"Jimmy, I don't know if you ever received my voice mails—but I want to apologize in person for how I acted, not only at Denny's that night but the phone calls after. I was just so messed up back then that—"

I waved away the rest of his words. "It's all right, Dwayne. That was a long time ago. I'm glad to see you're doing well."

"You look good yourself. You still go to that A.A. meeting on Monday night?"

"Well, right now let's just say that I'm in between recoveries. Again."

"I know how that is. I've been meaning to get back into some kind of support group but—"

"Dwayne, you don't owe me any explanations."

"Hey, you're going to love this house. It's got a great backyard that overlooks the association swimming pool. I almost leased it myself when it became available last month after Mrs. Bush died."

"Why didn't you?"

"It didn't have the right kind of steps to play stoopball."

"But there's a great stretch of sidewalk to play skelly. You have any good bottle caps?"

"Hold on. I've got some Heineken in my fridge—be right back."

Fifteen minutes and two beers later we were back again in the Brooklyn of our youth, laughing and pretending there had never been the slightest rift in our friendship. There had never been a Monster.

On that day—a very bad day—I was grateful to have my friend Dwayne back.

. . .

Dwayne was Mr. Helpful that first day in my new home on Maple Street. Although it was a workday, a Monday, he appeared to have nothing more important to do than insist upon carrying boxes to the F.W.'s designated areas. At a certain point in the afternoon I realized that someone had removed every single lightbulb in the house.

"No problem," Hassleman said. "There's a new Ace hardware store off of Hartz—I'll be back in a New York minute." And he was out the front door before I could give him the bill I was pulling out of my wallet. A compulsive list maker, I already had on my "Moving—To Do List" a trip to the hardware store, the post office, the supermarket, then some take-out Chinese food.

Through the large picture window in the living room I watched Dwayne race down the cobblestone path that led from the front door to the sidewalk. The stone walkway bisected a colorful front garden blooming and bursting with unknown (to me) varieties of plants and flowers. Parallel to the cobblestone walkway was my driveway leading into a two-car garage. Although our homeowners' association rules prohibited parking cars overnight in the driveways, most residents did it anyway—a suburban expression of civil disobedience.

The Monster's driveway across the street boasted a late-model silver Mercedes parked alongside a spanking new Range Rover. Dwayne paused a moment, examining his set of keys as if trying to decide on the appropriate mode of conveyance for the half-mile journey to Ace. He reached into a large pouch in his cammy pants and extracted one of those huge Banana Republic safari hats designed to deflect . . . what? Poisonous snakes dropping down from overhanging vines? Poison blow darts to the neck?

The Monster finally selected the Range Rover, a manly choice for a hardware store trip. The Mercedes would be kept in reserve for the early evening journey to Starbucks.

Or it would have been, except two minutes after Dwayne embarked on his suburban safari, a tow truck rolled up behind the Mercedes. Two burly guys wearing identical sweat-stained black tank tops over ragged Levi's emerged from the truck, one of them consulting a clipboard.

They looked like, walked like, and quacked like visitors from Planet Repo. I watched through my living room window (*have to get some window treatments*) as they seemed to verify information from the clipboard with the Monster's license plates and address. Apparently convinced the Mercedes was a rightful resident of Planet Repo, they quickly hooked it up and were towing it down Maple Street when the Range Rover pulled into the driveway.

Dwayne leaped out just in time to scream at the Mercedes' rapidly disappearing bumper.

"COCKSUCKERS! GODDAMN MOTHERFUCKING SHIT!"

Had my grandpa George been there, he might have remarked that "profanity is the crutch of a crippled vocabulary."

All raging army fatigues now, the Monster started jumping up and down on the sidewalk, directing a barrage of profanities so foul that my remaining notion of propriety prohibits me from listing them all here. Veins like ugly purple ropes suddenly popped out on the Monster's linebacker sturdy neck, pulsing and palpitating with the implied promise of payback for Planet Repo.

When the jumping and cursing failed to fetch back his beloved Mercedes, the Monster started beating first his fists and then, rage fading to sadness, his head against the Range Rover's windshield, tears streaming down his cheeks. It was a transformation so extreme and curiously poignant that it was like watching someone working his way through the "stages of mourning" at a lightning pace, moving from rage and denial to grief and acceptance in seconds.

The Monster must have really loved that Mercedes.

Dwayne finally extracted an Ace hardware sack from the Range Rover, crossed the street without looking first (only in California are people so trusting), and calmly strolled down my walkway.

I opened the front door. "Problem?" I asked.

Hassleman managed a weak grin, the affable mask firmly back in place. "No problem," he said, handing me a bag of lightbulbs. "I'll straighten it out tomorrow—hell, I paid eighty grand in *cash* for that car." On the journey to get my M.B.A. I suffered through a few financial management and accounting classes and I didn't recall ever hearing that cash had the downside risk of bouncing. Maybe I just wasn't paying attention.

I took out my wallet to pay for the lightbulbs, but Dwayne waved it off.

"Consider it a housewarming gift." He grinned, eyes still moist with Mercedes grief.

"Thank you. Listen, I have a lot of stuff to put away—"

"No problem, guy, I got a few things to take care of myself, a little business, but why don't you drop by later, say seven or so, and I'll barbecue us a couple of steaks in the backyard. I noticed your fridge is empty."

What was he doing looking in my refrigerator—we didn't put any food away. I had been planning to pick up some spicy-hot Mongolian beef and wonton soup (paying extra for the crispy noodles), but my back and neck were singing in pain after wrestling with boxes all day. The prospect of driving into downtown Danville (six whole blocks) exhausted me. The alternate plan of a delivered pizza (extra topping for the newly divorced) depressed me.

"That would be great, Dwayne. Listen, I appreciate your help today and thanks again for the lightbulbs."

"Hey, what are neighbors for?" he said brightly, all the rage of a few moments before nowhere in evidence.

Front door closing, Hassleman's jungle boots bouncing over the cobblestones, then making a diagonal cut at the curb to cross the street and reach his driveway. He stops by the Range Rover, considers.

Then backs the Rover into his garage.

Thwunk! Metal garage door meets the concrete below.

Somewhere in a never-imagined future a steel door is sliding open from a concrete wall. Two steel sleeping trays in an empty cell, a rusted metal toilet, graffitied cinder block.

Just waiting for me.

During the course of my first day in the house on Maple Street I unconsciously reenacted the housekeeping rituals of the Newly Divorced Guy. The furniture guys pulled up in a truck and delivered my brand-new black leather La-Z-Boy recliner. They placed it in the living room in front of my thirty-five-inch TV without my even having to tell them that was precisely where I wanted it.

I hadn't luxuriated in the comfort of a huge recliner since my bachelor days, fifteen years before. The wife considered recliners to be male barbarisms whose true subversive purpose was to destroy the tasteful communal decor of the family room. She preferred sectional sofa arrangements, not just for the aesthetics but to facilitate family bonding.

Recliners were the last refuge of the solitary scoundrel.

The cable guy arrived to ensure that I had twenty-four-hour access to old Rocky and Rambo movies, to Arnold and Bruce Willis, Steven Seagal, reruns of *Bonanza* (give me dark, brooding Adam over punk-ass Little Joe any day), *The Twilight Zone, The Prisoner,* and my all-time favorite, *Leave It to Beaver,* featuring network TV's first true sociopathic character (also a favorite), Eddie Haskell.

Could my childhood affinity for Eddie—that rascal!—account for my unthinking acceptance of the Monster's barbecue invitation?

I tipped the cable guy generously to hook up my VCR to my TV. Despite my M.B.A. in telecommunications management and my strategic "white papers" extolling technological "convergence," I could never manage to get the VCR to do anything more than play back rented movies. The F.W. had always handled the high-tech details of modern living. VCR hookup was her job. I was clueless.

The movers arrived with more stuff from my "old house" that the F.W. thought I could use. Two big beer-gutted guys from the furniture company arrived and installed a new king bed in the master bedroom, two twin beds for the girls in "their" bedroom. (I hoped they didn't mind sharing a bedroom.)

I tried to replicate the amenities of their bedrooms at home—a Nintendo, a color TV, a telephone, a computer, a CD player. A mature and amicable divorce should never interfere with the spoiling of the children. The F.W. and I agreed on that. Though not Jewish, the F.W. had the heart and soul of a Jewish mother.

The phone guy came out and activated dial tone, added a second line to ensure uninterrupted Internet access (no way I was going to pay for the phone company's overpriced DSL connection), and passed on rumors he'd heard from the union that the phone company was an acquisition target for an even bigger Baby Bell. Another generous tip and twenty minutes later the computer, monitor, scanner, printer, and modem were happily interfacing in my bedroom.

The sun was setting in a velvet haze over Mount Diablo when I was finally able to take a break. I slothed out for a minute in my new La-Z-Boy, adjusting the level until my head was about an inch off the floor (optimal relaxation position) and my feet somewhere in the heavens. A serene bachelor moment except the blood was rushing to my head and I couldn't breathe.

Also too quiet. Way too quiet. With the exception of the occasional business trip or "marketing retreat" to learn how to Be Here Now, I hadn't been separated from my wife or the girls in many years.

As part of the joint custody and visitation schedule, the girls would spend every weekend and one weeknight every other week with me. That was the formal agreement; in practice the F.W. and I would be as flexible as circumstances required. If her job took her away on a business trip during the week or she just needed a few days to herself, I would gladly have the girls, and she would do the same for me. We both read the books and articles about how to minimize the trauma to the children. We were determined to have a collaborative, consultative divorce. No bickering in front of the girls and absolutely no behind-the-back bad-rapping each other to the kids.

Five more days till Friday, though. I tried to adjust the recliner lever to return me to a more or less horizontal position. Hopeless—my center of gravity had sucked me into a potentially critical condition. I rolled up and to my left and quickly received a reminder about the unresilient qualities of a hardwood floor. Have to buy some throw rugs or something. Meanwhile my back was killing me.

I had been in a car accident almost a year ago, shortly after receiving my two-year A.A. chip and horrifying the group with my "chair." A teenager driving his parents' monster SUV rear-ended me while I was stopped for a red light. It took two operations for the neurosurgeons to make what repairs they could. The first one was called a "cervical discectomy with fusion." The fusion involved removing a chunk of my hipbone and fusing it to my neck. The surgery wasn't successful. The pain, numbness, and lack of mobility persisted.

No problem for Dr. Feldman, the neurosurgeon. A few months ago he brought me back to the hospital for a second operation on the rest of the disks in my neck—"a laminectomy." Don't ask me the technical difference in the operations. All I know is that the first one, the fusion, left me with scars on my throat and hip. The second adventure into pain awarded me with a thin scar on the back of my neck. I spent months off from work on full benefits, wearing one of those hard collars, going to physical therapy, and eating pain pills.

I finally gave up the hard-collar habit but kept the pain pill addiction.

The La-Z-Boy was killing my back.

I went to the bathroom, where I had just put my Vicodin prescription into the medicine cabinet. The instructions on the bottle said "take one tablet every four hours."

Maybe it was selective dyslexia (or more likely, my Inner Dope Fiend), but I interpreted the instructions as *take four tablets every hour.* Sometimes even that wasn't enough to block out the pain. After almost a year of taking painkillers, my tolerance for the pills had increased to frighteningly high levels. When I mentioned this to the neurosurgeon, he increased the prescription strength and cheerfully suggested a third "procedure." The proposed third surgery sounded like even less fun that the first two.

Something about inserting titanium rods into my spinal cord.

Using big metal bolts and screws.

I decided to take a rain check.

I went back to the recliner and tried to read the newspaper. Gave up after catching myself rereading a paragraph about the expanding hole in the ozone. Like I didn't have enough problems.

The muscles in my arm started jumping and convulsing in electrical twitches. More annoying than painful. The neurologist said it was a "normal" side effect of spinal surgery. Called it a "fasciculation." Like the big medical word made it acceptable. *Normal.* Normal or not, I went back to the medicine cabinet and swallowed an abnormal dose of Soma tablets.

I tried calling the girls to see if they wanted to spend the night with me. I was prepared to bribe them with pizza, soda, popcorn, candy, and the R-rated movie of their choice from Blockbuster.

Of course, I got the answering machine: "Hi! We're not in right now but if you leave a message we'll return your call as soon as we can." I hadn't been gone twenty-four hours and already *my* greeting had been deleted, my masculinely firm (but friendly) words relegated to the digital dustbin of divorce.

After attending a phone company training session on Network

Security, Redundancy, and Survivability, I advised the F.W. that one *never* leaves a taped greeting proclaiming "We are not in right now." Very reckless. Might as well say, "Please come rob us—*now* would be a good time." I recall pontificating at length about this. Her eventual desire for a divorce did not surprise me nearly as much as the fact that she was able to endure me for fifteen years. She had the patience, kindness, and love of a saint. It was impossible for me to resent her or not think kindly of her.

A couple of months ago (using the surgeries as an excuse) I started drinking again. I congratulated myself on the fact that I didn't drink every day and I always waited until after 5 P.M., the gentlemanly cocktail hour, unlike *real* alcoholics, who have no control and think nothing of drinking Thunderbird for breakfast. As promised, the wife filed for divorce.

It was too quiet. I clicked on the TV. A minute later clicked it off. Turned on the CD player, popped in a Neil Young. Too whiny and depressing. Neil was going through some sort of artistic stage or something.

I switched to radio, then put the TV back on with no sound. No improvement.

Finally I reached for my briefcase and extracted the half pint of Chivas I had purchased on the way home from work. I also congratulated myself on not buying a full pint or a fifth like a real alcoholic would have done. I knew I couldn't get drunk on just a half pint. I would also sip my drink slowly. Like a gentleman.

I was determined to control my drinking. Once again.

A.A. members like to say that the definition of insanity is doing the same thing over and over and expecting different results.

I was insane.

. . .

At 7 P.M., after some lonely wallowing in delicious self-pity, I went down the street to partake of the Monster's barbecue.

Much has been written and sung of the things we do for love and friendship. Not as much about the mistakes we make trying to banish loneliness.

When Dwayne opened his front door, I was immediately over-whelmed by the stench of rot and mold and a mustiness so pungent I suspected wild animals were conducting dark orgies somewhere in the house. The only source of illumination was the eerie glow of a computer monitor on the living room coffee table.

"Excuse the mess," the Monster said. "My cleanup boy's been sick all week." (*Cleanup* boy? Where do I order one of those?)

The light from the monitor revealed a filthy beige carpet mercifully concealed by Kentucky Fried Chicken buckets, piles of dirty, stinking laundry, and Little Caesar's pizza boxes. There were unopened stacks of mail and *Soldier of Fortune* magazines nesting on top of other magazines with names like *Suck!, Sperm Productions,* and *Bloody Fists.* Through the doorless kitchen opening I could make out a three-foot-high pile of dishes congealing in what I deduced to be a sink.

"Come on—the backyard's this way." Dwayne urged me toward the sliding glass doors in the kitchen.

"You have mail," the computer announced in its upbeat female chirp.

I stopped to watch the pixels being rapidly downloaded—a blur of bytes which resolved itself into a monstrously engorged purple penis, followed quickly by a sexually ambiguous figure kneeling in a position I did not think was prayerful.

Hassleman grabbed my arm and pulled me out through the kitchen and into the backyard.

"Don't want those coals to die out. Don't know about you, Jimmy, but I like my steaks *sizzling.*" Dwayne was extremely nervous ("I don't get much company") but also happily excited as he hand-tossed two huge steaks on a grill that looked like it had last been cleaned during the Eisenhower administration.

"Sizzling sounds good to me," I said, my appetite suddenly gone. I sat down on a wooden bench in front of a rotting picnic table. The backyard was small, with nothing living in it. No flowers, no plants, no grass—just gravel and cement and the rusted black barbecue.

I accepted a beer while Dwayne poked and prodded and flipped the meat, occasionally shaking his head sadly—he must have been mourning the loss of the Mercedes.

"That crazy Joey—what a sick fuck! Loves to send me that pornographic crap over the Net, kind of a joke."

"To each their own, Dwayne." I managed to produce this platitude from some deep reservoir my family could draw from at will.

Halfway through his sizzling steak, Dwayne leaped up as if he had just remembered he left a taxi outside, meter running.

"Got to drain the lizard," he said. "The beer goes right through me." I watched him pass the tower of dirty dishes, then briefly study the computer monitor before turning off the power. Twenty minutes later he returned from "the bathroom" in an ebullient mood. Popped the top off another Heineken by placing the bottle cap on the edge of the table and smacking down hard with the palm of his hand. Very macho.

I was underwhelmed.

"This is *great*! Just great, having company, just kicking back with the guys for some steak and brewskis." I didn't know there were other guys present. Dwayne must have "drained his lizard" from his pet white rock—he had suddenly developed a severe summer cold. He dabbed at his nose with a handkerchief.

An increasingly bloody handkerchief.

"These summer allergies are a bitch," he said.

"Yeah, must be El Niño blowing in some pollen from Bolivia," I replied—out of the side of my neck.

"Excuse me?"

"Nothing important. Listen, let me give you a hand with this stuff, then I have to get going—big day at work tomorrow. Thanks for every-thing, Dwayne. The steak was great." It wasn't the drug use by itself that concerned me. I wasn't that much of a hypocrite. I even had a nice Chivas-Vicodin-Soma glow going. I wasn't casting any stones.

I was just worried about the Monster making an unpleasant ap-pearance. So far our conversation had adeptly avoided any mention of that night in Denny's—Dwayne's Fifth Step was the proverbial ele-phant in the living room that we chose not to notice.

Dwayne waved a hand dismissively when I rose to leave.

"These plates are nothing—hang out with me for a while." To demonstrate his housekeeping system, Dwayne grabbed both plates and silverware and tossed them on top of the reeking pile in the sink.

I followed him into the kitchen, planning a quick getaway, when, for the second time that evening, I felt an iron grip on the back of my arm.

"Look, Jimmy, don't go just yet. I haven't really made many new friends since Caroline filed for divorce and left with the kids."

"Caroline?"

"My wife. Well, my *ex*-wife. Come on, let me show you something."

Dwayne led me into a small bedroom that smelled even more mephitic than the living room. Bed unmade, more piles of dirty, stink-ing clothes on the floor, plastic prescription bottles on the bureau, the floor, the nightstand, and on top of his dirty clothes. Pills were scattered all over.

There was a stale cooked smell to the air. In the corner beside a pair of stiffened socks was a bloody piece of cotton. With the Vicodin and Chivas and Soma warmly embracing in my brain, I thought of one of the signs you see in every A.A. meeting: LIVE AND LET LIVE—the recov-ery version of "judge not, that ye be not judged."

Dwayne had one of those skillfully customized closets with a dozen small shelves for—who knows? Hatboxes? Shoes?

Handguns of every make and model shone darkly from the shelves. Swords and hunting knives were mounted on the closet walls.

"You wanted to show me your weapons collection?"

"No. Anyway, this is nothing—the good stuff is in the garage. Wanna see?"

"No thanks, I'm fine. I saw enough armor and artillery in the army."

This disclosure of my martial history seemed to ignite Dwayne into a frenzy. "The fucking *army*? Me too, man! What did you do?" Dwayne was vibrating with pleasant anticipation inside his army-surplus jungle boots.

"As little as possible," I said modestly. "What was your MOS?"

"My what?"

"Your MOS." Everyone who has ever been in the army knows, even decades later, his MOS—Military Occupational Specialty.

Dwayne searched the closet ceiling for the correct answer to the MOS trick question. "I was with the Rangers, you know, Special Forces." With the instinctual gesture of the pathological liar, Dwayne stared directly into my eyes. Earlier today his eyes had been bright green. Now they were brown. How many tinted contacts did he own?

"Oh, so you were a 12 *Zebra* MOS," I suggested, inventing a non-existent specialty.

Dwayne didn't even blink. "Exactly—but a lot of our MOSs were classified." A nice touch to the lie, that cagey qualification.

"I can understand that," I humored him. I knew the Monster was close—just one wrong remark away—and his right hand was just a few inches from his Closets 'R' Us armory.

"Jimmy, this is so great! Your being a veteran, like me. And also divorced. But I wanted to show you my Caroline and the kids."

Dwayne circled around the cesspool of his bed. Stood staring at the glass-framed photos that covered the wall. I stepped over a burned teaspoon and stood beside him.

A beautiful young woman, dark hair spilling down to her waist, reclined in a chaise lounge under a massive umbrella on a beach. Three small children in bathing suits, two boys and a girl, played with pails and shovels nearby. There was another photo of the same woman, this time on horseback. Another of her behind the wheel of a red sports car.

There was no sign of Dwayne in any of the pictures.

Tread lightly here, Jimmy-boy. You already pulled his covers on his bogus MOS. "She's beautiful, Dwayne. And those are your kids? You must be real proud."

"Thanks, Jimmy—I am. I just wish I had been able to get custody. I haven't seen the kids in a long time."

"I'm sorry to hear that."

"Well, it's been real tough." Dwayne seemed to brighten at the thought of how tough it had been for him. Must be that stoical Ranger training. "But I'm not going to lay my problems on you—you *just* got divorced. I know the beginning is the most painful part."

"Well, I'm hoping it gets better. Look, Dwayne, I have to run. I have a marketing presentation to the Board of Directors at eight in the morning and I have to review my notes."

"Sure, guy—hey, I didn't mean to hold you up. I know how it is. I used to be an office grind myself. The old nine-to-five."

"What do you do now, Dwayne? I remember you were a sales consultant or in computers?"

"I was. Right now I'm on disability again—the shoulder is permanently damaged—but I have my own network marketing business. Health care products. I have about seven hundred guys in my downline now. MLM is the wave of the future."

"MLM?"

"Multilevel marketing."

"Is that anything like a pyramid scheme?"

"Not one bit—that's a common misconception. MLM is the most powerful sales distribution channel ever developed to move products. You don't sell a product, you sell a business *opportunity*!"

"That sounds great," I said, wading over and through the *Suck!* debris and dirty clothes in the living room. Get the door open. Must have fresh air. Behind me Dwayne called out, "Hey, Jimmy, want to do this again tomorrow night? I really enjoy your company. I think we have a lot in common."

"Thanks, Dwayne, I'm busy tomorrow night," I called out from the safety of my stone walkway.

"How about Wednesday night?" Dwayne yelled.

"I'll call you if that works for me, Dwayne. Thanks again."

"Night, buddy."

"Good night, Dwayne."

Of course, the Monster called me.

After escaping relatively intact from the Monster's putres-cent parlor, I attacked the last of the boxes stacked in the living room. Beneath a pillow and some cans of tuna fish the F.W. had thoughtfully packed for me, I uncovered the ivory chess set. The F.W. had bought it for me on our tenth anniversary and I loved it. The chess set and the piano were the only two items I had wanted from the accumulated debris of a fifteen-year marriage.

I decided against calling the girls—too late—made my bed, locking the sheets down tight with hospital corners the way my drill sergeant had taught me long ago. I took a Trazodone and a Restoril and was sleeping when the phone rang.

"Jimmy? Hey, guy, hope I didn't wake you." I glanced at the lighted alarm clock on my nightstand—two in the morning.

"Dwayne?"

"Yeah, buddy, look . . . I'm just calling to see if you want to be my guest at the Yankee–A's game on Saturday. I got two box seat tickets behind home plate and I thought we could really have some fun." The Monster was clearly shifting pharmaceutical gears now—he was slurring.

"Dwayne, it's two in the morning. I have to be up for work in a few hours."

"Yeah, well—sorry, buddy. I just wanted to offer a ticket to you first before one of my other buddies grabbed it."

"I appreciate that, Dwayne, but I spend the weekends with my daughters." Then it struck me that my new phone number had just been activated this afternoon. I hadn't yet given it to anyone except my girls. It wouldn't be listed in directory assistance's database for at least three more days.

"Dwayne, how did you get my phone number?"

A long silence. I imagined the Monster was accessing a mental file named *Mendacity*—probably the entire subdirectory.

"Uh . . . got it from information, how else?" The lie came across something like, *gofith fromasion, howse?*"

"Good night, Dwayne." I hung up and punched 411. Gave my name and address to the operator. A moment later she came back on the line.

"Sorry, sir, we have no listing for that name."

"Well, it's a new listing."

"As of when, sir?"

"As of today."

"Then it won't be in the database for at least three days."

Sometimes I am so tired of being right about certain things that I make myself sick. Directory assistance operators are overworked, underpaid, and unappreciated by our corporate finance folks, who are forever looking to fire them all and replace them with interactive voice mail.

"Thank you for your help," I tell the operator.

"Thank *you* for choosing . . ."

I went into the living room, picked up the receiver, and there was my new number, hastily scribbled in by the installer. I couldn't get back to sleep, so I spent the rest of that night reviewing my viewgraphs and notes for the morning.

At five in the morning I logged onto AOL to check my e-mails— maybe the girls had sent a message last night. There was the usual spam, nothing from Rachel or Alana, but the last message was from an unfamiliar screen name: GDNAYBR.

I clicked open the message—sent at 4:52 A.M.

"Hey, buddy, sorry I woke you. I forget sometimes, having my own business, that you office drones go to work in the morning." This was followed by the little smiley face that is supposed to convey cyberhumor. "Anyway, please accept my apology and let me know if you want to go out for breakfast at Denny's before you go to work." And another smiley face.

I deleted the message.

How did he get my screen name?

At 6:30 in the morning I placed a briefcase full of view-graphs and my proposed "vision statements" on the passenger seat of my trusty Camry wagon. I had wanted an SUV or at least a minivan, but the F.W. showed me an article in one of her consumer magazines disclosing the increased risk of these vehicles flipping or rolling over. We went with the old-fashioned, earth-hugging station wagon.

I looked forward to my presentation. I had happily suckled at the titty of AT&T—the original Ma Bell—for years, and I was no less de-

voted to draining the bloated bureaucratic bosom of her California off-
spring, Baby Bell of the West. Although I didn't want to alarm the
phone installer yesterday, it was common knowledge to much of management that our more aggressive (and profitable) sibling Baby Bell of
the South was in the final stages of swallowing us up. Our public rela-
tions people euphemistically referred to our predaceous sister as a "vi-
able merger candidate."

This was a merger in the way that democracy is asking six foxes and
one chicken to vote on what they want for dinner.

However, we tried to be good soldiers—at least for a few days. We
all parroted this official party line with varying degrees of virtual enthusiasm. Here and there, however, at the water coolers, the cafeteria,
the T-word was whispered: *takeover.* The latest mission of my anxious
corporate tribe—Strategic Planning and Market Assessment—was
meant to ennoble the imminent staff firings with a Delphic spin designed to comfort shareholders and confound employees. We were
already talking about "identifying redundancies and duplicative, non-
value-added functions."

I sensed I was a non-value-added function. It's not a feeling con-
ducive to enhancing one's self-esteem (which is what Bay Area living is
all about).

As Peon Spinmaster, I was selected (not unlike that lamb of old) to
dazzle the Board of the West with sparkling scenarios of future syner-
gistic suckling on both titties of the newly "merged" company.

I placed my suit jacket on top of the briefcase, adjusted the Windsor
knot my father had taught me to tie long ago. My father was now re-
tired in Florida after many years of practicing medicine in Brooklyn.
His office on 320 Empire Boulevard (just a few shouts from the old
Brooklyn Dodgers' Ebbets Field) stubbornly remained open in the
midst of an increasingly blighted neighborhood that grew more dangerous every year.

An old-fashioned "general practitioner," my father made house calls on any day or night of the week. To anywhere. Year after year, as neighborhood businesses boarded up their storefronts and all the professionals fled, my father hung on. All around him the lights were going out. He just kept showing up at his office every day, kept making house calls in the middle of the night. If a patient didn't have the money to pay, that was all right. He could pay when he could.

For my father the practice of medicine—*being* a doctor—was a privilege. A sacred trust. Despite graduating from college summa cum laude, he was turned down by every single medical school in the United States that he applied to. A few of the more forthright schools expressed regret but explained that they had already filled their "Jewish quota" for the year. He once showed me some of the rejection letters he kept in a file.

The letters were all dated 1942.

Undeterred, my father went to medical school in Montreal. He became fluent in French. He returned to Brooklyn to open his own practice.

And he never forgot the letters or the thinking behind them.

He stubbornly refused to join the "white flight" to Long Island or Westchester County. He and my mother were liberals before the term became a pejorative. Liberals of the activist variety, particularly my mother, whose father (my grandfather George) had left newly Bolshevik Russia as a young man and taken with him a lifelong admiration for Lenin and communism. My mother's commitments went beyond the membership in SANE or the subscriptions to *I. F. Stone's Weekly* newsletter, the *New Republic,* and later, that radical new upstart, *Ramparts* magazine.

My mother marched with Martin Luther King and was there whenever Dr. Benjamin Spock rallied the faithful (usually with Peter, Paul and Mary inspiring the crowd) against war and injustice. She organized interracial neighborhood action committees, and our house became an informal headquarters for left-wing causes.

She recovered from her disappointment over Adlai Stevenson's loss to Ike in time to become an enthusiastic volunteer for Eugene McCarthy and then George McGovern. (I don't recall her ever supporting a politician that actually won an election.)

Even when my father's office was burglarized three times in five months, he still refused to relocate. "The people in this neighborhood have a right to medical care beyond the hospital emergency room."

It took a couple of neighborhood junkies in search of narcotics to change his mind. They broke into the office one afternoon when my father was out on a house call. They stabbed his nurse, Judy, before fleeing with the drugs.

Judy recovered but the practice did not. My father had seen enough. He closed the office and a few months later was in Florida with my mother. He quickly became busier than ever, finding new challenges in local government and environmental issues.

My father, a nonobservant Jew, whom I don't recall ever attending synagogue, liked to say that "a man can preach a better sermon with his life than with his lips."

I looked in the Camry's rearview mirror and fixed the Windsor knot the way my father had shown me.

The Monster was in the mirror.

Maybe thirty yards distant, he was busy scooping up the morning newspaper that had just been deposited on the front doormat of a town house across the street. The Monster had on yesterday's jungle warfare costume, perfect for suburban newspaper pilferage.

I managed to accelerate down Maple Street before Dwayne could intercept me with whatever morning demons were dancing inside the safari hat. In five minutes I was at my—the F.W.'s—house to pick up the girls for school. Since my commute to work was only a few minutes, I was glad I would get to continue the long-standing routine of taking the girls to school in the morning. I liked the idea of seeing them both every day. The F.W. had already left for her job in San Francisco when I pulled up to the house.

The girls acted like my arrival was routine, carrying on in the back-seat with their usual spirited insults.

"You're so *lame,* Rachel—you're such an *idiot!*"

"*Daaad,* Alana called me an idiot."

"Because she *is*! She's trying to—"

"Girls, please, I'm trying to drive here. Can you please kill each other *after* you're out of the car?"

"But, *Da-ad*!"

"But nothing. Hey, did you know that a pig's *butt* is made of pork?"

"Dad, that's *so* stupid."

"Now you know how you both sound. Listen, just try to get along for five minutes."

"Whatever."

At the board meeting I showed my viewgraphs full of little bubbles and arrows and converging markets. A team of hit men consultants flown in from Boston facilitated the meeting to ensure we had a "rich interaction relative to structural opportunities and value-adds in the new empowered Corporate Culture."

Usually I resonate to this type of talk. Except when it might culmi-nate in my department's destruction and scattering to the winds of leveraged opportunity. Mergers are tricky—one empty suit's "value" is another's "redundancy."

I left the boardroom wondering how things had moved so fast. I hoped I would get a chance to liberate my personalized stapler and some other supplies before my desk was designated as ground zero for the "repositioning of duplicative management layers." After almost twenty years a man gets attached to his three-hole puncher and (fake) brass business card holder.

Wives come and go. Children grow up, get married, and leave. Love fades. But Corporate Culture is forever.

Until it changes.

In the wake of the board meeting our trusty Rumor Control Center went to work, triggering a feeding frenzy focused on the contemplated corpses in the executive offices. Pagers chirped and vibrated, phones trilled, and laptops lured the idle with the promise of delicious e-gossip, the more savage the better. My own voice mail box announced, "You have seventy-three new . . . and nineteen saved messages."

Old friends and even new enemies dropped by my cube (six square feet larger than any FNGs) to exchange information and paranoid speculations about the projected Baby Bell body count.

"Hey, Jimmy—did you hear about Don Lee, the quality veep?"

"Not yet, Paul. Why?"

"He's fucking history!"

Chirp! I return the page.

"Yeah, Barry, what are you hearing?"

"I hear Joe Stankus in H.R. is history. What does Rumor Control say? You're on headquarters staff."

"We're hearing Stankus will elect to leave to pursue outside opportunities."

"Yeah, I hear he's talking about becoming an *entrepreneur.* The moron can't even *spell* it."

Chirp, beep, briiiiing!

"This is Lerner, Strategy and Planning."

"Jimmy, it's Rick. I hear they're relocating headquarters staff to San Antonio."

"Nah—we're hearing they're just going to outsource the entire de-partment to our crack consultant firm from Boston."

"Hmm . . . actually that might make some sense."

And on and on.

All week we massed like lemmings by the fax machine, bloated ré-sumés in hand. We scrutinized the fractional fluctuations in the stocks of Baby Bells West and South. The closing prices on a secretly desig-nated date would affect the golden and silver parachutes. Possibly my bronze one.

Chirp! Rick's home number appears on my display.

"Jimbo, they're talking about a 20 percent premium for Baby West. What are you guys hearing?"

"Rumor Control says 16 percent plus a juicy cash-benefit buyout package for us peons." I was excited. A few of my oldest friends in mar-keting had just formed ("launched") a dot-com start-up in San Francisco and were urging me to join them. This was a chance for me to jump ship with a bunch of cash, stock, and health benefits and fi-nally do some challenging and interesting work.

The timing was perfect. After many years as a workaholic, a model cubicle slave and kiss-ass extraordinaire, I was drained, bankrupt—emotionally, intellectually, and spiritually. In the last year, actually the last few months, I had completely burned out. I had lost all desire and ability to focus on phone company business.

And I knew it hadn't gone unnoticed. I just couldn't get myself to care.

Dr. Shekelman regarded my lack of energy at work and my inabil-ity to concentrate as "just part of the depression." The pills would take care of it. Eventually.

My buddy Rick (who, nearing forty, recently started spelling his name "Ric") was happily shouting over the phone at me.

"All *right*! Sixteen percent! That would be just *too* fucking much! What are they doing with the geeks over in R&D?"

"Forty percent cuts—clear out your desk today and get an 'accelerated incentive payout.' Like one thousand bucks for each day you leave before the deadline."

"No fucking *way*, Jimbo!"

"Way, Rick—the elevators on their wing are jammed with future dot-com gazillionaires, plastic pen protectors stuffed with credit union checks for twenty grand."

"Those fucking lobs can *find* the elevators?"

"Sad but true. Who knows, next week we may be calling them *Mister* Lobs."

We were having the time of our lives! Cushioned by 401(k)s that had skyrocketed in the "irrational exuberance" of the nineties or vested stock options or just the expected cash-benefit buyouts, we were corporate rats scurrying about the carpeted corridors, drunk on rumor and chaos. The sheer pleasure of watching some of the empty suits drown in panic outweighed the hypothetical pain of our own diaspora.

We were survivors, dwellers forever in the cracks of the vast organizational chart. Disperse us, downsize us, squash us, transfer us, and we will reassemble someday, somewhere, to once again build new layers of redundancy, waste, and glaring irrelevance.

At a certain point in my musings I made a worried note in my corporate-financed leather Day-Timer:

Appt with Dr. Shekelman re adjusting Prozac.

Shekelman had recently increased (once again) the dosage to "help smooth out some of the rough edges of divorce."

The pills made me a tad excited.

After an exhilarating afternoon of tapping into Rumor Control's bottomless reservoir of misinformation, I left Cube World behind at 3 P.M. to go pick up the girls for their dental appointment. The F.W. didn't get back from San Francisco (the City, as Danvillites called it, and not fondly) until about six, so I made sure the girls (and sometimes two or three of their friends) adhered to their hectic postschool schedules.

Orthodontist appointments, soccer, softball, track, Girl Scouts, choir rehearsal—these kids were busy! Plus we had to make time for a McDonald's Happy Meal after all the errands.

School summer vacation was fast approaching, and both girls would go off to camp for two weeks. It was the first time both of them would be away from home at the same time. I missed them already.

After depositing the girls into the far more capable hands of the F.W.—a wonderful mother, I would also like the record to reflect—I arrived at my new crib on Maple Street.

Where the Monster, pick and shovel in his hands, is digging up my front garden.

So intent was he on his digging (was there oil beneath my leased property?), he never heard me pull into the driveway.

"Dwayne, what the hell are you doing?" I step out of the Camry and tap his shoulder, then jump back quickly, out of range of the pick.

"Hey, buddy! You sure put in the hours for the old phone company—hey, I see in the newspaper that your Baby Bell's been taken over. Are you out of a job?" Dwayne tosses the pick and shovel on a flower bed that a moment ago was pacifically producing baby buds and pleasant fragrances.

"Just a rumor, Dwayne. Why are you digging up my garden?"

Dwayne is in full gardening bloom today, shirtless in the summer heat but wearing the same green-brown camouflage pants favored by disgruntled postal workers and kids who think Vietnam was a video game. He even has an ammo pouch on his belt to hold his cigarettes.

"Just putting in your sprinkler system, pal. Want a beer?" The Monster takes off his work gloves and pulls a Heineken out of a cooler.

"No thanks. I don't recall asking the owner to install a sprinkler system." I remove my briefcase and suit jacket from the car.

"You didn't, pal—it's for the previous renter, Mrs. Bush. If it's the money you're worrying about, don't sweat it. Old lady Bush already paid me eight hundred bucks before she died." My leasee predecessor, Mrs. Bush, had conveniently died just as the F.W. and I were scouring the classifieds in search of a suitable residence for me and the girls.

"Dwayne, help me to understand. Mrs. Bush is currently a resident of the Heavenly Gardens Gated Community—why are you tearing up my garden?"

Dwayne responds to this question by unsheathing a bowie knife from his webbed "infantry" belt. The knife is long enough and sharp enough to remove the hump from a whale.

I'm still not sure whom I'm talking to: my friend Dwayne, fellow Brooklynite and stoopball aficionado, or the Monster. Just in case, I raise the briefcase slightly to my chest. I have packed enough bullshit on the viewgraphs inside to stop a surface-to-air missile—it should at least slow Mr. Bowie down a bit.

Dwayne flicks the tip of the blade upward, fast as a cobra, popping off the bottle cap. Takes a sip and studies me. It's the Monster who speaks next.

"Because Mrs. Bush *paid* me, buddy, so I *owe* her the sprinkler system. It's a question of *honor*—and I always pay back my debts."

"Well, Dwayne," I say, lowering the briefcase, "that's a very . . . honorable attitude."

"Bet your ass it is, pal! If that lying fuck Nixon had kept his word, all that shit about 'peace with honor,' this country wouldn't have left its balls on some stinking swamp of rice paddy in Viet Fucking Nam!"

His eulogy to America's lost honor apparently over, the Monster turned his wrath on me.

"Speaking of honor, of keeping your word, why did you rush off this morning? I thought we were going to Denny's for breakfast." The

Monster's tone has suddenly taken on the injured air familiar to any parent with small children. "Hey, I know it's not *Nathan's,* but it's closer." Dwayne is back now, smiling ruefully.

"Dwayne, I got your e-mail and definitely did *not* respond that I could make it for breakfast. In fact, I deleted the message."

Dwayne starts whining. "But on Mondays they have the western omelet special." He has conveniently shelved the issue of my nonresponse.

"How did you get my e-mail address, my screen name, Dwayne?"

Dwayne starts rummaging for the lie in the ammo pouches on his belt. Decides instead to delay by extracting a Marlboro.

"Fuck, all this shoveling shit really aggravates my shoulder injury." Next, I'm sure he's going to tell me how he "caught some shrapnel" in Vietnam. Instead he pulls a couple of prescription pill bottles out, drops two or three from each bottle into his mouth.

"No big mystery, Jimmy. It's not a password or anything. I simply did a keyword search on your AOL profile. You might think about not putting your real name and address in the profile fields."

"I don't, Dwayne. All I have in my profile is 'Jimmy,' my age, and the town of Danville."

"That's all I needed, pal. You should really adopt some stronger security precautions if you don't want your friends e-mailing you."

I'd had enough of my new neighbor (and former sponsee) for the day. I needed to go inside, shower, then call out for a substandard California pizza.

"Look, Dwayne, the sprinkler system is appreciated—I could use it. Gotta go now."

I had the front door open when Dwayne called out.

"Hey, buddy, how 'bout some steaks again tonight?"

"I'll take a rain check, Dwayne, but thanks anyway."

As I closed the door the Monster was on my front porch, shouting.

"Hey, you gotta eat! I'll bet you haven't even gone to Safeway yet. How about those steaks, buddy?"

I locked the door. Then put the chain up.

I needed a drink.

By myself.

The two burly visitors from Planet Repo returned a few days later, early in the morning. Their tow truck touched down dead center in the Monster's driveway. The two black tank tops marched directly to Dwayne's front door. After a few polite pushes of the bell they quickly resorted to the more natural rhythms of their planet:

Savage pounding.

Then the alien wolf tickets.

"Come on out, asshole! We know you're in there!"

"Give up the *Rover*, Grover—Repo Man taking over!"

"Don't be a fucking pain, De-*Wayne*!"

I've always been partial to street performance artists, so I clicked off *Good Morning America* and eased (fell) out of my La-Z-Boy to watch from the window. Resplendent in my ratty old bathrobe, I sipped cold instant coffee and gnawed at a piece of frozen Domino's pizza with icy anchovies embedded in the crust.

Breakfast of Champions for a soon-to-be "cash-benefit buyout" bachelor.

"Yo! De-*Wayne*! Come on out, you deadbeat piece of shit!" Silence from the Monster's lair. Not a creature stirring.

Till the Monster's garage door rumbled open and the Rover rocketed out in reverse, tires—and driver—shrieking.

"YO REPO COCKSUCKERS! EAT SHIT AND DIE!"

The Monster waved a middle finger, his face a clenched fist. His exit blocked by the tow truck, the Monster lurched the Rover into drive, spun, then escaped alien capture by fashioning an alternate route through his front garden. The Rover bounced over the curb, then skidded uncontrollably across the street before leaping the opposite curb and extending the escape route through my front garden, over the crushed bodies of innocent little flowers.

By the time the repo invaders had retreated to the radio in the tow truck, the Monster had shifted into warp three, screaming "cocksuckers" out the window as he vanished. The tank-topped invaders got on the radio and reported back to the mother ship.

I shaved, suited up, and went to pick up the girls for school. I spent much of the day talking to Rumor Control, then spreading fear and loathing throughout Cube World.

Score so far: Repo Planet 1, the Monster 1.

Less than zero for my little flowers.

Although I didn't see the Monster for a few days after that I knew he was hiding in his foul cave—like Grendel's mom nursing her hatred. Late at night, from my living room picture window, I could look across the street and see cars pulling up, people getting out, going into the house for a few minutes, and then taking off. Then the next car would pull up.

Sometimes I could see silhouettes moving back and forth behind Dwayne's semitransparent living room window treatments.

On a Tuesday night I was returning from a late evening with the girls. We had gone to the nearby Blackhawk movie theater to see *Little Women.* We stuffed ourselves with popcorn and soda and Gummi Bears (they taste better at the movies) and played the pinball machines in the game room afterward. I dropped them off at about eleven at the F.W.'s and was cruising down Maple Street when I heard the shouts coming from the Monster's house. A solitary silhouette behind the curtain was stalking the living room floor, arms flailing at the air. The Monster was apparently alone.

And screaming.

Curious, I eased the Camry to the curb and idled.

"COCKSUCKERS! THINK YOU CAN COME DOWN TO MY HOUSE! TO MY MOTHERFUCKING *HOME*?!" The Monster was a spinning shadow behind the front curtains. The raving was acoustically enhanced by the occasional crash of a dirty dish against the wall.

I put my cigarette out in the ashtray. Didn't want to give away my position in case the Monster looked out his window and decided to try a little target practice with his closet arsenal. I paid attention at the jungle combat and night-fighting courses they put us through in Panama. And *my* MOS was 11B—11 Bravo, Infantry, also known as "eleven bang-bang"—a.k.a. Combat Arms.

Crash!

"...LIKE IT'S ALL RIGHT...WELL, LET ME TELL YOU MOTHERFUCKERS SOMETHING—IT'S *NOT* ALL FUCKING RIGHT. NOBODY FUCKS WITH ME! YOU DON'T COME TO MY HOUSE AND FUCK WITH *ME!*"

It wasn't clear to me if the motherfuckers in question were the tangible ambassadors of Planet Repo or the generic kind of motherfuckers that plague all of us: the sluggish, sullen supermarket checkout girl; the octogenarian driver doing thirty-five directly in front of you when the highway is clearly marked fifty-five; the telemarketer who somehow knows precisely when you are sitting down for dinner.

So many motherfuckers. So little time.

Craaaash! go Dwayne's dishes against the wall.

"BUT *YOUR* DAY IS COMING, MOTHERFUCKERS! OH, YEAH, YOU CAN MAKE FUCKING BOOK ON THAT. YOU CAN TAKE THAT TO THE FUCKING BANK AND . . ."

And on and on.

The Baby Bell "merger" was temporarily delayed by our regulatory "stakeholders" (the FCC, PUC, and Justice Department), who were starting to ask intrusive and irritating questions about the potential benefits to consumers. They even invoked the M-word—*monopoly*—like this is a *bad* thing.

While the regulators met with the empty suits, I, along with a thousand or so of my cubicle world soulmates, resumed my rightful place at Ma Bell's titty. It took all of us working together to exhaust the still generous residue of the conference, supplies, training, and travel budgets.

Like ravenous bums at a free buffet, we gorged till we resonated and burst! Air and hotel reservations were booked to critical "interdisciplinary" seminars and market-focused workshops in Puerto Rico, London, Brussels, New York, and Hawaii. I ordered (through a "preferred minority vendor") multiple copies of cutting-edge, A.I.-based software and shameless quantities of "home office" supplies to support my "telecommuting" effort, concluding my orgy with a four-star-hotel reservation in Miami for an upcoming Strategic Planning conference in November.

Travel, conferences, and conventions are critical to periodically refresh the old "skill sets" and "knowledge base." So is networking over the free cocktails they give you at the receptions before the seminars.

Wouldn't want to be considered *noncompetitive*!

. . .

When I rolled up to my driveway on a hot Friday afternoon, the Monster was back at it, running sprinkler wires from the small trenches he had dug in the front yard to the side door of my garage. Dwayne was in full battle safari regalia with a cowboy twist. The flexible Banana Republic safari hat was pulled down to shade his eyes, and instead of the webbed army contraption around his waist he wore a wide cowboy belt. The belt encircled the baggy camouflage pants, cinched by an enormous brass buckle.

"Hey, pal, you're right on time! Open up the garage door and I'll install your control box and then it's a wrap."

I emerged warily from the Camry, again armed only with my briefcase and suit jacket. I had removed my tie the moment I exited the phone company complex. Danville was about an hour inland from the bay, and by late May it was not unusual for temperatures to approach 100 degrees. Dwayne wore his favorite long-sleeved safari-style shirt, with the sleeves buttoned tight at the wrists.

When he approached, his eyes (blue today) bespoke a world of remorse. I had seen the same look in the faces of countless newcomers to A.A. meetings—before they found their Higher Power and relapsed into self-righteousness, drunk on false spirituality.

The A.A. old-timers would just chuckle when they shared and advise them to "keep coming back."

"Jimmy, I want to apologize for running over your flowers the other morning—I was in a bit of a rush."

A *bit* of a rush? Must have been a Costco special on tinted contact lenses. I accepted his outstretched, oversize hand. Once again he did his best to crush my pianist's fingers. There was a track of dried blood on his left sleeve.

I gave back as good as I received. "Dwayne, why don't you save that grip for someone at the gym that might be impressed."

Dwayne ignored the barb—he was on some kind of twelve-step inspired "amends" mission.

"Listen, buddy, I'm gonna make it up to you. I'm putting in a *digital* sprinkler control box, *top-a-da-line*! You can program your watering days, your hours. Cost you just two hundred extra. The labor is on me—for the flowers and all."

Gone was the false sincerity. Another mask the Monster could don or discard at a whim. We stood in my driveway in the shadow of Mount Diablo, squirrels racing up and down the trees that glutted Maple Street with green life.

"*Extra?* Dwayne, I thought old lady Bush had already paid you eight hundred bucks. What happened to all that inspiring rhetoric about Vietnam and 'honoring debts' to the dead, not to mention honoring your word to the living?"

Instantly abashed (another mask?), the Monster's blue eyes du jour stared down at the jungle boots, seeking some credible semblance of a truthful reply. His right hand slid down, gunslinger style, to the belt buckle.

The cowboy buckle was a massive rectangle of metal, engraved with an eagle. The eagle seemed to be soaring above the barbed-wire fences and watchtower of a POW camp. Above the watchtower the inscription FREE OUR MIAS; below—OUR EAGLE FLIES IN CHAINS.

The thought of paper eagles *not* flying into his wallet as expected must have shocked the Monster into an answer. In two strides he was upon me. In my face.

"That's right, pal—I *always* pay my debts and I always honor my word! Forget about the fucking money!"

In the next instant came that amazing transformation. The Monster sat down hard in the dirt. Clasped his arms around his knees and started rocking. When he finally looked up, Dwayne's eyes were a damp pool of pain.

"What the fuck is *wrong* with me? I'm sorry, pal. Things are just going straight into the toilet—financially. I don't know what the fuck is—"

"Dwayne, listen to me." I dropped my briefcase and put a hand on his shoulder. "It's the drugs, the coke talking, not you. You have to clean it up, you have—"

The Monster was immediately on his feet, the blue vein starting to flutter in his forehead.

"Hey, pal, don't you fucking *dare* to lecture me! You're not my sponsor now. You think I don't see what *you're* doing? Better clean your own house before you start pointing fingers at my mess."

He was right and we both knew it. I went to safer ground.

"Dwayne, why not just forget about the sprinklers? Keep the digital box. I don't need any of this stuff. The garden hose works just fine."

But the Monster had already turned back to his bundle of wires.

"Too late now, pal. I'm done. Just open the garage door and I'll be finished in ten minutes. I gave my word." Sulking worse than a child, the Monster started gathering up his pick, shovel, and other assorted tools. I pulled the clicker out of the car's visor, pushed the button, and let the Monster enter with his *top-a-da-line* two-hundred-dollars-*extra* digital box.

My refrigerator was near empty again. The F.W. would be bringing the girls over in a couple of hours and I needed to prepare dinner. No problem. I called Tony Roma's and reserved a table. The girls loved Tony Roma's, the baby back ribs chased down with Shirley Temples.

Actually the girls loved McDonald's and Burger King. Every now and then *I* just had to have some real food.

The F.W. drove up with the girls just as the Monster finished digitizing the water so my dead flowers could benefit from a high-tech res-urrection. The F.W. and the girls looked like three dark-haired beautiful sisters coming down the cobblestone path. They were lugging enough backpacks and suitcases and soccer paraphernalia to sustain the girls for a year of weekend visitations.

Dwayne emerged from the garage side door as I was relieving the F.W. and the girls of their lighter burdens. The hip-to-neck fusion had never taken properly, and I was careful to avoid lifting anything too heavy.

"You're in business, pal! I'll come back for my tools and stuff tomorrow." Dwayne was talking to me but staring at the girls and at the F.W. with the incredulous manner of a death row inmate in Texas who has just been granted a last-second pardon by the governor.

"Thanks, Dwayne." Ignoring his unspoken plea for an introduction, I hustled my former family inside, where the F.W. immediately went to the girls' bedroom, followed by an inspection tour of the bathrooms and kitchen. She took note of the empty refrigerator.

Alana took immediate advantage of having both parents present.

"Dad, can't I just sleep on the living room floor? Mom can bring over my sleeping bag. No way I'm sharing a room with Rachel—she's so *gross!*" Alana, pretty as a fresh-minted penny, all of fourteen, athletically slender, and already drawing her battle lines.

But I was still a general.

"No, honey, I've set up a nice bedroom for you and Rachel. Only crack addicts and refugees sleep on living room floors."

"But, *Da-ad*! Rachel's so *disgusting*. She does things just to annoy me. She's so *sick*, she—"

"Shut *up*, Alana!" An outraged Rachel, a beautiful thirteen-year-old version of her sister (and her mother). "You're the one who's *sick*. Why don't I just tell Dad who you—"

"Girls," I interrupt in my most authoritative manner, "there will be a minimum of bickering in this house—a new rule for a new house." I could almost hear their eyeballs rolling up to the backs of their heads—the adolescent antidote to parental pompousness. I ignored them.

"You girls are sharing a bedroom and that's final. I had to share a bedroom with your Uncle Michael for years, and he used the wallpaper above his bed for a booger vault. Now, *that's* disgusting."

"*Da-ad!*" Both girls now in whining unison: "*Booger vault? That's so* sick!"

The F.W., laughing, picked up her purse and headed to the door.

"Enjoy the weekend, girls. Jimmy, don't forget about the soccer games at nine tomorrow—it's the first round of the play-offs."

"How could I forget? I tried to schedule an optional root canal procedure instead, but all the other dads beat me to it."

The F.W. closed the front door behind her. I glanced around to see if any windows of opportunity had magically opened. You never can tell.

"Dad, what are we having for dinner? I bet you didn't even buy any food yet. Can we go to McDonald's?"

"Special treat tonight, Alana. We've got reservations for Tony Roma's."

"All right! Can we get those tall Shirley Temples?"

"Anything you want."

And Alana hugged her little sister and squeezed her affectionately until Rachel howled in protest.

God, how I loved those girls.

The following week on Saturday morning both girls went berserk at the same time. I attributed it to the stress of the final soccer play-off games. Or maybe they were nervous about leaving for summer camp in a few days.

Or maybe just the fact the sun had risen again.

"Dad, I can't find my soccer shoes—that idiot Rachel probably *hid* them!"

"Don't call me an *idiot,* Alana. I've got *my* soccer shoes on. You're just a *retard!*"

"*Da-ad*—Rachel called me a retard."

This time the bickering only lasted ten minutes.

After a hurried breakfast we raced out to the station wagon—late, of course—loading up the back with the tons of equipment necessary for landing on Omaha Beach.

The car, parked overnight in the driveway, wouldn't start.

Just a feeble *click.*

I turned the ignition key again.

Click.

This had never happened to the Camry before. I maintained both our cars—the Camry and the (F.W.'s) Honda Accord—with the fear-driven fanaticism of the mechanically hopeless. I grew up with subways and buses and Keds sneakers. One time I took a ferry out to Staten Island. You didn't have to know about auto repairs.

Click.

"Da-ad! We're going to miss the game!"

"No we're not, baby."

Click.

"Forget it, Dad—can't you just call Mom?"

"She's already at the game, honey—she's helping set up."

Click.

Clueless, I wondered if the clicking noise indicated carburetor arrhythmia, or worse, a terminal transaxle disorder.

"I'll call Triple-A," I finally reassured the now-hysterical girls.

"That will take, like, *forever.* Can't you check under the hood? It sounds like a dead battery." My daughter Alana the mechanic.

Everything under the hood looked fine to me (it always does). All the important stuff seemed to be in the usual places—the engine, the battery, and God only knows what the rest of those things are. Like I said, I took the subway during my formative years.

"Hey, pal, need a hand?" Dwayne was approaching from across the street, a long-sleeved flannel shirt over tiger-striped fatigue pants, safari hat, and shades. We had gotten together once during the week after I got off work. We went to a new Chinese restaurant in downtown Danville so we could criticize it later—"In New York you can get *real* lobster Cantonese." After dinner we drove in to Berkeley for a revival of *Midnight Cowboy*. When Dustin Hoffman, as an outraged Ratso, slammed his hand down on the hood of that car and proclaimed, "Hey! *I'm wah-kin here,*" we both shrieked with delight. *Ratso Rizzo!* That was a *real* New Yorker.

"Morning, Dwayne. It won't start. I think it's the transaxle fluid or something."

"Dad! *Da-ad!* We gotta *go*—the game's starting in like five minutes!"

Dwayne took a look under the hood and listened to the *click*.

"Jimmy, do you have jumper cables? I'll go get the Rover and get you started." Dwayne went jogging off, disappearing around the block.

"Dad, who is that huge creep?"

"My new neighbor, Alana."

"When did they let him out?"

The Range Rover roared down Maple Street, freed from its temporary hiding place. After a quick battery juice transfusion the Camry came to life and we were racing toward the park. Dwayne insisted on following in the Rover in case we stalled out on the way.

Both girls' teams were in the play-offs, on separate fields. I was the designated sufferer for Alana's game. Whenever the girls had games at the same time, the F.W. and I would switch off, alternating teams over the season. We wanted to quash any adolescent charges of favoritism.

So we both suffered equally. Or at least I did. The F.W. genuinely enjoyed watching the games. Must be a New Jersey thing.

The girls charged across the field as soon as I opened the Camry's door. Then Dwayne came over and leaned down to the window. He

was apparently experiencing another attack of summer allergies, snif-
fling and dabbing at his nose with a slightly bloody handkerchief.

"It probably won't start up again after you turn the ignition off. I
better hang out, follow you to a garage after the games. You can get the
battery recharged or a new one at Exxon."

"Thanks, Dwayne, you saved the day."

But Dwayne was gone.

It was the Monster who snarled down at me.

"Sure, pal, guess I did save your ass—the ass of a guy who just last
week thought he was *too fucking good* to introduce me to his precious
little girlie family." The Monster leaned into my window, removed his
shades, and directed a green laser glare at me. The eyes glittered in the
sun's reflection.

Like an ax.

"Dwayne, I'm sorry about not introducing you—we were in a
huge rush."

The Monster receded. "All right then, buddy, apology accepted."
Dwayne reached down and tightened the laces on his jungle combat
boot. What was he expecting? Hand-to-hand combat with a deranged
soccer ball?

From the field came semihysterical screams and shrieks.

From the parents.

They thought of this as "encouragement."

"Thanks again, Dwayne." I escaped from the car, taking my cell
phone. "You don't have to hang out. I'll call Triple-A from the game.
One of the soccer moms will give me a boost if I need it."

"Hey, there's no problem, pal. I'll just wait with you until the games
are over. I'm a big soccer fan."

"I appreciate that, Dwayne, but it's not necessary."

"Neither was giving you a boost or making sure you made it here."

So the Monster sat beside me on the splintered wooden grandstand,
just two guys, the *only* guys, neighbors, in a sea of frenzied, encourag-

ing soccer moms. The moms prowled the sidelines, cheering on every misplaced kick, every misguided pass.

The players, the girls, were just happy to be out in the sunshine, kicking it with their friends and basking in the adulation of their moms. The rare ball that actually squirted past the defending goalie was regarded as a not unpleasant bonus.

"Hey, pal, check out the little babe with the blue sweatband." The Monster elbowed me in the ribs. The "babe" in question was a good friend of Alana's named Courtney. She'd been over to the house dozens of times.

"What about her, Dwayne?"

"What *about* her? Are you blind? The little bitch's tits are bobbing around like fucking grapefruits." The Monster was also bobbing around the bench, clearly excited by his belated discovery that many thirteen-year-old girls had well-developed breasts.

Unbidden, the downloaded image of a naked and kneeling adolescent on Dwayne's computer monitor swamped my brain.

"*Shut the fuck up, Dwayne!* That girl's a friend of the family, and even if she wasn't, she's *thirteen,* for Christ's sake." A few of the cheerleader moms stopped prancing on the sidelines to look reprovingly at me. The Monster, unaffected by my remark, squeezed my elbow, leaning into my face.

He whispered.

"So what are you saying, pal? Look at the fucking tits, the *ass* on that little bitch! You saying you wouldn't stick a bone up that tight little ass? Maybe slap her around a little bit first, get her in the mood, ya know?"

My friends say that I am slow to anger, very slow, but when I get there, people usually know it.

"Get the fuck out of here, Dwayne! Move your ass—*now!*"

The Monster didn't move. Just gave me that injured look, then the slow twist of a smile. My friend Dwayne was long gone and far away.

"Or *what,* Jimmy," he said softly. Calm and cold as a rock. "Let me tell you something, pal—back in Brooklyn, if I had seen your skinny ass on the streets when we were kids, I would have taken your lunch money. You think you're gonna *do* something? You going to hit me in front of your daughter, in front of all these fine ladies?"

I jumped off the bench, startling the ex-cheerleaders.

"No, Dwayne, I'm not going to hit you. But if you're not out of here in three seconds . . . I WILL BREAK YOUR FUCKING NECK!" The cheerleader moms all scurried away down the sidelines.

The Monster feigned fear, mocking me, before sliding off the bench and strolling casually toward the parking lot.

It was the F.W. who later gave me the battery jump.

The girls begged off for the rest of the weekend, having accepted invitations for sleep-overs. On Monday morning they would leave on buses for a two-week camping trip near Lake Tahoe. They wanted to be home on Sunday night to pack.

After buying a new battery from Exxon (the teenage battery specialist determined that my three-month-old one would not hold a charge) I spent the rest of that Saturday at my computer, chain-smoking and putting together financial projections for the new dot-company I would shortly join. The instant that the phone company offered me the cash buyout (Rumor Control said my group would "receive coverage" this week) I was gone. Out the door. Good-bye, Empty Suits.

My friends (all phone company marketing guys but without the bell-shaped heads) had already received their cash buyouts and leased office space on Market Street in San Francisco. Initial funding would come from our cash buyouts, and we were confident of quickly picking up venture capital once we firmed up the business plan.

We were going to make millions through an on-line telecommunications management company. We would guarantee to save businesses 20 percent off their phone bills, and our fee would be a percentage of those savings. A slam-dunk, no-brainer proposition.

We would simply follow the model of traditional "resellers" and billing "aggregators" who made high-volume (and highly discounted) wholesale toll purchases from long-distance carriers and then resold it to business customers. My Lotus spreadsheet profit projections were very simple to build: buy millions of MOUs (minute-of-use) at three cents a minute and resell at five to seven cents. Not *too* profitable—ha!

The bankers or venture capitalists would resonate and salivate.

Bill Gates would want to either buy us or crush us.

From my phone company supplied "workstation" in the living room I watched the mailman screech his van to a halt in front of the mailbox. I watched him stuff it and then returned to my fantasies of dot-com deification and millions in equity ten minutes after the IPO. The mail could wait.

Sunday morning, sporting my old ratty bathrobe (with fresh cigarette burns), I unhinged the mailbox to release the new bills and advertising circulars ("$2.00 off your 2nd large pizza!"). Mostly junk except for the comp offer from the Excelsior Hotel in Las Vegas. I had played blackjack there a few months ago with my marketing buddies, and we had made our usual donations, losing maybe two hundred dollars in total.

No good deed goes unpunished. The Excelsior was going to make it even easier for me to lose money in the future. The Excelsior "VP Staff" had just elevated me to "Diamond Player" status. As a "preferred Diamond customer" I (plus a friend) could avail myself of "two complimentary nights in our Diamond Executive 2-bedroom/living room suite." Any two nights of the week.

As long as they fell between a Sunday and a Thursday.

And it had to be during the off-season—in the blazing-hot summer.

I suspected there were levels even higher than "Diamond."

I spent the rest of the day and early evening with Dr. Blackjack, practicing my counting techniques. Dwayne called twice to apologize. I hung up both times and let the third call go to my answering machine. I screened the call—it was not an apology:

"*COCKSUCKER!* DON'T YOU FUCKING HANG UP ON *ME!* NOBODY TALKS TO ME LIKE YOU DID AT THE SOCCER GAME! NOBODY THREATENS ME. THIS IS *WAR,* COCK-SUCKER, AND YOU ARE A *DEAD* MAN!"

Without thinking about it I pressed Message Save and then massaged the surgical scar on my throat. I made a trip to the medicine cabinet and then returned to Dr. Blackjack, quickly amassing $3,000. Within an hour I was up almost $10,000. This called for a celebration.

I opened up a bottle of cabernet and poured myself one glass. No harm in just one glass of wine. The key was to control the intake. The problem with the alcoholics in A.A. was that they just hadn't figured out a good control strategy. I would sip the wine. Like a gentleman.

By nightfall I was up $40,000, my dot-com projected profits were up to the billions, and the bottle of cabernet was down to nothing.

Life was good.

When the Monster called again at 9 P.M. to apologize again, I didn't hang up. He had just been kidding at the soccer game and carried it too far. *Really sorry, pal.* For all those offensive remarks. He certainly hadn't meant that last call as a *threat.* No, we were *pals,* he'd never threaten me. He was just frustrated, pissed off at himself and letting off steam.

After five minutes I accepted his apology and begged him to shut up already. We talked about a pool hall in Brooklyn—Spinelli's on Church Avenue. With my girls gone to camp we decided to go to nearby Oakland this week to a pool hall. Shoot some *New York*-style pool—*straight* pool, a game of skill, none of this eight-ball slop so beloved by Californians.

I told him about my dot-com billions, my new Diamond status, and my Dr. Blackjack winnings. Maybe we'd even go to Las Vegas together.

How could I stay mad at a guy when life was so good?

On Monday morning I was so hungover I forgot the girls had left for camp. I was almost at the F.W.'s house when I remembered they were gone for two weeks. I made a U-turn and raced back toward work. My mouth was a foul thicket of cotton, and an invisible hammer was pounding out a bass line inside my skull.

This has to stop, I thought. *You're losing control. No—you've already lost it.* I resolved right then and there to return to A.A. To raise my hand and start all over—on Step One if necessary. Right after work I would go to a meeting.

When I arrived at Cube World, there was a message (a Post-it note stuck to my computer monitor) from the secretary to go see my boss for the "cash-benefit coverage." (She was familiar with my message "aging" system and knew better than to send me an urgent voice mail.)

So today was the day. A cornucopia of cash and stock just to say bye-bye! My only thoughts were *yes, yes, and YES!*

An hour later I emerged from my Empty Suit's office with an obscene grin and a stack of forms including one whereby I waived my "exit interview." I was taking the money and running. I technically had thirty days to clean out my desk; however, I had elected the "accelerated departure option." Imagine. They would actually pay me a bonus for each day that I left under the thirty days.

It took me only two hours to get out of the building.

I first spent a few minutes on the phone to make arrangements to roll my 401(k) over into an IRA. I then called my new dot-com comrades in San Francisco. I would join them in one week, bringing my final marketing and financial plans.

Feeling more excited, more hopeful than I had in many months at the office, I visited the cubes and offices of the few friends who were still left. I shook lots of hands, gave and received hugs, exchanged numbers, and then piled my personal belongings in a cardboard box.

I took some books, my personalized stapler, my three-hole puncher, and my (faux) brass business card holder. There were *lines* of people holding boxes up and down the corridors, waiting for the elevators. They were all smiling. Unlike all our previous downsizings, this was a sweet deal.

For me this felt like *redemption.* Like a new beginning.

I drove directly from work to an A.A. noon meeting in Danville.

I was relieved that none of the familiar faces (like Luther or Doris) from my Monday night meeting were there. When the secretary asked if there were any new members or any members in their first thirty days of sobriety, I raised my hand and stood up.

Everyone clapped for me and there were shouts of "Welcome."

I sat quietly through the meeting, leaving a few minutes before the closing prayer. I didn't want to talk with anyone.

Back at the house I went through the kitchen cabinets. I emptied out what remained from a pint of Chivas. I uncorked a full bottle of cabernet and poured the contents into the sink. There was a half-empty can of Foster's beer in the cabinet under the sink—I tossed it. I was stunned to find an empty half-pint bottle of vodka hidden behind the box of Frosted Flakes. I didn't remember buying it. The vodka was inside a brown paper bag.

Where did that come from?

I was scared. No, I was *beyond* scared—I was totally freaked out.

I thought I had this problem under control. Well, if not under *complete* control, at least there had been no blackouts. It was like discovering that the alcoholic monster you thought was secured safely in a cage had somehow managed to sneak out undetected a few times.

Late at night. When no one was looking.

Like the rebellious teenager grounded by his parents who waits until midnight and then slips out through his bedroom window to meet his friends and go party.

I was filling a plastic garbage bag with the evidence of my insanity when the phone rang. I picked it up warily, heart pounding. I wouldn't have been surprised if it was the police telling me not to leave town because I was the chief suspect in a hit-and-run.

Instead, it was the A.A. police.

"Welcome back, asshole."

"Luther?"

"I was wondering when you'd get sick and tired of being sick and tired. How is it *Out There*? Did the booze work for you this time? You know in all my years in A.A. I have yet to hear anyone come back and tell me how great it is to go out, how great it—"

"Luther, it's so nice to hear your warm and supportive voice. How the hell did you know I was at a meeting?"

"I got spies, Jimmy. A.A. in a small town is the same as getting drunk in public in a small town. Everyone knows about it right away. You realize you got to start all over again and your first step better be to quit hanging out with that guy Dwayne. Doris says she saw you with him at the movies in Berkeley. He's a drug dealer. This time around in the program you better get a sponsor right away. Forget about that drug-dispensing shrink of yours. Get rid of all your pills. Get rid of that quack doctor. A.A. is all about *one alcoholic talking to another.* About *sponsorship*! As a matter of fact I'm not doing anything right—"

"Luther, I appreciate your calling but you caught me in the middle of a project here. Let me call you back later."

"All right—just remember HOW."

"How?"

"Honesty, openness, and willingness! The three things you never brought with you when you came into recovery. Probably the reason you slipped and—"

"Luther, let me—"

"And HALT, Jimmy, don't forget that."

"Halt. Uh, let me guess. This is not a Lutherism, it's another A.A. acronym, right?"

"And this one might just save your life, smart-ass. Just remember HALT: never let yourself get too *hungry,* too *angry,* too *lonely,* or too *tired.* And don't even think . . ."

And on and on until my head hurt. I was almost sorry I had just dumped out the Chivas.

The next morning was trash pickup day, so I dumped the empty bottles in the garbage can in my garage and wheeled the can out to the curb. Across the street, in front of Dwayne's house, a slender young black man was also setting out the trash, struggling to balance several plastic bags on top of the cans. He wore bright red gym shorts under a yellow T-shirt that had been torn to display a bare brown midriff.

The moment he spotted me he waved and seemed to light up with smiles. He balanced two huge cans against the curb, then scurried

across the street, swinging his hips and ass in what he must have supposed was a girlish gait.

"You must be Jimmy. I'm Hakeem, Dwayne's housekeeper. Dwayne
called and asked me to tell you that he's sorry but he won't be able to
go shoot pool with you. He'll be out of town on business for a few
days." Hakeem was barely out of his teens, and his voice had that pleasant musical lilt of the Caribbean.

This was good news since I had planned to cancel anyway. Hanging
out with Dwayne could not possibly fit into my recovery plan.

"Thanks, uh, A-*Key*?"

"*Ha-keem.*" He spelled it for me. Hakeem was very slight and short,
and his eyebrows had been plucked out and painted back in. He looked
past me to my house. "I understand you just moved in. If you need any
cleaning or laundry done, just let me—"

"Thanks, Hakeem, but I'm fine for now."

"I could use the money. Dwayne hasn't paid me in almost two months
and I'm practically broke. And his place is a *total* pigsty. He should pay
me triple just to *enter* this pisshole. Have you ever been inside his house?"

I nodded.

"And now he says I have to be a *house sitter* until he comes back—
like I'm supposed to guard his little treasures, his stashes, for nothing
when he hasn't even paid me yet for all the cleaning. Well, I just don't
know." Hakeem clucked his tongue and released one of those exasper-
ated sighs that said, "Life is unfair."

"When is Dwayne coming back?"

Another dramatic sigh and roll of the eyes. "Like he would tell *me*.
Besides he would just lie like he lies about everything. Lately, when I
ask him about anything—*especially* for my money—he goes crazy. I
thought he was going to tear me apart this morning when I asked him
to pay what he owes me. I swear the man is a *monster*!"

I went back inside and thought about what Hakeem had said.

A *monster*. The word was spat out from Hakeem's lips. In the days and months to come I would look back on this conversation, and the part I remember most vividly is that one word:

Monster.

I woke up early on Tuesday morning—trash day—to the sound of garbage cans being emptied into trucks. I hoped the bottles I had stuffed into the cans (after wrapping them in newspaper) didn't shatter on the curb. Where all the neighbors could see.

I spent the entire morning working on the dot-com (we were thinking of calling it Bellboys.com) business plan. I massaged some of the revenue forecasts and wrote a section on the "competitive landscape." For the benefit of our potential lenders I built a series of spreadsheet scenarios with even the "worst case" showing a break-even point after a scant twenty months.

My "probable case" would, of course, shower the investor with fabulous returns in only twelve months. We had no doubt about attracting capital. Our concern was how to retain as much equity for ourselves as possible.

By 5 P.M. some of the members of the committee that lives inside my head started talking to me. I recognized a few of the familiar voices: Mr. Jack Daniel's and his pals, Mr. Johnnie Walker Red and Mr. Johnnie Walker Black.

They talked softly, reasonably.

Seductively.

They always did.

Señor Cuervo and Comrade Smirnoff even weighed in with encouraging and friendly comments.

At 6 P.M. I jumped into the car and went to an A.A. meeting. In Oakland. It was a forty-minute drive, but I didn't want to run into anyone I knew. Again, I raised my hand when they asked for newcomers. Again, I left early, before anyone could talk to me.

On the way home it occurred to me just how foolish I was being about the whole drinking situation. I was definitely overreacting. The alcohol wasn't the problem. It was the stress of the job! Well, guess what, Jimmy? The job is now history. So the underlying reasons that led to (perhaps) drinking too much (occasionally) are gone.

I was on the precipice of a whole new life. Dot-com millions! No more empty suits looking over my shoulder. I'd be my own boss. None of the old phone company *aggravations*! This was certainly no time to abandon faithful old friends like Jack and Johnnie. I thought of all the great men—all the great artists and leaders and visionaries throughout history—that drank alcohol. In fact, alcohol often *fueled* business genius and creative accomplishment.

Just ask any alcoholic, I thought crazily.

The key, the secret, was all in moderation. Ancient philosophers knew this.

Aristotle knew it. I would simply employ the Aristotelian Golden Mean.

My (dwindling) inner voice of sanity piped up: *Jimmy, this is insane thinking. Why don't you call someone? Your brain is a very dangerous place. Like a really bad neighborhood. You shouldn't be in there all alone.*

And as I took the I-680 exit to Sycamore Road in Danville I was temporarily restored to sanity.

For about two minutes.

Then my Camry, on its own volition, made a sudden right turn and steered itself into the parking lot of Liquor Barn.

Hello, Johnnie. Hello, Jack. Who's up first?

. . .

I woke up at dawn on Wednesday morning. Years of habit pulled me out of bed and into the shower. I was accustomed to going to work with a hangover and I wanted to finish the Bellboys.com plan. In just a few more days I would be expected to lead the dog and pony shows for the benefit of prospective investors.

I wanted to be thoroughly prepared, ready for any and all questions. I wanted the marketing and financial plans to be absolutely perfect. The same way I always wanted an A on my school papers.

Four hours, three cups of coffee, and a half pack of cigarettes later, I had to stop and get up. Had to move around. My muscles were quivering like a bowl of Jell-O in an earthquake. One of the many joys of two less-than-successful surgeries is unexpected jolts of searing pain. The pain was sharp and sustained, like someone plunging an electric cattle prod into your neck—and then holding it there for a half hour.

Dr. Feldman, my neurosurgeon, referred to this bit of unpleasantness as "normal postsurgical radiculopathy." *Normal,* like its muscle-convulsing first cousin, Mr. Fasciculation. Feldman said not to worry, though. Just some temporary (probably) side effects. They would disappear. Eventually.

I went to the medicine cabinet and then sought the comfort of my La-Z-Boy to smoke and await a temporary respite from the stabbing pain. I knew a shot of Jack or Johnnie would work faster than the pills, but I was adhering to the Golden Mean—moderation and balance.

There would be absolutely no drinking until 5 P.M. Part of living in the Golden Mean was adhering to a gentlemanly cocktail hour.

The pills kicked in twenty minutes later, and I hunched back over the monitor and resumed my number crunching. I stayed that way all afternoon, trying not to glance at my watch every few minutes to see if it was getting close to five.

At 7 P.M. Mr. Daniel's and I were battling Dr. Blackjack when the doorbell rang.

Dwayne Hassleman stood there grinning, a purplish-black shiner under his swollen right eye. He was wearing brown eyes and green cammy pants with his favorite long-sleeved Banana Republic shirt. He had on his jungle boots and his huge cowboy belt buckle.

The swollen eye looked to be of recent vintage. "Who did you piss off?" I asked.

Dwayne ignored the question and poured himself a shot of Jack Daniel's. He wandered over to the computer to admire my latest blackjack winnings.

"Looks like you're getting to be a master card counter. Think you could handle a real casino situation? At the table there will be other players who will screw up your counting strategy by taking stupid hits."

"I think I can adjust for that."

"How the hell do you get comfortable in this thing?" Dwayne was struggling to adjust the La-Z-Boy lever. "It's a medieval torture rack."

I took a deep swallow of Jack.

"Yeah, but without the reward of eventual death. Hey, your, uh . . . house sitter, Hakeem, said you were out of town on business. How did it go? Was that your multilevel marketing deal?"

"Jimmy, if I told you the truth I'd have to kill you."

"Then please lie to me."

We laughed and drank and then Dwayne was idly thumbing through the junk mail on the kitchen table.

"Is this the free Las Vegas trip you were telling me about?"

"Are you impressed? I'm a *Diamond*-level VIP."

"Impress me with your Dr. Blackjack program."

We took turns playing blackjack against the computer and were up $5,200 after an hour. Dwayne was excited about all the money we were making, and after a prolonged trip to the bathroom he was even more excited. He studied the comp offer from the Excelsior.

"Jimmy, why don't we go for the real deal? This Vegas comp is good any two weeknights. We could leave now and be breaking the bank at the Excelsior by lunchtime tomorrow."

"Sorry, Dwayne, but I'm not up to driving to the airport. Besides I've got to—"

"Gotta *what*? Didn't you just tell me your girls are at camp in Lake Tahoe and you don't have to be at your new job until *Monday*? Screw the airport. Why waste our blackjack money on airfare. We'll drive— it'll be fun. Fear and loathing and all that."

Dwayne sat down at the piano bench and started banging out "Chopsticks," stabbing at the keys like he was learning to use a manual typewriter.

"That's barbaric! Keep your paws off my piano."

"Not until we're in the car and on our way."

"Dwayne, there's no way. I'm practically falling asleep now and—"

"Hold on a second, pal."

Dwayne fumbled at one of the zippered compartments in his shirt, and a moment later there was a small mirror on the piano bench.

Reflecting a thick white line of cocaine.

"That's all I have left, pal, but you go ahead and do it. I've got a great connection in Vegas."

I looked at the line as the small dim voice of sanity inside my head finally spoke up:

This way lies madness.

A small solitary voice, instantly and decisively overruled by the noisy committee.

It had been a long time since I had done any coke, but I remembered the basic principle. The Monster even lent me a tightly rolled-up dollar bill. The committee cheered.

Toot-toot and away we go!

A few minutes later I was not as tired but still in no shape to drive.

"All right, Dwayne, but you have to drive and we take the Rover. I'll call and make sure this comped Diamond Executive suite really exists."

The Monster leaped off the piano bench and thrust a fist into the air.

"All *right*! The Rover is in the shop right now but I'll tell you what—we take the Camry and I'll drive the whole way. Hell, you can even crawl into the backseat and fall asleep if you like."

Which is just what I did. Either the coke wasn't very strong or it didn't stand a chance against Mr. Daniel's and his friends from the pharmacy.

I slept like a dead man.

Slept through the night and the miles and the endless black ribbons of desert highway.

Slept like death.

I woke up in the backseat of the Camry to find myself in New York City—with a blazing desert sun overhead.

Dwayne had the air-conditioning on full blast and was singing along with the radio. Something about breaking rocks in the hot sun. 'Cause the law won.

I blinked to clear the shimmering haze of heat outside and watched the Manhattan skyline go by—or the Las Vegas version of it—complete with a Statue of Liberty and what appeared to be a slightly scaled-down Chrysler Building. Construction crews were dangling in the air, busy wrapping a roller coaster around the entire hotel. It was an amazing spectacle.

Dwayne turned the radio off and grinned.

"Morning, pal—or afternoon actually. Damn! It's almost one o'clock. Made great time. You checking out the New York New York hotel, huh? The Big Apple in fucking Las Vegas! You just gotta love it."

"Yeah, start spreading the news."

"I'm leaving today."

We dissolved in laughter as we pulled up to the front entrance of the Excelsior. The valet parking area had two cars in front of us. After a New York minute Dwayne said "fuck it" and backed up.

We found a spot in the hotel parking lot in seconds. Stepping out of the car was like being suddenly thrust into a sauna bath. We slung our overnight bags over our shoulders and marched through the colossal glass doors, into the cool air, in search of the registration desk.

To reach the craftily hidden check-in counter, we had to first navigate a maze of dollar slot machines. Then another jangling labyrinth of five-dollar machines. Ten minutes later we reached the registration desk and were greeted by a clerk who looked too young to even be allowed in a casino. He wore a huge button on his lapel: HAVE A MEGA-BUCKS DAY!

"Welcome to the Excelsior, Mr. Lerner. You gentlemen are reserved for the Diamond Executive suite." He rang a bell, and instantly a leggy young woman sporting a VIP HOST button and beauty queen good looks came out from an office behind the front desk. She handed us "Welcome Packets" (containing "free" tokens for a pull on the Megabucks machine) and then two tall glasses with diamond patterns and the hopeful injunction to HAVE A MEGABUCKS DAY!

"Enjoy your complimentary diamond screwdrivers," she said, smiling. "Would you gentlemen like your free pull on the Megabucks now?" The beauty queen motioned to a nearby slot machine.

"Maybe later, thank you." I was anxious to take a shower and then do battle with the flesh-and-blood version of Dr. Blackjack. Dwayne nervously jangled my car keys, dismissing the Megabucks offer with a wave of his hand. Sipping our diamond screwdrivers, we spent the next five minutes on a circuitous journey to the elevators. To reach the elevators from the registration desk, it was necessary to take a forced tour of most of the casino. We passed the roulette wheel, blackjack and poker tables, and all of the latest new slot machines with themes like "Elvis" (he sings "Hound Dog" when you win money) and the *Wheel of Fortune* TV show (get a "free" spin!).

As promised, the Diamond suite had two bedrooms, each with its own bathroom, separated by a spacious living room. The carpet was a plush blue with diamond (what else?) patterns. The living room boasted a wet bar, a refrigerator (with those five-dollar bags of cashews and six-dollar airline bottle drinks), a big-screen television, a large writing desk, a matching couch and chairs (diamond patterns), and a Jacuzzi large enough for three adults and their Megabucks machines.

On opposite sides of the living room were adjoining doors to the two identical bedrooms and bathrooms. Both bedrooms and the living room had door exits to the hallway. After verifying that the snacks and drinks in the refrigerator weren't comped ("Diamond players must not be a very big deal around here"), Dwayne picked up his bag and arbitrarily selected a bedroom.

"Hey, pal, I have to run a quick errand, go get a check cashed."

"Dwayne, you're in a casino—they'll happily cash your check."

"No, my credit isn't what it used to be, but I know a place. Why don't you jump in the Jacuzzi and I'll be back in less than a half hour and we'll take on these blackjack dealers together."

By 2 P.M. Dwayne still had not returned. I went downstairs, got some cash from an ATM, and went in search of a five-dollar table to see just how much I had learned from Dr. Blackjack over the last few months. I looked for and found an empty table (plenty of seats for Dwayne when he got here) and exchanged smiles and greetings with the dealer, a hard-eyed young man wearing the HAVE A MEGABUCKS DAY! button.

I bought fifty dollars in chips and was proud of myself when the cocktail waitress came over with the free drink offers and I ordered a Coke. There were no Cherry Cokes, but she said she would toss in a couple of cherries from the bar. Las Vegas knows all about service quality and customer satisfaction.

I was determined to carefully monitor the drinks I would consume at the blackjack tables. Follow the path of the Golden Mean.

Moderation and balance were my new watchwords. Counting cards, gambling, and getting drunk didn't mix.

I didn't see Dwayne or my car keys again till after midnight.

Which is when I next saw the Monster.

I played blackjack for hours, counting both cards and comped Excelsior screwdrivers, somehow managing to reach about two hundred dollars in winnings. Close to midnight (when I realized I was losing track of the cards and the drinks) I decided to get something to eat at the coffee shop. Rare prime rib would be good. Maybe a beer with it. Or two. Reward myself for my discipline at the blackjack table. Then call it quits for the night. Quit while I was ahead.

The moment I reached my bedroom I put my glasses, cigarette pack, and wallet on the nightstand. I then dropped facedown on the bed and passed out. I dreamed every card counter's fantasy: I was facing the blackjack dealer with a 19. A huge (and admiring) crowd surged behind me, shouting encouragement. I knew the dealer was sitting solid on a 20. I asked for a hit and the dealer shook his head. Nobody hits on 19. I motioned again (imperiously this time) for a hit and, of course, it was the deuce: 21!

The crowd went wild, cheering, shouting, pounding me on the back.

"Jimmy, wake up! *Wake the fuck up, man!*" The Monster was shouting, pounding me on the back.

I rolled over and tried to blink away the fog. The lighted digital display on the nightstand clock read 1:45 A.M.

"Dwayne, where the hell you been? What's wrong with—"

"I need you to give me a hundred bucks—*fast!*"

I sat up and switched on the lamp.

The Monster was still in his jungle cowboy mode. Hopping from one combat boot to another in his cammy pants and wide leather cowboy belt.

"Where's the fire, Dwayne? Why don't you—"

"Come *on,* pal, I got someone waiting downstairs for the money!"

"What are you talking about? Where—"

"I'm *talking* about your fucking *debts*! Talking about the money you *owe* me for the *sprinklers,* for the fucking *lightbulbs*! The motherfucking *barbecue*! You think New York steaks are *free,* cocksucker? Not where I come from."

"I think that if you need a *loan* you can—"

"I DON'T HAVE THE FUCKING TIME FOR THIS!" The Monster snatched my wallet off the nightstand and removed most of the bills, stuffing them into his cammy pants pocket.

I was trying to get off the bed.

"Put the wallet down, Dwayne. If you need some money—"

As I was rising off the bed, the Monster's fist streaked out and struck me in the chest, driving me back against the headboard. I was still struggling to get up when his other fist connected with my forehead.

Whack! The back of my head met the wall with predictable results.

My lights went out.

When I came to, it was 2:30 A.M. Pain radiated in sharp electric waves from my head and neck down to my fingertips. The muscles in my right shoulder were jiggling and jumping in their version of a Saint Vitus' dance. I reached over for my glasses, lit a cigarette, and said hello to Messieurs Radiculopathy and Fasciculation.

Then I took my own inventory.

I stilled the clangorous committee in my mind long enough to allow that small solitary voice of sanity to be heard. The one voice in my head that wasn't trying to kill me: *Jimmy, get up, get packed, get the hell out, and most of all, get sober. Get the fuck away from this maniac and don't look back! Get your sanity back, your life back before you hit that next YET. I'll help you but you've got to do this NOW!*

It was my long-delayed "moment of clarity."

I scrambled off the bed and made sure everything was packed in my overnight bag. I put my wallet in my back pocket and was reaching for the bedroom door when my heart began pounding with a sickening realization.

The Monster still had my car keys.

And my car.

A half hour later I was sitting on the living room couch still considering my options (*will Triple-A bring out duplicate car keys?*) when I heard the plastic key poking into the door slot of Dwayne's bedroom. I was instantly on my feet in a high-alert adrenaline rush (the Monster would not sucker-punch me again) when Dwayne staggered into the living room, clutching his ribs and moaning. He fell into a chair, doubled over in obvious pain.

"Cocksucker busted my ribs, Jimmy."

"Save your bullshit and give me the car keys, Dwayne. I'm out of here—*now.*"

Dwayne hugged himself and tried to stand. He cried out in pain and sat down hard. I didn't know what the purpose of these theatrics were and I didn't care.

"Dwayne, give me my car keys."

Dwayne rocked himself in the chair, arms hugging his rib cage.

And suddenly his face contorted in genuine agony and he was sobbing uncontrollably.

"Jimmy, I'm sorry about the money. I was out of my mind. Have to be crazy to hit my best friend." His breath came out in strangled gasps.

"Dwayne, what the hell is wrong?"

Dwayne groaned and a fresh flood of tears coursed down his cheeks.

"That asshole busted me up. Right outside the hotel. I reported it to hotel security too. Even demanded my money back for the suite."

"Dwayne, the suite is comped."

"Yeah, that's what the bitch at the front desk said. Told her I'd fucking sue for injuries, though. I got beat up on hotel property. They're fucking *liable*!"

Dwayne's doubled over again, wheezing, his breath becoming a harsh rattle. I could no longer believe that he was faking.

"Listen, Jimmy, you got to get me to a hospital, I'm having troubling breathing. I think there's a busted rib stuck in my lung or something." To demonstrate, Dwayne starting coughing violently, the copious flow of tears increasing. The image of a shattered rib bone sticking through a soft moist lung galvanized me.

The only thing I hate more than seeing a grown man cry is seeing a woman cry.

"All right, all right, just hold on. I'll call 911, get you an ambulance—"

"*No!* No ambulance. No cops. Jimmy, you got to help me—get me to an emergency room."

"Okay, no cops. Can you stand up? We'll catch a cab in front to the hospital."

Dwayne half stood, then motioned me over to help.

"I can make it if you lend me your shoulder."

I got an arm around him and hoisted him to his feet. He leaned heavily down on my shoulder and together we staggered into the hallway. We made it to the elevator and down to the valet parking and taxicab area without anyone falling down.

I got in the front seat and told the cabdriver to take us to the nearest hospital emergency room. He started the meter and sped off without a comment. Dwayne curled up like a fetus and moaned in the back-seat. I wondered if the cabbie would turn the meter off and offer me a deal. Or maybe they didn't use pancakes in Las Vegas.

Less than five minutes later we were at the emergency room entrance. I paid the driver and helped Dwayne inside. I had spent a lot of time in hospitals in the last year, and the smells that filled my nose were depressingly familiar—bleach, rubbing alcohol, urine, and the faint underlying odor of rotting flesh.

Directly in front of the admitting nurse's desk, Dwayne slipped from my grip and fell heavily to the floor.

Then two male orderlies in white were lifting Dwayne onto a gurney and wheeling him behind a curtained examination room. The nurse urged me to come to the desk to help fill out the insurance paperwork.

I told her that Mr. Hassleman would be able to take care of all that. I had no idea about his insurance information. Despite her protests, I took a seat in the waiting area where I could watch the curtained entrance to Dwayne's room. Every few minutes he let out a pitiful piercing groan which would carry down the corridors.

About ten groans and thirty minutes later a young intern trailed by a nurse parted the curtain and went inside. A few minutes of silence were broken by Dwayne's shout.

"*Damn!* That really hurts! Yeah . . . right there, I think it's busted . . . oh, *please don't touch it . . .*" Then some more pitiful weeping.

I wondered if he had somehow sustained massive internal injuries. Maybe he was bleeding internally. I was getting increasingly worried.

The doctor and nurse left, and an orderly wheeled Dwayne back out and through two swinging doors marked X-RAY.

I found a *Time* magazine that was only seven years old and settled in to wait.

When Dwayne was wheeled back behind the curtain, I went inside. He was flat on his back, his face all white except for the fading black shiner under his right eye.

"Dwayne, how are you doing? What did they say? Are the ribs broken?"

Dwayne used an elbow to struggle up and groan in pain just as the young intern came in and consulted the clipboard.

"Mr. Hassleman? I have good news. There doesn't appear to be a fracture. However, I understand that you were mugged in front of your hotel—kicked in the ribs—and you are in a great deal of pain. Are you allergic to morphine?"

"No, Doctor, thank you." Beneath Dwayne's grimace, the mask of pain, I detected the outline of the Monster in a brief twisted grin. Then, quick as a lightbulb blinking out, the smile was gone, replaced again by the agonized expression.

The nurse came in and gave Dwayne his shot. As soon as she left the exam room, Dwayne was sitting up and effortlessly lacing his jungle boots.

A miraculous recovery.

The Monster smirked up at me like a little boy who has just gotten away with stealing all the cookies from the jar.

"Hey, pal, nothing like a shot of morphine to take the edge off the coke."

I was angrier with myself for being fooled than I was with the Monster. Too angry to even speak.

The Monster adjusted the knife in its hidden ankle sheath and then bloused the cammy pants back over the boots, securing them with green elastic bands.

"Come on, pal, let's get the fuck out of here—let's go play some *blackjack*!"

The Monster ignored the shouts of the admitting nurse, who

wanted to know whom to bill, and strode past me toward the exit. He pushed the glass doors and he was outside, immediately lighting up a cigarette. When I reached the glass doors, I crashed through them so hard that when they swung back the glass almost shattered.

I never saw the two hospital security guards trailing me out to the parking lot.

The Monster was waiting for me outside, grinning and smoking. I got up right in his face.

"Dwayne, I knew you had problems, but until tonight I didn't realize *just how fucked-up* you really are—you better find your own way back to Danville. Give me the car keys now!"

The Monster patted all the little pockets in his long-sleeved safari shirt and then went through the same process with the cammy pants. More a pantomime than a search.

"Sorry, pal, I must have left them back at the hotel." The Monster snickered and then I was shouting.

"You lying sack of shit! You're a *pathological* liar, Dwayne. You should be fucking killed!"

"Who should be *killed*?" Two security cops stood right behind me in the semidarkness of the parking lot. The older of the two, a heavyset man with wisps of gray hair peeking out from his cap, was addressing me.

The Monster had instantly metamorphosed back into the injured mugging victim, seeming to shrink before my eyes as he again clutched his ribs and moaned.

The younger guard shone a flashlight into my eyes.

"Did you know you almost broke the glass doors back there? *What* is your problem?"

The Monster, still clasping his waist, backed up from me as if in terror, limping in pain. He circled warily around me and got behind the guards and cringed—a frightened man seeking protection. When he spoke, his voice was soft and quivering with a mixture of fear and pain. Here was an injured man, a peaceful, soft-spoken man who was clearly being terrorized by a lunatic.

"Officers, I'm glad you're here. This man is threatening me, talking crazy, saying he's going to kill me."

"We heard." Both flashlights beamed into my eyes.

I couldn't believe this was happening. "*He's* the one who's crazy—hey, get that light out of my eyes!"

"Sir, have you been drinking?"

During the interrogation that followed, the Monster simply limped away into the darkness and got into a waiting cab in front of the hospital.

It took me a few minutes to calm down and convince the rent-a-cops that yes, I had been drinking, but no, I wasn't drunk and I wasn't threatening to kill anyone. All I wanted to do was get in my car and go back to California.

The promise of my imminent departure from Las Vegas finally seemed to satisfy the security guards. After checking my driver's license ID, they told me I was free to go.

After giving a warning about almost breaking glass hospital doors.

And threatening to kill people.

It was four in the morning when I hailed a passing taxi to take me back to the Excelsior.

I would grab my bag and my car keys and leave this nightmare behind. Leave the Monster behind. If the Monster wouldn't give me the car keys, I would call Triple-A.

That was my plan.

It seemed like a good plan.

But you know what they say:

If you want to make God laugh, just tell him your plans.

. . .

I entered the Diamond suite through the bedroom door and grabbed my overnight bag. Dwayne was not in the living room.

Silence. Then a series of smacking sounds.

The Monster was in his bedroom. Behind the closed door.

I knocked and stepped back quickly. "Dwayne, I want the car keys. If you still want to play games, fine, 'cause either way I'm out of here."

Silence again. Then a rapid staccato series of chopping sounds. Followed by a more measured series of snorts. The Monster simply pausing to refuel the Colombian Express. Next stop: a town called *Rage*.

I was headed for the living room exit when the Monster yelled through the door.

"Hold on, pal, I got your fucking keys. Give me a second."

A minute later the Monster called out from behind his door. A singsong voice. Both mocking and menacing.

"Hey, pal, I hope you're not thinking of leaving just yet. Did you remember to turn your sprinklers off? The forecast calls for rain later. *Red* rain. Like maybe where your little bitches go to camp. Yeah, pal, the forecast is for *red fucking rain* up at Lake Tahoe."

A chill went through me like an ice pick. I dropped the bag (*keep your hands free, Jimmy*) and pounded on the Monster's door.

"What the hell are you talking about?"

Getting near the Monster's door was a bad idea.

Bare-chested and screaming, the Monster burst through the door and crashed into me like a linebacker on a steroid rage, knocking me halfway across the room and against the wall beside the big-screen TV.

I got to my feet slowly and watched the Monster take a few steps back and pull out a knife from the ankle sheath. His bare chest was like the heaving hull of a small ship, knotted and bulging with ropes of muscle.

The Monster advanced in his tiger-striped cammy pants and jungle boots, the knife slashing arcs in the rapidly shrinking space between us.

"HOW DO YOU *WANT* IT, COCKSUCKER!" The Monster was closing in behind the chest-high swings of the knife blade.

Screaming:

"I SAID, *HOW* DO YOU WANT IT? UP THE *ASS* FIRST? HUH? CAN'T *HEAR* YOU, PAL? NOT TALKING YOUR SOC-CER FIELD SHIT NOW, *ARE* YOU, *COCKSUCKER*? HOW ABOUT IN THE BELLY? THAT WAY I CAN HEAR YOU SCREAM FOR A COUPLE OF HOURS BEFORE I CUT OUT YOUR FUCKING EYES . . . *THEN* YOUR BALLS! OH, YEAH, YOU COCKSUCKING SPRINKLER-STEALING PIECE OF *SHIT*! FAKE SPONSOR *HYPOCRITE* MOTHERFUCKER! THE KNIFE IN THE BELLY FIRST, NICE AND SLOW . . ."

The Monster was trying to back me up into the corner by the TV. I didn't dare take my eyes off the knife, now just an extended arm swipe from my stomach. But I knew if I backed up another step against the wall, it was highly unlikely I would ever have another Megabucks day.

The Monster raved nonstop, knife slicing the air between us.

"CALL *ME* A *PATHOLOGICAL* LIAR? *NOBODY* FUCKING TALKS TO ME LIKE THAT . . . I'M TALKING ABOUT A DIGI-TAL TOP-OF-THE-LINE SPRINKLER SYSTEM! NEW YORK *STEAKS*, YOU *COCKSUCKER*! I THINK YOU WANT THIS KNIFE UP THE *ASS* FIRST!"

I backed up, eyes on the knife, heart pounding like a trip-hammer.

"Put the knife down, Dwayne. We can work this out, whatever the problem is." Hoping to calm the Monster, talk him down. Try to get Dwayne back in the room. Or at least back on this planet.

The Monster slashed at my face with the knife.

Missing by an eyelash.

I felt the wall against my back now. Old rock song lyrics rattling crazily in my head—*nowhere to run, nowhere to hide.*

The Monster was pulling off his wide leather cowboy belt.

"OR MAYBE I'LL JUST *WHIP* YOUR MOTHERFUCKING ASS FIRST. COCKSUCKER TELLING ME TO GO TO— *WHAT*?—FUCKING *FAGGOTS* ANONYMOUS? BET YOU AND LUTHER AND THE A.A. BOYS AND GIRLS GOT A GOOD LAUGH WHEN YOU TOLD THEM ABOUT MY *FIFTH* STEP!"

The Monster roaring, knife flicking in constant motion like a snake's head. Slashing the air in front of my chest. His eyes had the color and expression of mud.

"YEAH, *FIRST* THE BELT, THEN THE KNIFE . . . YEAH, HOW 'BOUT MR. KNIFE DEEP *UP YOUR ASS!*"

Right hand still waving the knife between us, the Monster yanked off the belt with the OUR EAGLE FLIES IN CHAINS buckle. Holding me at bay against the wall with the knife, he whirled the belt in a circle above his head—just another drugstore cowboy looking to rope himself a sprinkler-munching steer.

Then *gut* it.

The big brass buckle struck my forehead, the sharp metal edge tearing open a gash in the flesh. Another savage swing and my right eyebrow split open, raining blood.

The forecast is for red rain.

Blood was pouring down into my right eye. And the belt was swinging again.

"ARE WE HAVING *FUN* YET, COCKSUCKER? I'M GOING TO POUND YOU LIKE A FUCKING *PIÑATA* BEFORE I STRING YOUR GUTS ACROSS THE ROOM! THEN I'M GO- ING *CAMPING!* GOING TO TAKE MR. KNIFE TO VISIT YOUR LITTLE BITCHES UP IN LAKE TAHOE. OH *YEAH*, PAL, THEY'RE GONNA *LOVE* TAKING MR. KNIFE UP THEIR

TIGHT LITTLE ASSES! HEY, WHAT'S WRONG, MR. *SPON-SOR*? NOT TALKING NOW ABOUT MY GOING TO A *SPECIAL INTEREST* A.A. GROUP, *ARE* YOU, COCKSUCKER?"

Smack!

This time the heavy buckle smashed against my nose, and there was an instant geyser of blood. Blood filling my mouth, soaking my chin, my chest, turning the blue diamond carpet a bright red.

I timed the next swing.

When the brass eagle descended again at my battered face, I snatched the belt in midair.

And pulled. *Hard.*

Yanking the Monster—and the knife—toward me.

Off balance, the Monster lurched forward and I did my best kung-fu Bruce Lee imitation, kicking him squarely in *his* belly.

Mr. Knife dropped to the carpet.

And I was all over him, my fists, fists of fury fueled by a raging flood of adrenaline, by a horrifying image in my head of my little girls screaming in their bloody and shredded pajamas beneath the Monster.

I no longer felt the pain in my neck or my back. I pounded the Monster's face, delivering a whirlwind of blows to the mouth, the eyes, the nose, until red rain misted the air and soaked us both. My hands, hands that coaxed "Heart and Soul" from ivory keys, were strangers to me—dual juggernauts savagely hammering the Monster to his knees.

I *was* the Hammer.

And I hammered away until the Monster fell back hard on his camouflaged ass, his right hand searching blindly for his buddy, Mr. Knife. I kicked the knife across the room, but the Monster was snatching up the eagle belt. Still on his ass, he had no leverage to swing.

I drove two more solid rights into his nose and heard the crunch and snap of bones—*his* bones. More red rain.

And then he was on his back, still groping around for a belt, a knife, anything—still raving through his bloody mouth.

"BETTER NOT LET ME GET UP, *COCKSUCKER!* 'CAUSE WHEN I *DO* GET UP, YOU'RE FUCKING *DEAD—THEN* YOUR PRECIOUS LITTLE TIGHT-ASSED BITCHES!"

I believed him.

In seconds I had the cowboy belt cinched around the Monster's neck, eagle buckle tight against his throat as I pulled the makeshift noose—tight. The Monster tried scuttling ass-backward on the thick, blood-soaked carpet.

With one powerful wrenching motion, using both hands, I broke the Monster's neck. It made a sickening cracking sound, like a rotted branch being snapped from a tree by a vengeful wind.

And I was the wind.

I dropped the end of the belt.

Sat down on the blood-soaked carpet. Beside the Monster. Wondering why I was so cold. Shivering and shaking so hard I thought I was going into convulsions.

Wondering when I would wake up from this nightmare.

Wondering when I would be able to breathe.

Wondering if I was having a heart attack.

When the violent tremors subsided a bit, I opened my overnight bag and pulled out my shaving kit, where my small pharmacy was located. My hands shook so bad that to get the childproof cap off the Xanax bottle I had to use my teeth.

Got two blue pills under my tongue. Dr. Shekelman said they work faster if you let them dissolve under the tongue.

Eventually I went to the living room phone.

I tried to remember the telephone number for one of my A.A. sponsors. The only number that came to mind was Luther's.

He picked up after three rings.

"Jimmy, it's six in the morning—are you drunk?"

I told him what had happened.

I don't remember much of the conversation except Luther telling me to call 911. The receiver became too heavy to hold. My eyelids too heavy to keep open. I hung up after telling Luther that I would call the police.

I woke almost two hours later. Kept my eyes closed. Praying that when I opened them I would be home, safe in my bed in Danville. Delivered intact from this horrible nightmare.

When I opened my eyes, my pants and shirt were still soaked in blood.

The Monster was still sprawled bare-chested on his back. The cowboy belt still wrapped tight around his broken neck.

Not a nightmare. Oh dear God in heaven, please no, no, no, no!

I had to get the blood off. I was soaked in it. The copper taste filled my mouth.

Moving like a zombie, I started the Jacuzzi, climbed in, and the water soon bubbled red. I put on fresh clothes and called 911. The police dispatcher kept me on the line, asking questions until the police arrived. I told her everything that had happened.

The police arrived, took one look at the Monster's bloody and battered face, the cowboy noose around his neck, and put handcuffs on me. Said they were taking me to the hospital. First we just had to make a short stop at the police station.

Where I waived my rights. Waived my right to remain silent and then waived my right to have an attorney present. I knew that once the detectives heard the whole story, once I told them all about the Monster, once I explained it all, they would understand. They would take the cuffs off and let me go. I didn't need a lawyer.

They didn't understand.

They arrested me for murder.

They initially booked me on charges of "open murder," later amending the charges to "murder in the first degree," with the "use of a deadly weapon." A capital offense. Punishable by lethal injection.

I used my phone call to reach Freddy Shapiro in New York. My old college friend and attorney said he would be on the next plane. The detectives then drove me in handcuffs to the hospital.

Then to the jail. To Suicide Watch Cell No. 3.

I never did get my free pull on the Megabucks machine.

Shapiro and I met in the small conference room the jail provided for attorney visits. The walls were thick glass, and two deputies stood guard outside the door. Attorneys, unlike other visitors, received "contact" visits. They didn't have to talk to their clients separated by a Plexiglas partition and shouting through a defective wall phone.

A small man lost in a calculatedly cheap suit, Freddy Shapiro still affected what he thought of as the sixties Radical Lawyer Look: two stringy shoulder-length curtains of gray hair descending from both sides of an otherwise bald pate.

Freddy had been very busy, reviewing the "discovery"—the evidence provided by the district attorney—and putting together my defense. He had also hired a private investigator to check Dwayne Hassleman's background. Freddy opened a folder that grew thicker by the hour.

"Jimmy, *nothing* about this guy Hassleman checks out. Nothing he told you anyway. He was never married. He has no ex-wife or kids back in New York. We couldn't even find any record of him ever attending Saint John's in Brooklyn or New York University. Definitely no military service. No employment history that we could find unless you count selling cocaine in Oakland. Apparently he likes to go after people with knives—he was arrested a few years ago for attacking a hotel maid with a knife. She dropped charges."

Nothing about the Monster could surprise me any longer.

"Freddy, what about getting me bail?"

"I'm working on it—they don't have to grant bail in a capital case. But all that's about to change. So are these bogus 'murder' charges. The D.A. likes to overcharge and then plea-bargain down from that. Sort of like charging someone with dumping nuclear waste and ending up fining them twenty-five bucks for littering a candy bar wrapper. I've got a meeting with the judge and the D.A. later today. I'll be presenting them with a dramatically different version of events and evidence than the one the D.A. is using to bargain with. The autopsy report shows this Hassleman was a walking narcotic salad: morphine, cocaine, codeine, barbiturates, methamphetamines. The Excelsior desk clerk says he was acting crazy that night, claiming he was mugged and insisting the hotel compensate him for injuries. When the assistant hotel manager refused to give him any money, he miraculously recovered and demanded a comped trip to a whorehouse. Talk about chutzpah! Nice people you like to hang out with, Jimmy. I'll bet you've already befriended all the psychopaths in jail."

"Freddy, could you possibly refrain from the editorial comments— I already know I have a seriously flawed character. Look, I'm in *deep* shit here."

Freddy waved an impatient hand in the air, as if to swat away my concerns.

"Nah, you'll be fine. Not to worry. I'm also going to play your phone answering machine tape for them—Hassleman raving and ranting."

"Which one?"

Freddy chuckled and read from the folder.

"Oh, I think the one from his album—Dwayne Hassleman's greatest psycho outbursts. The song begins with . . . let me see . . . 'This is *war*, cocksucker, and you are a *dead* man!'"

"Freddy, why haven't they dropped the murder charges yet?"

"The D.A. says he has two eyewitnesses, the hospital security guards, ready to testify that you threatened to kill Hassleman just hours before you killed him. Bad timing on your part, Jimmy. Also that you smelled like a brewery and almost smashed in the hospital doors."

"Yeah, but, Freddy, I—"

"Jimmy, I'm on *your* side, remember? I'm just telling you what they've got. It's not in the discovery yet, but based on what you told me I suspect the D.A. also has a few soccer moms in the wings. Who will say that you threatened to break this guy's neck. Hmm . . . now, *that* was an unfortunate remark. Why couldn't you just *shoot* him? It would look better—less blood too. Juries don't like looking at pictures with bloody victims. And cowboy belt neckties. Makes them want to punish the defendant."

The cop rapped on the glass, signaling today's meeting was over.

"Freddy, can't you at least get me out of this suicide watch cell? It's truly making me suicidal."

"Just hang in there a few more days. All this will be resolved. The D.A. really does not want to go to trial."

The cop took me to a small holding cell. I stripped, which was simple—just pulled the white paper suit over my head. I spread cheeks, coughed, and opened my mouth. Showed the cop the back of my hands, the soles of my feet, and behind my ears.

What really terrified me was just how familiar this humiliating ritual was starting to become. My life was becoming a living nightmare.

Then things got worse.

EPILOGUE

In the days following my Parole Board denial I am in a daze, a thick fog in which I stumble and then sleep. In my still private cell I sleep around the clock.

The prison nights are the worst. The nights are when my personal demons like to come trampling into my dreams. I know all their names now—Fear, Loneliness, Despair, and Death, my very own Four Horsemen. I have even learned to distinguish the hoofbeats so I can mentally prepare for the arrival of any particular horseman.

They especially like to ride in all at once. They somehow know that they are most powerful, most fearsome in a herd, thundering through the landscape of my nightmares of the Monster.

I trudge through the days like a blind man wading through hip-deep mud. I am indifferent to Kansas and the Car's loud fantasies about exacting some payback from Stanger and the Dirt.

I am bone weary, muddy, sluggish, buried deep beneath a dark mountain.

It is quiet here.

It is quiet here, down in the abyss.

. . .

Belinda died today.

C.O. Fallon took the dead cat away in a black plastic garbage bag. He promised Chico he wouldn't just toss it in a Dumpster somewhere. Belinda was grandfathered—no more cats.

Then Chico's day got worse.

He received another denial from the Pardons Board. His sentence is Life Without, and the Pardons Board is going to make sure it *stays* Without.

Now Chico's looking for a chess game to get his mind off his troubles. And listening to his problems has suddenly lifted me at least partially out of my own abyss of self-pity. There's nothing like the incomparable misery of a friend to put one's own concerns into perspective.

So I have a few more years to do. So what? It's not like I had any grand plans for the new millennium other than becoming a dot-com billionaire. Chico will live out the rest of his life here. He will die here. Alone.

I shake off some more of the mud from the abyss.

Chico's chess game is also getting competitive. This time, playing black, I unveil the Hyperaccelerated Dragon Variation—pushing a pawn to G6 on my second move, hoping to sucker him into advancing in the center.

"I see you laying in the cut, O.G."

"Seeing and doing something about it are worlds apart."

We're both sitting, lotus style, on Chico's bunk, Saint Mary's Hospice blankets sheltering our butts from the harsh slab of metal. It's over 110 degrees out in the yard, only slightly less in the cells. The cinder block walls are literally sweating.

"Yogee, how 'bout I do something about your sideways-talking mouth? Oh, *excuse* me, Mr. M.B.A. Convict, permit me to rephrase that wolf ticket—how about I respond in an optimal manner relative to your punk-ass pawn play?"

"I'm resonating. Come on wid it—I'm down wid dat, my little Hispanic meat puppet!"

We pass a pleasant evening pushing pawns and insulting each other. Chico temporarily forgets about the aching vacancy in his upper bunk. My own mud creature is out of the abyss and climbing the banks of a river in purgatory. The creature reaches the top of the bank, shakes off the remaining mud, and stands tall and clean for the first time since my Parole Board results.

Kansas pounds on the cell door, then comes in.

"Aiight, O Fucking *Gee*! Welcome back to the land of the living! Listen up, dawgs—the Shit's Jumping Off tomorrow, so you might want to stay close to your houses, unless you want to get up in the mix. Y'unnerstan' what I'm sayin'? Punk-ass Stanger and some fucking Dirtboys are due some getback."

We tell Kansas we're down wid dat and he moves on to another cell.

Chico looks up from another untenable chess position.

"O.G., the only thing jumping off tomorrow is a lockdown. Probably going to be a shakedown, so if there's anything in your house, you might want to get rid of it tonight."

"What do you mean?"

"I mean Kansas opened his big mouth to too many cons. The Shit Jumps Off on some C.O.—even Stanger—and they'll have us in a lockdown for months, maybe years. Get everybody crossed out. Well, some of us don't like the idea of being put in a cross. Maybe somebody dropped a dime."

"Chico—some of *us*?"

Chico took a deep breath and then concentrated on rolling a supertight cigarette from a can of Bugler. Rolled it slowly, as to buy time to resolve some intensely private conversation in his head.

"Jimmy, you're still a fish, although you've learned to talk some righteous shit and I love you like a brother. And I trust you, so listen: Lifers have a lot to lose—maybe even the most to lose. When all you have is time, when you got nothing coming, then you don't want to do *hard* time. You don't want *any* shit jumping off. And I *know* you understand what keeping something 'on the D.L.' means, so I won't insult you with the usual *know what I'm sayin'* nonsense."

"Yes I do. And I will." I brought my rook down across the board. "Now—do *you* understand the meaning of *checkmate*?"

"Shit! This losing is developing into an annoying trend."

"Chico, this goes way beyond *trend*. It's practically a lifestyle."

"How 'bout I just bitch-slap you and then see how you *style*?"

And we laughed and joked and wolfed away the day.

It's good to have a brother in prison.

On the morning Kansas thought he would coax some shit into jumping, the Dirt have a different thought. I'm doing my laps, kicking dirt, and counting my steps when sirens begin to shriek and the loudspeakers crackle.

"EMERGENCY COUNT! RETURN TO YOUR CELLS AND *LOCK IT DOWN!*"

Black-clad Dirtboys stand with rifles and shotguns on all the roofs to provide encouragement if necessary. Despite today's scorching desert sun, they are in full battle regalia, including bulky black vests and helmets.

The "emergency count" is a pretext for getting everyone locked down so the Dirt can conduct an Inmate Health and Welfare Inspection. The vibrations from Chico's dropped dime are reverberating throughout the yard, and I can't say I blame my friend.

Like Eloi to the Morlock slaughter, we stream in from every hot and dusty corner of the yard. When we are all massed in front of cellblock 4, the Bubblecop inside hits the switch and the double steel slider doors hiss open.

Instead of C.O. Fallon in the pod, this is someone we have never seen before. A smooth-faced rookie—very young and very nervous.

In minutes we are all in our houses, locked down.

From my cell window I can see half the cells across the hall, most of them with the pissed-off faces of convicts at the windows. This lock-down is interfering with the morning routines of the Wood Pile and the Yard Rats.

The new Bubblecop hits the button and the huge crash gates rumble open. Clutching his clipboard like it's a life preserver, he walks quickly down our corridor, pausing briefly before each cell window to conduct his "emergency count."

When Bubblecop approaches the cells, the faces at the windows disappear as convicts drop to the floor to start shouting and barking under the doors. Then they innocently pop up again, grinning before the cell windows. Convict jack-in-the-box. This is payback for the lock-down. The idea is to screw up the cop's count, make him start all over. Or at least get him totally pissed off.

That's part of *our* job description.

"Hey, See-Oh! *See-Oh!* Why you got to lock a motherfucker down? Ain't nothing going down up in here." The Bone's face is at the window. Then gone. Replaced now by his cellie Big Bird's gray beard.

The young Bubblecop continues down the corridor, trying to count heads without making eye contact. The dawgs pick up the scent of his fear and play off it.

Skell hissing under his door.

"Hey, *rookie!* Why don't you bring that pretty little mouth of yours over here? And don't try to tell us you don't smoke *that* brand!"

The cop's smooth white face goes bright red and the cellblock explodes in laughter.

Now Kansas, pounding a huge fist against his cell door.

"Yo, *Fishcop*. Hey, *fish*! Didn't Fallon teach you how to crack open the cell doors? Or just your *asshole*?"

Fishcop or not, the C.O. can't let another convict insult go unanswered.

"Get *back* on your trays! You're all on *lockdown* till further notice!" he yells in a high-pitched voice that scares absolutely no one.

Kansas ignores him and pounds twice as hard against the door.

"Yo, Bone! *T-Bone!* Send over the Cadillac with a rollie for me. I'm all out, bro."

The Bone, yelling back through the air vent. "I ain't trying to give up none a mines, Kansas. Ain't got but a little bit of tobacco left."

Kansas, who ain't trying to accept a "no" from the Bone (or anyone else), wolfs under the cell door. The threat is only half in jest—what convicts call "kidding on the square."

"Bone, if you don't kick down some tobacco *now,* your homeboys will be playing pickup sticks with a little black *splinter* of bone—y'unnerstan' what I'm sayin' to you?"

I have come to really appreciate the way Kansas employs this phrase as a feedback loop to test for understanding. He averts lots of communications problems this way.

Then the Cadillac is rolling out into the hall, swerves across Kansas's front porch, and pulls in under his cell door.

"*Aiight,* Bone, it's all good. Thanks, bro." The Bone pulls his end of the line, and the Cadillac backs slowly out of the house.

Fishcop, who must have just driven up to the gate this morning, freezes, bewildered by this laundry string with a piece of soap slithering across the concrete floor.

Fishcop can't remember what rule bans this type of behavior, so he decides to invoke that old standby Article 22 and enforce the nonexistent "no yelling under the door" rule.

Against Kansas.

A bad choice.

"Hey, 26 cell! Shut the fuck up and get back on your tray! You are on *lockdown*!"

Telling Kansas to shut the fuck up is like tossing a gallon of kerosene on a fire and then hoping it will go out. Kansas explodes, hammering at the cell door.

"SHUT THE FUCK *UP*? Who the *fuck* you think you're *talking* to, punk-ass *Fishcop*! Come into my *house* and try talking your shit. I'll peel your fucking *onion*, PUNK-ASS FISHCOP *BITCH*!"

Now Fishcop is moving very fast, the emergency count apparently forgotten. He jogs past the open crash gate, and then we hear him locking himself into his bubble, fastening himself in for the journey like a Gemini astronaut in a space capsule.

The bubble radio crackles and in moments we know the Dirt are on the way.

Arf, arf, ARF AAAARF! Along with the German shepherds.

THWACK!

The giant crash gate closes, sealing us in the cellblock.

It's not quite the way Kansas had planned it, but the Shit Is Jumping Off. Throughout the cellblock the dawgs are pounding fists and feet against the steel doors, screaming threats and curses down to the bubble. Steel flush buttons are pushed, and dozens of toilets stuffed with paper roar to life and start overflowing, flooding the cells, spilling under the doors, and running out across the concrete floor. Assorted contraband, from shanks to syringes, are launched from under the cell doors, skittering into the flood.

From his steel bubble sanctuary, Fishcop yells, trying to save face. Or maybe to impress Stanger and the Dirt who are pouring through the steel sliders.

"GET *BACK* ON YOUR TRAYS! THAT'S A *DIRECT* ORDER."

Kansas, kicking the door, screaming back, "ORDER THESE FUCKING *NUTS,* PUNK-ASS *FISHCOP!*"

Even our new arrivals are getting into the act. The inmates who just arrived from kitchen duty in the Inferno—still regarded as fish—start screaming. Relatively new to general population, these cons are astounded by the unabashed brazenness, by this incredible, scary, *wonderful* display of sheer *Stand-up Balls!* They are smashing fists and Hard Time mugs against the steel doors, contributing their own lunatic hoots to the general madness.

"Come on *wid* it! Take us on down *through* it, Fishcop!"

"Whatchu gonna do, *See-Oh*? Put us in fucking *prison*? Fuck you, punk-ass *bitch!*"

Then Stanger assembles his Dirt into a staging area in front of Fishcop's bubble.

Sergeant Stanger, perhaps perceiving an opportunity to hone his communications and leadership skills, makes a speech to the troops. Some incoherent raving about "convicts got nothing coming." About "taking back our prison." And "taking no prisoners." The speech is confusing, but the psychotic passion behind it is unmistakable.

Fishcop, finally feeling safe, hits a button and the crash gates roar open.

Here come the Dirt.

And the Dirt are dressed to kill!

All in black, from gleaming jackboots to the dark visored helmets. They have Plexiglas shields and lethal-looking black billy clubs. A dozen savagely barking German shepherds strain against their leather leashes.

As Yogi Berra is reported to have said: *It's déjà vu all over again.*

The Dirt release the German shepherds, the signal for all righteous dawgs to drop to the floor and start howling under the doors. I don't know if the objective is to irritate the dogs to the point of madness or it's just good primal scream therapy for us.

I do know that you don't ask *why*—it's just something that *we* do.

I also know I have shaken off the last remnants of depression, of self-pity. Left the dark Mud Man behind. And did it without a drink or a drug or a prescribed dose of Prozac. Left the Mud Man back there at the edge of the abyss where I once peered down into a monster's face and saw my own reflection.

I keep pounding the flush button until the waters rise to my sneaker tops.

The wolves are almost at my door.

I am wonderfully, wondrously, *electrically* alive, and as the Dirt and the dogs charge down the corridor, I am smiling with the humble, heartfelt gratitude of a man who is inexplicably thankful for the simple gift of another day.

Kansas, literally bouncing off the walls, kung-fuing his door, screaming, barking, howling, having the time of his life.

"O.G.! Do the *cat*! Do your fucking cat noise—*now*!"

The Dirt dogs racing toward my door, nails clattering and clicking on the concrete. Full riot-geared Dirt in black close behind them.

ARF! ARF! ARF! ARF!!! shout the Dirtdogs just outside the cell door.

They are in perfect range.

Chico shouting, "O.G.! O.G.!!! *Do it now!*"

I slowly pull the last drop of air up from my diaphragm. Take a moment to visualize a cat—*Belinda*—to Be Here Now.

Then I *am* the cat.

"BREEEEEEEEEEEEEEEEEE—OOOOOOOOOOOOOOO-OOW!!!"

And all the dawgs go wild!

ABOUT THE AUTHOR

Jimmy Lerner was born in Brooklyn, New York, in 1951 and attended Erasmus High School, Brooklyn College, and Chapman College. He has been a cabdriver in New York City, a soldier in Panama, and a corporate cubicle slave in San Francisco. After obtaining an M.B.A. from Golden Gate University, he worked for many years as a marketing and strategic planning manager for Pacific Bell. A former resident of Danville, California, he is the divorced father of two teen-age daughters. Convicted of voluntary manslaughter in 1998, he currently resides in a Nevada prison where he is working on his poetry book, entitled *It's All Part of the Punishment.*